THREE WHO MADE A REVOLUTION

VOLUME ONE

THREE WHO MADE A REVOLUTION

A BIOGRAPHICAL HISTORY

BERTRAM D. WOLFE

WITH A NEW INTRODUCTION
BY ALLEN DULLES

RTP TIME Reading Program Special Edition
TIME INCORPORATED · NEW YORK

TIME-LIFE BOOKS
EDITOR *Norman P. Ross*
TEXT DIRECTOR *William Jay Gold*
ART DIRECTOR *Edward A. Hamilton*
CHIEF OF RESEARCH *Beatrice T. Dobie*
ASSISTANT TEXT DIRECTOR *Jerry Korn*

EDITOR, TIME READING PROGRAM *Max Gissen*
RESEARCHER *Ann S. Lang*

PUBLISHER *Rhett Austell*
GENERAL MANAGER *John A. Watters*

TIME MAGAZINE
EDITOR *Roy Alexander*
MANAGING EDITOR *Otto Fuerbringer*
PUBLISHER *Bernhard M. Auer*

COVER DESIGN *Norman Green*

FOR
ELLA

CONTENTS

LIST OF ILLUSTRATIONS

EDITORS' PREFACE

"The past is never dead," said William Faulkner; "it is not even past." The three heroes of this book, though physically dead, are politically alive and still making history both inside and outside their native Russia.

In 1961 Nikita Khrushchev moved Joseph Stalin's eight-year-old corpse from its Red Square public tomb to a grave by the Kremlin wall. By this theatrical act, Khrushchev claimed to be restoring the due authority of Lenin, Stalin's hitherto co-equal tombmate. Some in the world audience thought they also heard a spectral flutter in the wings, hinting that Lenin's earlier colleague in revolution, Leon Trotsky, might one day return to life in that official Soviet history from which Stalin had so thoroughly expunged him.

These three powerful ghosts were in life responsible for the most momentous political event of the 20th Century, the Communization of Russia. In death the unceasing minuet of their reputations reflects real changes in the policies and power structure of world Communism. Lenin, Trotsky and Stalin are at once the puppets and the incubi of their heirs.

History did not thrust this ghoulish immortality upon them; they earned it by force of character, conviction and intelligence. All three were outsize samples of the ruthless, brain-ruled, future-intoxicated breed of Old Bolsheviks which has managed but dimly to reproduce itself in the later leadership of Soviet society. It seems fantastic to liken these men to the American founding fathers, but one thing is true of both groups: it is essential to understand them in order to understand the political system in their country. And thanks to this book, Americans are in a better position to understand the founders of Soviet Russia than most Russians are.

These three men all believed in Karl Marx's so-called "laws" of history and served them with awesome dedication. By so serving, they made the "laws" seem partly or temporarily true. Why and how they were able to do this is the subject of *Three Who Made a Revolution*. It is a book with three heroes but also with four themes: men, ideas, Russia and revolt. Wolfe's great achievement is to have kept these four themes distinct, while weaving them and the three heroes into a pattern that has the life, color and texture of historical truth. Edmund Wilson, whose *To the Finland Station* did notable pioneering for American readers in the same historical and ideological jungle, has called Wolfe's the "best book in its field in any language." The book is all the more remarkable for having held up so well; it was written in 1948, when Stalin was still alive and Khrushchev was a minor functionary all but unknown in the Western world. (Though this edition was revised after Stalin's death, Wolfe retained the present tense in many of the passages about Stalin.)

Wolfe opens with a vivid set piece, a compact history of Czarist Russia, which prepares us for the revolution that took so many Western statesmen by surprise. It also took Lenin by surprise, but it did not catch him unprepared. His whole life had been spent in preparation for the seizure of power. He had mastered the political arts of oratory, propaganda and vituperation; the manipulation of crowds, committees and individuals; the uses of terror and of force; even a smattering of military technique. He was, says Wolfe, the only Russian Marxist of high theoretical capacity who also had the will and ability for systematic attention to organizational detail.

He had still another weapon: what Wolfe calls his "almost unconscious Russianism." The historical determinism of Karl Marx was originally a heretical offshoot of Western philosophy, having been concocted in the British Museum under the influence of Hegel. But Lenin Russified it by making it at once concrete and uncompromising, yet adaptable to the circumstances that confronted him in his self-appointed mission of the conquest of power. The first proletarian revolution, according to Marxist theory, should have taken place almost anywhere but in Russia, which was not ripe for it. Yet Russia was certainly ripe for some kind of revolution, as Wolfe makes vividly clear; and it was Lenin who, though a Marxist, made it a primarily Russian revolution and saddled that unhappy country with a dictatorship that still owes as much to Russian history as to Marxist theory. Trotsky contributed a more Western accent, and Stalin a more Asian one. These accents have fooled a lot of observers, which was in part their purpose. But Lenin, in whom as in Russia itself both the Western and the Asian accents sound intermittently natural, remains the gyroscope of Russian Communism. And his favorite words were "relentless" and "irreconcilable."

In part Wolfe's story is novelesque. It does full justice to the gunrunning, the counterfeiting, the bank robbing, the underground journalism, the street fighting, the conflict-management, the espionage which preoccupied the European socialist movement until 1917 and have preoccupied its Communist wing since. The established governments of the time contributed to the lurid tale; had France not needed the Czar of Russia's vote at the Algeciras Conference, for example, French money might not have shored up the Czar's regime after 1905, or brought it into the alliance whose war was fatal to it. The ubiquitous deviousness of the Czarist police is part of the story, setting an example which only Stalin's secret police would surpass. It is worth knowing that the "40,000 clerks" who by Czar Nicholas' own admission ruled his doomed empire for him were not stupid men; "no set of governing officials in history," says Wolfe, "has ever given a clearer account of the situation facing it." They had plenty of agents inside the socialist conspiracy to give them the facts; to the most notorious of these, Roman Malinovsky, Wolfe rightly accords a whole chapter.

But this is a story of political ideas as well as of conspiracy. Endless doctrinal arguments and factional infighting were the daily bread of the professional European Marxists, especially the Russian exiles; year after year in Geneva, Vienna, Stockholm,

London, they sharpened their revolutionary fervor by drawing one another's blood with every hair they split. Trotsky, whose great year was 1905, established himself for a time above these doctrinal squabbles; but Lenin used them as steps to his own absolute personal power in the Bolshevik faction. Succeeding dictators have followed Lenin's example and have continued the feuds by doctoring the documents to suppress their rivals, enhance their own roles and justify their policies. The result is an almost hopeless maze for historians who hold the Western view that truth is to be discovered, not decreed.

To thread this maze properly, a rare kind of historian is needed: he should be a trained Marxist who has emerged from that training with his critical intelligence unimpaired. Bertram Wolfe has this unusual qualification. He is both a Slavic and a Marxist scholar who served an apprenticeship also in the American Communist Party. There he encountered the Byzantine ruthlessness of Stalin's management of international Communism at first hand. Young Wolfe was an American delegate to the Comintern Congress in Moscow in 1929, the year in which Stalin, having exiled Trotsky, was borrowing Trotsky's policy of absolute Leftism and imminent revolution abroad. The American party was ordered to prepare for the collapse of capitalism, to set up political "dual unions" outside the indigenous bread-and-butter union movement, and to expel all spokesmen of "American exceptionalism," a doctrine akin to what is now called "peaceful coexistence." When Wolfe and others demurred, Stalin gave the American delegates his famous "graveyard" speech: "There is plenty of room in our cemeteries." This lurid ultimatum triggered the departure of one entire faction from the American Communist Party. Wolfe's last words as a party member explained why he could not expound the new Stalinist line to the faithful in the American hinterland: "I cannot persuade others to believe what I do not believe."

His early disillusionment with Communism—well before the more publicized defections that followed the Moscow trials and purges of 1934-1938—helped make Bertram Wolfe one of the coolest and wisest of American fighters against tyranny, especially Communist tyranny, a fight he has waged for 30 years. *Three Who Made a Revolution* is his most distinguished work in this field. It is a work of scholarship, not of polemics, and is within the best canons of scholarly fidelity to sources and evidence. Yet in this field the best scholarship is also the best polemics. Note that *Three Who Made a Revolution* is a thoroughly non-Marxist title; a Marxist would give more credit to history's so-called "laws." By putting ideas and men, Russia and revolution, all in their due perspective, Wolfe has demonstrated that the Western tradition of intellectual responsibility and love of reality can still transcend and surround the Communist assault.

—THE EDITORS OF TIME

INTRODUCTION

Important historical events are generally the products of men and opportunity. A leader appears when the stars in the heavens are in the right conjuncture—at a crucial moment in history when he, and possibly he alone, can exert a decisive influence. The course of events may then be decided for good or evil, depending upon the type of man who emerges and the environment in which he seizes the initiative.

Hitler, if he had been in his prime 20 years earlier or 20 years later, might never have come into the pages of history at all— let alone have been the man who caused the bloodiest and most destructive war of all history. It took the German military defeat in 1918, the Versailles Treaty, and a depressed and frustrated people to create a climate of politics and opinion in which a Hitler could rise to power.

It also took an extraordinary combination of events to bring Lenin to the fore. Here, too, there was war weariness and deep popular unrest; moreover, the leadership in Russia was weak and vacillating. Lenin, in the earlier days of his underground activities within Russia and his exile in Siberia and abroad, had doubted whether he would live to see the triumph of the revolution he was planning. Nor was he sure where in Europe the revolution would come.

But here I am getting a little ahead of the story. Bertram D. Wolfe's *Three Who Made a Revolution* does not deal with the days in 1917 when the Bolsheviks took over power. It is rather an account of how Lenin, Trotsky and Stalin used their years of underground activity, exile and confinement to prepare and steel themselves for the day of decision should it come; how they planned to seize the power in Russia, to control and direct the revolution, and to give Communism the thrust which has made it such a sinister influence in the world.

In these days, when "the world is too much with us" and time for quiet thought escapes us, one wonders whether a period of exile or imprisonment—if honorably come by—would not help one to think through some of the problems of the day. Certainly, as Mr. Wolfe's book shows, Lenin and his two co-conspirators had an extraordinary preparation for the task they had set themselves.

To my mind, one of the most fascinating passages of the book is the chapter dealing with what was called the Unification Congress, the meeting of almost 60 Russian revolutionaries held in Brussels in the summer of 1903. Lenin was the directive force; Trotsky, one of the chief protagonists; Stalin, then in his early twenties, was not to meet Lenin until two years later. In the platform that Lenin helped prepare for the Congress was this plank:

"The essential condition for the social revolution is the dictatorship of the proletariat, i.e., the conquest of such power by the proletariat as will allow it to suppress all attempts at resistance on the part of the exploiters."

The opposition to Lenin asked how this principle could be reconciled with other sections of the revolutionary platform which appeared to sponsor a democratic republic. "How," they asked, "do you square it with your demands for a constituent assembly elected by free, equal, direct, secret and universal suffrage? With your demand for freedom of speech, press, parties, organization, conscience, movement, occupation? for equality of all citizens regardless of status, sex, race, religion, nationality? Is not democracy an absolute good? Is it not a matter of principle? One of the desiderata for which we are fighting in every field? Shall we, representatives of those who suffer from dictatorship, countenance its use ourselves?"

Lenin remained silent—for good reason—but Trotsky tried to answer:

"The rule of the working class was inconceivable until the great mass of them were united in desiring it. Then they would be an overwhelming majority. This would not be the dictatorship of a little band of conspirators or a minority party, but of the immense majority in the interests of the immense majority, to prevent counter-revolution. In short, it would represent the victory of true democracy."

Fourteen years later, when the Bolsheviks seized power in Petrograd, Lenin demonstrated how little he was interested in "true democracy." Since he did not dare—or was not able—to prevent the scheduled elections for a Constituent Assembly, the Russian people had at last a relatively free vote. The Bolsheviks obtained only one fourth of the 36 million ballots cast and 175 of 707 seats in the Assembly. When an attempt to intimidate this body failed, Lenin brutally dissolved it by force, commenting:

"Everything has turned out for the best. The dissolution of the Constituent Assembly means the complete and open repudiation of the democratic idea in favor of the dictatorship concept. This will be a valuable lesson."

In this fashion, dictatorship of the proletariat became a dictatorship of naked power. And so the Communist dictatorship has remained ever since.

Since Lenin's death, under Stalin and Khrushchev, this power has been exercised by a single man. It is true that during the interregnum before Stalin had liquidated all his rivals and then between Stalin's day and Khrushchev's take-over, the men in the Kremlin had a kind of "collective leadership," and that after Stalin died they attacked—as they still do—the cult of personality. This does not change the fact that today Khrushchev has power like that of a Stalin—even though he exercises it in a less brutal manner.

Thus the question posed by the revolutionaries in 1903 as to how to square the dictatorship of the proletariat with democratic principles was answered by Lenin in 1917 with a resounding repudiation of these principles. Thereafter, the Communists never even tried to find another answer because there was none which satisfied the ambitions of a Lenin, a Trotsky or a Stalin, or met what they considered to be the requirements of the revolution. Here was the basic cause for the Social Democratic split with the Communists years ago.

It is interesting today to look back on the fate of the three men who made the revolution. When Lenin died in 1924, he left behind some correspondence and a testament evaluating the Communist leaders. Of Stalin, he said that he had concentrated enormous power in his hands and did not always know how to use it with sufficient caution; he proposed that Stalin should be removed from his position as General Secretary of the party because he had become "insupportable" in that office. After Lenin's death, in the struggle for control, Stalin conspired to have the document suppressed.

Trotsky's fate is well known. Forced by Stalin to flee from the Soviet Union, he was hounded by Stalin's agents and finally hacked to death by an assassin in Mexico City on August 20, 1940.

Although Stalin, the third man who made the revolution, ruled the Soviet Union for some 30 years, he was denounced by Khrushchev in 1956 as having betrayed the principles of the revolution by his reign of terror. Now in the Soviet Union they are trying to blot Stalin's name and memory from the pages of Soviet history.

But for us in the free world, the memory of these three men will remain and will be bound up with the view we take of the Soviet system and all its works. If one is to understand the course of our own dealings with the Soviet Union, with all its frustrations and deceptions, it is of vital importance to study the careers of these three men. Undoubtedly the influences of their early days played a great part in determining the nature of their actions when they came to power. One could wish that those in the Western world who negotiated with Stalin with such optimism during the war and early postwar days had taken the time to study his character and antecedents and those of his two fellow conspirators. Bertram Wolfe gives us an opportunity to do just this.

There is even some disagreement among the Communists today as to the conclusions to be drawn from the teachings of Lenin. He left behind him so much dogma that the protagonists of differing views can always find some quotation to support their particular thesis. While Khrushchev has cited him in support of his doctrine of coexistence, Molotov, a deeper scholar and more intimately concerned with the origins of the revolution, is reliably reported to have submitted his own doctrinal thesis disputing Khrushchev's conclusion.

And so the revolution consumes its children. But what these three have done affects our lives today and will affect future generations for years to come. It is well that we should study their careers, and this we can do through Bertram Wolfe's excellent work. One lesson I found mirrored in his pages: These three, while they could be flexible in tactics, never compromised on their goals. Nor can we today defeat their evil purposes by so doing.

—ALLEN DULLES

AUTHOR'S INTRODUCTION

The work of one who writes a history of some large event of his own time is never done. Sealed archives are opened; colleagues publish books and monographs on various aspects of the same event; survivors grow old and write memoirs that reveal matters only a participant could have known. The very events that make up the large pattern keep revealing themselves in a new light as new consequences continue to flow from them; the ever-shifting kaleidoscope of time gives new shape to what seemed fixed and settled.

Internally as well, one's book begins to seem unfinished as soon as it is completed. Things said in closing chapters suggest changes in earlier ones. If it is a first volume in a contemplated larger study, later research keeps turning up fresh materials and inspiring new viewpoints concerning parts of what is already published. While the book is on press, the writer is already making changes in proof. When he looks at the first bound copy, his satisfaction diminishes as *"typos"* leap out of its pages, and fresh questions arise in his mind about things which yesterday seemed so certain.

Then come the reviews, the observations and corrections of colleagues. The meticulous reader—and every serious book merits one or more meticulous readers—finds an incredible number of minor errors. The author has barely seen the first copy off the press before he is longing for the entire printing to be sold out so that he can revise it.

In this regard I have been fortunate. The book's use as a university text over the past fifteen years has permitted three editions in cloth, eight printings in paper, and two printings for book clubs. Printing costs being what they are, corrections and alterations have had to be made by counting letters and spaces for each change so that the same pagination could be kept. Within this typographical straitjacket I have attempted to incorporate the suggestions of colleagues and critics (and the meticulous reader), and my own new insights and discoveries. But a number of methodological questions have been raised which do not permit of this skimped treatment, hence in this, the most sweeping revision, I have ventured to discuss some of these questions here, in a belated introduction.

Many readers have objected that the three protagonists, Lenin, Trotsky and Stalin, did not contribute in equal or comparable measure to the "making" of the Revolution. If to "make the Revolution" means to conceive and build the machine that seized power in 1917, then Lenin is without peer. If the strategy and tactics of the *coup d'etat* on November 7, 1917 is what is meant, then Trotsky as Chairman of the Petrograd Soviet and the Military Revolutionary Committee, made the chief contribution. Some critics have argued that Stalin merely inherited the power, having played a negligible role in the seizing of it. They are, of course, correct. Others have urged that Stalin "unmade" the Revolution, after Lenin and Trotsky "made" it. To resolve this matter is to go into metaphysical, ideological, quasi-theological definitions of what "the Revolution" was or was supposed to be; beyond the ambition pragmatically expressed by Lenin on its eve: "The point of the uprising is the seizure of power; afterwards we will see what we can do with it."

But the sense in which the title was originally conceived was quite different. The book was written during the years when Joseph Stalin was *Vozhd, Khozyain,* Leader. He was Boss and Dictator over the Party, the State and the People of Russia, setting his unmistakable imprint on the Revolution organized as Power, and on the new society it was shaping. In that sense, all three of these men "made" the Revolution for all three have set the imprint of their personalities, doctrines, passions and wills upon it. It is this impress of their personalities upon their time and land which explains the title, and also explains why it was sub-titled "A Biographical History."

Crane Brinton in a review of this work said of "biographical history":

> It is a good kind of history, even if, indeed probably because, it is a kind men have been writing since the ancient Greeks and Hebrews. By his practice and by an occasional methodological aside, Mr. Wolfe indicates his belief that the character of the leaders has a great and abiding influence on the course of history.

To this I must add that in our present "time of troubles," when thrones tumble, empires break up, new nations come to life, regimes are transformed, "new orders" are introduced, and new men of power conduct ruthless experiments on their people, biographical history takes on an especially large importance.

Because in the century from 1815 to 1914, institutions and economic and political structures were, comparatively speaking, more stable, it was possible for the historian to believe that it did not matter too much which president, premier, sovereign, or political leader was in the key position. One of the weaknesses of much nineteenth-century historiography was the belief that one could write history largely in terms of institutions and impersonal social forces, though, of course, the great historians knew how to combine the man and the age.

Now, in an age when change is rapid and dizzying, when newly born nations have to construct their institutions *de novo,* when new men heading new movements come to power armed with the determination to remake human beings according to their blueprints, then the character, the passions, the theories, the spirit of the man who sets his stamp upon his movement and his land—in short his "biography" and his personal impress upon history—become vastly more important. He may never be as all-powerful as he fancies and the past may have sly and devious ways of reasserting itself, yet even from the past he selects kindred elements and neglects or combats those that he finds distasteful. Indeed, even the traditions that persist despite him, even the unintended consequences of his actions, and the very deeds and spirits of those who react against him, bear the marks of his impress.

How different India is today because Gandhi was murdered at the moment of independence and partition, leaving Nehru to set his quite different stamp upon India's spirit and institutions. How different was the Chinese Revolution under Sun Yat-sen than it is under Chiang and Mao, each of whom claims to be his heir.

If, in time of peace, the stability and efficacy of the Tsarist administration was so different under a Stolypin than under a Goremykin, how much deeper, in a time when everything was in chaotic flux, was the difference between a Russia with Kerensky at the helm and one ruled by Lenin. What a difference it has made in the history of the "new Russia" that a Stalin had the biological constitution to outlive a Lenin, and not the reverse.

It was considerations such as these which prompted me to combine with the study of social forces, institutions, traditions, a close study of the ideas and the persons of the men who were the prime historical actors in the Revolution of 1917, and who set their imprint upon the regime which emerged from it. That is why, too, the study of their opponents is usually a mere vignette, while that of the prime actors is something of a full-length close-up.

The protagonists of the revolutionary movement were ideologues, essentially men of a single idea, which motivated them and to which their lives were dedicated. If they invoked the name of the people, or a class, or the masses, it was not the people that they loved, but their idea. It is for that reason that the present volume might with equal justice have been titled not a "biographical history" but an intellectual, or more narrowly, an ideological history.

"Revolution," wrote Mussolini, "is an idea which possesses bayonets." Lenin did not misprize bayonets, but to *idea* and *bayonets,* he added something peculiarly his own: namely, *organization.* In the world of ideologues, Lenin's *idea* was an idea concerning the nature and role of organization. Not the organization of the entire people or an entire class, but a special type of organization of men who were to be specialists . . . specialists in revolution, and then specialists in the administration of power. As for the rest of the population, he was ready to content himself with the words of Lasalle to Marx: *"Hate* in the *multitude* is sufficient for everything, if there are five people in the country who also *understand."**

For this reason it was impossible to write the history of the Russian revolutionary movement without trying to render comprehensible to the reader the obscure and unfamiliar world of inter-party and intra-party controversies, of fine-drawn doctrinal differences, of splits and splinterings, the world of the Russian underground.

Some have urged that in this work I have presented the Mensheviks as too doctrinaire, and Lenin as somewhat less despotic and totalitarian than in the end he proved to be. Perhaps this is so, if we examine Menshevism after it had assimilated the bitter lessons of defeat and gotten a clearer notion of the mischief in the ways of its adversary. And certainly it is so, if we contemplate what became of Lenin's doctrines and how they developed after they were implemented with the terrible instruments of absolute power. Bearing this in mind, I have introduced some corrections into the text in its latest revision. But because of the historical method I employed, these "ultimate" implications of character and doctrine had in the main to develop out of the events, and along with the story itself.

Those who read this work attentively will recognize that I have tried an extremely difficult historical design, but one necessary in my judgment to the living presentation of a historical sequence. The historian's most challenging task is to put himself, and his reader, back into the events he is treating as if they had not yet occurred and he did not yet know the

---

* From a letter dated September 11, 1860. It should be added that this thought was marginal in Lasalle, but central in Lenin.

"ultimate" outcome. Rejecting the deceptive omniscience of hindsight, he must look forward with his characters toward their future, which is to him already in the past. Only thus can he reopen what now appears to be closed, put himself in their places, see things as they looked to his protagonists before they made their choices among the possibilities of action. Only thus can he comprehend their dilemmas, appraise their achievements, misjudgments, errors, responsibilities, the consequences of their choosing to do one thing and not another, the results of their failure to foresee what might follow from what they do and leave undone. Only thus can he give to his story the breath of life, and extricate its human—that is to say, moral—significance.

Looking backward, the historian is seduced into regarding any large event as having been inevitable, is inclined to regard the consequences of the acts of willful and powerful men as having been all along intended. But looking forward, he cannot fail to see multiple possibilities all along the road ahead.

Backward or forward, more than the tidy historian likes to admit, he finds at every turn the unexpected and the unpredictable: contingency, historical accident, biological accident intruding itself into history, as when the death of a history-making personage brings a change in direction; sudden changes of mood; emergence of totally new situations; leaps that seem to turn an accretion of ambiguous little events into a definitive big event; the complicated interaction of multiple and various determinants in every happening; the unintended consequences of intended actions, and the unexpected consequences which were not foreseen even when the event itself was foreseen and forewilled.

Huge events like wars and revolutions are so multiply determined and so fraught with striking consequences, that in retrospect decades may seem to have been preparing for this and no other outcome. The vacillations and uncertainties, the ebbs and flows, the countless actions and counteractions, the striving for quite other results that the event finally gives forth

—all this tends to get lost from view. Choices of action and inaction have been made along the way, unnoticed or misapprehended, so that when the huge climax comes, it has the deceptive air of having been inevitable all along.

Afterwards, the historian can go back for decades, industriously picking and choosing among the welter of ambiguous and contradictory events just those actions, trends, forces, and proposals, which appear to have led up to just this denouement. He can ignore the ebbs for the now irreversible flood, overlook the turns not taken, the chances missed, that might have led better or more foresightful or luckier men to another outcome.

Be that as it may, the method I have used in *Three Who Made a Revolution* has been to put myself and the reader back into the time of the protagonists, looking forward and moving forward with them toward a future in essential respects still open. For this reason, the same problems pose themselves again and again in this history, each time on a later, more advanced and more explicit level of complication and meaning, as the "living dead" whose deeds and thoughts I treat face these issues under constantly developing and changing conditions, and add to their solution the ingredients of their own choices and perceptions.

Only in one respect, as I should here confess to the reader, have I consciously deviated from this method. When a man undertakes a large work, he does not know how much of it he will live to finish and publish. Therefore, after looking forward with my characters toward an issue or an event, every so often (or so seldom), I have permitted myself a side remark, or a leading question addressed to the reader to carry his thought beyond that of the protagonists and the action. Thus on page 510, for instance, the reader will find the story of the expulsion of Bogdanov, Lunacharsky and other Bolsheviks by Lenin:

> By a small and safe majority [I wrote], Bogdanov and his associates were declared to have 'placed themselves outside the faction.'

'Not outside the Party,' Lenin explained precisely. 'A party can include a wide range of opinions, the extremes of which may be diametrically opposed to each other . . .'

This was as far as the method of "looking forward toward the future" with my protagonists would have carried the story. But I could not resist the temptation to add two "hindsight" sentences to the episode:

But in 1912, Lenin's faction was to declare itself the Party! And after 1917, he was to make even the State a mere instrument of the Party. What then would happen to the 'wide range of opinions?'

Finally, this introduction would be incomplete without a word on sources, annotation, and my indebtedness to various colleagues. I have often been reproached for the lack of systematic footnotes. The reproach is well taken. Certainly the sequels (beginning with *Marxism: Ambiguous Heritage*—a work now on press which treats of aspects of the intellectual history of Marxism and Marxism-Leninism) will be annotated according to the prevailing rules. By way of extenuation if not disculpation, I should like to point out that many "footnotes" are not at the foot of pages, but in parentheses and asides in the text itself. If the text says, for example: "wrote Lenin in *Proletarii* of such-and-such date," any experienced researcher can find the passage in a moment in the corresponding (dated) volume of Lenin's *Sochineniya*. Especially where the reader might be inclined to doubt or where the interpretation appeared most novel, I included the sources in the text. And in my revisions for this edition I have followed the usual practices of historical scholarship.

I am deeply indebted to those Russian men and women whom fate has thrown on our shores, and whose spirits are irreplaceable human archives of all they have lived through. Only now are we beginning to get some of their memories in writing in such publishing ventures as the Inter-University Project on the History of the Menshevik Movement. When I did the first edition of this book, I had to depend on their time and patience in the granting of repeated personal interviews.

I owe a great debt to those who read the original manuscript in whole or in part before publication, and to the much larger number who read it in print, and kindly sent me their comments, suggestions and encouragement from many lands:

To Solomon M. Schwartz, who read the manuscript twice over.

To Vera Alexandrova, my guide into the intricacies and glories of the Russian tongue and Russian literature.

To Nikolai Vladoslavovich Valentinov, who read the work in French and, despite his illness, sent me many long letters concerning various aspects of the work.

To Wladimir Woytinsky, who read it on the bed of his last illness, and communicated his suggestions orally.

To Michael Karpovich who read the difficult opening chapter and gave his encouragement to publish its generalizations concerning the historical heritage and the intelligentsia.

To Boris Nikolaevsky, himself a living archive, for reading the chapter on Roman Malinovsky.

To Rafael Abramovich, who read the sections concerned with his own personal experiences.

To Angelica Balabanoff, who answered all questions I had the wit to put to her.

To Leo Borochowicz, who offered many valuable suggestions.

To Sidney Hook, who read in manuscript the chapter on "Lenin as Philosopher."

To David Shub, who sent me evidence which left its traces on the revisions I have made in the chapter on Roman Malinovsky.

To Iraklii Tseretelli, who made many valuable suggestions and gave me the priceless encouragement of saying, "As I read it, I cannot believe that you did not live in our movement."

To Boris Dvinov, Boris Sapir, Raymond H. Fisher, Warren

Walsh, Marc Szeftel, Max Nomad, Walter Goldwater, Mark Vishniak, all of whom made valuable suggestions and corrections.

To a number of Russians here and in the Soviet Union, who had best remain nameless, who answered questions put to them.

To the Slavonic Division of the New York Public Library, to the Hoover Library in Stanford, the Columbia and Harvard Libraries, the Library of Congress, and the British Museum, for the friendly cooperation of their staffs and for making materials available to me that were hard to come by.

To Leon Kramer, bookseller, who searched the Russian colonies of the world from Shanghai to Prague in an effort to secure for me obscure and out-of-print papers, pamphlets and books which might enable me to confront the "official truth" with the "truth of the defeated," so that out of the confrontation more of the historical truth might emerge.

To Edmund Wilson for lending me his valuable library of Leniniana which he had collected to write his own *To the Finland Station.*

It goes without saying that the defects in this book are my own and that none of those who so kindly helped, or sought to help, bears any responsibility for any of them.

The tentative large generalizations concerning Russia's history offered in the first chapter are my own, but I must acknowledge a debt to many Russian historians and thinkers, particularly to Klyuchevsky and his school, to Karpovich, Vernadsky, Berdyaev, and Milyukov, and to the sudden flashes of deep self-knowledge that abound in the nineteenth-century literature of the Westerner-Slavophile controversies and in the Russian novel. In order to "get back" into the vanished world I spent two years reading or rereading Russian novels and the literature of those great controversies.

The chapters on Lenin are based primarily on his writings and his letters, on the notes provided by the Third Russian Edition of his *Sochineniya,* on the memoirs of his wife and his sister Anna, and innumerable other memoirs friendly, hostile and hagiographical, concerning him. Special acknowledgment is due to Leon Trotsky for his brilliant fragment, "Vie de Lenine: Jeunesse."

The chapters on Stalin owe much to Boris Souvarine's ground-breaking biography, and to Trotsky's unfinished biography of Joseph Stalin. I am indebted to Charles Malamuth, editor and translator of Trotsky's *Stalin* for making available to me much unpublished documentation. Much more than for Lenin and Trotsky I have had to use for Stalin the "archaeological method" of uncovering successive layers of falsehood and juxtaposing them in the hope of extricating the truth. The reader can find a detailed account of these excavations in my article in *Foreign Affairs,* "Operation Rewrite: The Agony of the Soviet Historian." And I should record my thanks to Nikita Sergeevich Khrushchev for confirming much of my previously so hotly contested version of the truth concerning Stalin in his *Secret Speech* at the Twentieth Congress, and public speeches on the same theme at the Twenty-Second Congress of the Communist Party of the Soviet Union.

—BERTRAM D. WOLFE
January 1, 1964

CREDO

"Time in its irresistible and ceaseless flow carries along on its flood all created things and drowns them in the depths of obscurity . . . But the tale of history forms a very strong bulwark against the stream of time, and checks in some measure its irresistible flow, so that, of all things done in it, as many as history has taken over it secures and binds together, and does not allow them to slip away into the abyss of oblivion."

—ANNA COMNENA

"The historian has a duty both to himself and to his readers. He has to a certain extent the cure of souls. He is accountable for the reputation of the mighty dead whom he conjures up and portrays. If he makes a mistake, if he repeats slanders on those who are blameless, or holds up profligates or schemers to admiration, he not only commits an evil action; he poisons and misleads the public mind."

—ALBERT MATHIEZ

"History does nothing, possesses no enormous wealth, fights no battles. It is rather man, the real, living man, who does everything, possesses, fights. It is not 'History,' as if she were a person apart, who uses men as means to work out her purposes, but history itself is nothing but the activity of men pursuing their purposes."

—KARL MARX

"Society can never think things out:
It has to see them acted out by actors,
Devoted actors at a sacrifice—
The ablest actors I can lay my hands on."

—GOD TO JOB, IN ROBERT FROST'S
"The Masque of Reason"

CHAPTER ONE

THE HERITAGE

Russia, whither flyest thou? Answer! She gives no answer. The ringing of bells melts into music; the air, torn to shreds, whirs and rushes like the wind, everything that is on earth is flying by, and the other states and nations, with looks askance, make way for her and draw aside.

—NIKOLAI GOGOL

The tradition of all the dead generations weighs like an incubus upon the brain of the living.

—KARL MARX

The greatness of today is built on the efforts of past centuries. A nation is not contained in a day nor in an epoch, but in the succession of all days, all periods, all her twilights and all her dawns.

—JEAN JAURÈS

The great Eurasian Plain opposes few obstacles to frost and wind and drought, to migrant hordes and marching armies. In earlier centuries the plain was dominated by vast Asiatic empires, Iranian, Turkish, Mongolian. As the last of these melted away, Muscovy expanded to take their place, expanded steadily through several centuries until it became the largest continuous land empire in the world. Like the tide over limitless flats, it spread with elemental force over an endless stretch of forest and steppe, sparsely settled by backward and nomadic peoples. Wherever it met resistance, it would pause as the tide does to gather head, then resume its inexorable advance. Only at the distant margins does the plateau end in great mountain barriers: the snowy summits of the Caucasus; the Pamirs, roof of the world—where two of our three protagonists have peaks named in their honor, thrusting up over four miles each into the sky; the Altai, Sayan and Stanovoi mountains forming China's natural wall. How could a people not be great and not aspire to greatness, whose horizon was as unlimited as this Eurasian Plain?

By the time our story begins, the empire of the Tsars sprawls heavily across two continents, from the Gulf of Finland to the distant Pacific shore. It includes most of the land area of the frozen Arctic to within twelve degrees of the Pole, and stretches southward into hot desert sands and semi-tropical slopes bordering on Turkey, Persia, Afghanistan.

History presents no parallel to this vastness. The Roman Empire at its height would have been lost in it. The other great continuous land areas, the United States, China and India, do not equal its extension, when all three of them are added together. Its European portion is equal to all the busy lands of Western Europe combined, yet two-thirds of its vast bulk lies outside that continent, on the Asiatic tundras and steppes. It embraces over 8,500,000 square miles of contiguous territory—approximately one-tenth of the human race and one-sixth the total land surface of the globe.

It gives us fresh perspective on the wars of our time to follow backward through the pages of history the ebb and flow of peoples over this limitless plain, recalling that the Elbe (Slavic *Laba*) was a Slav frontier in the time of Charlemagne, Hamburg a fortress erected to hold the Slavs in check, Prussia (anciently Borussia), once a Lithuanian land, and Breslau (formerly Breslavl, now Wroclaw), along with Dresden and Leipzig, once Slavic towns. Or to remember that Mongolia, now being torn from China, once ruled alike over China and what is now Russia and the whole Eurasian Plain.

Against every powerful invader, the chief defenders of this great open plain have ever been General Distance (with his aides, General Mud and General Winter) and his age-old strategy of the "scorched earth." No invention this, as recent "discoverers" of Russia have proclaimed, of socialism, or state property, or Stalin's military genius, but so venerable as to be known in Russian history as "Scythian tactics." For it has been used against every would-be conqueror from Hitler and Hindenburg in the twentieth century, Napoleon in the nineteenth and Charles XII in the eighteenth (Charles, be it remembered, got as far as Poltava in the Ukraine), to Darius the Great of Persia, who invaded the plain through the Pontic steppes in 512 B.C. Then the Scythians, as the inhabitants of what is now the Ukraine were called in those days, retreated inland, driving away their cattle, burning the grass and poisoning the wells. They drew the hosts of Darius inland until he was too deep within the scorched land, then counter-attacked, helping to save an Athens of which they had never heard, even as the Tsar's armies saved Paris in 1914 and the Soviet armies London in World War II.

At the beginning of the nineteenth century, one European in seven was a Russian; at the beginning of the twentieth, one in every four. As I write, the ratio is still changing in Russia's favor. If we include all the newly annexed lands, and all those being brought under the sway of occupying armies and puppet governments. approximately one European out of every two is today under Russian rule.

The three holy capitals of the Russian Empire—wrote the Pan-Slavist Tyuchev—are Moscow, Saint Petersburg and Constantinople. Where are her boundaries in the North and East, in the South and West? Destiny will show that the path of the future will lead us to the seven inland seas and to the seven great rivers, from the Nile to the Neva, from the Elbe to the Yangtze, from the Volga to the Euphrates, from the Ganges to the Danube—this is the Russian Empire, and it will last through the ages. . . .

And fearfully Lord Palmerston, that same Lord Palmerston whom Marx denounced as a "hireling" of Russia, responded:

The policy and practice of the Russian government have always been to push forward its encroachments as fast and as far as the apathy or want of firmness of other governments would allow it to go, but always to stop and retire when it met with decided resistance, and then to wait for the next favorable opportunity to make another spring on its intended victim.

The unity and expansive force of Muscovy have had about them something elemental, largely independent of differences in leadership and régime. The spread of the Russian people in earlier centuries was more the work of Cossack bands, fugitive serfs, outlaws, adventurers, freedom-seekers, than of the state itself. Sometimes the state sought to check or contain this process of overflow, yet, in the long run, it always reaped the harvest which swelled it into the super-state we know. Only at brief intervals, particularly in the later nineteenth century, has it been consciously expansionist. The Bolshevik leaders we are to meet will find in Russia's great distances the salvation of their revolution in its days of peril. Beginning with a sincere attempt at rupture with Russia's imperialist-expansionist past, in the end they will take over and develop further, under other forms, the same expansive force, the same far-flung centralism, ubiquitous bureaucracy, million-headed standing army, leviathan state, the whole imposing apparatus which binds this many-colored conglomerate of races into a single, ever-expanding domain.

An empire so huge and cumbersome is hard to tie together, inept at times in bringing its overwhelming force to bear at any given point. Yet four times in the eighteenth and early nineteenth centuries, victorious Russian armies stood upon the Rhine. They took Paris from Napoleon and Berlin from Frederick the Great. Even under the palsied leadership of Nicholas II, they crushed the imposing forces of their Austro-Hungarian neighbor in 1914-16, compelling Germany to abandon its drive on Paris in order to contain them in East Prussia. Thus it is mere legend that Russia's armies were never great till now.

Behind the legend lies the fact that in the last two centuries the countries of Western Europe have made up for their inferior numbers by advancing technically faster than Russia. Therefore, five times did Muscovy meet checks in its slow expansion. Yet the expansion did not cease, while contact and conflict with the West gave rise to tremendous transformations, as if the law of Russia's being were to progress through defeats.

The first such encounter began in earnest Muscovy's modernization, when Peter the Great saw his armies melt away on the Narva, and answered with the forced "Westernization" and industrialization-for-war of his backward land. The second impulse came from the French Revolution, Napoleon's march on Moscow, and Russia's march on Paris. Out of these were born such diverse things as the moral unity of the nation, the early plans of Alexander I and Speransky for reform, the military-agricultural "communes" of Arakcheev, and the abortive revolt of the Decembrists, which opened a century of revolution. The third impulse came when the small forces of the Concert of European Powers defeated Russia's far-larger serf-formed armies in the Crimean War, leading to the emancipation of the serfs and an era of attendant reforms. The fourth was the defeat by Japan (this time, General Distance went over to the enemy), which precipitated the uprisings of 1905 and gave rise to the beginnings of a constitutional régime. By none of these clashes, be it noted, was Russia's secular expansion more than given pause. At the end of each encounter, Muscovy was in possession of more territory, and mightier than before.

The fifth such event forms the central core of our story, when Russia's enormous military machine bogged down in East Prussia and Galicia because of demoralization in the rear and exhaustion of matériel, with no possibility of lend-lease to supply the deficiency—a defeat which helped to bring on, and was accelerated in turn by, the revolutions of 1917. This time the transformation was to be the most sweeping of all and would in the end provide the greatest dynamic power for expansion that Russia had known since Muscovy first swept through Siberia in the sixteen-hundreds. Such a record of mighty offensive force and stubborn staying power in the face of adversity makes it perennially impossible to "write off" Russia in the hour of her reverses, or to contain her within her old limits in the hour of her victories.

In Russia, Europe and Asia meet. Throughout its history, East and West have striven for its soul. How often has it stood between Europe and Asia's migrant hordes? How many times saved Europe from conquest at the price of its own partial ori- entalization? Still today, as at the dawn of history, it stands at the boundary line, embracing half of the lesser peninsula called Europe and more than a third of the greater mainland called Asia, serving as the channel of the ebb and flow of Eastern and Western influence, partaking of both in its make-up. Though the center of gravity has long shifted from Asia to Europe, still Russia remains, in body and in spirit, a double nature, a Eura- sian land.

Its window on Europe is narrow and small, and, even as its tiny casement *fortochkas,* likely to be nailed tight shut in win- ter. Behind that little vent upon the West (growing larger now), lies the overwhelming hinterland, stretching eastward a quarter way round the world. It is a hinterland localistic and passive enough to be held in control, but vast enough and sufficiently resistant to stifle or distort the most powerful movements for change. Again and again mighty impulses have come from the

West only to weaken and lose themselves at last in the endless eastward-stretching plain, which again and again has reconquered its conquerors or transformed their dreams into something more in accord with its own patient and timeless image.

Though predominantly a European land it has long stood on the periphery of Europe. It formed a part neither of the Roman nor of the Holy Roman Empires. In its formative period, its culture came from the Near East, from the "Eastern Rome," Byzantium, and from the Caliphate of Baghdad. This did not then spell backwardness, for in the tenth century when these Eastern cultures rippled through the Balkans and the Caucasus into Russia, their centers were not behind but ahead of Western Europe. But, shortly thereafter, the life of Baghdad and Byzantium seemed to freeze into rigidity, and consequently their spiritual child, Russia, lagged behind too. The sudden shift of the currents of historical dynamism westward to the Mediterranean and then the Atlantic shore, left Russia outside the main stream. As the Arab Caliphate and the Byzantine Empire both fell to the Ottoman Turk, Russia retained for a while a precarious connection with the West through the Baltic and the Black Seas, then lost that to the Germans, Lithuanians, Swedes and Turks. But the decisive events which cut Russia off from Western Europe were the schisms between the Byzantine and the Roman Church, and the Tartar-Mongol invasion, followed by two centuries of Mongol domination.

The Mongol invasion was but one—the last before the formation of Muscovy—of a long series of such elemental floods of migrating peoples. Norsemen from Scandinavia, Poles and Livonians and Germans from the West, Greeks and Turks and Persians from the South, Ugro-Finns from Asia, Slavs from the Carpathians, Khazars, Kalmucks, Tartars and other nomadic hordes from the East, have rolled in endless succession over the great open Eurasian Plain, now as conquerors, now in flight, planting their successive deposits of race and custom, rooting up and scattering again and again the slow accumulations of settled civilization, retarding the progress of economy and laying on all the land the ineradicable imprint of pillage and enslavement and the sword.

Yet, when the age of the great migrations ceased in Europe, Russia, under the dominance of the Slavs, no less than the Western lands, developed its unifying language and culture and seemed ready, along with the rest, to make its first steps toward the economy and civilization that characterize the modern Western World.

The unifying impulses which radiated outward during the later Middle Ages from linguistic-cultural centers like Paris, London, Tuscany, Castille, and made French, English, Italian, Spanish dominant over neighbor dialects and languages within great regions of national cohesion, have been but obscurely studied. One thing, however, seems certain: that markets and trade routes and consequent cultural interchange have played an important role in begetting these centers. And yet another, that the experience of a common struggle for existence tended to give their leadership over "national" regions a permanent form.

The Little-Russians (Ukrainians) and the Great-Russians (Muscovites) were not behind the rest in developing the trading towns of Kiev and Novgorod, in exhibiting that potent expansive force of one tongue and people, in Russifying quite without compulsion the conquered Finnish peasants in the central plain and the conquering Viking boyars and princes who ruled the land. Russia-Ukrainia, no less than other countries, became an early highway of medieval commerce in men and things and ideas. At the very dawn of the Middle Ages, its network of broad, slow-running rivers, navigable by ships of trade through much of the year, connected by easy portages, and serving as smooth sledgeways for winter traffic, provided the main highway of the East European medieval world—the long continental route "from the Varangians to the Greeks," i.e. from Scandinavia to Byzantium. The river road ran through a land of forests and steppes. The nomads of the steppes provided the first trading-piratical bands. The forests supplied primitive forest products: honey and wax; pelts and furs; agricultural products crudely cultivated with wooden plough and hoe in the clearings around towns that raised the first armies to defend the highway; and the human animal, hunted in forest and steppe to be sold as a slave. Young Russian girls were famed in Arabia as concubines, while the very word slave is declared by most philologists to be related to Slav.

How far this early commerce might have carried ancient Russia toward urban culture and democratic or patrician town government we do not know; for in the thirteenth century the course of inner transcontinental trade was suddenly and permanently deflected to other routes. When the Crusaders took Byzantium in 1204, the Orient trade ceased to follow the route of the Black Sea, the Dnieper and the Baltic. It was diverted to the Mediterranean, going through Venice and Genoa to Syria, Palestine and Egypt, and through the passes of the Alps to the Rhine and northern Europe. Italian cities flourished while the great river highway from the Varangians to the Greeks became a turbulent backwater; the young Slav towns withered, the nascent burgher or aristocratic democracies died, the forest and steppe prevailed in Russia once more. The Renaissance flowed through other waterways, passing Russia by. It alone of the great nations never knew that spiritual stir, never felt the full force of the Reformation, never developed the widespread culture and individualism that those movements brought in their train. Indeed, it became a strangely silent land. In the centuries when Italy had its Dante and its Petrarch, when England had its Shakespeare, Spain its Cervantes, France its Corneille and Racine, Russia remained silent. The mighty land did not find its voice until the nineteenth century, when suddenly full throated, it astonished the world.

At the moment when the river highway was becoming a backwater and the dying towns had grown too feeble to offer successful resistance, came the last great Mongol-Tartar invasions from the Asiatic steppes. The moribund centers of trade were

pillaged, burned, laid waste, their "principal men" extermi-
nated or carried off as slaves, their primitive liberties and feeble
shoots of lay culture destroyed. Urban and mercantile Russia,
"bourgeois" Russia, received a blow from which it did not
recover for several centuries. And then it was another Russia,
centering in Muscovy, and not the old Russia, or Ukrainia
rather, centering in Kiev.

> One *Rus*—writes Tolstoy—has its roots in universal, or at
> least in European culture. In this *Rus* the ideas of goodness,
> honor and freedom are understood as in the West. But there
> is another *Rus:* the *Rus* of the dark forests, the *Rus* of the
> Taiga, the animal Russia, the fanatic Russia, the Mongol-
> Tartar Russia. This last Russia made despotism and fanati-
> cism its ideal. . . . Kiev *Rus* was a part of Europe, Moscow
> long remained the negation of Europe.

Not that the Mongols contributed nothing positive. If, unlike the Arabs who invaded Spain, they brought with them
"neither Algebra nor Aristotle," they did bring a technique of
statecraft eminently suited to a great land empire. Guided by
Chinese sages, these nomads of the Asiatic steppe had developed a considerable skill in bureaucratic administration of
great areas, greater areas than had ever been held together by
any people from a single center. They it was who contributed
the loose and easy tolerance of local religions, local adminis-
trations and local customs, which enabled both Tsars and Soviets to hold together a diversity of peoples by varying com-
binations of centralism and autonomy. All they asked was
submission from the indigenous, autonomous ruler, or, failing
to get that, they set up a puppet from the same indigenous
ruling layer. Provided they secured tribute and a military levy
(the only centralist aspirations of that simpler day), they were
content to let dukes and priests and elders remain in their posts.
Finding that they could use the Russian Orthodox Church and
the Grand Dukes of Muscovy as instruments of their rule, they
favored them, while they destroyed the more advanced and

democratic cities like Kiev, richer in booty and more zealous in their resistance. Moscow was aided by the Tartars against the West, and elevated into a collector of tribute, a center of religion, and a Tartar viceroydom. As the power of the Golden Horde began to disintegrate, the Grand Duchy of Moscow succeeded swiftly to the headship of the great vacant empire extending over the Eurasian Plain. Its sudden growth brought the other princes to the Muscovite Court, made Moscow into a holy city and a patriarchate, reinforcing the Byzantine principle of Caesaro-papism with the Mongol principle of unquestioning submission and universal obligation of service to the absolute military leader and the state.

But it is too frequently forgotten that this military autocracy had deep popular roots. Its successive struggles for Christian reconquest from the Tartar Khans, then with Roman Catholic Poland-Lithuania, and much later with Sweden and Germany, made the Church into its banner and earned for tsardom as deep popularity among the masses of Muscovy as was won by the Spanish monarchy in its long struggle with the Moors. Thus a capital of popularity was accumulated that it would take until the twentieth century to disperse. In the year 1905, as we watch a gowned and bearded priest, Father Gapon, lead a procession of the most skilled and advanced workers of Russia, those of the famous Putilov machine and locomotive works, on a march to the Palace to petition the Dear Father Tsar, bearing on high the images of the beloved monarch, we will have cause to remember how deep were the roots of popular support of tsardom. It was the firing of the troops upon these unarmed and reverential workers that broke at last the Tsar's spell. But a feeling so deeply rooted is more likely to be displaced and transferred to other objects than utterly disintegrated. Still, today, as in the past, Russian workers march in all their processions bearing on high the images of their ruler and call him *Rodnoi Otets,* "Our Own Dear Father," or "Father in the Flesh."

After Muscovy shook off the Tartar yoke, all serious threats to Russia's existence were destined to come from the West— from the German knights, from Poland-Lithuania, from Sweden, from Napoleon, from the Concert of Powers, from Germany under Wilhelm II and under Hitler. Thus the bonds of loyalty that bound the people to the state and its military autocrat were continually being reinforced. And the barriers of Byzantine heritage and Tartar rule that had cut off Muscovy from the West were as constantly strengthened by the ever-present sense of Occidental threat and national danger.

Indeed, war, virtually unending war, was an all-powerful factor in shaping the Muscovite state structure and spirit. In the years from 1228 to 1462, the years conventionally given for Western Europe's Renaissance, Russian historians list 90 internal wars and 160 foreign invasions! During the seventeenth and eighteenth centuries, Western Europe's "Enlightenment," Russia fought three great wars with Sweden, ending with the annexation of Finland and the Baltic lands, and seven desperate struggles with Poland, ending with the Polish partitions.

Muscovy was slower to develop feudal bondage than the countries of the West, because, unlike those smaller realms, it possessed in the Eurasian Plain limitless reaches of free land. Whereas serfdom was reinforced in France and England and Germany by the absence of unoccupied lands, in Russia, with its boundless steppe and river bottom and Black Sea shore, fixity had to be created by law. It was the drain and strain of unending war which caused the Tsars to decree bondage (the Russian word for it, *Krepost,* literally means "fixity"), fixity so that tax collector and recruiting sergeant might always know where to find each individual and might hold each village communally responsible for its share of money and men. Bondage began to develop under Peter and Catherine when, in Western Europe, the institution of serfdom was already being abolished. In England and France, at the very moment when medieval institutions began to develop into a juridical system, feudalism was already beginning to decay. The same century which undertook to codify the variegated patchquilt of Western medieval life saw the fabric wear thin and show great rips and tears. But in Russia, several centuries later, the fabric was sewn solid, reinforced, stiffened to outlast the storms of the French Revolution. There were woven into it rich and unpliable materials from the dying Byzantine East, bright metallic strands contributed by the Tartar hordes, dark ones worked into the warp and woof by never-ending war.

Still primitive and crude, the Muscovite state—cut to the pattern of a mere dukedom—became the head of a great Eurasian empire long before it possessed an apparatus or a technique equal to such massive tasks. In the words of Russia's greatest historian, Klyuchevsky, "the state swelled up; the people shrank." Or, as Karpovich has put it, "the body of Russia grew too fast for its soul." The military budget and the costs of the apparatus were always too big for the productive economy (and are so still). Hence people had to be fixed in their jobs and tied to their places, where tax-gatherer, military levy, and army supply commissariat could find them. On this military-feudal foundation Russia put into the field great standing armies while the Western powers were still contenting themselves with little companies of mercenaries or volunteers.

Thus, what today has come to be known as totalitarianism, product of the gearing of modern life to modern total war, with its perpetual sense of emergency and its omnipotent state, has deep roots in the formative history of the Russian land. "All through the state, nothing against the state, nothing outside the state"—today the doctrine has a new technological base and completeness, but the spirit is not altogether new. Universal obligation to service, universal fixity created by decree—*krepost* and *nevolya*—have for centuries been characteristics of Russian life. Other peoples, it has been said, consist of two parts, Body and Soul, but the Russian of three: Body, Soul and Passport. Prior to World War I, only two countries required passports for foreigners, Russia and Turkey. Now, as all lands move towards leviathan statism, documents and passports multiply. But today, as in the past, the internal passport, occupational fixity, prohibition of the free movement of the individual from factory or farm, distinguish Russia from other countries still. The countless reports on the "New Russia" have not even posed the problem: how much of this is socialism or Stalinism, and how much the heritage of Russia's past?

The greatest industrializer of Russia prior to Lenin-Stalin was Peter the Great. His modernization, like that of his successors, was intended primarily for the purposes of war and the state. Industrialization was an aspect of militarization. It came from the top downward. It lifted, shoved, dragged, drove, booted the Russian people toward Western technique by fiat of the state. Overnight, Peter created alongside the cottage industry, a great textile and clothing industry to produce uniforms in millions and a great iron and steel industry to produce bayonets, cannon and the munitions of war. The industries were created by state plan and *ukaz*. Sons of the nobility were ordered to study science and technology; capital was invested by royal command; a laboring class was created by assigning state serfs from the Crown estates. Thus, long before Marxian socialism was so much as dreamed of, the Russian state became the largest landowner, the largest factory owner, the largest employer of labor, the largest trader, the largest owner of capital, in Russia, or in the world. The needs of its huge armies made it the largest customer for private industry as well.

This brought into being the world's largest apparatus of bureaucracy. The destruction of the hereditary nobility, begun by Ivan the Terrible in the sixteenth century with his substitution of a security-and-service-to-the-state *Oprichnina* (curiously suggestive of the GPU), was completed by Peter the Great in the eighteenth. The bureaucracy was arranged in a fixed hierarchy, and the slow ascent in the service from copying clerk to high dignitary was largely dependent upon mere length of years spent at a rigidly determined series of desks, each with its well-defined routines, duties, associates, grade and titles, salary and prerogatives. Nobility itself was now so rooted in service to the state that it was automatically attained by a plebeian who had put in a definite number of years in possession of a government inkpot. The bureaucracy was graded by Peter into a hierarchy of *chinovniki,* a ladder of precisely fourteen *chins,* or rungs, not as a rule to be ascended by impetuosity or merit, but rather at an exact and monotonous pace, which could be varied only by the arbitrary decision of some higher being.

To this structure of state capitalism, Alexander I and Nicholas I added a system of military state farms, termed by Vernadsky an "experiment in military socialism." Its aim was to engage Russia's huge armies in productive labor and thus reduce the monstrous war budget. Whole regiments were settled in farming areas, whence the native peasants were deported. Whole villages had their male population put into uniform and drilled, while continuing to work the fields. New communities were constructed to plan, with farmhouses, barracks, communal buildings. They received cattle, horses, subsidies, tax exemptions, and were subject to discipline and continual drill. Though spiritually galling, physically they prospered, piling up a reserve of 32,-000,000 rubles. Begun in 1810, by 1825 when Alexander I died, they embraced 138 infantry battalions and 240 cavalry squadrons: over 200,000 soldiers and their families, one-third of the standing army. The system continued for over 40 years, being abolished as part of the "loosening of the bonds" by Alexander II. It is suggestive of the militarized labor communes attempted by the Bolsheviks in 1920; many of its features can be found in today's state and collective farms and in Khrushchev's dream of the *agrogorod.*

After the emancipation in 1861, there was at last a rapid development of free labor and capital. But the state continued to expand economically, too, and to take on additional enterprises:

notably, a vast construction of railroads and telegraph lines, with state operation; new trade monopolies; and large-scale state banking. Alexander III, according to Count Witte, declared in language befitting Lenin or Khrushchev: "The existence of Railroad Kingdoms ruled by little railroad sovereigns is incompatible with the dignity and security of the Russian autocratic empire." (Witte: *Vospominaniya,* p. 352.) In 1869, the state owned 23 percent of the railways; in 1890, 60 percent. Then it undertook the construction of the Transsiberian, in ten years completing a greater mileage than any government before or since. In the twentieth century it was also the leading banker, the State Bank having a turnover of 234,009,000,000 gold rubles in 1913. During the War it continued to build railroads at a more rapid rate than the Bolsheviks have ever been able to achieve in a like period of time. About one-third of the pre-war tsarist budget was appropriated for government-operated industries and construction, another fourth for army and navy, the rest for the usual purposes of a vast state apparatus. The state's leading position in the economy (its possession of what Lenin would call "the commanding heights") was further strengthened by the conversion of industry to war after 1914. What the Bolsheviks really took over in 1917, even before they had nationalized a single industry on their own, was the largest state economic machine in the world.

"Europe is necessary to us for a few decades," Peter is supposed to have said, "and then we can turn our backs on her." But the new techniques, the new administrative forms, required new attitudes and were imported with an invisible aura of a new way of life and thought. Technologically one borrowed an end result without the organic cultural development which had engendered it. Or one borrowed the latest idea, wrenching it loose from the competing ideas which held it in check and the shadings which qualify it. From Peter's time to the present, Russia has often imported her ideas along with her machines, and often not known how to operate with one or the other. To import technicians along with techniques solved one problem only to raise another: offended national pride. The sudden injection of "Westernism" by "Eastern methods," by command from on high, did little to prepare the people spiritually for what was commanded, and much to offend them. The enforcement of the strange ways caused a deep split in the Russian psyche: a crisis in religion, culture, politics, feeling and thought, which has lasted three centuries and not ended yet. It deepened the schism between Old Believers and State Church, the cleavages between throne and people, nobility and peasant, bureaucracy and people, intelligentsia and people, and finally, inside the intelligentsia itself. In the nineteenth century the intelligentsia became conscious of this fissure in the Russian spirit, giving form to it in great battles of the Westernizer-Slavophile controversy.

In the present century, the same dualism expressed itself in the proliferation of splits among the opponents of the régime: between Miliukov and Maklakov in the Liberal camp; between Slavophile Social-Revolutionaries and Western Marxists; between Bolsheviks and Mensheviks—endless variations of the same psychic tug-of-war. The crowded years of the Revolution show a peculiar symbolic displacement: zealous Westernizers dominating the first three-fourths of the year 1917; then Lenin, whose complex blend of "Slavic" and "Western" we shall examine in this work. Next the Great-Russian from the Central Volga is succeeded by Stalin, a Georgian from the Caucasus, where Europe ends and Asia begins.

Yet even within the soul of Stalinism appeared the same schizoid inner war: between the Stalin of the twenties and early thirties who imported foreign technicians and machines and worshipped foreign techniques, who defined his "holy of holies," the very "style of Leninism" as "the harmonious union of Russian élan (*razmakh*) with American practicality in getting things done"— and the Stalin of the forties who feared and denigrated everything foreign and created the new thought-crime of contact with, admiration for, or "slavish kow-towing to the West." Now the more mercurial spirit of Khrushchev, his disciple, shuttles visibly back and forth between the same two poles of tension.

Suddenly, in the dawn of the nineteenth century, long-mute Russia found her voice and became aware of the rival spirits struggling for the possession of her soul. The first stirrings had come in the preceding century, but it was the contact with the West and the sense of national peril and national triumph in the Napoleonic Wars that gave new impulse to Russian industry and culture, brought young aristocrat-intellectuals of the officer caste into the camps and capitals of Western Europe, awakened the aristocratic intelligentsia to national self-consciousness. Not among the masses, but among these young noblemen of camp and court, stirred the first impulse to freedom.

> *We wait, our anxious hearts are beating,*
> *We yearn for sacred liberty,*
> *As a youthful lover yearns to see*
> *The lagging hour of sweetheart greeting*

sang the youthful Pushkin. Characteristically, it was from the Tsar that he expected the precious gift:

> *And shall I see, my friends, a people freed from burdens*
> *And serfdom's yoke struck off by royal hand,*
> *While at long last the sacred dawn of freedom*
> *Sheds its bright glow o'er our dear fatherland?*

For a time, the Autocrat on the throne seemed to share the bright dream. But then Alexander the liberal dreamer became Alexander the reactionary mystic. He who had written to Thomas Jefferson for advice on a constitution, commissioned Czartoryski to plan the charter of Polish freedom, and the commoner Speransky to draft a constitution for Russia itself—now fell under the influence of such reactionary figures as Arakcheev in domestic, and Metternich in foreign, affairs. Thereafter there was a displacement of the center of renovation from monarch to enlightened aristocrats, though these young radicals of the Court long continued to center their hopes on a revolution from above because they dared not think of a revolution from below. For a whole decade after Alexander withdrew his favor, they waited, dreaming, planning, plotting, in their secret societies and Masonic leagues, hoping for a change of heart, for death to bring a change of autocrats, for a palace revolution.

Most interesting of the officers' secret societies were those known as the Northern and the Southern. The program of the Northern Society, written by Colonel Muraviev, provided for a liberal constitutional monarchy on the English pattern, for federal decentralization, and individual civil rights. Muraviev would have preferred a republic; however, the people would have to be consulted, and their will could only be determined through a constituent assembly. The program of the Southern Society, on the other hand, was conceived in the spirit of French Jacobinism, curiously foreshadowing the ideas and methods of those twentieth-century Jacobins, the Bolsheviks. Pestel, its author, was determined to establish a republic by any and every means, in the interests, of course, of the people, but, if necessary, against the will of the people themselves. The members of his society were divided into a triple hierarchy of responsibility and initiation: a leading layer of conspirators that would alone know all secrets and make all important decisions; a middle layer that would participate in some degree in the knowledge and determination of these matters; and a lower layer whose duty it was merely to execute instructions. Below them was to be yet another group of "friends" or sympathizers, a species of fellow-travelers who were not to be initiated into any of the secrets of the society's existence. Pestel's plans involved a conspiracy which would overthrow the autocracy, execute the Tsar and all the members of the imperial family, then take power and set up a temporary military dictatorship as the lever for a sweeping program of social reform. The dictatorship was to be equipped with all the instruments of power, including police, spies, censorship. The serfs were to be freed, class distinctions abolished, the land was to be nationalized and divided into two equal portions, one of which was to be in the communal possession of the peasants, the other at the disposal of the state for fiscal purposes, or for sale or distribution as private holdings. In eight or ten years, Pestel thought, the dictatorship would have sufficiently transformed Russia and eliminated the danger of counter-revolution so that the land might become a firmly centralized republic with a popular council or *vieche* (the word is etymologically related to "soviet") as lower house, and a higher ruling body in the shape of a directory of five, a sort of Politbureau which would concentrate the administrative power in its hands.

When Alexander I died, the young radical officer nobility undertook a military coup, known to history by its date (December, 1825) as the Uprising of the Decembrists. It was the last of a long series of attempts at palace revolutions, and the first attempt at a socio-political revolution. It ushered in the period of Russian revolutionary history.

But the very sweep of its program made it less likely to succeed than previous palace revolutions since it involved the fate of the masses and they remained indifferent and unaware of what was planned for them. Nicholas I easily suppressed it, personally conducting the inquiry into the conspiracy. His temperament combined with the alarm attendant upon his accession to the throne to make his long reign (1825-55) a period of reaction. Seeing that a stay in foreign parts had proved so unsettling, he forbade Russians to go abroad except by special permission or on missions for the state. Regarding the discussion of ideas with suspicion, he set up rigid standards as to what must be taught and printed and discussed. As his chief instrument of rule he set up a secret "Third Section" or political police, with himself as chief judge and inquisitor, chief censor and policeman, and, in his own words, "first official"of his realm. Thus the autocracy set itself against the awakening nation, and entered upon the final and fatal stage of its existence.

With the Decembrist uprising of 1825, the frozen crust was broken. In vain did Nicholas, "The Cudgel," seek to stifle change under his iron rule. His own construction of the first railroad (characteristically, he drew two straight lines across a great map, ignoring towns and cities, and said, "Let it run so"), and his own policy of furthering industrialization and a modernized bureaucracy, were more disturbing in their effects than any plot that might have been conceived. When he died in 1855, literally of a broken heart because his rigid social setup had failed ignominiously in the test of the Crimean War, all the stout props he had put up against the work of time collapsed of their own weight. His son, Alexander II (1855-81), was to resume the work of transformation at a rate as rapid as that of Peter, going down in history as "the Tsar Emancipator." But he was to perish by a revolutionist's bomb. For the rest of the century, Russian life would be an unequal race between the waning force of reform from above and the waxing strength of unrest from below.

Inevitably, those who sought the way of revolution had to turn their attention to the still slumbering Russian folk. All possible attitudes mingled in their feeling concerning the people: self-abnegation, repentance, humility, mystic worship, blind hope, fascination, fear. Some appealed timidly and reluctantly, with incomprehensible hints and equivocal gestures; others with reckless abandon. But all appeals fell on deaf ears. The people neither stirred nor comprehended, or, worse still, indignantly turned in the would-be revolutionaries to the authorities, for the peasants' faith in the benevolence of the Autocrat was as deeply rooted as was their distrust of his officials, and of all refined, lettered, and city folk. Thus, the "way to the people" became the central problem of every movement for freedom. Many, even as they sought to approach the masses, felt an obscure foreboding that the entrance of this million-headed actor upon the stage of history might crowd the intelligentsia itself forever off that stage. This feeling is expressed again and again, from the Decembrists to Maxim Gorky, but

even those who held it did not refrain from approaching the
folk, and seeking to stir it to wrath. Five years after the crushing
of the Decembrists, the sixteen-year-old Lermontov in his fearful "Prediction (1830)" gave voice to the darker side of the
ambivalent hopes and fears involved in that way to the people:

> *A year will come for Russia, a dark year*
> *When Royalty no more his crown will wear,*
> *The rabble who loved him once will love forget,*
> *For Blood and Death will richest feast be set;*
> *The fallen law no more will shield the weak,*
> *And maid and guiltless child in vain will seek*
> *For justice. Plague will ride*
> *Where stinking corpses fill the countryside,*
> *And flapping rags from cottages demand*
> *Help none can give, while Famine rules the land.*
> *Dawn on thy streams will shed a crimson light;*
> *That day will be revealed the Man of Might*
> *Whom thou wilt know. And thou wilt understand*
> *Wherefore a naked blade is in his hand.*
> *Bitter will be thy lot; tears flood thine eyes,*
> *And he will laugh at all thy tears and sighs.*

Russian patriarchalism was rooted in the "undivided family"
and the communal village *mir*. The village was dominated by
its council of its elders, and each family by its patriarch. So
long as he was in the years of his vigor, he was the autocrat
of the family domain, where he ruled with absolute authority
over grown sons and daughters, their spouses and children and
their children's children. Both institutions, the undivided family and the communal village, survived into modern times.
They set their unmistakable patriarchal, communal stamp on
much of Russian life. To them is largely ascribable the peasant
disposition to submit to authority and to give love, and faith
and obedience to the patriarch of patriarchs, the "Dear Father
Tsar." To them is attributable the corporateness of Russian

rural life, the comparative speed with which the village could be collectivized into the *kolkhoz,* the readiness with which bolshevism was transformed from a program of rule from below into rule by a small élite and then into a personal dictatorship, once more of a "Father of the People." Perhaps, too, these forces help to explain such practices as the taking of hostages and the holding of an entire family legally responsible for the acts of any one of its members. The practices of taking hostages and of family responsibility were taken for granted by Russians, Red and White, during the Civil War, and became basic tenets of the new régime. Even such a "libertarian" as Leon Trotsky professed himself to be during his last years, still stubbornly defended to the end his use of hostages in the Civil War. To be sure, in Nazi Germany, too, and even in the unconscious thought of Western Europe and America, the doctrine of collective responsibility of entire families and peoples has been growing again, as a by-product of the modern total state and total war. Yet family and collective responsibility has not figured in our conscious thinking since we permitted to fall into desuetude the theological doctrine of the sins of the father, while our first statement of fundamental law specifically set it down that "no Attainder of treason shall work Corruption of the Blood." So alien has it been to our way of thinking that the average American does not even know what the words mean.

In a certain sense, all of olden Russia was one vast patriarchal family, with a single autocratic head. To the "Dear Father" of his people, every Russian owed obedience, material and spiritual. All partook in varying degrees of *nevolya*—absence of freedom or of self-determined will—excepting only the Tsar. He was at once self-willed and the sole source of will for all. In a world of universal hierarchical subordination, he alone knew no superior. He was constrained neither by binding law theoretically superior to his person, nor by theoretically unalterable institutions. For others his will was law, until he might alter it, proclaiming the law and cancelling it by simple decree or *ukaz.* Until 1905, all efforts of the nobility, or the Senate, or of the earlier

Sobor, to put definite restrictions upon that power had ended in nullity. Even the constitutional *ukaz* extorted from Nicholas II by the Revolution of 1905 contains the revealing ritual expression, "it is our inflexible will." *Samoderzhetz,* self-holder of power, was his untranslatable Slavic title, itself a Russian version of *aùtokpátwp,* employed by the Byzantine emperors of the late Roman empire of the East. In the nineteenth century, the so-called "Fundamental Laws" still designated the Tsar as "unlimited autocrat," the fourth article thereof stipulating:

> To the Emperor of all the Russias belongs the supreme autocratic power. To obey his commands not merely from fear but according to the dictates of one's conscience is ordained by God himself.

The Tsar might, if strength and interest permitted, regulate all matters throughout his vast domain, all details large and small, make all appointments, dictate or overrule all verdicts, set aside or impose all commands military or civil, take over a court of inquiry, as Nicholas I did with the Decembrists, or command of the armies in the field, as Nicholas II did in 1916. The only limits on his power were those of tradition and wont, plus those dictated by the possibility of rebellion or palace revolution, and those dictated by the need to delegate authority to officials and to rest his power on some social support beyond the mere apparatus of police, army, clergy and bureaucracy. "Russia is not ruled by me," said Nicholas I modestly, "but by my forty thousand clerks." And his Chief of Police wrote to him:

> The landowner is the most reliable bulwark of the sovereign. . . . No army can replace the vigilance and the influence which the landowner continuously exercises in his estates. . . . He is the most faithful, the unsleeping watchdog guarding the state; he is the natural police magistrate. . . . If his power is destroyed, the people will become a flood endangering, in time, even the Tsar himself. . . .

And, of course, there were the inevitable limits imposed by nature on the ubiquity, omnicompetence and powers of even the mightiest of autocrats. "This is Her Majesty's will," Catherine II had written in a characteristic *ukaz* intended to make Russia independent of imported silk. "Silk factories shall be established in Astrakhan . . . to which shall be sent those who were found at the previous census to be idlers, and those who do not remember their origin." But the peasants did not take kindly to silk culture, nor the worms to the Russian climate. "The works were founded by *ukaz,*" Prince Shcherbatov commented shrewdly, "and maintained by *ukaz,* but silkworms cannot very easily be multiplied by *ukaz.*"

Like the benevolent despotism, the cruelty that characterized Russian life had in it a patriarchal element, too. In Western Europe the last refuge of the flogging of adults was the navy, where the captain is absolute autocrat on his vessel. But in Russia, flogging continued as a dwindling device up to this century. Until 1904, it was legal in rural penal law and in the armed forces. A strange counterpart was to be found in the self-flagellation of the *khlysty* as a mystical discipline of the spirit. Torture as an investigative device disappeared after the judicial reform of 1864. The torture introduced by the Cheka, and raised to a nightmarish system in the purge trials and extraction of "confessions" which the accused could not conceivably have committed, is in degree and principle somewhat new in the history of mankind. It is not to be derived from earlier despotism but from totalitarianism, which holds that for its apodictically noble ends "all things are permitted." The "scientific experiment" to remake man totally according to an infallible blueprint is modern. Only the cruelty has roots that are age-old.

An eighteenth-century "apostle of enlightenment," the landowner Bolotov, author of a *Guide to Happiness,* relates, not without pride, how he administered five successive floggings to a peasant suspected of theft, to force him to confess and divulge the identity of his accomplices. When at last he named names, their bearers were flogged in turn to extort confessions, but in

the end they proved to be innocent. Fearing that a further flogging might kill the original suspect, Bolotov records:

> I ordered that he should be tied hand and foot and thrown
> into a heated bathroom [a brick chamber such as is used for
> "Russian baths"], after he had been made to eat the saltiest
> kind of fish; and a strict watch placed over him to see that
> he had nothing to drink, and that he should suffer the tor-
> ment of thirst until he spoke the truth. . . .

Nowhere in his memoirs does he suggest that there is anything unusual or reprehensible in the flogging of suspects who
later turn out to be innocent.

The advanced Peter, creator of academies, hospitals, museums, industries, settled the revolt of the *streltsy* by the simple device of having twelve thousand of them decapitated on
a single occasion. "The violence of his punishments for neglect of duty or for offenses against his policy," writes Klyuchevsky of Peter, "produced a neurasthenic condition in his
subordinates."

Similarly, a century later, accounts of the reign of Catherine II, liberal blue-stocking and friend of the Encyclopedists,
are full of floggings with rods and whips, and of tortures
more refined and more abnormal. Wrote the visiting French-
man, Passenans:

> I have taken precautions to avoid witnessing these cruel
> proceedings, but they occur so often, they are so habitual in
> the villages, that it is impossible to avoid hearing the cries
> of the unfortunate victims of inhuman caprice. Their cries
> followed me in dreams. Many times I wished that I had not
> understood the Russian language when I heard orders being
> given for punishments.

Not only revolution and counter-revolution have been accompanied by outbursts of violent cruelty. Terror and torture, physical violence, arbitrary, capricious and unrestrained, have been
a regular feature of much of normal, peaceful, benevolently

patriarchal life in old Russia, and part of the unconscious heritage of the new. The legendary-seeming acts of madmen related of so many Tsars were indeed not legend. "The trade of autocracy," as Mavor has written, "was an exhausting and dangerous business, imposing a severe strain upon the physical constitution and tending to the disturbance of mental equilibrium." And from that center of often well-intentioned and generous but as often brutal despotism, the same manners and methods filtered downward to manorial lords and overseers, army captains and factory foremen and provincial police chiefs.

During the latter half of the nineteenth century, the bonds that tied every serf to his land and lord, every man to his estate and occupation, began to dissolve. It was the hope of all democrats and lovers of the people that Russia, having "reached the limits of her natural expansion" and being comparatively secure from attack, might now turn from super-armies and military super-budgets to the "loosening of the bonds" and to the development of the cultural and physical well-being of its own people.

The last four decades of the nineteenth century, and the first two of the twentieth, were bright with this hope of the "loosening of the bonds." In 1861 serfdom was abolished by fiat of Alexander II. If that seems "late" in history, it is sobering for us to remember that the same year marked the outbreak of a great civil war in America, rooted in Negro slavery, and that Lincoln's Emancipation Proclamation of 1863 failed to endow the freed slaves with any of the land they had tilled, as Alexander did the freed serfs.

Followed the introduction of local zemstvo rule, trial by jury, irremovable judges, reduction in censorship, expansion of public education, town councils, factory inspection, social security legislation, shortening of the former "life-term" of military service, freedom of movement from the countryside into the cities, freedom to emigrate, freedom for foreigners to enter and move about the land. True, many of these reforms were incomplete, and were partially undermined by the reaction which followed the assassination of Alexander II. But, after 1905, they were further extended, a limited constitution was granted, a Duma or legislative parliament set up, a large measure of parliamentary immunity granted. In 1907 a new and sweeping land reform was initiated. In 1912, the revolutionary parties, not excluding the Bolsheviks, were permitted to establish legal daily papers. Finally, in the first revolution of 1917, literally all the bonds were loosened at once—save only the overweening bond of war. Why freedom did not come to flower and fruit in that swift growth is one of the tragic problems with which we shall have to deal.

Not stagnation, then, but the very rapidity and unevenness of change made increasingly intolerable all that was left of the old order. All through the latter half of the nineteenth century it continued to disintegrate, yet a new Russia seemed powerless to be born. Gradually, a sense of impending doom took possession of the ruling class and of the Court. The reform movement spread from the top downward, the history of the century presenting itself as a progressive widening of the circle of those who felt that change was necessary, and an increasing audacity in their conceptions of the nature of the change. Awakening from its millennial slumber, Russian public opinion took as its banner the words of a Dostoevsky: "In all things I go to the uttermost extreme; my life long I have never been acquainted with moderation." The reformer Tsars ended up in disillusionment. They were succeeded by lesser autocrats, unable to lead the nation boldly along the new uncharted ways, until at last the autocracy ceased to show signs of further adaptability, becoming the rallying center of opposition to change. Thereby it sealed its doom, handing over the initiative to the intelligentsia.

The Russian intelligentsia is a specific formation of nineteenth-century Russia, not to be identified with the "educated and professional classes" of the Western lands, or with the officials, technicians, and managers of present-day Russia. It was extruded out of a fixed society of medieval estates into which it no longer fitted, an ideological sign that that old world of status had been outgrown. It was recruited simultaneously from the more generous sons and daughters of the nobility, and from the plebeian youth: from above and from below. Its members were held together, neither by a common social origin and status, nor by a common role in the social process of production. The cement which bound them together was a common alienation from existing society, and a common belief in the sovereign efficacy of ideas as shapers of life. They lived precariously suspended as in a void, between an uncomprehending autocratic monarchy above and an uncomprehending, unenlightened mass below. Their mission as independent thinkers was to be critics of the world in which they had no place and prophets of a world that had not yet come into being, and might have no place for them either. They were lawyers without practice, teachers without schools, graduate clerics without benefices and often without religion, chemists without laboratories, technicians, engineers, statisticians for whom industry had as yet no need, journalists without a public, educators without schools, politicians without parties, sociologists and statesmen rejected by the state and ignored by the people. They anticipated and oversupplied in advance the requirements of a world that was too slow in coming into being, and sought to serve a folk that had no use for their services. In the decaying feudal order they found neither scope nor promise; in the gross, timid, and backward mercantile bourgeoisie neither economic support nor inspiration; in the slumbering people no echo to their ardent cries. Even while they sought to serve the unreceptive present, at heart they were the servants of the future. With all their being they longed for its coming, and all possible and impossible futures for Russia mingled together in their dreams.

Almost involuntarily they were forced into open enmity to the old order that had no use for them. Beginning as gentle dreamers, reformers, and humanitarians, they were constantly being punished for mere dreaming and forbidden to dream. In despite of themselves they were driven into open rebelliousness, a mood so general that the very word "student" would finally become synonymous with revolutionist. The better to regiment them and set them apart, the state devised a student uniform for them, and, sometimes, before their formal education was completed, exiled them to their native village, or to Siberia, for a "higher education." Many were lost and broken, many more forsook their generous vision as they grew older and adapted themselves to a career under the existing order. The noblest and the best sought to merge themselves with the people—who did not receive them; or hurled themselves single-handed, or in desperate little bands, against the still unshakable régime; or finished out their lives dreaming of home and freedom, in distant lands.

Their very culture was a source of torment to them. Their inherited or acquired privileges burdened them with a sense of guilt. How could they enjoy things of the spirit while around them the people remained in darkness and Russia decayed? Their deep love of their native land was transformed into a passionate hatred of all that was evil, backward, and degrading in it, and into a fierce belief in the nobility of its future destiny and mission in the world.

> *Thou art black with black injustice*
> *And slavery's yoke has branded thee. . . .*

wrote the Slavophile Khomyakov, welcoming the humiliation of his country in the Crimean War as a just punishment for its evils and a hope of its repentance and purification. In this he became the prototype of that apparent contradiction in terms, patriotic defeatism, which thenceforth was to characterize a good part of the intelligentsia.

When their efforts to rouse the people remained unanswered and their first attempts to shake the autocracy ended in deeper reaction, they came to be tortured by a sense of their own powerlessness, or they became more reckless in the scope of their dreams. Thought and feeling accumulated potential like a dammed-up stream. Over and over again they solved in agonizing theory the problems they were forbidden to touch in practice. They constructed grand systems, vast as Russia, embracing the whole of humanity. Their awareness of Russia's backwardness and lack of liberty mingled with their sense of Russia's grandeur, expansive force and imperial strength. That Slavic messianism which, after the fall of the Eternal City on the Tiber and the Eternal City on the Bosphorus, had seen in Moscow a "Third and Last Rome," now took on a new, a radical form. Even as they envied Western Europe they rejected it. The gospel that was destined to save and transform Russia would exalt that which made backward Russia different from and superior to the West; would make Russia capable of saving Europe from the evil which her own critics saw in her; would give to Russia the leading role in the salvation and transformation of the world.

Each decade, each half-decade, saw a completely new version of that evangel of universal salvation: through science, through the negation of tradition and convention, through literature and criticism, through nonresistance to evil, through a return to primitive Christianity, through the village commune, through love of the people and adoption of their way of life, through anarchism, agrarian socialism, Marxism—whatever the gospel of the moment, its disciples were ready to live by it and die for it and remake the world utterly in its image.

Not having much else to live by, they acquired the power of living by ideas alone. "The thoroughly true-to-type intolerance of the Russian intelligentsia," observes Berdyaev, "was self-protective; only so could it preserve itself in a hostile world; only thanks to fanaticism could it weather persecution."

It was a fanaticism that served as a surrogate for the older religions. It idealized Russia, the peasant, the proletariat, science, the machine. It made a true gospel of its particular brand of salvation. It possessed singleness, exclusivism, dogma, orthodoxy, heresy, renegation, schism, excommunication, prophets, disciples, vocation, asceticism, sacrifice, the ability to suffer all things for the sake of the faith. Heresy or rival doctrine was worse than ignorance; it was apostasy. To the disciple even of so rational a doctrine as that of Marx, an *ipse dixit* was an irrefutable proof.

This energy of dammed-up thought, prevented from overflowing into action, invested Russian literature with its peculiar intensity. A charged atmosphere, a sense of coming storm and apocalyptic revelation pervades the great works of nineteenth-century Russian literature. They are full of forebodings and prophecies, bear demonic charges of inhibited energy, give glimpses of ecstatic heights of hope, fearful depths of gloom. Their characters are driven by obscure compulsions into the most violent gestures and grimaces; their events take place against a background of preternatural darkness, illuminated by sudden flashes of blinding light; their sunlit passages seem brighter than the light of day.

Even the humor of Russian literature, without losing its gaiety, is yet grotesque and savage, full of violent and incomprehensible actions, fantastical gesticulations, terrible caricatures that come close to tragedy, laughter that verges on hysteria. What is *Dead Souls,* a humorous masterpiece? a sanative satire meant to heal Russia of deep maladies? the voice of a religious holy man, crying of wickedness, salvation, and doom? Not only the critics, its very author could not make up his mind or know what it was that he had done, or ever finish the work.

The intensity of these works took the whole Western world by storm; their love of humanity moved generous spirits everywhere; their self-determined and almost unconscious technique became the envy of every great novelist in a century of great novelists and in lands with a far older literary tradition. As the grand century of peace and progress came to a close, their forebodings began to seem prophetic for a world that was moving

toward universal war and social upheaval. Now in retrospect
we can see that not Dickens, Thackeray, or Hardy, not Balzac,
Zola, or Galdos, not even Turgeniev or Tolstoy, but Dostoevsky—whose voice sounded a trifle mad—was the prophet who
came nearest to foretelling whither both Russia and the optimistic, self-confident, progressive West were blindly driving.
The sufferings of his demon-ridden spirit enabled him to see
depths in human psychology that were covered over, to discern
the fearful outlines of the age in which at this moment we live,
to express the compulsive, uncontrollable furies of our war-
ridden, breakdown-tortured, totalitarian time—when an old
order, dying, seems powerless to die, and a new order, aborn-
ing, seems powerless to be born.

Since direct political discussion was prohibited, all literature
tended to become a criticism of Russian life, and literary criticism itself but another form of social criticism in the second
degree. If the censor forbade explicit statement, he was skilful-
ly eluded by indirection—by innocent-seeming tales of other
lands or times, by complicated parables, animal fables, double
meanings, overtones, by investing apparently trivial events
with the pent-up energies possessing the writer, so that the
reader was compelled to dwell on them until their hidden
meanings became manifest. Men found means of conveying a
criticism of the régime through a statistical monograph on
German agriculture, through the study of a sovereign four
centuries dead, the review of a Norwegian play, the analysis of
some evil in the Prussian or some virtue in the British state.
There developed that peculiar "Aesop language" which would
enable Lenin to fight Russian imperialism in wartime by a
statistical, theoretical analysis of the German variety. Still later
Bukharin was to employ the same device to circumvent a more
vigilant and ruthless censorship, when he wrote a pamphlet
attacking the Vatican, in which his criticisms of Loyola and the
"corpselike obedience" and discipline of the Jesuits implied his
criticism of the Stalinist régime.

Not only literature was charged with peculiar intensity and allegorical meaning. Often the most trivial acts became in some obscure fashion overpowering symbols. Whether to eat vegetable or animal food, whether to leave beard and hair uncut, whether to wear a peasant blouse or a flowing tie or a workman's shirt, might easily become, did become, matters of passion and banners of devotion.

The same energy charged the most abstract theoretical debates on philosophy or program and the most minute discussions of petty organizational detail. Conversation consumed the Russian intellectuals as a fever. They spent days and nights, weeks and months and years on end, discussing and rediscussing actions on which they were as yet powerless to embark.

If the peasant revolts of earlier centuries had been doomed for lack of urban leadership and thought-out program, now the situation was for several decades reversed. Russia was seething with programs and her cities crowded with would-be leaders; but the masses remained passive and indifferent, the countryside gave no sign. However, as the nineteenth century drew to a close, the atmosphere became charged with electricity. All signals presaged a coming storm. Theory and physical might, intellectual program and mass movement, city and countryside, began to approach each other.

The revolutionary intellectuals sensed that their day of isolation was drawing to a close; tomorrow they might find themselves captains of multitudes and determiners of Russia's destiny and perhaps the world's. With fiercer passion than ever, they fell to engaging in controversies of a minuteness, stubbornness, sweep, and fury unheard of in all the history of politics. At socialist congresses in 1903 and 1907, men who were hunted together and exiled together and shared a common basic program, yet wrangled endlessly with fanatical fury and subtlety—in the one case for three and in the other for five whole weeks of days and nights on end, reckless of financial cost, drain on health, buzzing of spies, and the fact that they were actually driven during the course of the exhausting debates from one land to another. Even on the boat going over the English Channel, they never stopped the argument for a moment.

The controversies of the period carried over into the underground movement inside Russia, into the prisons and places of penal exile in Siberia, into the cafés and hovels and lodging-houses of distant and alien cities. So great was the turmoil and the chatter, so unearthly the hours kept, so furious the quarrels, that it became a commonplace in hospitable Geneva and Zurich to see advertisements reading: "Roomers Wanted, No Russians."

The angry, intolerant battle went on under the very eyes of the tsarist police; government archives filled up with reports of positions and faction documents; police spies were as energetic as others in taking sides. Even as the revolutionists began the opening skirmishes with the common enemy, their war with each other continued to gain in fury.

The three with whom we are to deal grew up in the midst of it, and it absorbed their major energies for more than a quarter of a century. It was the touchstone by which they selected their followers and associated or quarreled with each other, the whetstone on which their minds were shaped and sharpened. With brief periods of truce or enforced silence, their whole lives were one long series of controversies. The aim they held in common was so easily realized, apparently, that the outlived institutions, drained of their content by a half century of intellectual mining and sapping, were to fall of their own weight. But not for that reason did the debate cease. The continued "discussion" was to make up the principal content of the two decades of Russian history from the Revolutions of 1917 to the purges of 1937, and its echoes were to shake the foundations not of Russia alone, but of all the world. The disinterested clash of theories was transformed into the interested clash of parties and factions, implemented by the terrible and categorical implements of power. Their lives were a duel to the death not merely with tsarism and capitalism, but equally with each other—with each other and with almost every one else whose name we shall meet in these pages. That struggle is an essential aspect of the revolution they made, and of the stuff their own lives were made of.

CHAPTER TWO

VLADIMIR ILYICH ULYANOV

Whoever wanted to learn to detest feudal barbarism should be born in Simbirsk.

—LEON TROTSKY

Let no one say that Lenin is an expression of some kind of allegedly Asiatic 'elemental Russian forces.' I was born under the same sky, I breathed the same air, I heard the same peasant songs and played in the same school playground, I saw the same limitless horizons from the same high bank of the Volga, and I know in my blood and bones that it is only by losing all touch with our native land, only by stamping out all natural feeling for it, only so could one do what Lenin did in deliberately and cruelly mutilating Russia.

—ALEXANDER KERENSKY

Surely thou couldst only have been born among a spirited people—in that land that does not care to do things by halves, but has spread a vast plain over half the world, and one may count its milestones until one's eyes are dizzy.

—NIKOLAI GOGOL

The Volga is a slow, monotonous river that takes its rise at the heart of Russia midway between Petersburg and Moscow, majestically winding its way eastward to Nizhni Novgorod and Kazan, thence southward through the Tartar country, past Simbirsk, Samara and Saratov down to Astrakhan, where it empties, still unhurried, into the vast landlocked Caspian Sea. Around it cluster the songs and legends of the Great-Russians. The land's few revolutionary traditions—the fierce peasant and Cossack revolts of the seventeenth and eighteenth centuries—are indissolubly linked with its name. The true history of Russia, in contrast to the intrigue and turbulence surrounding the Muscovite court, is as slow and monotonous and uneventful as is the course of this river. It, rather than the Urals, forms the true boundary separating Europe from Asia. On the "European" side, the shore rises into hills and bluffs as if nature had constructed palisades to aid in repelling the Mongol invader. On the other bank there are only the low plains and endless expanse of the Asiatic steppe stretching out to the horizon.

On this river, as befits a leader and ruler of the Great-Russian people, Lenin was born; on the hills of the "European" bank he spent his childhood and youth; in his veins flowed its mixed bloods of Tartar and Great-Russian and Volga German. From Astrakhan his father came, and his mother from the province of Kazan. In Simbirsk he was born, studied in Saratov and Kazan; near Samara he lived through his brief experience as a landowner and exploiter of peasants; in Samara, too, he began and ended his short career as a law clerk or junior attorney and engaged in his first activities as a revolutionist. When at last he left the banks of the Volga for Saint Petersburg he was grown to man's estate, a fully formed Marxist who had chosen revolution as his "profession."

Simbirsk, where the future Lenin was born, in 1870, was then and still is a backward, desolate provincial capital. Its wooden buildings are scattered in disorderly fashion up the sides and over the summit of one of the more commanding hills of the "European" bank, standing guard like a fortress against the endless steppes to the East. On the "crown," as it elegantly called itself, were a few unimpressive buildings of stone: the governor's palace, the cathedral, the *gymnazia,** the prison, and the little library dedicated to the memory of the historian Karamzin. Its climbing roads were ruts of sticky mud in the spring and repositories of light-flying dust in mid-summer, yet it did not lack moments of physical beauty. No town on the hills overlooking the Volga and the steppes can be altogether devoid of beauty. "From the summit right down to the waterside," writes Alexander Kerensky, who was born there ten years later than Lenin, "stretched luxuriant apple and cherry orchards. In the spring the whole mountainside was white with blossom, fragrant, and at night breathless with the songs of the nightingales. . . . With the melting of the snow, the river used to leave its banks and flood the low-lying lands on the left, stretching like an endless sea over the fields which, later, in the heat of the summer, would be gay with the songs and games of peasants and townspeople come to mow the rich fragrant grass. . . ."

Vladimir Ilyich Ulyanov—the boy whose underground name was to ring round the world—was at birth one of a mere thirty thousand souls who lived their quiet, undistinguished, routinary lives in this most conservative and stagnant of the river capitals. No railroad connected it with the rest of the country; one had to go many miles by horse to Syzran to take the train. It was not even a significant river port. Its peasants were more backward, its handicraft industries more local and insignificant, its nobility more impoverished and stubbornly reactionary, its life more stagnant than that of the other Volga capitals.

It was young, too, as river towns went, and poorer than the rest in history. It possessed no fabled past like Nizhni Novgorod, Kazan and Astrakhan; it was, indeed, scarce two centuries old when Vladimir was born. The revolutionary traditions of

* The Russian *gymnazia* was a type of intermediate or university preparatory school roughly corresponding to our senior high school and junior college.

Pugachov, the Cossack pretender, and of Stenka Razin, the Russian Robin Hood—traditions which haunted all the rest of the length and breadth of the Volga valley—had no foothold here. Rather did Simbirsk find cause for boasting in the fact that its serfs had been too impoverished and apathetic to rebel, and that it alone had held out against Cossack and peasant risings as a bastion of reaction, while those two great movements swept by and around it to their short-lived triumphs and inevitable doom.

Its intellectual glories, too, were symbols of sloth and social backwardness. Its two great men before the time of Lenin were the historian Karamzin and the novelist Goncharov: that Karamzin who was the literary antagonist of the modest reform proposals of Speransky and who became the leading historian of reaction, creating in his works a vast and stately monument to despotism, written, Pushkin declared, to show the Russian people "the necessity of autocracy and the charms of the knout"; and that Goncharov whose one great fictional creation, Oblomov, had become a symbol of all that was torpid, apathetic, and impotent in the sprawling Russian spirit. It was here, in the shabby elegance of the nobles' quarter of Simbirsk, that Goncharov formed his melancholy impressions of the decaying gentry whose soul he embodied in the elephantine apathy of his anti-hero. Oblomov consumes over two hundred pages of the novel bearing his name in the mere effort to get out of bed and dress, and spends most of the rest of it in moving sluggishly from decrepit sofa to slovenly dressing gown, dreaming, amid intermittent snores, of the possibility of better things, of improving the lot of his peasants and the income of his broken-down estate, of wedding the girl he passionately adores, yet never rousing himself sufficiently to lift a finger toward the realization of his dreams.

But the boyhood years which Lenin spent in Simbirsk were far from unhappy. His father, Ilya Nikolaevich Ulyanov, was a solid and respectable figure in the bureaucratic and intellectual life of the provincial capital. Until the latter's death the family knew neither want nor rebellion. Their household was one breathing order, peace, conscientious devotion to duty, domestic simplicity and quiet affection. The boy, unsuspecting of the symbolism that might one day be read into his Christian name of Vladimir ("Lord of the World"), enjoyed the boyhood that goes with a healthy body, a lively brain, an ironical sense of fun, an ability to excel easily in studies and sports and childish tests of strength. He knew the peaceful and untroubled existence that springs from a modest and assured economic foundation, parents who respected themselves and each other and were respected by the community, and an atmosphere of family harmony in which brothers and sisters loved and cared for each other. There was fishing and swimming in the river, wandering over its hills, skating, sliding, sleighing on its frozen surface in winter, hunting as he grew older. There were long summer sojourns with mother and aunt and cousins of like age, at his mother's paternal estate in the village of Kukushkino in the Province of Kazan. There were games of sport and imagination and stories told or read aloud by the mother. She sang to her children and played for them on her pianoforte, and taught Volodya (affectionate for Vladimir) to play on it, as she did her other children. She and her husband were their first instructors in reading and writing. Volodya and his older sister, Anna, were each taught to read at the age of five, and his precocious older brother, Alexander, at the age of four. There were high marks at school and honors and prizes and the intellectual joys that come from the exercise of an able brain and entrance into possession of a goodly portion of the accumulated cultural heritage of the race. From his mother's example and teaching, the boy early learned to love books and learning, to find solace and absorption in the great Russian novels and poems that this remarkable century was creating, and to find deep joy in music.

In short, in all the reminiscences of brothers and sisters and family friends, as in Lenin's own occasional references to his childhood, there is nothing to accord with the fashionable "psychological" explanations of the careers of the world's great rebels, nothing to document the formula of mother or father fixation, no unhappy family life, maladjusted childhood, youthful rebellion against domestic tyranny, no traces of a sense of inferiority due to failure at school or in childish competitive sports, no sign of queerness or abnormality. True, the hanging of his older brother, Alexander, for an attempt on the life of the Tsar when Vladimir was only sixteen, was an event to put iron into his adolescent soul, but that only moves the question a little further back: what made brother Alexander into a plotter and a rebel? We shall have to look elsewhere than to the maladjustments of a miserable childhood for the motive forces that drove them to hate feudal barbarism and despotism and to choose revolution as a way of life.

Friends and enemies alike who knew the Ulyanov family have left testimony in their memoirs as to the bright and industrious harmony prevailing there. Its head, Ilya Nikolaevich,* was somewhat given to the quiet exercise of patriarchal authority within the home (while he lived his wife looked up to him as her intellectual superior and the family's undisputed head). But the patriarchalism was no more, rather much less, than prevailed in other families of the same region, time and social class. Ilya Nikolaevich must have had a capacity for anger, since his eldest daughter, Anna, in a work of unmitigated piety, speaks of Lenin's having inherited his father's love of work, his gay, sociable nature and inclination to humor and jest "and also his quick temper." But there is ample evidence that his influence was exerted chiefly by the force of example rather than by coercion. The children did not remember ever having witnessed a quarrel between their parents or a disagreement in their presence.

---

* The Russian custom is to give the Christian or given name and the patronymic or father's first name with an ending signifying "son of." Thus Lenin's father was Ilya Nikolaevich Ulyanov, signifying Ilya, son of Nikolai Ulyanov. Lenin's name, Vladimir Ilyich Ulyanov, means Vladimir, son of Ilya Ulyanov. "Lenin" is of course one of the pseudonyms he adopted in his prolonged duel with the police. His older sister Anna's married name is Anna Ilyinishna Ulyanova Elisarova, signifying Anna, daughter of Ilya Ulyanov and wife of Elisarov.

All his life the head of the Ulyanov household bore on his spirit the sobering mark of a hard, orphaned childhood and a consciousness of how much an older brother had sacrificed and how he himself had labored to secure an education. From his pupils, his subordinates and his children, he expected the same devotion to duty, diligence and application, and the same respect for study that he had himself. Anna records that he feared for his young son, Vladimir, because learning seemed to come a little too easily to him, without arousing sufficient tension and effort. But if he had lived to see that son's bulldog intellectual tenacity and powers of sustained application and prolonged exertion in later days, he would have been satisfied that his fears had been vain.

Ilya Nikolaevich was universally reputed to be industrious, intelligent, respectful towards authority, and philanthropic in the older sense of that word. He was a deep believer in the meliorative value of education, unselfishly devoted to his profession, first as teacher of physics and mathematics, then as provincial inspector and superintendent of schools. He had come of a modest plebeian family of Astrakhan (his father is believed to have been a tailor), which distinguished itself from its similars only by a certain devotion to learning and zeal for advancement. Astrakhan, at the mouth of the Volga, was an old Tartar town and the family, Great-Russians, had some Tartar blood in their veins. It showed in the high cheekbones, flat nose and deepset, small, slanting eyes of both Ilya Nikolaevich and of his son, Vladimir Ilyich (Lenin), who so closely resembled him.

The father of Ilya Nikolaevich (that is, Lenin's paternal grandfather) had died when Ilya was only seven. Grandfather, father and son were alike destined to die at a fairly early age. When Ilya became an orphan, an older brother, thirteen years his senior, dropped his own schooling to support the family and to see Ilya through school. Thus Lenin's father began, on behalf of the family, the upward climb that was to lead from the plebeian estate to that of nobility, by the only avenue of ascent open to it: service to the state.

The school career of Ilya Nikolaevich more than justified his elder brother's sacrifice. He graduated with honors from the *gymnazia* at Astrakhan, and then, also with honors, from the University of Kazan. Here Ilya attracted the favorable attention of a mathematics teacher, Lobashevsky (world-renowned today as the founder of non-Euclidian geometry), on whose recommendation he was given the post—unpaid—of director of the Meteorological Station of Penza. His living he earned as instructor in physics and mathematics at the secondary school of the Institute of the Nobility in Penza. The devoted filling of such unremunerated posts was typical of the fashion in which the old-time Russian intelligentsia built up Russian science and culture, and Russia's knowledge of her own resources.

When Ilya Nikolaevich left Penza at the age of thirty-three for a similar post as instructor in the *gymnazia* of Nizhni Novgorod, he took with him his newly acquired bride, Maria Alexandrovna Blank, twenty-nine-year-old younger sister of the wife of a colleague at whose home he had boarded in his bachelor days in Penza. In Nizhni, this secondary-school instructor founded a family, and there his first two children, Anna and the ill-starred Alexander, were born. In the sixth year of his marriage he was promoted once more, this time to the post of inspector of schools in the Province of Simbirsk. Simbirsk was a comedown from the great town of Nizhni Novgorod, but the new appointment meant advancement in grade and compensation and the abandonment of teaching and meteorological research for a bureaucratic career. It is not on record that Ilya Nikolaevich hesitated to accept. His daughter Anna explains the change on the ground that the emancipation of the serfs by Alexander II (in 1861) and the subsequent reforms in local self-government and education had made possible the opening of new schools and the spread of instruction to new sections of the population. By the reform of 1864 the zemstvos were given the supervision of local schools, and, by the efforts of such enlightened and devoted officials as Ilya

Ulyanov, public education spread—despite occasional setbacks
—so that by 1914 there were fifty thousand zemstvo schools
and a planned expansion of the educational budget envisaged
universal education by 1922. The war of 1914 and the civil war
of 1917 delayed but did not permanently hinder the realization
of the dream of universal education and general literacy, the
foundations of which were laid by the generation of zemstvo
educators of which Lenin's father was one.

When the Ulyanov family moved to Simbirsk in 1869, the
new school inspector was thirty-nine years of age, his wife
thirty-five, and they took with them two children. A third was
on the way. That third child, born on April 22, 1870, they were
to name Vladimir, after the saint who was the first Christian
ruler of Russia. One day the backward provincial town to
which the Ulyanovs were moving was to have its name changed
from Simbirsk to Ulyanovsk, in honor of the son who was
born to them soon after they arrived in their new home.

Maria Alexandrovna Ulyanova, the mother of this little
family, had more time than ever to devote to her children. She
had few friends at first, and Simbirsk was much slower and
duller than Nizhni Novgorod. The schools were scattered, the
roads bad, the distances great; arduous trips by horse and sleigh
or horse and carriage kept the new inspector away from wife
and children for long stretches of time. His homecomings were
remembered as festive occasions. The care, education and upbringing of the growing family—there were to be six children
in due course, not counting one who died soon after birth—
were largely left to the mother, and, as the family fortunes improved, to a hired tutor.

In the beginning the inspector met with little interest on the
part of the local governmental régime in his efforts to improve
the quantity and quality of the scattered schools of Simbirsk
Province. He himself gave courses in pedagogy to prepare new
teachers. In time, his self-denying zeal and devotion to duty
attracted the attention of influential superiors so that he was

promoted once more in the rapidly expanding school system to
the new post of director of primary schools for the entire province, with several inspectors under him. His reliability and respectability made him acceptable to the authorities even as they
were beginning to have misgivings about the spread of popular
education, while his reputation among those really interested in
education began to spread beyond the confines of Simbirsk.
His ascent up the bureaucratic ladder now brought with it the
honorific title of "Actual State Councillor" accompanied by
hereditary nobility for him and his children.* Thus, in 1874,
when Vladimir was three years old, the lad's status changed
from that of plebeian to nobleman; so that all the ink that has
been spilt in discussions as to whether the future Lenin was of
one origin or the other has been spilt in vain, since he was each
in turn. By the time he was old enough to fill out school or police questionnaires—and he filled out many of the latter in his
lifetime—he was privileged, even obliged, to record himself as
a member of Russia's state-created or bureaucratic hereditary
nobility. Not from his father's title, but from his mother's
modest estate, he was also, for a time, a landowner.

Bolshevik prudery is reticent concerning the youthful Vladimir's slow mastery of the "political facts of life." Nowadays, he
is habitually treated as if he were born a Bolshevik, and as if
his father had been a revolutionist before him. The persistence
of such a legend in his official biographies is illuminating. In a
land where hereditary status is ingrained in the very texture of
life, where one's right to schooling was denied under the old
régime if one were "the son of a cook," and was later to be
denied under the new régime if one were "the son of a kulak,"
such legends are more than an attempt to evade the problem of
tracing the development of their subject's views. Moreover,
the current cult of the infallibility of the leader and the apostolic succession requires him to have sprung, ideologically fully

* "Actual State Councillor" was one degree higher than "State Councillor" and carried with it the title
of "Excellency" and the privilege of hereditary nobility. It corresponded to the rank of major general
in the army.

armed, from the womb, as the Greek goddess of wisdom from the forehead of Zeus.

Leon Trotsky in his brilliant study of *The Youth of Lenin* (the first volume of a life destined never to be completed) has examined all the evidence available in this matter. With patient and ironical persistence he reduces the official legends to foolishness. For the facts are, as he amply demonstrates, that Lenin's father was orthodox in religion—without that strain of mysticism which sometimes challenges the authority of the hierarchy and institutionalized church; a champion of domestic order and discipline—without that excess of tyranny and cruelty which, when it does not break the spirit, is conducive to rebellion; a sincere servant of the state devoted to improving its foundations by the spread of religion and popular education —without ever dreaming for a moment of calling into question the established order, the authority of his immediate superiors, or the autocracy of the Tsar.

Ilya Nikolaevich was an earnest man of good will. Devotion to his duties in a land where popular education itself was frequently regarded with suspicion, represents the sum and substance of his "liberalism." Former students of his, who later attained sufficient importance to write their memoirs, mention with respect this hard-working instructor in mathematics and physics, who put his heart and soul into his teaching, and voluntarily gave up part of his Sundays to tutor the more impoverished and backward of his pupils without charge. Teachers who served under him as he advanced in official position speak favorably of his inspectorship and subsequent directorship. But there is no record—quite the contrary—of his having defended any of his subordinates from dismissal for radicalism. Indeed, his daughter relates how a niece came to him to complain of the unjust dismissal of a teacher by his superiors. Ilya Nikolaevich, she reports, listened without saying a word, "his head lowered, he kept his thoughts to himself."

Official documents reveal that in seventeen years of service as an education official he was credited with the construction of some 450 new tiny school houses in his backward province, and a doubling of the number of pupils enrolled. However, the period of his inspectorship coincided with a general period of growth of zemstvo or local educational facilities throughout the country, so that the achievement, while genuine, must not be writ too large, or ascribed too exclusively to his individual zeal and ability. Still, he was sufficiently above average to stand out among his peers so that a liberal zemstvo nobleman of his *gubernya* could write of him as a "rare, exceptional phenomenon," and, describing his tireless efforts in the face of difficulty and apathy, could say: "Such strength and vigor can come only from a devotion bordering on abnegation." (*Vestnik Evropy,* 1876.) Not every provincial official was sufficiently noticed to have himself written about in a metropolitan paper in Saint Petersburg! And even as late as 1906, in a history of public education in Russia published more than a quarter of a century after the inspector's death, and before his son's fame could give him retroactive importance, it was still recorded that among the educators of the Province of Simbirsk "the first place belongs, according to the unanimous opinion of his contemporaries, to Ilya Nikolaevich Ulyanov."

The very unanimity and continuity of official approval, however, is sufficient refutation of the theory that Alexander and Vladimir Ulyanov, and the other less celebrated children of Ilya Nikolaevich, "inherited" their revolutionary tendencies from their father. What they did derive from him were such things as a good head, an ability to move familiarly in the world of books, a tendency to application, hard work, unswerving devotion to duty as they might conceive it. But their conception of duty would likely have shocked their good father had he lived long enough to learn of it. That this is so, the available evidence leaves no doubt.

Thus we find that the zealous inspector of schools, Ilya Ulyanov, went beyond the obligations of his post to report to his superiors a lack of zeal on the part of the village priests in the teaching of the catechism. And the catechism of the Russian

Lenin's family

Portrait of Alexander Ilyich Ulyanov, Lenin's brother, taken shortly before he was executed

Lenin as a child

Krupskaya
when Lenin first met her

Lenin in 1895

Martov,
Lenin's closest associate until the split

Plekhanov, Lenin's teacher

Orthodox Church goes beyond the simple rendering unto Caesar of that which is Caesar's, as the following passage will suffice to demonstrate:

Question. What does religion teach us as to our duties to the Tsar?

Answer. Worship, fidelity, the payment of taxes, service, love and prayer—the whole being comprised in the words, worship and fidelity.

It is interesting to pursue the legend of the revolutionary character of the elder Ulyanov a little further, since it provides a relatively innocent example of the retouching of the past to fit the dominant folklore, which makes so difficult the work of biographer or historian who must deal with Soviet sources. Trotsky quotes with angry irony from biographies of Lenin which portray his rather timid and moderate father as one who "regarded the revolutionary movement with great sympathy," and which make of his home on Moscow Street in Simbirsk a sort of revolutionists' club in which "the tone was given by Alexander (Lenin's elder brother)," while Vladimir also "participated frequently in the discussions and with great success." At that time, the youthful Vladimir must have been all of thirteen or fourteen years of age, since his father died before he turned fifteen! Even Lunacharsky, who was a more scrupulous writer than most and who wrote before a respect for historical truth had been completely purged from the printed page and from the heads of men, sets it down as fact that the father of the Ulyanov household "sympathized with the revolutionists and brought up his children in a revolutionary spirit."

Against this retroactive revision of ancestral traits, we have the testimony of Lenin's elder sister, Anna. "Our father, who was never a revolutionary, during those years—being more than forty years of age and head of a family—wanted to protect us, his children."

The state, too, as we have seen, gave ample testimony to its confidence in the reliability of Ilya Nikolaevich. From teacher

to inspector of other teachers, from inspector to director of
primary instruction for an entire province and superior of
various inspectors—such watchdog posts were not knowingly
given, in the reactionary Russia of the seventies and eighties,
to men of doubtful loyalty. As early as 1859 the earnest teacher
had received a bonus of 150 rubles "for his excellent services
and his zeal." Though there were repeated investigations of the
teaching staff for germs of sedition, Ilya Nikolaevich was never
called in question. The creation of the posts of inspector and
director of primary schools, which posts he filled from the moment of their respective creation, were steps in the calculated
subjection of local educational institutions to the bureaucratic
center at Saint Petersburg. All through the closing years of
the reign of Alexander II, who was assassinated by revolutionists, and especially during the reign of his son, Alexander III,
this process of curbing the autonomy of the institutions of local
government, the zemstvos, continued as a part of the growing
reaction. Years later, Lenin was to write of this reactionary
process, and to pick out two symbolic dates, of both public
and biographical interest, as mileposts in this backward march
from the great reforms of Alexander II's earlier years. The dates
he selected as markers on that road were the years 1869 and
1874. They were the dates when the posts of inspector and director of primary schools were created, and the very dates, as
Lenin knew, when his father had been appointed to each of
those posts in turn!

In 1869—Lenin wrote in an article on zemstvo liberalism,
published in 1901—the office of inspector of elementary schools
was created for the purpose of taking the effective management
of elementary education out of the hands of the zemstvo. . . .
In 1871, instructions were issued to the inspectors of elementary
schools empowering them to dismiss teachers who are deemed
politically unreliable. . . . In 1874, a new regulation was passed
which placed the management of the schools entirely in the
hands of the school directors. . . . [Zarya, No. 2-3, Dec. 1901,
signed T.P., Lenin's Collected Works, Vol. IV, pp. 133-4.]
Who does not know—Lenin was to write eleven years after

his father's death—how easily is accomplished in Holy Russia the transformation of a radical intellectual, of a socialist intellectual, into a functionary of the imperial government—a functionary who consoles himself by thinking that there is "a certain utility" within the limits of the routine of office—a functionary who justifies by that "utility" his own political apathy, his obsequiousness before the government of the *knout* and the *nagaika*.

Clearly there is more than an accidental touch of family biography in these two passages. "It would be unjust," comments Trotsky on the second passage, "to apply without reservation these severe words to Ilya Nikolaevich Ulyanov, but only because he had been neither socialist nor radical in his youth."

Thus, while educational reaction grew apace, Ilya Nikolaevich continued his unwavering devotion to his career, ascending with unbroken regularity the slow grades of civil promotion, until he received in good time the decoration of the Order of Saint Vladimir, the title of "Excellency" and the hereditary nobility of which we have already spoken. There is nothing to set in doubt the official epitaph written of him by the subsequent Deputy from Simbirsk to the Second Duma, Delarov:

"I. N. Ulyanov was a man of conservative views, but not reactionary or conservative in the ancient way—he had his personal aim in life . . . zeal in serving the good of the people." This zeal, and this alone, is the social heritage of Alexander and Vladimir Ulyanov from their father. The rest is legend, stupid, mendacious legend, serving no purpose the historian or the biographer can honor.

To this social heritage of zeal in the service of the people, respect for education, and ease in moving through the world of books, Vladimir added a physical and personal inheritance which he did not share with his older brother. Vladimir resembled his father in features and constitution; Alexander his mother. If Lenin in the prime of his maturity had let the fringe of reddish hair around the great bald forehead grow a little longer and his beard assume statelier flow and dimensions, if he had dressed himself in the respectable outfit of a late nine-teenth-century functionary in the employ of the state in place of his own unvarying and no less respectable outfit of a bour-geois *bonhomme* of the early twentieth, old-timers in Simbirsk might well have thought that His Excellency, Ilya Nikolaevich Ulyanov, Director of Primary Schools and Actual Councillor of State, had returned once more. The same tiny, slanting, pale, chestnut-colored Mongolian eyes with the same little wrinkles of fun-loving laughter around the edges, the same plump cheeks and high cheekbones, the same strongly marked features, the same broad, flat and slightly curved nose, the same high fore-head made yet higher by premature baldness in the days of young manhood, the same somewhat flattened back of the skull, the same short, pudgy, rotund, muscular body, the same hunch to the shoulders, the same solid, self-contained physique and spirit, suggestive of great physical and moral force, the same reddish hair—where there was any—and grayish complex-ion, the same hint of plethora of the blood, almost the identical winding up of the clock of life—a tense spring capable of run-ning strong for some fifty years and then destined to snap sud-denly—in both cases by a hemorrhage in the brain.

Much has been written of Lenin's wearing himself out in the hard exertions and cares of running one-sixth of the earth in the midst of universal ruin and chaos, and of the shortening of his life by the bullet from Dora Kaplan's gun. Trotsky has even hinted, in his last article in *Liberty* (August 10, 1940), that Stalin hastened the death of the bedridden man by administer-ing poison. Certainly, any of these theories would greatly in-crease the drama and the conventional biographical suitability of Lenin's death. But the "evidence" which Trotsky adduces is too thin and insubstantial, too like the Moscow trials "evi-dence" against Trotsky himself. And while the ruthless pace of self-driving whereby this man, who died in his fifty-fourth year, seemed to crowd fivescore years of living into little more than half a century, may well have shortened his life, yet the biogra-pher cannot help but note that his father, of whom he was the "spit and image," died in his fifty-fifth year and that the medical certificate offers cerebral hemorrhage as the cause, even as in the case of the son.

Lenin's mother remains a mystery in Soviet literature; and there are not presently available unofficial sources from which an inquiring biographer might safely learn anything to fill the great gaps in the otherwise prolix flood of memoirs and biographies. Her maiden name was Blank, Maria Alexandrovna Blank. The family name is obviously not Russian, but there is no hint in all the official literature as to the national origin of that Alexander Blank who was Lenin's maternal grandfather. The silence suggests deliberate reticence, for such matters are easily ascertained in a land where every man registered with the police, bore a passport for internal travel, and had all his goings and comings recorded from the day of his birth to the day of his death.

Alexander Blank was a medical doctor and landowner of the Province of Kazan. He married a girl from the German colony on the Volga, and their daughter, Lenin's mother, was brought up in the German tradition. This fact is more hinted at than stated in the existing literature. Decisive are the memoirs of Lenin's elder sister, Anna—though even she is strangely vague on her mother's family origin. From Anna we learn that her mother did not manifest the same religious orthodoxy as the father, that the sum and substance of her religious tradition lay in the solemn-sweet observance of the Germanic tradition of the Christmas tree, and that "she visited the Russian church as little as the German temple." This implies that her family religion might have been Protestant. For the rest, Anna makes clear, her piety was an inward force which moved her to prayer only in moments of great trial. Twice, Anna records, her mother besought her to "pray for Sasha" (diminutive for Alexander, the oldest boy). The first time, he was desperately ill and the doctors had told his mother that he might not live. The second time, Anna was facing her mother through the double grille of bars through which prisoners are permitted to speak to their visitors. The girl hung onto the prison bars and inquired anxiously concerning the success of her mother's efforts to save Alexander from the hangman. Actually, he had already been hanged, but Maria Alexandrovna did not tell her daughter. Her only answer to the question was once more, "Pray for Sasha."

Lenin's mother came, it seems clear, from a higher social layer than the young secondary-school teacher whose bride she became, for she brought as dowry a modest landed estate in Kukushkino, presumably one-fifth of the estate of her father. Her education, like that of most women of her time, had been received entirely at home: a little desultory tutoring when tutors could be hired, instruction in languages and music and the domestic arts and the graces proper to her class. She knew German, French and English and taught the rudiments of these languages to her children. She early learned to read and love books, an affection which she communicated to her children, also. Reading aloud of an evening to her family circle was a common custom, so that the future Lenin acquired in childhood a wide acquaintance with the Russian novel and a love for the great classics of its sudden heyday, which he carried with him all his life. His plain, usually pedestrian writings display as almost their sole adornment an occasional illustration of some political trait by reference to a character known to the readers of Russian literature. These unostentatious literary allusions are to Gogol, Saltykov-Shchedrin, Griboyedov, Pushkin, Goncharov, Tolstoy, Krylov, and Turgeniev, whose newly written novels must have been coming into Lenin's home during his childhood, and whose work he loved best of all.

The one characteristic which stands out in the meager material on Lenin's mother is the steady, warm flame of her unquestioning devotion to her children. The family was—after the German rather than the Russian fashion—not a demonstrative one. There was little kissing or embracing, few tears at parting or in time of misfortune. But Maria Alexandrovna Ulyanova was devoted to her children and tireless in bearing, rearing and training them and watching over them in illness and adversity. She sheltered them to the best of her ability from the difficulties of somewhat reduced circumstances after her husband died. She humiliated herself by pleading with the officials her husband had served under, when it was a question of getting her expelled son Vladimir reinstated in the university, shortening or moderating terms of prison or exile for one or another child, or shielding them from persecution as a result of their activities. All of her children were arrested at one time or another, sometimes several of them at once, and always if she could she moved near the prison, or into the town of administrative exile, of the one who seemed most in need of her ministrations. She never professed to understand the activities which brought her eldest son to the gallows and her two daughters and two other sons into the hands of the police on various occasions. But she sympathized in a general way, was even proud, as so many parents in those days were, of the abnegation, devotion to society and to freedom, which she understood to be the content of the activities that got them into trouble. She asked no questions, made no reproaches, wasted little time in lamentation and none in efforts to persuade them to abandon the paths onto which their consciences had led them. To her they were children who had grown up and were old enough to decide their own conduct. Her task was to follow their fate with anxiety or pride, to stand by them in their hour of need, to send them money, books, clothes, food, delicacies, to visit them when authorities and regulations permitted, never to waver in her loyalty however much official society branded them as criminals and monsters.

Maria Alexandrovna outlasted her husband by thirty years, all the years of her children's adversity. She went twice abroad to see her long-exiled son Vladimir Ilyich—the last time in 1913 —and died in Russia at the age of eighty-one, a little more than a year before his return to become head of the new Russian state.

CHAPTER THREE

LIFE
AND
DEATH
OF
ALEXANDER
ILYICH

To you who desire to cross this threshold, do you know what awaits you?

I know, replied the girl.

Cold, hunger, abhorrence, derision, contempt, abuse, prison, disease, and death!

I know, I am ready, I shall endure all blows.

Not from enemies alone, but also from relatives, from friends.

Yes, even from them . . .

Are you ready even to commit a crime?

I am ready for crime, too.

Do you know that you may be disillusioned in that which you believe, that you may discover that you were mistaken, that you ruined your young life in vain?

I know that, too.

Enter!

The girl crossed the threshold, and a heavy curtain fell behind her.

Fool! said some one, gnashing his teeth.

Saint! some one uttered in reply.

—IVAN TURGENIEV

Vladimir had been backward in learning to walk. He took his first steps at the same time as his younger sister, Olga, some eighteen months his junior, and then his efforts were not altogether successful. For some time, each adventure in toddling was likely to end in catastrophe, a fall on the nose and a howl that resounded through the neighborhood. "Probably his head was heavier than his body," is the explanation offered in the memoirs of his older sister, Anna.

Despite his diminutive height he began to show great prowess in trials of strength and speed. When those of like age did not offer sufficient competition, he chose to emulate his brother Alexander, four years his senior. Soon the effort to pattern himself after his older brother was reduced to a formula.

"Volodya," his mother would ask him, "how do you want your kasha?" (It is worth noting in passing that the family régime was not so stern as to permit of no selection by the children.) Volodya waited to see whether his older brother would take his cereal with milk or with butter, and then: "I want mine like Sasha." When Alexander came home from the *gymnazia* wearing his new student's uniform, his younger brother became fired with enthusiasm for learning: he too wanted to have a uniform like Sasha's.

Yet, in physique as in temperament they were as different as two brothers could possibly be. Alexander's face was long and brooding; his skin milky white; his hair, thick, turbulent, frizzy, deeply rooted, stood up in all directions from a line far down on the forehead. His eyes, set deep and on a strange angle in a nobby, overhanging brow, seemed to turn their gaze inward. It was the strongly chiseled face of a dreamer, a saint, a devotee, an ascetic. But Vladimir's head was shaped like an egg, and the thin fringe of reddish hair began to recede from the forehead before he was twenty, leaving him bald, like his father, in young manhood. His complexion was a blend of grayishness and full-bloodedness; his eyes tiny, twinkling, Mongoloid. His whole aspect, except in moments of intense thought or anger, was jovial, humorous, mischievous, self-confident, aggressive. Not knowing him, one might have taken him in later years for a hard-working kulak, a rising provincial official, a shrewd businessman. There was nothing in his build or appearance or temperament to suggest kinship with his brother Alexander.

The young boy was noisy and boisterous, a player of practical jokes, an inveterate tease, quick at repartee, sharp of tongue. He loved to exhibit the growing powers of his mind by raillery at the expense of his little brothers and sisters, young cousins and playmates. The one bad mark in his high-school record came for playing pranks on a French teacher whose pomposity he disliked. Various people testify to the fits of ill-temper to which young Vladimir was subject on occasion, while his mockery and intellectual superiority created a certain wall between him and the other lads of his age. ("Vladimir Ilyich enjoyed the love of his schoolmates," writes the pious Anna, "although he had no very close friends.")

But the older boy was habitually silent and reserved. Throughout his school career there is not one bad report by any of his teachers recorded against him. He rarely spoke unless addressed, and then to the point, directly and briefly. No one, not even his mother or his sister Anna, the two that were closest to him, ever knew what was going on in his head. The great moments of his life came as a bewildering surprise to them. Even when they reviewed it all in retrospect, they could remember few signs that might have foreshadowed his destiny. He read much, meditated much, studied in solitude, thought through his perplexities alone, then acted resolutely to carry out his conclusions.

The polarity of these two temperaments is symbolized in their choice of favorite authors—a polarity which characterized the entire nineteenth century Russian intelligentsia: Alexander's favorite was Dostoevsky; Vladimir's was Turgeniev and the realistic, "preconversion" Tolstoy. In Dostoevsky the older brother found the brooding introspection, the morbid saintliness, the terrible humility and compassion, the compulsive urge to self-immolation that were to reveal themselves as having been at the core of his character, in the early hour when it was put to the test.

Each lad was invariably the best student in his class and they received uniformly high marks in all subjects. Each won the gold medal as the Simbirsk *gymnazia's* "best student." But here too they showed marked differences in intellectual character. Alexander's predilection was for science, Vladimir's for Latin, history and literature. Both were thorough in their preparations, but the younger boy was so swift that he seemed to finish his homework before he was well settled down in the house, and then his noisy ebullience disturbed his older brother. Sometimes his father put him through his paces to ascertain whether he had mastered his lessons, and did not know whether to be pleased at his speed or fearful that because things came so easily, his son might never acquire the powers of prolonged application.

Writing compositions was Alexander's most difficult exercise in school. He labored long over them, then the ideas came out direct, naked and stark. Vladimir went in for elaborate outlines, as a preliminary to vigorous and workmanlike expression of his thoughts.

Even when his feelings were hurt, Alexander was silent. Almost in infancy he ceased to shed tears at anything. When he felt wronged, or saw wrong done to others, the force of his unshed tears accumulated within him.

Little Volodya was made of noisier stuff than his older brother. His howls when learning to walk made enough noise to get themselves recorded in family memoirs. His boisterous shouts on the Volga steamer when they were headed for the summer estate brought a rebuke from the quiet mother: "One doesn't yell like that on a steamer," she told him. "Well, the steamer is yelling loud enough," cried little Volodya.

At least one childhood lie was recorded as having been told by young Volodya—he had broken a decanter belonging to an aunt while racing through her rooms, but at the solemn family inquest denied all knowledge of how the bottle had met its fate. Three months later, Anna records, he came to his mother in tears to make voluntary confession. Obviously, lying did not come easy to him, as his detractors were to insist when they discussed his later advice to use lies on occasion as a stratagem in the revolutionary struggle. But to the older boy, lying was an utter impossibility: it was absolute truth—or silence—for him from earliest childhood. Once some adult, probably a school inspector, asked him to name the two worst vices. "Lying and cowardice," was his answer. The response was not something drilled into him; it came from the depths of his own nature, to which untruth and cowardice were utterly alien.

"Very characteristic it was," writes his sister Anna in her memoirs, "that he was unable to lie. If he did not want to say something, he remained silent. That particular quality of his showed itself brilliantly before his judges."

> One feels like adding—comments Trotsky on the above— what a pity! In an implacable social struggle, such a mentality leaves you politically defenseless. Austere moralists, liars by vocation, have reasoned well, the lie is the reflection of social contradictions, but also, at times, a means of struggle against them. One cannot, by an individual moral effort, escape from the context of the social lie. In type, Alexander resembled a knight more than a politician. And that created a psychic separation between him and his younger brother, considerably stronger, considerably more opportunist in the questions of individual ethics, better armed for the struggle, but in any case no less intransigent in his attitude toward social injustice.

Trotsky's comment is interesting, not for what it adds to that of Anna concerning her two brothers, but for the indirect light it throws upon the attitude of Trotsky, and upon the ethics of Bolshevism—a subject to which we shall have to return.

Sometime during his early adolescence—the exact age is not recorded—Alexander suddenly ceased to be religious. The change, characteristically, was preceded by no discussion with parents, teachers or spiritual advisers. Whatever debate there was went on within him, until, one day, he stopped going to church. "Aren't you going to vespers tonight?" his father asked. The "no" was so firm and decisive that Ilya Ulyanov did not venture to pursue the subject further. "Devoted teachers," the school inspector had written, "do not need to have recourse to punishment." Whether it was his disbelief in coercion, or respect for the budding personality of his son, or hope that he "would get over it," Ilya Nikolaevich never raised the matter again, and from that day forward Alexander did not set foot inside a church. Yet he made no demonstration when the priest conducted services at the *gymnazia,* and his record for outward conduct there continued to be perfect. There was, as we have noted, not one complaint recorded against this quiet and studious lad by any of his teachers during his entire life. Always his marks were of the highest; always his lessons were prepared with perfection; always he kept his doubts and disagreements to himself. He graduated with highest honors, and was awarded the gold medal. Though he was good in all subjects, his intellectual predilections were already formed: he was determined to follow in his father's earlier footsteps and become a scientist. He looked with eagerness to Saint Petersburg, city of a great university, distinguished scientists, well-equipped laboratories. During his last vacation before leaving for the metropolis he spent all his time in a homemade laboratory on the maternal estate, performing chemical experiments, too absorbed for conversation, for meals, for sleep. The only time which he took off from his scientific pursuits was for hunting, and for shy courtship of a young cousin with whom he had fallen in love.

When they succeeded in assassinating Tsar Alexander II in 1881, the mysterious Executive Committee of the Narodnaya Volya ("The People's Will" or "The People's Freedom"—the word *Volya* has both significations) seemed to be all-powerful. The new Tsar, Alexander III, a corpulent giant of a man, wept on the bosom of his confessor as he implored guidance on how to answer the Executive Committee's ultimatum offering peace in exchange for a constitution. His adviser strengthened his anger and pride. After a brief period of vacillation, Alexander III answered by recalling the moderate constitutional rescript which the dead Tsar had been about to publish, and by multiplying the police, enlisting spies, closing the feeble liberal newspapers, purging the libraries, supervising professors and curricula, reducing the local self-government of the zemstvos, prohibiting student organization, setting up the *Zemski Nachalnik* (rural chief) as a permanent guardian over the peasantry, strengthening the restrictions on the Jews, and in general tightening all the chains in the great prison house of peoples.

The Narodnaya Volya felt that it had no choice but to give out the watchword: "One Alexander after the other!" But the new Tsar had shed his frightened tears for nothing. The Executive Committee was no longer anything but a signature on an ultimatum. Six prior unsuccessful attempts on the life of Alexander II had cost them twenty-one executions. "We are consuming our capital," Zhelyabov, chief organizer of the successful assassination, had exclaimed in anguish. And now, two years after their great success (in 1883, the very year that young Alexander Ulyanov went to Saint Petersburg to enter the university), one Degaev, an informer in their ranks, betrayed to the police the last surviving member of the Executive Committee, Vera Figner. Next year she was condemned to die, but, being a woman, her sentence was commuted to life imprisonment in the Schluesselberg fortress prison. The dread Executive Committee no longer existed, nor any party to which it might serve as executive.

In a land of secrets and mysteries, there were many who did not know that. Here and there, for the next few years, little groups sought to act in its name, even though they had no contact with it. But they moved now in a nightmarish vacuum. The village had not responded to the deed, many peasants even believing that the nobles had killed the Tsar-Emancipator as an act of vengeance for his Emancipation Proclamation! And liberal public opinion, which at first had celebrated the assassination, later execrated it as the bringer of reaction. The police noose pulled ever tighter, the mighty body of Russia stiffened and grew still, its great voice choked on the gallows.

"The eighties cut across the history of Russian civilization like a belt of darkness," wrote the historian Pokrovski. But even in the darkness, here and there the heart of youth, being young, continued to glow. Everything about the next conspiracy, six years later, was naive and inexperienced. The continuity of the generations had been ruptured. The technique of conspiracy and the programs of freedom alike had died on the gallows, or been buried beneath tons of masonry in the dungeons of Peter-and-Paul and the Schluesselberg fortress. The young men of generous vision had to begin afresh spelling out the first letters of the revolutionary alphabet.

Not until 1886, five years after the assassination of Alexander II, was there any new activity amongst the students, and then— a measure of its modesty—it was but a decision to go to a cemetery (the Volkov Cemetery in Saint Petersburg) to lay wreaths upon the tombs of the thinkers and officials of the reign of Alexander II who had prepared and carried out the emancipation of the serfs. It is a measure of the change of mood that the older generation had declared war to the death on Alexander for what they considered the inadequacies of his reforms, and now the student youth was paying tribute to a time that seemed blessed in comparison. Of course, in their hearts some were perhaps paying tribute, too, to those martyrs and rebels who had gone before and whose deeds and dreams had helped to prepare the loosening of the bonds in the sixties. At any rate, the police made no move to prohibit or dissolve the demonstration. Some four hundred students, with no support from the older intelligentsia, marched to the cemetery, had a prayer said by a priest, chanted the requiem service and laid their wreaths on the tombs of the tsarist officials. Among the young men was Alexander Ulyanov. It was his first act of public participation in the student movement.

When Alexander Ulyanov went to Saint Petersburg in 1883 he had had no interest in student circles. They wasted his precious time, they violated his innate reserve, they were engaged in frivolities and dissipations which did not attract him, or in discussions of social questions on which he felt that he—and they—knew too little for profitable discussion. He was absorbed by science, and, unlike most Russian intellectuals, not given to the feverish pleasures of conversation.

At the university he had plunged into biological research, pored over the microscope, made observations on earthworms, made laboratory notes, read deep in the literature of science, accumulated knowledge enough to last a long lifetime.

His father had provided a comfortable monthly allowance of forty rubles. Alexander assured him that thirty would be sufficient, then ceased to insist, perhaps because he did not wish to embarrass his sister Anna, who received the same stipend. When he came back to Simbirsk at the end of his first school year he silently returned to his father the sum of eighty rubles, the excess saved from his pocket money. The episode was characteristic, and gives evidence both of his abnegation and the fact that he kept away from the rest of the students and their activities, else he would easily have found ways of spending the spare rubles. At the end of 1885, some of the students had approached him to join one of their clubs. His answer, as remembered by one of them: "One talks a lot there, and learns nothing."

In January, 1886—he had not even given up his research to return with his sister to Simbirsk for the Christmas vacations— the mails brought him the news that his father had died suddenly of a cerebral hemorrhage. "For various days," one of his schoolmates records, "he neglected everything. He walked up and down from one corner of his room to the other, deeply wounded." But he did not abandon his work, nor even then return to Simbirsk. A few weeks later he wrote to his mother: "For my zoological study on annelid worms, I have won the gold medal." The zealous school inspector would have approved his son's devotion to duty and rejoiced at his prospects for a brilliant future.

Freud has offered the theory that young men do not often undertake significant independent activity until after the deaths of their fathers. Be that as it may, the independence of spirit of Alexander had developed earlier. The first, almost the only, observable change was that during that next summer, for the first time in his life, he rebuked his younger brother, Vladimir, for rudeness to their mother, as if he felt himself now the responsible head of the Ulyanov household. There was one more change which might give support to Freud's theory: the year of his father's death, without slackening his scientific studies, Alexander decided to go with his fellow students to the Volkov Cemetery for the memorial services to the officials who had brought about the peasant emancipation. And that same year, when the students united into a single federation the only organizations not prohibited by the police: the regional clubs (they were mere groupings of the students by their province of origin)—the name of Alexander Ilyich Ulyanov figured as one of the leaders of the union of clubs!

A few months later they essayed again the sheltering device of a funeral demonstration. This time they chose the occasion of the twenty-fifth anniversary of the death of the radical critic, Dobrolyubov. Encouraged by success, they brought out greater numbers—estimates vary from six hundred to one thousand—but they found the cemetery barred by a cordon of police. They sought to break up and return to the city, but they were surrounded by mounted police and kept two hours in the rain. Forty of their number, alleged ringleaders, were expelled from the university and from Saint Petersburg!

Alexander was once more among the participants. He was not among the expelled, but he felt that if they were guilty of any crime, he too was guilty. If they should suffer, he would suffer also. Such was his nature. He brooded quietly and deeply upon the experience. He discussed it with several earnest young men who, like himself, could not forget the indignity or the unjust and arbitrary punishment.

What to do? The students drafted a "protest to society," but the police went from mailbox to mailbox, collecting the crude circulars. "Society," if it received any of them, gave no sign. Write? There was no liberty of press. Speak? It was not even permitted to hold a memorial meeting with priest and requiem in a cemetery! How make one's protest heard? There seemed to be only one possible answer. On a pitifully diminutive scale, only half realizing it, he and his young comrades were repeating in a few months the evolution of a great generation that had preceded them. "Peaceful methods had been forbidden me," the gentle Vera Figner had told her judges at her trial only two years previously, "we had of course no free press, so that it was impossible to think of propagating ideas by means of the printed word. If any organ of society had pointed out to me another course than violence, I would have chosen it. . . ."

Alexander Ulyanov, a young man of integral character, who could not accept the conveniences of a gulf between thought and action nor leave to others the dangers of things he thought needed doing, now added laboratory experiments with nitroglycerin and magnesium to his studies on annelids and sea spiders! Press and speech being choked off, dynamite, that democratic invention of the Swedish chemist Nobel, perfected twenty years earlier, would guarantee that their protest would at least be heard in the shameful silence. Once more they chose the anniversary of a death for their demonstration, but this time it was to link themselves onto the great tradition that had just perished on the gallows. They chose the date March 1, 1887, the dreadful anniversary of the day when, six years before, the Party of the People's Will had laid low the Tsar-Emancipator, Alexander II.

The plot was in all things pitiful. Scarce knowing the meaning of the words, they resoundingly called themselves "The Terrorist Section of the Narodnaya Volya." Before one has "sections" one must have a whole. There was no Party of the People's Freedom any longer. There were only seven earnest young men, the oldest twenty-six, the youngest twenty; four of them, including Alexander Ulyanov, just turning twenty-one.

Alexander was not the leader or organizer of the attempt. That post was assumed by a sickly and intense young man, Shevreev by name, aged twenty-three. But Alexander became the official chemist of the little group, and his conscientiousness made him into the drafter of its vague, immature program. Still in love with life and his personal future, he could hardly tear himself away from a study he was even then completing, dealing with the habits and physiology of the sea spider, to pore uneasily through the pages of Marx's *Capital* and other forbidden and ill-comprehended books—it takes time to carve oneself out a revolutionary *Weltanschauung,* and time was pressing. On the very days that he felt might be the last of his young life, he still divided his time between sea spiders, chemical experiments with dynamite bombs, and Marx's *Capital.* The seven young men classified themselves, theoretically, into three "Social Democrats," three "Narodovoltsi" and one who took no part in the programmatic controversies. Young Ulyanov, despite his studies in Marxism, declared himself a member of the Narodnaya Volya or "People's Freedom" group. They pooled their meager resources to send one of their number to Vilna to purchase some nitric acid, which proved too weak to be usable. A pistol that one of the bomb-throwers possessed, intended to supplement the dynamite or aid his escape, likewise proved unserviceable when he tried to use it. Alexander's poor bombs were so inadequate that, when one of the students hurled one at a policeman who was placing him under arrest, it did not even explode! In order that one of the organizers of the plot might escape abroad, Alexander pawned the gold medal he had won in the *gymnazia* at Simbirsk. Such were the weapons and the resources, material and intellectual, with which seven young students set out to overthrow the mighty Alexander III, Tsar of All the Russias!

Even then the conspiracy was thwarted only by the merest accident. Its very obscurity escaped the vigilance of an overconfident police. On March 1, 1887, police agents followed a young man onto the Nevsky Prospekt, the broad boulevard to the banks of the Neva that runs past the Tsar's Winter Palace. He was carrying a thick "Dictionary of Medicine." The astonishment of the agents was boundless when they found that the "Dictionary" was hollow and contained a crude dynamite bomb. Two other students with him proved to have dynamite bombs in their possession and one an unserviceable pistol. The police had followed the young man almost as a mere matter of routine. Only the day before they had received a tip from the police in Kharkov that the youth they were shadowing had written a letter—six weeks earlier: there was little speed in the Tsarist bureaucracy—to a friend in the latter city. The letter, being opened by secret agents, proved to be a confused hymn to terror. The student Andrushkin, the carrier of the "Dictionary of Medicine," was the author of the letter. "To enumerate the qualities and the advantages of the red terror, I shall not attempt," reads a typical sentence, "for I would have enough of them to take centuries, since it is my hobby, and it is from that, no doubt, that my aversion for the Social Democrats is derived." The police themselves did not dream that the young man who needed centuries had actually allowed himself only one more day for enumeration and exemplification together. The Tsar's thanks for "having watched well and acted efficiently" were not deserved by his loyal police.

Alexander Ilyich was not on the Nevsky Prospekt, for he had not been chosen among the three bombers. The police raided his lodgings and found his sister Anna there on a purely personal visit. They arrested her and posted a guard to waylay her brother, who was arrested the same day at the house of another student. To young Vladimir in Simbirsk, not yet seventeen but henceforth the acting male head of a fatherless household, a former teacher of the Ulyanov children wrote a letter telling of the danger to his older brother and sister and bidding him break the news as best he might to his mother. He didn't get far before she snatched the letter out of his hand. She made instant plans to join her two oldest children in their peril, leaving Vladimir in charge of the younger children in Simbirsk. All the friends who but a year ago had paid such eloquent tribute to the school inspector at his public funeral, those who had visited him, played chess with him, drunk his tea with him, shrank away from the accursed and perilous household.

> When we had become closely acquainted—Lenin's wife wrote in her memoirs—Vladimir Ilyich once told me about the attitude of the Liberals towards the arrest of his elder brother. All acquaintances shunned the Ulyanov family. . . . There was no railway at Simbirsk at that time, and Vladimir Ilyich's mother had to go by coach to Syzran in order to go on to Saint Petersburg, where her eldest son was imprisoned. Vladimir Ilyich was sent to seek a companion for the journey. But no one wanted to travel with the mother of an arrested man. Vladimir Ilyich told me that this widespread cowardice made a very profound impression upon him. This youthful experience undoubtedly did leave its imprint on Lenin's attitude towards the Liberals.

At the trial, each played the part that corresponded to his character. Some turned state's evidence. One, a young Pole who had lent his home to Alexander for the printing of their program, denied all sympathy for the movement. His name was Bronislaw Pilsudski. His brother Josef, future dictator of Poland, being brought in as a material witness, denied all knowledge of the affair, but was shown to have sent a coded telegram to Vilna for the conspirators. The organizer of the conspiracy, Shevreev, had disappeared from Saint Petersburg. Alexander Ulyanov took upon himself full responsibility. To a fellow-prisoner in the courtroom he whispered: "If you need to, you can put all the blame upon me!" "There is no finer death," he told his judges, "than death for one's country's sake; such a death holds no terror for sincere and honest men. I had but one aim: to help the unfortunate Russian people."

His power of speech in the prisoner's dock astonished his mother and sister. So this was their silent Alexander! "How well Alexander speaks!" his mother whispered. But she could not stand the new-found eloquence, and fled the courtroom before his address to his judges had come to an end. To his sister Anna, he confessed that he was torn between the desire to shield the others by taking all blame upon himself, and the fear of hurting their feelings by belittling their role and magnifying his own—a true character out of that Dostoevsky who had been his favorite author!

Even the prosecutor was touched by his nobility. "I concede full confidence," he said, "to the declarations of the accused Ulyanov, whose admissions, if they are at fault, err only in taking upon himself what he has not done in reality."

A few weeks later, the mighty Tsar who was the target of this impotent conspiracy carefully read the entire record of the case, scribbling in the margin his loutish commentary. But when he came to the words of the accused Ulyanov, insisting that his was "the most complete moral and intellectual responsibility . . . all that my abilities and the strength of my knowledge and convictions permitted," alongside this sentence the Emperor wrote: "This frankness is even touching!!!" Whereupon the touched Emperor approved the hanging by the neck until dead of young Alexander Ilyich Ulyanov and four of his comrades. Their lives ended before they had well begun.

And with them ended the "Terrorist Section" of their "Party of the People's Freedom"—the last, faint, childish echo of the heroic age of the populist terror, the pitiful *reductio ad absurdum* of its methods of seeking to revolutionize society behind its own back. Alongside the many mightier and more significant attempts and celebrated trials that had preceded it, it scarcely deserves to be mentioned at all. Its real importance to history lay in the deep impression it made upon Josef Pilsudski, brother of defendant Bronislaw, and upon Vladimir Ilyich, sixteen-year-old brother of defendant Alexander Ilyich Ulyanov. It loaded young Vladimir with a man's responsibility; it put iron into his soul; it barred his path to respectability; it opened an unbridgeable gulf between him and the régime that had taken his brother's life. And it inoculated him with a profound contempt for the "liberal society" which had abandoned the Ulyanov family in its time of trouble. That contempt found far more frequent and eloquent expression in his writings than did his opposition to the Tsar. It drew the line of distinction between him and most of his associates in the socialist movement. Though, in the abstract, he would frequently preach the strategy of a common alliance of all "democratic and liberal and socialist oppositional elements," yet at every crucial point in his career when there was a serious proposal to implement that strategy, his fury knew no bounds. Greater than the anger of his denunciation of the régime would be his anger at the "unreliable and treacherous liberals," and greatest of all his anger at those of his comrades who proposed agreement with them. Again and again he did not hesitate to break with all and sundry on this issue, even his closest associates and the men he had most admired. Again and again he would split away from a movement he himself had helped to build, standing isolated and alone, as if he were repeating symbolically the tragic scene of the isolation of the Ulyanov family from all of Simbirsk "liberal society," at the hour of his bereaved mother's greatest need.

CHAPTER FOUR

AGAINST
A
STONE
WALL

Repression is the only lasting philosophy. The dark deference of fear and slavery, my friend—observed the Marquis—will keep the dogs obedient to the whip, as long as this roof shuts out the sky.

—TALE OF TWO CITIES

Their well-deserved hangman's fee
My son and my sire received.
But, a specter of ancient slavery,
I ride through all eternity
Derided by humanity.

Other monstrosities were torn down by the cleansing wave of revolution, but on the pedestal of the equestrian statue of Alexander III—a huge-buttocked rider on a huge-buttocked horse that seems to sag under the rider's weight—the Bolshevik art commission merely carved these lines, and left it standing as a monument to the late autocracy's bad taste. The father of Alexander III died by a bomb. His son Nicholas would be shot to death with all his family in a cellar in the Urals. But he himself lived heavily and died heavily in his bed, and heavily weighed all his life upon the Russian people. With those powerful royal hands with which he could unbend a horseshoe (it was one of his proudest accomplishments), he personally horsewhipped his grown-up son, the future Nicholas II, so as to train him in obedience, and, no doubt, fit him for command.

His father had been "the Emancipator" and had even dreamed of issuing a moderate constitution. The reward had been Grinevitsky's bomb. For his part, therefore, Alexander III would "not grant Russia a constitution for anything on earth." He would maintain peace, as a graveyard is peaceful. He would freeze, for all eternity, the sluggish current of Russian public life. His Polish, and other non-Russian subjects would be made to talk Russian though it choked them.* Over the villages he would set his *Zemski Nachalniki* (rural chiefs) to curb the zemstvos and to keep the peasants "eternally under age" even as he kept his son Nicholas up to the day when death took from him the crown and set it on the twenty-six-year-old boy's head. Alexander's Minister of Education, Delyanov, issued the celebrated *ukaz* directing that "the children of coachmen, servants, cooks, laundresses, small shopkeepers, and suchlike should not be encouraged to rise above the sphere in which they were born."

For spiritual advice, and for the education of his son,

---

* Contrary to general belief, Russification was intermittent and sporadic under the Tsars. For some time the Poles retained a wide measure of autonomy, and Finnish autonomy still sheltered Lenin from the Tsar's police in 1907. The conquered peoples of Central Asia were despoiled of their best lands but retained their local customs and leaders and were exempt from military service until 1916. Only the last two tsars were persistent and irreconcilable Russifiers.

Alexander turned to the lay Supreme Procurator of the Holy Synod, the state's watchman over the Church, "a thorough despiser of human nature who had turned reaction into a system of philosophy." From this counsellor the Tsar learned that representative institutions are "the greatest falsehood of our time . . . serving only to satisfy the personal vanity, ambition and interests of the representatives"; that liberty, equality, freedom of thought, civil rights, trial by jury, are alien importations, elaborate deceptions and utter failures; that general education should be limited to reading, writing and arithmetic, beyond which "all else is not only superfluous but dangerous"; that fear was the sovereign principle of statecraft and that "fear of, not love of God, and fear of, and devotion to the Tsar, are to be cultivated as aids to government."

But the walls Alexander set up against change were so many dams behind which fresh pressure accumulated. The subsidies and tariffs he bestowed upon industry, the great network of railroads he constructed, called into being great concentrations of workingmen. At the very moment when his triumphant police were putting the finishing touches upon the Narodnaya Volya in 1883, an obscure "Union for the Liberation of Labor" was being founded by a few exiles in Geneva. In 1886, at the height of the period of stagnation and abject surrender of all liberal circles, the régime of granite and iron found it advisable to make its first social security concessions to the nascent working class. In 1891 a great famine, one of those periodic famines which had always been taken passively as incomprehensible acts of God, caused men to stir uneasily as if they were about to awaken from a nightmare. Three years later, when Nicholas II (1894-1917) succeeded to the throne, a sensitive ear might already catch sounds which told that the long sleep was coming to an end.

Thus Alexander III's "eternal" régime proved but to be a parenthesis of sagging reaction between the rising movement of the People's Freedom that had laid low his father, and the rising movement of the Social Democrats and Social Revolutionaries that would lay low his son. It was during this parenthesis of reaction that Nicholas Romanov, born 1868, and Vladimir Ilyich Ulyanov, born 1870, received their respective educations and came to maturity. From its increasing industrial expansion, and from its rigid tyrannies, Lenin derived his political conceptions. Its very immobility sheltered him from premature exposure such as had cut short his brother's life, and taught him to estimate soberly the difficulties of the task to which he was to dedicate himself.

In the preceding chapter—following Lenin's own reminiscences to his wife—we portrayed the Ulyanov family as completely deserted by respectable Simbirsk society in the hour of its trial. But, among the colleagues of the deceased school inspector, Ilya Nikolaevich, there was at least one honorable exception who stood by the family. Feodor Kerensky (father of that Kerensky who will play a large role in our story) was the director of the *gymnazia* of Simbirsk, instructor in literature and Latin, and headmaster of the graduating class in which, at the moment Alexander was hanged, his younger brother, Vladimir, was completing his high-school studies. Even while scandalized whispers still remarked the uses to which Alexander had put his gold medal (according to sister Anna, Kerensky received a reproof from his superiors for having given the medal to one so unworthy), the director had the decency and courage to award the gold medal once more to an Ulyanov for excellence in studies. He advised with Lenin's mother on the boy's future, suggesting that Vladimir apply to the University of Kazan rather than to that of one of the two capital cities, and that she accompany him to Kazan as a safeguard for his good conduct. Setting aside any fear of what might come of praising the brother of a would-be assassin of the Tsar, he wrote the following recommendation to help young Vladimir Ilyich get into the university:

> Very gifted, always neat and industrious, Ulyanov was first in all subjects and, upon completing his studies, received the gold medal as the most deserving pupil in ability, progress and con-

duct. Neither in the school nor outside of it, has a single instance
been observed when he has given cause for dissatisfaction by
word or deed to the school authorities and teachers. [A white lie,
this, for Vladimir had gotten into trouble for ridiculing his
French teacher!] His mental and moral instruction has always
been well looked after, first by both his parents, and, after the
death of his father in 1886, by his mother alone, who devoted all
her attention to the upbringing of her children. Religion and discipline were the basis of this upbringing, the fruits of which are
apparent in Ulyanov's behavior. Looking more closely at Ulyanov's character and private life, I have had occasion to note a
somewhat excessive tendency towards isolation and reserve, a
tendency to avoid contact with acquaintances, and even with the
best of his schoolfellows outside of school hours. Ulyanov's
mother intends to be with him throughout his university career.

Even the mild stricture on his excessive isolation and reserve
(which incidentally confirms what his sister Anna records about
his lack of close friends) was intended to convince the authorities that the boy lacked the qualities which might make him into
a ringleader and troublemaker.

At first glance, the above document does not seem to have
anything remarkable about it. Why should an innocent youngster suffer for the crimes of an elder brother? Why not be rated
on his own merits? Why deny him a gold medal merely because
the previous winner in the same family had sold his to finance a
conspiracy against the Tsar? But it is well to remember that in
Medieval England, and to some extent in pre-nineteenth century
Russia, the blood of whole families was regarded as "attaint-
ed" if one of their members was guilty of treason. And in the
Soviet Union today, far from having declined, the doctrine of
family responsibility has received unheard-of extension and
legal codification.* In order to see in its true perspective Director Kerensky's act on behalf of the lad who was one day to
become the leading antagonist of Kerensky's own son, we need

---

* See, for instance, the decree of June 6, 1934, making all the adult members of a military deserter's
family responsible, even though they did not know of his intention to desert, and making them liable
to a penalty of not less than five years' exile in a Siberian forced labor camp (*Izvestia*, June 9, 1934).

only try to imagine an official of present-day Russia writing such a letter concerning the younger brother of one who had plotted to assassinate Stalin!

One hundred and fifty miles or so north of Simbirsk, Kazan was the main capital of the middle Volga. Presiding over the Tartar country, it had thirteen mosques scattered among its old streets. Its university, not yet a century old, had been established to serve as a fount of Slavic Orthodoxy and a place where the lesser provincial nobility and bureaucracy might send their sons.

But for the young Vladimir Ilyich, whose seventeen years had been passed within the confines of backward Simbirsk and rural Kukushkino, the journey up the Volga to his father's *alma mater* in Kazan was an entrance into an ampler, more modern world. On May 20 of that same year (1887), his beloved older brother died upon the scaffold. Just as Alexander had stayed in Saint Petersburg without interrupting his studies when he heard of the death of his father, so Vladimir had not ceased his scholastic work when his brother was tried and hanged. On June 22, a month after the execution, he graduated at the head of his class. Bearing the certificate, medal and recommendation of the headmaster, he applied for admission to Kazan. To the disappointment of Director Kerensky, his promising pupil did not heed his advice to choose letters or history, but entered the faculty of law and political economy. Was his interest in legal defense aroused by his brother's fate? Did he feel that some such profession as law would be more promising now that he was the male head of the twice-bereaved household? Or was it, as his sister Anna conjectured, the beginning of a newly awakened interest in public affairs?

Before we follow the Ulyanov family—all but Anna, who was rusticated by the police at Kukushkino as a dangerous person— to their new home in Kazan, we must examine the reminiscences collected from old-timers in Simbirsk, concerning Vladimir Ilyich's seventeen boyhood years, spent in that narrow provincial capital. We have little enough to go by for those crucial formative years, and from that little we must endeavor to squeeze the last drop of ascertainable truth. Our sources are the memoirs of the oldest Ulyanov girl, Anna, of two younger children, Dmitri and Maria, of a teacher or two, and some family acquaintances, none of whom suspected then that this stocky, homely, slant-eyed, mocking boy had greatness in him, or was one day to be the ruler of Russia. Thirty years and more would pass before they would rack their brains for memories of him.

Anna Ilyinishna, on whose memoirs we have to depend most, was six years Vladimir's senior. Moreover, it is significant that she had not even known of Alexander's revolutionary activities, although there was but two years' difference in their ages, until she was arrested in his lodgings. Clearly we will not learn much from her of what went on within the head of Vladimir. Dmitri, on the other hand, was four years younger than his famous brother; his memories yield nothing of interest beyond some superficial childish impressions. As for young Maria, born in 1878, when Vladimir Ilyich was eight years old, she records little more than that she was tutored by Lenin in various subjects and was impressed by the long, silent, solitary hours he spent in poring over books. For the rest, she remembers what is expected of her, or what might be "remembered" by one who has heard about things at second hand, years after they occurred.

If we go outside the family, we are no better off. Alexander Kerensky, son of the *gymnazia* director and one time Premier of Russia, has introduced a few sparse "memories" into his autobiographical writings, concerning the man whom he came to detest more than any other on earth. Though they were born in the same town and their parents moved in the same bureaucratic and pedagogical circles, there was eleven years' difference in their age. Kerensky's hostile reminiscences, like those of the adulators, are recalled *ad hoc* to fit a preconception, more than three decades after the events to which they refer.

> Lenin was cruel by nature—he writes.—As a boy he liked to shoot at stray cats, or to break a crow's wing with his airgun.

That Lenin went hunting as a boy, we already know. But a curious coincidence makes the above "memory" a bit suspect. In a novel written by Eugene Chirikov (schoolmate of Vladimir Ilyich in Kazan) we find the following passage:

> He—Ulyanov—always had moist hands! And yesterday he killed a little cat with a rifle shot. . . .

Kerensky's other memories do not stand textual criticism any better. He is at great pains to testify to the noble character of Alexander Ulyanov, the better to contrast him with Vladimir. But all he can actually recall of the martyred older brother is "a carriage with drawn green blinds; that carriage which mysteriously drove through the town at night and took people away into the unknown" when they were placed under arrest. Remarkable memory, since Alexander was not arrested in Simbirsk, but in Saint Petersburg!

> I have a strange, eerie feeling almost of mysticism—reads the longest of the passages concerning the boy Vladimir in Kerensky's memoirs—when I call to mind that scene: the school chapel —I picture it before my eyes on a festive occasion—a solemn service: the Holy Gates are opened, the headmaster's two little sons are led up to him: they are in white, with pink bows under their Eton collars; and behind them, from among the orderly rows of schoolboys, dressed in a tight-fitting blue uniform with silver buttons, looking at them, is the exemplary pupil—religiously educated and first in his class—Vladimir Ulyanov. . . . Who would have thought by the looks of that precise, exemplary schoolboy living in the God-forsaken Simbirsk of fifty years ago and brought up in the best tradition of the humane and liberal Russian culture, that one day he would be the gravedigger of that culture?

"Who would have thought," we might as well ask the author of the memoir, "that the little, eight-year-old headmaster's son in white with a pink bow under his Eton collar in that God-forsaken Simbirsk of fifty years ago would one day become

Premier and War Minister of Russia, flirt with the idea of taking full power into his hands, and then let it slip so easily into the hands of the 'exemplary pupil'?" Such memoirs throw more light on the rememberer than on the one remembered.

As against the Chirikov-Kerensky story of the cat and the crow, we have a statement of Anna's that Vladimir was always an indifferent hunter. ("At bottom, like my other two brothers, he was never a hunter.") Trotsky, a passionate devotee of hunting, disputes Anna on this score, while Krupskaya (Mrs. Lenin) in her memoirs of their stay in Siberia sets her husband down as "an ardent huntsman." Yet, in an immediately following passage she has this to say of his role in a foxhunt:

> We placed the hunters in such a way that the fox ran straight at Vladimir Ilyich. He grasped his gun and the fox, after standing and looking at him for a moment, turned and made off into the wood. "Why on earth didn't you fire?" came our perplexed inquiry. "Well, he was so beautiful, you know," said Vladimir Ilyich.

Finally, we have Vladimir Ilyich's own words in a letter to his mother from Siberia: "There is plenty of game but without a dog and I being such a bad shot, shooting is a difficult sport" (letter of May 18, 1897).

Whichever version we accept, the whole matter is not very illuminating and proves nothing about his real relations with ideas and men. But it will serve to give the reader a notion of the difficulty with sources, friendly and hostile, which are really an inflation of meager materials, recalled to order more than a quarter-century after they occurred, when Lenin was already leader of the Soviet Government, or still later, when his death called forth a steady stream of publications made up of the most insubstantial memories of his formative years.

Besides being trivial, they are often demonstrably false. Founders and leaders of states and faiths are customarily surrounded by edifying or enhanced legend. It is the way of the folk in dealing with a figure that has captured its imagination, and the lowliest adherent thereby feels himself somehow enlarged. Moreover, in Lenin's case such retouching has been a matter of plan and an affair of state. Yet the very legends in his case are few and feeble. His personal sobriety and modesty, his lack of fire and color—there was little of the Promethean about him as there was about Trotsky, or of the secretive and adventurous as in the case of Stalin—lend themselves ill to legend. During his life he was sparing in personal reminiscence, and, unlike Stalin and Trotsky, not at all concerned with the editing of his future obituary.

To make matters worse, as a lad Vladimir "never brought a friend home with him" (Anna); had "a somewhat excessive tendency towards isolation and reserve, a tendency to avoid contact with acquaintances and schoolfellows outside of school hours" (Director Kerensky). When cousins, or his brothers' and sisters' playmates called, he frequently climbed out of the window into the yard, or, if escape were cut off, he could be heard to say with mock courtesy, "Kindly oblige me by your absence" (Anna).

Indeed, all through his life there was a faint envelope of aloofness separating him from even close associates. In later years, as Edmund Wilson has put it, there was always about him something of "the respected headmaster who deals directly and frankly with his charges yet who stands on a higher ground and always preserves a certain distance between him and them." None of the intimates who shared his perils and his triumphs ever called him "Volodya," except his wife. The others, however close, limited themselves to the grave, formal intimacy of "Vladimir Ilyich" or the more patriarchal "Ilyich." In many a village, there was a respected elder thus addressed by patronymic alone, as a mark of intimacy, respect and affection. In Lenin's case, the intimacy was lacking. Both *Ilyich* and *Starik* were signs of his authoritative, charismatic predominance over a group which was unconsciously saturated with ways derived from the Orthodox folk. Even Krupskaya called him *Ilyich,* more like a worshipful disciple than a wife.

The import of the few legends concerning Lenin's youth that have received official sanction is invariably the same: they all tend to increase the precocity of his intellectual development. It is deemed unfitting to tell Komsomols and Pioneers (members of the Communist Youth Leagues and Boy and Girl Scouts) that their great exemplar did not cease to be religious and a faithful attendant at church until he was sixteen or over. Krzhizhanovsky, the old Bolshevik engineer who knew and worked with Lenin in Saint Petersburg when they were both young men in their twenties, has produced a more "suitable" memory, according to which Vladimir Ilyich told him how he had become irreligious when he was fourteen and "thrown his cross into the dungheap." But Anna records that during the autumn after their father's death she and the sixteen-year-old Vladimir were drawn more closely together, and took long walks in each other's company. Apparently due to first-hand experience with death, Vladimir showed a disposition to question religious teaching. Their father's closing years as an educator had been embittered by the tightening régime of reaction and he had suffered a premature pensioning off, without the customary five years of grace accorded to a faithful servitor. This, too, must have contributed to Vladimir's mood. At any rate, Anna notes that she found in him "for the first time an oppositional spirit on the direction and instruction of the *gymnazia,* as well as on religion." The words are fairly sober and specific. They do not speak of Marxism or revolution, merely of a mood of opposition concerning the things directly within the orbit of his youthful world. In any case, the question of the exact moment of his rejection of religion would seem to have been settled by Lenin himself, for on one of those party questionnaires which he himself invented and which he took very seriously, in response to the question: "When did you cease to believe in religion?" he had written in his own careful hand: "At the age of sixteen." This would correspond with Anna's testimony, whatever its deficiencies as exemplary instruction to the Russian youth of the present day.

Anna's memoirs tend to destroy yet another favorite "cherrytree" legend of Soviet hagiography, which, in despite of historical materialism and suchlike trifles, would hold that great revolutionaries like Lenin are born, not made. Even the comparatively sober Lunacharsky portrays the boy Vladimir in earnest discourse with his father and elder brother on matters of revolutionary strategy and theory. Since Ilya Nikolaevich Ulyanov died at the beginning of the New Year, 1886, the discussions with his sons would have had to take place when the untalkative Sasha was eighteen or nineteen, and the bumptious Volodya (who "participated with considerable success") was fourteen or fifteen. But that should not surprise us too much since one of the recent official biographies of Stalin (by Yaroslavsky) has the latter also, "while still a schoolboy"—in this case at the age of fourteen or fifteen—often conversing with workers and peasants and "explaining to them the causes of their poverty."

One anecdote, repeated by Lenin's wife Krupskaya, has the boy Vladimir shaking his wise young head over his elder brother's deep interest in natural science. "No," Krupskaya reports him as having said to himself, "my brother will never make a revolutionary—a revolutionary cannot devote so much time to studying annelid worms!" According to the old Bolshevik Shelgunov, when Vladimir read the telegram announcing the execution of his brother, "he rubbed his forehead and said: 'Very well then, we shall have to find a more efficacious path.' " To whom did Vladimir address these sage words? his biographer, Trotsky, ironically inquires. Obviously not to Shelgunov, whom he did not meet until years later. Nor to his father, who had died the year before. Nor to Alexander, who had just perished on the scaffold. Nor to Anna, who was in prison. Nor to his mother, who had gone to Saint Petersburg to beg from ministerial door to door in an effort to save her boy. "Evidently," writes Trotsky, "Vladimir confided his revelations as tactician to Dmitri, who was thirteen, and Maria, who was nine!"

As against these portents of precocity we have the narrative of Anna, who has written, "Our father was never a revolutionary," and who places Vladimir's first oppositional questionings on the ways of school and Church in the autumn following the school inspector's death. To this we can add the report of another old Bolshevik, Lalayants, who got to know the future Lenin as a student in Kazan, while he was thus far more celebrated as the younger brother of a martyred would-be regicide than as a leader of men in his own right. Lalayants naturally questioned him on his memories of the affair. "For all of us," Vladimir Ilyich responded, "the participation of Alexander in a terrorist act was completely unexpected. Perhaps my sister knew something. As for me, I did not know a thing about it." Nor did Anna, as her later memoirs were to make clear.

According to Steklov, former editor of the Soviet organ *Izvestia,* Vladimir received a copy of the first volume of Marx's *Capital* "directly" from Alexander's hands. "Thus, Alexander Ulyanov installed not only his successor," observes Steklov, "but the inheritor and continuator of Marx as well." When we contemplate the role that the theory of apostolic succession was to play in the faction struggles of the Bolshevik Party, this anecdote takes on significance. Actually, however, Alexander did not begin to study Marx's *Capital* until the winter and spring that preceded his arrest. Copies of it were rare even in Saint Petersburg, and hard to lay hands on. He would have had to send the volume to his brother in Simbirsk by mail or messenger, since young Vladimir never stopped his schooling during the trial and never saw Alexander again. It is not unreasonable to suppose, however, that he first heard the fateful name of Marx in connection with his brother's trial.

In reality, Vladimir Ilyich was not one for sudden conversions. He resembles but little those romantic revolutionaries who preceded him: that generation of noble young men who brooded briefly on the people's wrongs, rushed swiftly from brooding to conspiracy, and died on the scaffold or by their own explosives within a few months of their first impulse to action. Alexander was fashioned thus, but not Vladimir. His was the kind of nature that grows slowly and robustly, sending its roots deep into the ground, solid and stout and destined to endure. He was not so much the man of action as the shaper of the actions of men. There were four years between Alexander and Vladimir which, in the discontinuity of the experience of the seventies and the eighties, was the equivalent of a revolutionary generation. The depth of the reaction through which Russia was going combined with Vladimir's temperament to favor this slow, organic growth, this capacity to give material force to his ideas not by enacting them into passionate drama but by making them take possession of great masses of men. Strange to relate, these official legends, which appear to exalt him, actually do injustice to his strongest qualities, his habit of many-sided examination of the matters he had in hand, his depth and solidity, his continued growth and flexibility to the end of his days, a certain scientific experimentalism toward the problems he faced in applying the certainties, which he in good time acquired, to the uncertain world of day-to-day affairs.

Young Vladimir did not last long at the University of Kazan. The year 1887, in which his brother was killed and in which he entered into the law school, was the very nadir of the prolonged reaction, and the doctrine of family responsibility, though it had been relaxed slightly in favor of his youth, was operative nonetheless. Alexander Ulyanov and his four comrades died on May 20, 1887. A spasm of fear and horror took possession of the student body of Saint Petersburg when he and three of his co-plotters were hanged. When the rector of the University of Saint Petersburg sought to improve the occasion by a sermon denouncing these "miserable creatures who had insinuated themselves into our charming university family to dishonor it," there were murmurs of indignation. The next day an anonymous leaflet appeared saying that it was the university which had dishonored itself by falling servilely at the feet of despotism. The summer vacation intervened to stop the wave of muted protest. In the autumn, the measures which the government took to control the student body after the scare occasioned by the recent plot, served to start a new wave of student protest, travelling slowly from university to university, until it reached Kazan.

On December 4, of that same year, 1887, in which Alexander died and Vladimir entered the university, the students of Kazan met in assembly, drew up a series of demands, or rather respectful petitions, and sent a committee to invite the provincial inspector to listen to their requests. Flanked by provosts, he ordered them to disperse. For a while, they refused. The official eye was on the alert for "ringleaders." In the front row it remarked the round head, flat nose and Kalmuck eyes of the stocky little first-year student from Simbirsk. As he walked out, he like the others was asked to show his registration card. It bore the fateful name Ulyanov! That very night police invaded the lodgings of young Vladimir Ilyich Ulyanov and placed him under arrest.

No doubt the more active older students had tried to draw in the boy who was surrounded by the aura of martyrdom as younger brother of a hero who had just died on the scaffold. But apparently Vladimir had had nothing to do with the calling of the assembly or the drafting of demands. He had not said so much as a word during the meeting, only sat "impudently" in the front row.* However, the authorities had been keeping their eyes on him from the outset of his university career. The rector now sent in a report to the effect that Vladimir Ilyich Ulyanov had conducted himself during his brief three-month stay at Kazan "with deceit, dereliction, and even discourtesy." The vagueness of the terms, their anticlimactic order, indicate that he had probably done nothing. "In view of the exceptional

* A recent prize-winning painting in Russia portrays the freshman Lenin organizing the whole demonstration and gathering students of all ages, some heavily bearded, in a corridor to march at their head into the auditorium. (Water color by P. Alyakrinsky, reproduced in the Soviet Embassy Information Bulletin, January 28, 1948.)

circumstances surrounding the family Ulyanov," the report continued, "such attitude of Ulyanov in the meeting has given the inspectors reasons to judge him quite capable of all sorts of illegal and criminal manifestations." The young offender was expelled from the university and ordered to leave Kazan. Because of his three-month stay there, the university would one day be rechristened with the name of Vladimir Ilyich Lenin, but of course, only after his death, for he would never have permitted such self-glorification while he was alive. Neither Simbirsk was renamed Ulyanovsk, nor Petrograd Leningrad, nor the Rumyantsev Library called Lenin State Library, nor the University of Kazan the Vladimir Ilyich Lenin University, until he was in his tomb.

According to an account of his official biographer, Adoratsky, accepted by Vladimir's sister Anna, the boy got into an argument with the policeman who supervised his expulsion from Kazan.

"Why do you revolt, young man?" the agent asked. "You are up against a stone wall . . ."

"A wall, yes, but a crumbling one, and one which will soon collapse," Vladimir is reported to have answered.

This anecdote, too, is probably apocryphal, but certainly the wall was there. Within a matter of some three months his university career had begun and come to an end. Thus did tsarism tend to drive young men into the profession of revolutionary by closing all other professions to them.

But Vladimir was only seventeen. His widowed mother, whose oldest boy was in his grave and whose oldest girl was in disgrace, had set her hopes on his career. He did not give up easily. During the next few years he made repeated attempts to gain readmission to the university, or, failing that, to get permission to take the professional qualifying examinations as a self-taught or external student, and thus win admission to the bar.

CHAPTER FIVE

MATRICULATION
IN
MARXISM

The very air of Russia seemed to be saturated with an intense desire for liberation. We became the enemies of the Autocracy almost as soon as we entered the university, and this seemed to happen naturally . . . there were no arguments among the students whether the Autocracy was to be fought or not . . . the only argument was as to where the real truth was to be found, with the Marxists or with the *Narodniki*.

—ALEXANDER KERENSKY

The youth who does equally well in all subjects is as yet lacking in intellectual personality. It may be taken as a fair measure of the slowness of Vladimir's spiritual development—as well as the athletic prowess of his mind—that at seventeen he still liked Latin and excelled in it; for in student circles at that time one's attitude toward Latin was regarded as a reagent to test for the critical spirit. The study of Latin had been deliberately enlarged by the authorities to convert the schools into more suitable houses of correction for the turbulent student movement. "Knowledge of the dead languages"—the Minister had explained in his circular—"by the very difficulty of success in its pursuit, gives a lesson in modesty, and modesty is the first sign and prerequisite of a true education." To the student generation just preceding Vladimir's, the idolization of science and contempt for the dead languages were the badges of enlightenment. But to Vladimir's robust and still undiscriminating mind it was a pleasant exercise, a kind of linguistic chess.

As with his other subjects, young Ulyanov found the prescribed pace too slow for him. When he tutored his sister Anna in Latin during their enforced rustication in Kukushkino, he told her that two years were more than enough to master the conventional eight-year course in the language. Under his tutelage, two years seem to have been sufficient. Some notion of how he might have gone about it is suggested by an anecdote told by Albert Rhys Williams apropos of Lenin's advice on the study of Russian.

Mr. Williams spoke to him at the historic session of the Constituent Assembly in the early winter of 1918, which ended with that body's dissolution.

> "And how goes the Russian language?" Lenin asked in the midst of all the turmoil. "Can you understand all these speeches now?"
>
> "There are so many words in Russian," I replied evasively.
>
> "That's it," he retorted. "You must go at it systematically.

You must break the backbone of the language at the outset. I'll tell you my method of going at it."

In essence, Lenin's system was this: First, learn all the nouns, learn all the verbs, learn all the adverbs and adjectives, learn all the rest of the words; learn all the grammar and rules of syntax, then keep on practicing everywhere and upon everybody.

The advice seems humorously exaggerated, but Lenin mastered a number of living European languages, among them English, French and German, by some such method. When he tried to practise his attainments on the people he met in the streets of the various European cities, he was amazed to find that they did not understand a word he was saying. Yet his reading knowledge was excellent, his translations into Russian workmanlike, and he kept at it until he could make himself understood and understand spoken discourse also. The same direct and unsubtle but overpowering method of "breaking the backbone at the outset" he applied to the study of law, to the extrication of the socio-economic outlines buried in the maze of Russian statistics, to the works of the Marxists and their opponents, to philosophy when he found himself forced to concern himself with it, to the chaos that was Russia when he took over the helm of the Empire in 1917.

Expelled students were not allowed to live in university towns, nor in industrial centers. Mild cases were directed to go to their birthplaces, if these were rural, or to lesser towns and villages; severe cases were remanded to the wilds of Siberia. Vladimir was permitted to join his sister Anna in Kukushkino, both under police supervision. Their mother took the younger children with her and went to keep house for them. There the youthful state criminal concealed from himself his uncertainty and restlessness by long spells of chess with his younger brother Dmitri, with his sister Anna's fiancé, the insurance agent Elisarov, with such neighbors as could hold their own with him and were not afraid to visit the twice-accursed household. As these did not supply enough opposition, Elisarov arranged for his future brother-in-law to play chess matches by mail with a distinguished amateur named Khardin, a liberal attorney-at-law in Samara.

At Kukushkino they shared a large old house with the mother's sisters. Here Vladimir found a library which had been gathered by a deceased uncle, one of those miscellaneous libraries such as enlightened provincial gentlemen of the preceding generation were wont to acquire. The books teased rather than satisfied his appetite. He went through the collection of old reviews of the sixties and seventies, finding there obscure hints of the turmoil of discussion among the Russian intellectuals concerning their country's future.

By mail, he borrowed entire boxes of books from the library at Kazan. In a grove of linden trees outside the house he spent the long spring and summer hours, reading, making summaries in a neat, diminutive hand of the books that interested him, reflecting on their contents and their implications; thinking, planning, dreaming of his own future and more and more frequently, of the future of Russia. But he was not sure yet as to either.

Immediately after breakfast he would leave the family circle and work by himself until dinner—taken at three in the afternoon. After dinner he would read novels or poetry, take a walk or a swim—he was a powerful and effortless swimmer—exercise on outdoor crossbars which he built himself, tutor Anna in Latin, help the younger children with their studies. In the evening after a light supper there might be family singing or reading aloud, but more often than not the boy would return to his studies until bedtime. Unlike many of the thus early "ruined" intellectuals, he had no intention of giving way to despair or blind rebellion. He was not sure of his future, nor what he wanted to study or prepare for, but he was determined to keep fit in mind and body and to strengthen the powers of both. The good mother eyed him uneasily from afar, pleased with his serene self-discipline and composure, but deeply worried over his career. What, she wondered, would come of all this reading?

In his vexation and uncertainty, he took to smoking—like chess—as a way of quieting his nervous tension. Apparently it was an alien habit in this somewhat puritanical household. The mother first remonstrated with him on the grounds of health, then suggested that, since he was earning nothing, he should not increase the expenses of the household by such practices. Without a word he abandoned smoking, never to resume it. Thus, years later, when he was convinced that chess was absorbing too much of his energy, he abandoned that taxing game permanently also. The same strict power of self-discipline was to shelter him later from the chief vice of the Russian intellectuals, fruitless and endless discussion. Participating only when there was someone to be convinced or something to be clarified and settled, he saved much nervous energy by avoiding discussion for its own sake.

Five months after his expulsion from Kazan, he made his first application for reinstatement. The district inspector sent it to the Minister of Education along with a report which warned that "despite his remarkable abilities, Ulyanov cannot for the present be regarded as a reliable person either as to morals or as to politics." The Minister had no use for unreliable persons. Without even reading the report to the end, he began scribbling his objections: "Wouldn't this be the brother of the other Ulyanov? He too came from Simbirsk." When he read further, finding that it was indeed the brother of the would-be regicide, "It is not at all desirable to readmit him," he wrote.

Two months later the mother of the expelled student sent in a personal petition in his behalf, hoping that her widowhood and her husband's good name and career might avail in softening the heart of the Minister. Again the answer was negative.

Then Vladimir made the first of his applications (under the Tsars, as under the Bolsheviks, people could not leave Russia without permission) to go abroad "for his health." This petition, too, was rejected. Still the local police captain, who came to the house from time to time to interview the probationers

Vladimir and Anna, continued to turn in uneventful reports. The boy's outward conduct was impeccable. Whatever might be transpiring in the household which could conceivably endanger the state, went on behind that brow which even then, in his eighteenth year, seemed to grow higher as the hairline began receding. In the autumn of 1888 he was allowed to return to Kazan, but was not readmitted to the university. Anna was not given the right to imperil Kazan with her gentle presence until sometime later. Her future, however, did not worry her mother, for she was engaged to her former schoolmate from the University of Saint Petersburg, Elisarov, and was making plans for her wedding. In Kazan, the boy joined a chess club, haunted the library, entered into an informal study circle for the consideration of social questions.

Maria Alexandrovna Ulyanova now went in person to Saint Petersburg to see if she could salvage the career of her son. She looked up the men who had known her husband. She begged one official after the other, pleaded her boy's youth, employed tears and whatever arguments a mother's heart could find. "It is a veritable torment," she wrote in one of her petitions, "to regard my son and see how the best years of his life slip unfruitfully away . . . such an existence must almost inevitably drive him to the idea of suicide." Nothing was farther from the boy's mind, but it was an understandable device, since the one thing that tempered the reactionary régime was an occasional burst of sentiment.

While Maria Alexandrovna continued her importunings, she kept an eye open for alternative careers for young Vladimir. Her widow's pension was not much: twelve hundred rubles— six hundred dollars—per annum. In addition she had the house they had lived in during their years in Simbirsk, and her share in the paternal estate at Kukushkino, which she had inherited together with her sister. Remembering her childhood in a German farm community on the Volga, she thought of making a farmer of her boy. She sold her home in Simbirsk and perhaps her share in her estate, in one way or another managing to assemble the necessary funds to purchase a farm at Alakaevka, near Samara. The purchase price was 7,500 rubles.

Alakaevka was a miserable village of eighty-four families, nine of which were without a single horse or cow, four without ownership of the huts they inhabited. The hamlet had no school. The village was a faded remnant of a once-bright dream for Russia's "redemption," part of a vast estate acquired many years back by the wealthy mine-owner, Sibiryakov, who had planned to establish modern model farms there. The venture had failed, leaving the region as backward and the muzhiks as miserable as it had found them. The new Ulyanov estate consisted of eighty-three dessyatins (roughly 225 acres) with a mill and a "manor house" (our quotation marks are intended to prevent the reader from picturing too much elegance).

Soviet biographers are strangely reticent about this little venture. Anna merely records the purchase of "a little farm in the province of Samara" and a request to the authorities that the young suspect and his family be permitted "to go there to spend the summer." An official biographer (Kerzhentsev) devotes to it only a tiny phrase: "He spent the summer in the country, first in Kukushkino and then in Alakaevka in the Samara *Gubernya.*" Most official biographers do not even mention Alakaevka.

What is the meaning of the taciturnity of these chroniclers concerning the several summers (at least three planting years) spent by Vladimir Ilyich in this miserable village? The answer is suggested by a sentence in the memoirs of Lenin's wife, Krupskaya. As brief as the others, her reference possesses a frankness and exactness lacking in the rest: "My mother wanted me to engage in farming," Krupskaya reports Lenin as saying. "I tried it, but I saw that it would not work: my relations with the muzhiks got to be abnormal."

It is a pity that we do not know more, but it is evident from little scraps of information available that the farm possessed, aside from the mill, no implements for direct exploitation, and had to be worked by some form of sharecropping or rental to the necessitous villagers. In other words, the future Lenin went through a brief period as a landowner and exploiter of peasant labor. The biographers who speak vaguely and at some length on how Ulyanov "got to know the agrarian problem at first hand" by walks in the countryside around Simbirsk, by summers in rural Kukushkino, by eager questioning of chance muzhiks with whom he came into contact, are silent on this deeper insight obtained from personal experience during several critical, formative years as a young landowner. Yet, to one not a slave to official legend it would seem not at all discreditable that the young Ulyanov, in quest of a career, tried his hand at running an estate and found it distasteful, deriving therefrom a deeper understanding and a deeper detestation of the relations of rural exploitation.

Fortunately, there was no need for conflict with his mother on the abandonment of the career of gentleman squire which, in her desperation, she had chosen for him. In the summer of 1890, almost three years after his expulsion from Kazan, she at last secured the consent of the Minister of Education to her son's resumption of the study of law. He was not to be permitted to reenter a university, where he might "contaminate" other students, but he was authorized to take the law examinations given in Saint Petersburg whenever, after study by himself, he should feel ready for them. Thereupon, this vigorous and systematic student, who liked to "break the backbone of a subject" at the outset, easily made up the time he had lost through his almost three years of enforced rustication. In little more than a year he ranged through the four-year university course in Jurisprudence, passing the first group of examinations in the spring of 1891 and the rest of them in the autumn, all of them with the highest possible grade. On November 27, 1891, he was granted a diploma, once more with honors. He had come out first in the examinations.

After some five months more of his mother's dickering, he even succeeded in getting the requisite "Certificate of Loyalty and Good Character" without which he could never be admitted to practice. In January, 1892, shortly before he turned twenty-two, Citizen Ulyanov was apparently travelling the road back to respectability as a junior attorney, having secured employment with his old chess opponent, A. N. Khardin, in Samara. Lawyer Khardin was a political liberal who would later join the Constitutional Democratic Party when it was formed, the party led by Professor Miliukov, which Lenin would outlaw and then destroy after 1917. Thus for the second time was Vladimir Ilyich Ulyanov helped in his career by a liberal. And still later, yet another liberal, the Saint Petersburg lawyer M. F. Volkenstein, took him into his office, although Volkenstein must have known then that he proposed to use the title of attorney as a blind for other activities. As we see, the tale that Lenin detested all liberals from the day they deserted his family when Alexander was arrested, is a retroactive legend. That traumatic experience must have affected him deeply, but he did not break completely with the liberals as a political current until the Revolution of 1905. And even thereafter, he was helped with funds, meeting-places, and cover addresses by well-to-do liberals. But psychologically this legend is sound, and behind it lies a truth: the memory of the way in which so many of his father's old friends and colleagues had deserted his widowed mother and her twice-stricken family undoubtedly colored Lenin's feeling toward so-called liberal public opinion, predisposing him to a harsher judgment and greater irreconcilability than characterized most of his associates in the leadership of the Social Democratic Party in the early years of the new century. Even while he and his associates were in theoretical agreement on the need to turn to the liberal opposition for a common alliance against tsarism, Plekhanov was moved to say to him: "We want to turn our face; you your behind."

His actual career as junior attorney was brief and undistinguished. The year and a half he spent at it in provincial Samara yielded him ten minor cases of pitiful defendants: ignorant, poverty-stricken, degraded muzhiks who had robbed a bit of

grain, held up a merchant, or stolen a few rubles, petty criminals all, the most serious complication being the additional
charge of "breaking and entering" when three defendants
opened a barn door to commit their thieving. All were clearly
guilty, and all but one were charged with crimes against property. In one case, that of a wife-beater, he refused to plead miti-
gation for the client which the court assigned to him. In not one
of the ten cases did he get an acquittal.

One case, however, he undertook without fee and without
court assignment—a case that, like a flash of lightning, illumined
the outlines of his future activities. In it he served as voluntary
public prosecutor, at his own cost, for a public that had long
accepted the abuse he challenged, and had neither fought it nor
asked him to fight it. He and his sister Anna had tried to cross
the Volga in a little boat, but a wealthy merchant named Arefeev was accustomed to collect tribute from all who crossed the
river at that point, by forcing them to hire his steam launch.
Arefeev's ship pursued the little craft the Ulyanovs had engaged
and drove it back to shore. His sense of justice outraged, Ulyanov brought complaint against the merchant. The latter contrived to have the case tried in distant Syzran—a trip of nearly
seventy miles from Samara for each hearing. He used all the
devices of the law and all his influence with the local courts to
have the case postponed and dragged out, hoping to weary the
young plaintiff. In the end, Ulyanov won his suit—it was his
only success as a lawyer!

The years 1886 and 1887 were the truly decisive ones in the
life of young Vladimir Ilyich, though it would take a half-
decade for the decision which they fostered to be transformed
from an unconscious to a conscious one. During those two
fateful years, the lad lost his father by sudden death (January,
1886), witnessed his brother's arrest, trial and execution on the
scaffold (May, 1887), entered and was expelled from the University of Kazan (December, 1887), had his first run-in with the
police, met his first arrest and rural, administrative exile. They

were, too, the years in which he began to put questions to the
world which he had hitherto taken for granted, the years in
which he lost his faith in God and Church, in school and state
authorities. They happened to coincide with the years in which
the passivity and reaction of the eighties had reached their ebb
and the outgoing tide of resistance was turning imperceptibly.
The famine year 1891 once more started the whole of oppositional Russian society into movement. It was the same year in
which Ulyanov passed his bar examinations. The rising tide
soon covered the tiny spot of "respectability" on which he
sought to stand, sweeping him along with the best of those who
were coming to maturity in the early nineties, into open rebellion against the régime of "eternal stability" that Alexander III
had erected.

"There can be no doubt," Alexander Kerensky has written
of Lenin, "that it was the cruel execution of the noble-minded,
brilliant Alexander which finally made Vladimir what he remained throughout his political career—an unsurpassed, sa-
distically revengeful cynic."

There can indeed be no doubt that the influence of Alexander's conspiracy and death was a profound one, and that Alexander's example imposed itself for several years upon the
imagination of his younger brother, even deflecting him somewhat from the path he was ultimately to follow. But the "vengeance on the Tsar" theory is as dubious as it is simple and
tempting. Vernadsky, not a friendly but a more objective biographer, has outlined (in his *Lenin: Red Dictator*) the obvious evidence against Kerensky's oversimplified viewpoint.
Lenin's detestation of capitalism, he points out, was no less
than his hatred of tsarism; he directed his blows no less against
the bourgeoisie than against the autocracy. During the seven
years that elapsed between the moment Alexander III signed
his brother's death warrant and the end of the Tsar's reign,
Ulyanov does not appear to have meditated any attempt on the
Tsar's life. And when Nicholas II, son and successor of the imperial executioner, fell into Lenin's hands in 1917, "he showed

no haste to square accounts so long as it did not seem necessary for political reasons."

What then was the influence on the seventeen-year-old boy of his brother's execution? It put him immediately before the dilemma: to accept his brother's deed in his heart, or to reject it. What doubts and struggles that may have meant we have no way of knowing. The only seemingly reliable report that has come down to us stems from the old family tutor of the Ulyanovs, Madam Kachkadamova. "Well it seems," the boy Vladimir said to her, "that Alexander could not have done otherwise." The judgment was personal and—at least in germ—social.

What Alexander's ardent, sincere and gentle temperament signified to all his brothers and sisters we can guess from Anna's letter to him while they were both in prison. "There is no one better than you, more noble on earth," she wrote to him. His forthright acceptance of responsibility, his refusal to beg for mercy, all the beautiful acts of his closing days and martyrdom, could only have served to enlarge the impression he made upon the other children.

For Vladimir the shattering experience put a sudden end to a hitherto joyous adolescence. At seventeen he was brought forcibly into contact with heavy problems of maturity. Before that year was out, in Trotsky's apt phrase, he had been expelled from the University of Kazan directly into the University of Marxism.

Yet the very spell of Alexander's person and example retarded the boy's entrance into the current of Marxism. He found ready acceptance in Narodnik circles as the younger brother of a martyred hero. He began his political thinking where Alexander had left off, as a theoretical populist and terrorist, and far from leading—as Soviet biographers invariably suggest—he lagged a year or two behind the sudden turn of the younger generation to Marxism.

For several years Vladimir Ulyanov continued to hold special views on terror, and, even after he became an active opponent of its employment, there was always a difference in his language from the more categorical condemnation of individual terror by most other orthodox Marxists.

> We have never rejected terror on principle—Lenin was to write in 1901—nor can we ever do so. Terror is a form of military operation that may be usefully applied, or may even be essential in certain moments of the battle—the point is, however, that terror is now advocated, not as one of the operations which the army in the field must carry on in close contact with the main body and in harmony with the whole plan of battle, but as an individual attack, completely isolated from any army whatever. . . . That is why we declare that under present circumstances such a method of fighting is inopportune and inexpedient; it will distract the most active fighters from their present tasks . . . and will disrupt not the governmental forces but the revolutionary forces [*Iskra,* May, 1901. *Collected Works,* Vol. IV. Part I: *Where to Begin.*]

All his life Lenin regarded objections to individual terror *on principle* as "pedantic" and "philistine"—the latter adjective, in his special vocabulary, is the equivalent of unrevolutionary. And it was boldness in connection with deeds of individual terror that first attracted his attention to Joseph Stalin and caused him to advance the latter to posts of importance.

In 1891, as so many times before, famine swept over Russia. The black earth fields turned gray, then cracked, then became dust; the grain burned to tinder on the stalks; hunger took possession of Europe's granary. Whole villages took to the roads in quest of food or employment. Or, gathering their rags about them, died quietly in dark corners, as animals die. Cholera, typhus, typhoid followed in the tracks that hunger had smoothed.

They are wrong who believe that the starving revolt. The countryside suffered in apathetic silence; it was "society" in the towns that was stirred to its depths. Hunger that comes from scarcity, they said, was a medieval phenomenon (not to be compared with that modern want, proper to capitalism, which comes from abundance). In this, as in other respects, Russia remained "medieval" even into the twentieth century—and we shall have to take note of two such "pre-capitalist" crises under the "post-capitalist" Soviets.

If Russia's backwardness and social structure could not be blamed for the failure of the rain to come, they could be held accountable for bureaucratic incompetence, for callous indifference to mass suffering, for stubborn refusal to acknowledge the famine and enlist aid in time lest prestige suffer, for greed which set greater store by price current than by human life, for the policy of continued grain export, for the abominable transport system which prevented shipment of bread from more favored areas, for the normal starvation level of the "good years" which left the peasants without reserves for survival.

"The gravest, the deepest difference on which we opposed ourselves to Vladimir Ulyanov," wrote the populist Vodovosov some thirty years later, "turned about the attitude to take to the famine of 1891-2." All of Samara "society" occupied itself with giving aid "except Vladimir Ulyanov and his family and a little circle which followed him." These, according to Vodovosov, found a perverse pleasure in the suffering and saw in it a progressive factor which "by destroying the peasant economy . . . creates a proletariat and contributes to the industrialization of the country."

Once more we seem to be in the presence of a retroactive legend. The view ascribed to Vladimir (and to his mother, sisters and brother!) is a distortion of an actual dispute—or rather two disputes—then raging between the Marxists and the populists (Narodniki).

One, a theoretical question, concerned the perspective as to Russia's future. According to the populists, Russia had a special destiny and mission: to lead the world to socialism without ever going through the hell of capitalism at all. To them the city was an alien importation, an ulcerous excrescence on the countryside; the proletariat was but a symptom of a social disease that might be avoided; the peasants were all instinctive socialists; the rural communes and cooperatives of village artisans were the road to a new social order. But the Marxists insisted that Russia was even then becoming a land of big industry; that the village commune was in full decay; that the small peasant was being ruined and proletarianized; that the village was differentiating into rich and poor, exploiters and exploited; that the proletariat and not the peasantry was the main hope of a movement for socialism. The idea that famine would strengthen Russian industry, however, was on the face of it an absurdity and caricature of Marxist argument: a single uprooted peasant may become a proletarian, but starving millions are only paupers, while a ruined countryside destroys the market for domestic manufactures.

The second dispute concerned an immediate practical question: how should the revolutionists invest their energies in connection with the famine? Here the more revolutionary of the Narodniks were at one with the Marxists, the line of cleavage being rather between revolutionary and moderate, than between Narodnik and Social Democrat. Ulyanov was not making a policy of his own in any case, merely following his new leader, Plekhanov, of whom he was even then in the process of becoming a disciple.* The alternative which faced the intelligentsia was whether to offer their services to the government (which the government feared and rejected) or to bring pressure to bear upon the government and expose its culpability. "For a socialist," wrote Paul Axelrod, close associate of Plekhanov, "an effective struggle against famine is possible only on the basis of a struggle against the autocracy." And the aged Narodnik leader Lavrov declared: "Yes, the only good work possible for us is not philanthropic work, but revolutionary work."

When Vodovosov, as he himself records, was defeated by Ulyanov, it was in a circle of local Samara radicals where he had proposed to send a telegram of congratulation to the governor of the province for his noble aid to the sufferers. Further

---

* Plekhanov enunciated his policy on the famine in two pamphlets: *The All-Russian Ruin* and *Tasks of the Socialists in the Struggle against Famine.*

light on the accuracy of Vodovosov's account is thrown by the fact that Anna Ulyanova actually did volunteer her services as a nurse.

In the end, the liberals were not successful in ingratiating themselves with the government, which brought charges of profiteering in spoiled grain against the zemstvo of Samara. Nor did they win the confidence of the peasants, who responded to the measures of forced inoculation, hospitalization and quarantine by attacking doctors and nurses and accusing them of poisoning those who died of plague. When seven years later famine recurred, even the moderate liberals spoke of charity as a miserable palliative, regarded haphazard pilgrimage to the stricken areas as ineffective, and demanded a reorganization of the basic structure of Russia. The viewpoint of Plekhanov and his associates had by then become the viewpoint of all Russian intellectuals.

The famine of 1891 marked a fundamental turning point in Russian public life, and it coincided with a rising tide that had begun in Western Europe a year or two earlier. There, too, the eighties had been years of reaction. The First International, headed by Marx and Engels, had perished in the seventies in a fury of police persecution and internal dissension. When Karl Marx died in 1883—the same year which saw the death of the Narodnaya Volya—there was no great organized labor movement anywhere to mourn his passing. But late in the same decade, Marxism began to haunt the capitals of Europe once more. The French working class, prostrate since the fall of the Paris Commune, which had cost them a hundred thousand victims, raised its head again. German Social Democracy, which Bismarck had sought to outlaw and drive underground, found means of surmounting the barriers of the law and rolling up a million and a half votes in an election in which, as a party, it had no legal existence! The British trade unions broke through the crust of routine and narrow craft interest to embrace for the first time great masses of unskilled workers. In Russia, the name of Marx and the prestige of Plekhanov began to take possession of an entire generation of young intellectuals.

The reviving organizations of the principal European lands came together in international conclave in 1889 and the Second International arose out of the ashes of the First. The Congress met under the inspiring influence of the German Social-Democratic victory over Bismarck. Vladimir Ulyanov, like all the Russian youth of his generation, read with passionate interest the meager accounts of German working-class triumphs and Reichstag debates as they appeared in the Russian press. For young Ulyanov the mighty German movement was long to be the model party of the International. In controversy he would quote not only Marx and Engels, but Bebel and Kautsky with a disciple's awe, as authorities whose *ipse dixit* virtually sufficed to decide issues. In the German Social Democracy, with its hierarchical centralization and rigid discipline, he was to find the model after which he hoped to mold the diffused, slack and localized Russian movement; from it he was to derive theoretical conceptions and ideas on strategy and tactics; its workingman leader, August Bebel, was to be the prototype after whose image he sought to fashion Russian workingmen leaders; its outstanding theoretical spokesman, Karl Kautsky, was to be in his eyes the chief defender of the orthodoxy of the Marxist faith. Though he translated all these features into Russian according to his own requirements and strong sense of Russian realities, for a quarter of a century he never doubted this ideal working-class movement at all . . . until, in August, 1914, the news reached him, incredible, unassimilable, that it had voted support of the Imperial Government of Wilhelm II in the war that was just beginning!

At the First Congress of the Socialist International* the leading spokesman for Russia was George Plekhanov. An ex-member of the movement that had given birth to the Narodnaya

---

* Its proper name is Socialist and Labor International. It regarded itself as the successor or continuator of the First International, founded in 1864 and disbanded in 1876. It came to be known generally as the Second International only after Lenin founded the Third or Communist International in 1919. Until then, it embraced all socialist parties and Socialist-inspired trade unions.

Volya, he had been living in exile in Switzerland since 1881. If ever there was a movement which could be said to owe its origin to one man, Russian Marxism owed its origin to this one. In Geneva he had gathered around him Vera Zasulich, heroine of the attempted assassination of Petersburg Governor Trepov, Paul Axelrod, and Leo Deutsch, all veterans of the Narodnik movement, and in 1883 they had formed the first Russian Marxist or Social Democratic organization: the group known as Ozvobozhdenie Truda ("Liberation of Labor"). Until the revolutionary revival of the nineties, it had vegetated in obscure and lonely exile, a handful of neglected thinkers cut off from any connection with Russia. Under Plekhanov's brilliant intellectual leadership it studied Western Marxism, and, in its light, examined critically the assumptions that had actuated the Narodnik movement. In a series of closely reasoned studies (*Socialism and the Political Struggle,* 1883; *Our Differences,* 1884; *Toward the Development of the Monistic Conception of History,* 1895), Plekhanov subjected to "Marxist"* criticism the favorite populist dogmas; the doctrine that the peasant was the driving force of the revolution; the hope of a peculiar path of non-capitalist development for Russia; and the tactic of individual terror. These works, and others of the eighties and nineties from the same hand, contain, in the words of the Bolshevik historian Pokrovsky, "practically all the basic ideas that formed the stock-in-trade of Russian Marxism up to the end of the century." The works of Lenin prior to 1900—so often treated by his followers as if they broke ground for these ideas—were little more than many-sided expansions of hints, or detailed proof of generalizations, contained in the work of this master who, in Lenin's ungrudging acknowledgment, had single-handed served to "rear a whole generation of Russian Marxists."

---

* If I have put the word Marxist in quotation marks here, it is because Marx himself was uncertain as to the possibility of a special non-capitalist path for Russia and warmly sympathetic to the Narodnaya Volya, whose recourse to terror he more than once justified as the only path open to it under then existing Russian conditions. And Frederick Engels, though he welcomed the foundation of the Marxist Liberation of Labor Group by Plekhanov and his associates and had anticipated many of their criticisms of the Russian populists, yet deplored the intolerance with which *Our Differences* treated "the only people who are doing anything in Russia at this moment."

When George Plekhanov addressed the foundation congress of the Socialist International in 1889, he told the delegates: "In Russia political freedom will be gained by the working class, or it will not exist at all. The Russian Revolution can only conquer as a workingman's revolution—there is no other possibility nor can there be."

To the representatives of the Western workingmen's parties that must have seemed a trite commonplace. It passed unnoticed, or they wondered at the air of dramatic revelation with which it was delivered. But as the dictum seeped slowly into the Russian underground, it marked the end of an epoch. With the aid of the vast sounding-board of a world socialist congress, it proclaimed that henceforward the Russian intelligentsia was to turn its face from the village to the city. For an entire decade it was to remain a subject of voluminous, acrimonious, and ever more triumphant controversy. Yet, when the system of ideas it summarized seemed completely victorious, a new wave of peasant riots and uprisings in 1902 was sufficient to revive the oft-buried revolutionary populism in the form of the strong Social Revolutionary Party.

In the course of the nineties, however, spurred on by the negative experiences of the famine and the dark passivity of the peasants, and by a gigantic leap in industrialization and a wave of strikes in the cities, the majority of the radicals among the younger generation—Vladimir Ulyanov's generation—went over to the new creed. They conceived for Plekhanov an admiration without limit, an admiration which, in young Ulyanov's case, would amount to "respect . . . reverence . . . infatuation."

It was in Samara that the young lawyer, Ulyanov, first made his acquaintance with *Our Differences* by Plekhanov, and it was in Samara that he made the transition from populism to Marxism. The town of Samara was a provincial river port with no industrial proletariat and no university. Hence the police considered it safe for the residence of men and women who had served out their time in prison and in Siberia but were forbidden to reside where they might come into contact with students or workingmen. If our provincial lawyer, who was just acquiring an intense theoretical interest in the proletariat, could not observe genuine industrial workers there, he could the world of tramps, vagabonds, migratories, bargemen and boat-haulers down at the waterfront—the world from which issued his future friend, Maxim Gorky. If he could not meet students except for a few expelled university men, he could himself enroll as a student to those past masters of revolutionary conspiracy, the veterans of the Narodnaya Volya whom the police permitted to reside there.

They were aging men and women, survivors of a movement that had failed and perished. They came to life only in their memories. A good listener and a tireless questioner, Vladimir came to them with credentials of younger brother of one of their own hero-martyrs. What were the great days like? he wanted to know. How had they themselves come to the movement and how won recruits for it? What was their program, how had they expounded it, how circulated it, how had the masses responded? How did one "go underground" and what could they tell him of the technique of conspiracy? What of chemical inks, secret codes, signals, false passports, jailbreaks, escapes from exile? How were the Narodovoltsi* organized, who chose the executive committee, what authority had it, how did it admit and instruct members, how limit their knowledge of each other to a minimum, how prevent the penetration of police spies? His questions were rigorous, searching, exact. He was not in quest of vicarious adventure, though his eyes must have burned when they told their heroes' tales. What he sought above all was information that might be useful in the future. Whenever he found that their answers lacked precision or that they were inventing and covering vagueness by verbosity, he ceased to question. When they were sentimental and romantic and seemed to lose touch with reality, his eyes smiled while his

* Narodovoltsi, members of the Narodnaya Volya.

face remained respectfully impassive, as if he were the old one and these aging men and women the youngsters.

As his slowly changing views led to growing differences with them on theoretical matters, he abstained from argument. He was restrained by veneration for their heroism and distaste for exacerbating and useless controversy with people not likely any longer to change their views. But it was not easy for him to break with them. He must have been speaking for himself, as well as for his generation, when he wrote:

> In early youth they enthusiastically worshipped the terrorist heroes. It was a great wrench to abandon the captivating impressions of these heroic traditions, and it was accomplished by the breaking off of personal relations with people who were determined to remain loyal to the Narodnaya Volya and for whom the Young Social Democrats had profound respect.

Toward the end of his stay in Samara, he ceased to seek them out. Then young intellectuals who still followed in their footsteps found him, in his sister Anna's words, "an exceedingly presumptuous and rude young man."

With the same speed and thoroughness with which he had mastered Russian law and come out first among those taking the examinations, the young attorney now absorbed Marxist theory. In Samara he sought out the forbidden works, mastered German to read the originals, obtained badly hectographed or handwritten Russian copies, tore out separate sections of outlawed books for more easy secreting. He plowed through the two volumes of Marx's *Capital* (the third was not yet published) and proceeded to apply its analytical method to Russian statistical material. He read all the government reports, all the economic studies, all the dissertations of liberal or populist economists and sociologists that he could lay hands on. During six silent years, he thought, studied, questioned, examined, soaking up knowledge like a sponge, organizing it in a mind as systematic as a library file, as dynamic and as sparely furnished as a power house. During all those years, except for notebooks, extracts, abstracts, brief or elaborate summaries, he wrote not a word. Not until 1893, during his last months in Samara, did he write anything intended to be read by others.

His first writing of which we have any record is a "book review"—itself almost book size—of a work on the agrarian question. The "review," loaded with statistics and written for legal publication, was rejected by the liberal *Russkaya Mysl* to which he submitted it, probably because it consisted too largely of quotation, paraphrase, tables and summaries from the already well-known book by V. E. Postnikov, *The Agricultural Economy of Southern Russia.* But he read the work aloud in the Samara study circle, where Postnikov's work was unknown. To the provincial circle it seemed a masterpiece of Marxist analysis by a twenty-three-year-old youth. It instantly established his authority. One of the two handwritten copies he prepared has come down to us thanks to those indefatigable collectors of manuscripts, the tsarist police. Not published until 1923, it takes up forty-six pages in the first volume of Lenin's *Collected Works.* The bulk of it was incorporated into his *Development of Capitalism in Russia,* written a half decade later, which also made liberal use of Postnikov's tables and analysis.

From the same last months in Samara dates another work which was circulated in handwritten copies among the youth of the town, but the police failed to preserve a copy for us. *Discussion Between a Social Democrat and a Populist* was its title. It took the form of a dialogue in which Vladimir rehearsed the arguments he had, first within himself, and then with young Samara populists. He wrote it out to clarify his own views, to seek for them a wider audience, and to compel his youthful opponents to listen to the end without interruption. He had too much confidence in his own ideas, even then, to tolerate disorderly and heated interruption by those whom he deemed less informed and in need of listening and learning, not arguing. He was to have recourse to this monologue method of "settling an argument" many times in his lifetime.

The theme of the two works was really the same: their personal basis was Vladimir Ilyich's own break with the Narodniki, their social basis the dispute that raged between the older and the younger generation of revolutionaries throughout the decade of the nineties. Whatever he was to title his future works, virtually all of them until the end of the decade, including the fat *Development of Capitalism in Russia,* were one long "discussion between a Social Democrat and a Populist."

As Vladimir Ulyanov became convinced that the proletariat was to be the driving force of the struggle against tsarism and that the industrial towns of Russia would be the directing center of the revolutionary movement, he began to feel that he had exhausted the possibilities of Samara. According to official biographers he delayed his departure for Saint Petersburg during two years, 1891 to 1893, because he wanted to comfort his mother in a new grief that had befallen her, the death of his younger sister Olga.

Yet the tale that he stayed two more years on the Volga to comfort his mother accords ill with the conception of devotion to duty which he had derived from his father. It fits the facts less than does the simpler, unsentimental explanation of his slow ripening to the point where he decided to make revolution his profession. Moreover, only five months after his sister's death, he again asked the government for a passport to go abroad. What was his purpose? Health, he told the police; but actually he desired to drink wisdom at the new source he had just discovered: George Plekhanov and the Liberation of Labor Group in Switzerland. Permission to go abroad was denied him.

What the young lawyer was like in the last months when he was preparing to leave the Volga, on whose banks he had spent his first twenty-three years, we can deduce from reminiscences of his contemporaries in Samara. "A profound faith in his truthfulness shone through all his speeches," writes the none-too-friendly Vodovosov. "Vladimir Ilyich was a stranger to all bohemianism," records Semenov, a member of his circle in

Samara. "In his presence, all of us restrained ourselves . . . A frivolous conversation, a dirty jest, were impossible in his presence." And young Samoilov, son of the liberal justice of the peace of the locality, recounts the impression Ulyanov made upon him when he visited the Samoilov household:

> When I went to greet the guests, my attention was suddenly attracted by a new figure (brought by Elisarov): at the table was seated at ease a very thin young man, marked with a lively red on his cheeks, his features somewhat Kalmuck, with sparse mustache and beard which had apparently not yet been in contact with the scissors, faintly touched with copper tint, looking at one out of deepset, lively, mischievous eyes. He spoke little but apparently that did not come from any feeling of being ill at ease in an unknown milieu. . . . On the contrary, I suddenly became aware of the fact that M. T. Elisarov, who ordinarily felt at ease among us, was not exactly upset by the presence of the new guest, but in some way intimidated. . . . In the midst of the conversation, after having made a deduction which seemed to him particularly well taken, he broke out suddenly in a little abrupt laugh, short, quite Russian. It was clear that in him there had just been born a thought, pregnant, piquant, which he had been searching for previously. That little laugh, healthy and not without mischief, emphasized by little wrinkles, equally mischievous, at the corners of his eyelids, remains in my memory. Everyone got ready to laugh, but he was already composed and once more listening to the general conversation, fixing on the speakers his attentive and slightly mocking gaze.

And in Krupskaya's memoirs we read:

> Some comrades told me that a certain learned Marxist had arrived from the Volga. Then they brought me an exercise book containing an article *On Markets* which was being passed around for comrades to read in turn. The notebook contained the views of our Petersburg Marxist, the engineer Herman Krassin, and the newcomer from the Volga. The pages were folded in half. On the one side, in a straggling scrawl with many crossings out and insertions, were the opinions of Krassin. On the other side, carefully written and without alterations, were the notes and replies of our newly arrived friend.

CHAPTER SIX

THE COMMON SOURCE

In Marxism there is a sense of fatality, but also the exaltation of a will. Every time fatality comes before will, I am suspicious.

—KYO GISORS, IN "MAN'S FATE."

Such was Krupskaya's introduction to her future husband. She was prepared to admire the man as soon as she had seen the notebook, but a number of months elapsed before she met him in person.

It was in the spring of 1894, five or six months after his arrival in the capital, that Nadezhda Konstantinovna* met Vladimir Ilyich. He was twenty-four and she twenty-six. They met at a pancake party, a traditional holiday festival occurring on Shrove Tuesday when the orthodox take their last fling with food and merriment before going into the lean, sad days of Lent. Almost all of the circle of Petersburg Marxists were there—intellectuals all, for there was as yet not one working-man amongst these representatives of the future "party of the proletariat."

The pancake festival maintained barely enough of a carnival air so that if the police should break in, the celebrants might put up the requisite show of gaiety. The table was spread with the traditional foods and drinks, but the solemn and unfestive talk turned around questions of "revolutionary tactics." Nadezhda Konstantinovna could not keep her eyes off the new arrival from Samara. What she saw was a serious young man with tiny, quizzical, ironic eyes, a high, boxlike forehead prematurely bald, a solid figure that was just beginning to grow stocky after a period of adolescent leanness—unprepossessing enough, but with a quiet air of self-confidence and self-mastery which she had already sensed in his notebook.

> Vladimir Ilyich spoke little and was more occupied in contemplating those present. People who styled themselves Marxists became uncomfortable beneath his fixed gaze. . . . Someone was saying—I think it was Shevlyagin—that what was very important was to work in the Committee for Illiteracy. Vladimir Ilyich laughed, and somehow his laughter sounded laconic. . . .

---

* Nadezhda Konstantinovna Krupskaya, that is, Nadezhda, daughter of Konstantin Krupsky. After her marriage to Lenin her legal name became Nadezhda Konstantinovna Ulyanova. By those who knew her she was normally addressed, and referred to, by her given name and patronymic, as Nadezhda Konstantinovna. Her immediate family and closest intimates, including Lenin, called her Nadya. Her first underground name was a nickname Lenin gave her, that of *Mynoga,* the Russian word for lamprey. Then she switched to the *nom de guerre: Sablina.* In later years she was always known simply as Krupskaya.

"Well," he said, "if anyone wants to save the fatherland in the Committee for Illiteracy, we won't stop him."

It was the same abrupt laugh that young Samoilov had noted in Samara; the same irreconcilability that Vodovosov had complained of during the famine. Nadezhda, who all her life loved children and untutored workingmen and took joy in teaching them, and who was working ardently in the Committee for Literacy (its proper title), was pleased with his scorn. It seemed to promise shorter and grander roads to the elevation of the masses. His contempt for their efforts to irrigate the desert of popular ignorance with spoonfuls of alphabet soup, completed the admiration that had been inspired by his notebook. His little, watchful eyes, searching the human material before him, must have noted the agreement and admiration showing in the face of the slight, large-eyed, snub-nosed girl, carelessly dressed, with hair cut almost boyishly short, as was the fashion with "emancipated" women. After the party, he walked home with her along the banks of the Neva. The walk is a lovely one; their talk did not make it seem less lovely. She told him about her evening and Sunday classes among the workingmen beyond the Nevsky gate. He spoke to her of his hopes and plans, and of the life and death of his brother Alexander. It was the first she had heard of the tragedy. Such was the beginning of their Marxist courtship.

Nadya was a typical representative of the female radical intelligentsia of the period. Both her parents were of noble birth, but orphans of families that had fallen into decay. Her father, Konstantin Krupsky, had entered the civil service, had risen to the rank of Collegial Assessor and been a provincial official in Russian Poland. There his liberalism took the form of attempting to shield the local population from Alexander III's policy of ruthless Russification. Charges of some sort were preferred against him and he was suspended from office. While his case dragged for ten years from court to court, he picked up his living as best he could as insurance agent, clerk, auditor, factory inspector. In the end, the charges were dismissed for lack of evidence. After his death, mother and daughter eked out the modest widow's pension by giving lessons. Thus her sympathy with the poor and the oppressed and her love of dispensing from her superior share of the world's cultural goods to the more needy, Nadezhda Konstantinovna had absorbed from the experiences of her childhood.

> We lived rather poorly, mother and I—she wrote in her memoirs—on what we could make by letting out rooms, copying work, and the like. Giving lessons took up all my time from morning to night, but all these lessons were but chance windfalls. The only regular work I had was an evening class at the *gymnazia,* but it prevented me from attending meetings and from working in the evening school, so I had to give it up.

This surrender of her one source of steady income in order to be able to give free instruction to the workers in the adult evening schools was typical of the abnegation that characterized her, as it did so many of the declassed nobility and radical intelligentsia. At the tender age of fourteen she had begun to teach. To get "to the people," she determined to become a village school teacher, but could not find a position. "It was only at the age of twenty-one," she wrote, "that I discovered that there was such a thing as social science . . . As soon as I began to understand the part that the workers must play in the emancipation of the working people, I felt an irresistible desire to be among the workers." Thus she became a member of the first Marxist circle in Saint Petersburg, two years before Ulyanov came from Samara. She continued teaching the workingmen common branches in the evening and Sunday schools, but increasingly her interest shifted from the mere spread of culture to making contacts for the Marxist intellectuals.

The Committees for Literacy, the free libraries and the adult education classes were a continuation of the *V Narod* ("to the people") movement of the preceding decades, with this noteworthy difference: that the "people" were now not peasants but workingmen. And with the further difference that among the latter was a readiness to receive the cultural ministrations of the intelligentsia, a deep hunger and thirst for knowledge.

At the end of 1891, when Krupskaya was preparing to join her first Marxist study circle, there were three free libraries in Saint Petersburg. Their readers were mainly skilled workers, artisans and poor students. Men and women trudged to the libraries from great distances, after long hours of labor and hastily bolted evening meals; sometimes they fell asleep in their weariness over books that seemed to promise unheard-of wonders. Most of them were but recently uprooted from the villages, newly freed from subservience to wind and weather and ancient communal tradition. The old rural content faded, but the mind, too, abhors a vacuum. Some, who performed the heavy labor, were likely to fill their few empty moments with drink. Others, generally skilled workers and artisans, stirred by the strange powers of the machines they tended, were beginning to have confidence in new laws of mechanism and power, of cause and effect, of man's dominion over the forces of nature. These drank as thirstily of science as the others of vodka.

Krupskaya's pupils watched their devoted school mistress with unlimited confidence shining from grateful faces. They told her everything. The usually gloomy workingman came beaming with the news that a son had been born to him; the consumptive girl from a textile factory brought her suitor along and demanded that he be made literate before she marry him; a Methodist artisan who had spent his whole life seeking God told her that "only on Passion Sunday had he learned from Rudakov (another pupil) that there was no God at all"; a conservative textile worker, wont to extol priest and Tsar, whispered: "Beware of that dark fellow there, as he's always prowling around on the Gorokhavaya."*

_____
* The name of the street where the headquarters of the tsarist secret police were located. Today men similarly refer to the G.P.U. or M.V.D. by the name of the street Lubyanka.

On Sunday afternoons Vladimir Ilyich would seek her out
after the classes were over, and they would take long walks together. She would tell him what she had learned about conditions in the factories and the mood and outlook of her charges.
He would question her minutely and exactingly, or sometimes
talk to her of the latest book he was reading or the progress of
his own thinking and writing. "Vladimir Ilyich was interested
in the minutest detail of the conditions and life of the workers.
Taking the features separately he endeavored to grasp the life
of the worker as a whole." It was no easy plight this, to believe
that the working class was the bearer of the future and yet not
be one of them nor have any real knowledge of their lives. Later, Volodya, as she had begun to call him, gave her elaborate
written questionnaires to guide her in eliciting information, got
her to bring trusted workers home with her for questioning,
made one of the chosen ones sweat (as the poor man afterwards
recorded), while he plied him with interrogation after interrogation on which to base a leaflet to be distributed in his factory. Then Nadya and some other woman comrades, masquer-
ading in working women's clothes, sought to slip the crudely
hectographed leaflets, printed letter by letter in Ulyanov's own
hand-lettering, into the workers' hands while shifts were changing. Or they left them on work benches, in toilets, or wherever
else the factory hands might find them. Thus with Krupskaya's
aid, did Ulyanov embark on the long course of trying to unite
the ideas of socialism with the spontaneously developing labor
movement, an effort which was his central preoccupation for
the next quarter of a century.

The Literacy Committees of which Ulyanov had been so
scornful soon began to absorb much of his attention. The Saint
Petersburg committee had about a thousand members. In more
backward Moscow it numbered four hundred. They included
Narodniks, Marxists, and all shades of democratic, liberal and
radical opinion. They established free libraries and reading
rooms, compiled bibliographies for popular education, taught

common branches to the unlettered, published cheap books for workingmen. Their funds came from donations, dues, lectures, concerts, benefit performances. During the two years of Ulyanov's stay in Saint Petersburg they raised the not inconsiderable sum of 25,000 rubles ($12,000). Members gave their time and their money with no other compensation than that which came from their hope that they might thus serve the people and "redeem" Russia. Ulyanov, despite his scorn for cultural philanthropy, was not slow to see in these committees a cloak for his own activities: a means of getting contact with workingmen and their teachers and learning what these workingmen were really thinking; a means of recruiting a few of the teachers and their most advanced pupils into the Marxist movement; of getting social contacts with well-to-do and friendly disposed liberals. Thus he and his comrades "penetrated" the committees and made of them one of the first of the many "fringe" organizations to which we have since gotten so accustomed in connection with the Communist movement. Its leaders and most active members became the first "innocents," "sympathizers," "fellow-travellers" and "angels."

The most outstanding of these "angels" was Mrs. Kalmykova. She was a friend of Krupskaya's and, like her, had taught in the Sunday school classes in the Nevsky gate district. Her outlook was similar to what Nadezhda's had been before she fell under the spell of Vladimir Ilyich. A woman of wealth and the wife of a high official of the capital, she despised the upper social circles which her wealth and position entitled her to move in.

Mrs. Kalmykova opened a bookshop and publishing house which became the leading center for the distribution of cheap popular books and progressive literature, and, surreptitiously, of underground literature also. Under the wing of her official respectability, radicals foregathered to browse among the books, or engage in hurried conferences in the back rooms. Soon her importance to the underground movement was such that she acquired an alias in their correspondence, being referred to among them as "Auntie." "Auntie" gave generously of her own funds, and collected much more from her acquaintances in Petersburg society. This, too, became important enough to receive a code designation: "the bucket."

After two short years of Social Democratic penetration, the police, who had their spies among the Marxists, closed down the Committee for Literacy. Once more, as in the days of the *V Narod* movement, the efforts of the intelligentsia to share their burden of culture with the masses was thus blocked by the government, and once more some of the most idealistic among them took up a direct struggle with the government. Mrs. Kalmykova was one of these. In 1903, when the Social Democrats split into Bolsheviks and Mensheviks, the news of the split distressed her deeply. She wrote to her friend Vladimir Ilyich, rebuking him for his share in the responsibility for it, telling how it disheartened her, and asking what she should now do with the "bucket"—the funds she was collecting for *Iskra,* which had been the periodical of the united movement. Lenin wrote her two letters in which he sought to justify himself and persuade her to his side of the controversy. Despite her discouragement, she remained a revolutionary sympathizer, returning from long voluntary exile abroad after the Revolution of 1917. Until her death in 1926 she continued a warm and friendly correspondence with Lenin and Krupskaya.

Gradually a number of Nadezhda's workingmen pupils were recruited for secret Marxist study-circle work, under the direction of Vladimir Ilyich. He would read to his little group from a popularization of Marx's *Capital,* interrupting frequently to explain the text, ask elucidating questions, illustrate from Russian examples. Then he would expound orally, without notes, some idea connected with the text they were studying, clinching the application to Russian realities. The second half of the long evening—these Russians were used to late hours in the pursuit of learning—he would devote to answering his auditors' questions, and questioning them in turn about their problems and conditions of work.

> He frequently tried to provoke us to speak or arouse us to start a discussion—wrote the workingman Babushkin*—and then he would urge us on, compelling each to demonstrate to the other the correctness of his standpoint on a given question. Thus our lectures were made very animated and interesting, and we began to become accustomed to speaking in public. This mode of study served as an excellent way of clarifying a given question for the students. All of us greatly enjoyed these lectures, and were constantly delighted by our lecturer's power of intellect, it being a standing joke among us that an excess of brains had made his hair fall out. At the same time, these lectures trained us to do independent work, and to find material. The lecturer would hand us lists of questions which required on our part close knowledge and observation of life in the factory and workshop.

These Marxist study-circles, too, were largely attended by intellectuals. The workers who came to them were precious few, but to Ulyanov those few were indeed precious. He saw in them "the future Bebels" who were to lead the Russian working class, the realization of the hope which that same year he expressed in one of his illegally circulated notebooks:

"The role of the intelligentsia is to make special leaders from among the intelligentsia unnecessary."

The future of Russia would in large measure depend upon whether or not, or to what extent, this aim would be realized.

Ulyanov's chief work of the year 1894 was entitled *What Are the Friends of the People and How Do They Fight Against the Social Democrats?* For good measure it bore the subtitle: *Answer to the Articles in* Russkoye Bogatstvo† *Against the*

---

* We are not here dealing with recollection embellished by knowledge of Lenin's subsequent victorious leadership; for Babushkin, one of the first workingmen Bolsheviks, was shot and killed by General Rennenkampf in Siberia in 1906, when he was caught transporting arms.

† *Russkoye Bogatstvo,* "Russian Wealth," was the leading journal of economics, sociology, philosophy and literature. Its editor, N. K. Mikhailovsky (1842-1904), veteran Narodnik and their outstanding theoretical leader, had just opened an ideological crusade against Marxism.

Marxists. It circulated in three stout, carefully written yellow notebooks, the first of which he read aloud to the Marxist circle of which he was a member. The notebooks created a remarkable stir in the Marxist microcosm and were soon hectographed and passed from hand to hand anonymously, under the alias of "The Little Yellow Books." In truth, they were far from little; only the first and third parts have come down to us, but these occupy 170 pages in Lenin's *Collected Works.* One can imagine the labor, intellectual, statistical, and physical, which Ulyanov spent in writing all this out in his neat, tiny hand in the manuscript notebooks, and then, all over again, letter by letter according to the printed alphabet, on the hectograph sheets. Here was a warrior of the pen if there ever was one! "How proud we felt," wrote the engineer Krzhizhanovsky,* "that such a man was marching in our ranks."

This, the first of Lenin's published volumes—or rather, of Ulyanov's, since the man Lenin did not yet exist—is a work of full maturity. In it are his mastery of Marxism, his ability to move familiarly in a maze of statistics and to distinguish the outlines of the basic structure of Russian reality without ignoring the multitudinous complicating detail. About it there is something of the freshness of youth, a bit of brashness, ever so light a touch of dreaming. Here, in germ, are many of Lenin's future deficiencies and weaknesses, but in full flower all his powers and sources of strength.

Unawed by the overpowering prestige of the venerable Mikhailovsky and his distinguished associates, this "presumptuous young man" studies and refutes their objections to Marxism, rectifies with caustic irony their misrepresentation of the views and aims of the Social Democrats, tears to shreds Narodnik theoretical conceptions and practical proposals. To their vagueness and sentimentality he opposes his rigorous exactness, to their wishful idylls his unvarnished description of the

---

* The *zh* which occurs twice in this, for us, so difficult name, is pronounced like the letter *z* in our word "azure." In the back of the book the reader will find some hints on the transliteration and pronunciation of Russian words.

facts; the problems they talk around he carefully defines. He expends whole pages on wearisome *argumenta ad hominem;* but the next moment, in no greater scope of pages, he lays bare the skeletal structure of that vast architectural construction, Marx's *Capital,* and disposes easily of objections which have formed, and still form, much of the stock-in-trade of professional Marx-critics.

As the awkward title suggests, there is no concern for adornment. The style is severely logical with an austere attraction where the great generalizations are propounded, didactic in repetitive schoolmaster fashion where ideas are hammered home, applied to instances, drilled in and repeated again and again with only slight variations. It is ill-tempered and scolding, or amused and scornful, where he catches his distinguished opponent in unworthy tricks of polemics. Occasionally it indulges in high good humor, like that of a muzhik laughing at the blown-up words and pretensions of the gentry:

> Yes, Mr. Mikhailovsky, any idea will be too general if you first take all the insides out of it as though it were a dried herring, and then begin to play about with the skin . . .
> The lap dog must be very strong indeed if he barks at the elephant . . .
> Apparently he feels very much at ease in this not overclean position: there he sits preening himself and splashing mud all around him . . .
> Naive attempts to make the bourgeois intelligentsia ashamed of being bourgeois remind me of the judgment of the pike which the court condemned to be thrown into the water . . .
> They are trying to devise arrangements whereby the wolves can eat themselves full, and the sheep remain uneaten . . .

Such are the simple and homely adornments of style with which the youthful combatant delighted his comrades, though the discriminating among them were more attracted by the austere rigor of the major outlines and the steamroller thoroughness with which the job was accomplished. Vladimir Ilyich was twenty-four years of age when he thus engaged in mortal combat with the great veteran publicist who for more than two decades had dominated progressive thought.

Plekhanov, too, had used his rapier-keen intellect in a duel with Mikhailovsky, but he was content with a few thrusts that drew blood and exhibited his own duelist's superiority. Ulyanov preferred rather to go to work on the systematic demolition of the entire thought structure. Before he is finished he seems to have used axe, hammer, saw, chisel, plane, file, sandpaper, and everything else in the tool kit. Plekhanov was too much the intellectual aristocrat and too much the stylist to relish the task of going in detail after all the trivia and absurdities of his opponent. Not so Ulyanov.

"George [Plekhanov] is a greyhound," Vera Zasulich was later to tell Lenin. "He shakes and shakes his adversary, then lets go. But you, you are a bulldog; you have a deadly bite."

"A deadly bite, eh?" he repeated to her with evident pleasure.

The intellectual war between Marxists and populists (Narodniki) was really a battle between two rival varieties of socialism. Populism was the older and more indigenous, having arisen out of the "To the People" (*V Narod*) movement of the Russian intelligentsia. It was Russia's own native variety of socialism: a humanitarian, agrarian socialism, which pronounced with reverence the sacred word: *people*—meaning thereby not just city workers but primarily the vast majority of the Russian people: the muzhiks. It had preceded Marxism by several decades. Its leaders had translated and helped to popularize Marx's works, respected them as a powerful scientific critique of Western capitalism, but, still and all, a Western importation, not fully applicable to non-capitalist Russia.

More than either of the two contendants realized, they were complementary to each other, rather than irreconcilable rivals, since the populists based themselves upon the rural masses, the Social Democrats on the urban. Never could there be a truly democratic transformation of Russia unless these two classes should join forces in mutual and equal partnership, and without either imposing itself upon the other. Since neither peasants nor workers were as yet stirring in response to the cries and conjurations hurled at them by the revolutionary intelligentsia, the actual struggle was not between those two classes, but between two little, all-or-nothing groups of intellectuals who were fighting for exclusive domination of the soul of the Russian intelligentsia, one trying to direct its attention to the working class, the other to the peasantry. Hence the ups and downs of the two tendencies coincided directly with the degree of stir in city and village. Whenever the peasants cut down forests, burned manor houses, drove out landlords or local authorities, as they had done for a decade before and a decade after the Emancipation of 1861, the hope of the intelligentsia in the peasantry flamed high, and the Narodnik movement became active and revolutionary. But for three decades, now, the village had been sullenly silent. It was despair at that passivity, even more than government brutality, which had driven the Narodniki to try individual terror. And, more than the police raids, it was the same despair which snuffed out the flame of the Narodnaya Volya in the eighties. What was left of populism became abstract and feeble and academically respectable.

Just at that moment, came the first great wave of industrial strikes of the middle nineties, turning the ever-hopeful attention of the Russian intelligentsia to the cities and the urban working class. The excitement caused by the great strike-wave was the emotional force that gave victory to the theoretical arguments of Plekhanov and his disciples, turning the attention of the entire younger generation, to which Ulyanov belonged, toward Marxism and Social Democracy. With characteristic Russian fanaticism, they excluded the peasantry from their thinking as a driving force of revolution.

Yet, early in the twentieth century, the village would awaken once more. Then the so-often routed Narodnik movement would rise again, phoenix-like, from its ashes, as the new Social Revolutionary Party. It would continue to grow in influence until, in 1917, its candidates for the Constituent Assembly would get

21,000,000 votes to the Bolsheviks' 9,000,000—indeed, a much larger vote than Bolshevik and Menshevik Social Democrats put together.

It was the doctrinaire, sectarian character of Russian disputation which turned these two groups, who might have been allies, into embittered enemies. Their theoretical controversy turned about this question: must Russia follow the course that the Western European nations have followed—from feudalism, through capitalism, and only then to socialism? Or might not Russia follow another road: from feudalism, by a "non-capitalist path," directly into post-capitalist socialism?

To answer this question it was necessary to know how long tsarism would last. More important, it was necessary to appraise the character of the peasant mind, and to estimate the nature and prospects of that peculiar Russian institution: the communal village or *mir*. The Narodniks contended that the communal village was "primitively socialist" in character and psychology, that it inculcated in its members the spirit of continuous redivision of property, of equality and fraternity, of collectivism and corporate feeling. The peasant mind, they held, was thus elementally or naively socialist, and well adapted—better even than the mind of the Western proletariat—to grasping the ideas and spirit of socialism. On the village *mir,* and the ideology it engendered, the Narodniks based their hopes that Russia might avoid the pangs of capitalism, and, shaking off the remnants of feudalism and absolutism, might build a socialist, free Russia. Was there an "iron law" which decreed that Russia must adopt a capitalism which was already showing its evils in the Western world? Or might not Holy Russia—the old messianic dream—from the last become the first, leading the whole world and showing it the way out of Western capitalism to a better and more humane order?

To these theoretical considerations, the Russian Marxists answered by making a banner of the name of Marx. They appealed to the schemata of Marx's *Capital,* which, they believed, "demonstrated scientifically" that all lands must "inevitably" go through the various stages from feudalism, through capitalism, to socialism. Moreover, was not industrial capitalism already developing with giant strides in Russia? Was not the village *mir* doomed? Was it not even then disintegrating into a "capitalist village"—extruding two new social classes: a landless, village "proletariat" and a rich-peasant, "capitalist farmer" class, or "village bourgeoisie"? This was the whole polemical point of young Ulyanov's first major theoretical work, his monumental *Development of Capitalism in Russia*. His examination of the real statistical trends of Russian economic development, an examination which was soon to win the admiration of all Russian Marxists, tended to prove that Russia was already taking giant strides along the path of capitalism, in agriculture, in industry and in trade.

But, most important of all—according to Lenin and his co-religionists—the mind of the Russian peasant was not "naively socialist" at all: but "naively bourgeois," or rather, "petty bourgeois," the mind of a small proprietor on-the-make. It was this distrust of, and unconscious antagonism toward, the peasant majority of the Russian nation which would, in the end, sterilize all Marxist protestations in favor of democracy. For, how can you have democracy where there is no trust in the majority of those who make up the nation?

Thus, with their characteristic thoroughness and abandon did the Russian Marxists unite statistical facts, theoretical logic, and temperament, to answer the over-all question concerning Russia's destiny. Yes, said they, Russia is fatally and inevitably destined to pass through the valley of the shadow of capitalism on its way to the heights of socialism! Moreover, such capitalism will be a step forward in Russia's march, a "progressive" development, both in that it will raise the productive powers of the nation and in that it will create an industrial working class or proletariat, which alone can be trusted and depended upon to develop a socialist ideology.

It is interesting to note that this view of those calling themselves Russian Marxists or Social Democrats was not necessarily
the view of Karl Marx himself concerning Russia's "inevitable
path." On the contrary, had he had to take his chances as a
Russian in the midst of the Russian controversy, without the
aura of authority that surrounded his name, he might well have
been condemned by his Russian disciples as an indifferent and
wavering Marxist, if not worse. In the last years of his life, he
began to study the difficult Russian tongue, chiefly for the purpose of seeking light on this specific theoretical question, and
he never could quite make up his mind as to which of the two
alternative paths Russia was more likely to take. In 1877, he
had written to a Russian magazine (*Notes on the Fatherland*) a
letter in which he spoke of Russia's having "the best opportunity that history has ever offered to a people to escape all the
catastrophes of capitalism." In 1881, only two years before his
death, he had written to Vera Zasulich, associate of Plekhanov:

> The analysis given in *Das Kapital* offers no arguments either
> for or against the vitality of the rural commune (*mir*), but the
> special study I have made of it . . . has convinced me that this
> commune is the *point d'appui* for the social regeneration of
> Russia. However, in order that it may function as such, it would
> be necessary first to remove the deleterious influences which are
> attacking it from all sides, and then to insure it the normal
> conditions of a spontaneous development.

And a year later, when he and Engels were called upon by
Vera Zasulich to supply an introduction to her new Russian
translation of the *Communist Manifesto,* they wrote:

> In Russia, alongside the capitalist system (which is growing up
> with feverish speed) and the bourgeois landowning system (which
> is in its early stages of development), more than half the land is
> owned in common by the peasantry. The question we have to
> answer is: Will the Russian peasant communes (a primitive form
> of communal ownership which is already on the downgrade) be-
> come transformed into the superior form of communist owner-
> ship of land, or will they have to pass through the same process

of decay we have witnessed in the course of the historical evolution of the West?

There is only one possible answer to this question. If the Russian revolution sounds the signal for a workers' revolution in the West, so that each becomes the complement of the other, then the prevailing form of communal ownership of land in Russia may serve as the starting-point for a communist course of development.

All these passages come at least as close to the hopes of the Russian Narodniki as they do to the asseveration concerning Russia's "inevitable path" made by those who called themselves Marxists and invoked Marx's name. Ten years after the latter's death, in 1893, his friend Engels drily refused to offer "authoritative opinions" on these Russian disputations:

> If you have followed the writings of the Russian exiles during the last ten years, you will know yourself how the various groups among them interpret passages from Marx's writings and letters in the most contradictory ways, just as if they were texts from the classics or the New Testament. And anything I could say on the question you propounded to me would probably be used in a similar way, if any attention were paid to it. (Letter to I. A. Hourwich.)

It is noteworthy that, from the time they first became aware of the revolutionary movement in Russia until the day of their respective deaths, Marx and Engels held that revolutionary terror had a special justification in Russia, and that both the Narodnik and Social Democratic (Plekhanovist) movements were entitled to consideration as legitimate expressions of the needs of revolution in Russia. When Plekhanov published his *Our Differences,* Engels wrote to express his approval of the contents but his dislike of the intolerant attacks on the revolutionary wing of Narodniki, "the only people who are doing anything in Russia at present." And to Vera Zasulich he explained that it was immaterial which sect might set a revolution going for which every condition, material and psychological, was present. He was pleased that the Marxists accepted so much of his and Marx's doctrine, but he never ceased to disapprove of their relegating the courageous and revolutionary Narodniks to the lake of fire and brimstone "with other reactionaries." It might be that the Narodniks were prone to believe some fairy-tales concerning Russia's future, but they were superior to the Social Democrats in their positive activity and in their aware-ness of the importance of the agrarian problem and of the vast peasant population.

In the spring of 1892, Engels actually arranged a meeting in his home in London between the leaders of the two groups among the Russian socialist refugees, in order to unite Narod-niks and self-proclaimed Marxists into a single party. But, what with the ardor of the Russian temperament in controversy, and the diffidence of Engels to intervene in a dictatorial manner, the plan fell through. Yet to Engels it seemed that it had failed only because these sectarians lived in the bitter "night of exile," in isolation from a mass movement. Thus his last word on the Russian question was a gently urgent plea for the unification of the Russian Marxists and the Russian populists, or, as they would later call themselves, the Social Democrats and the Social Revolutionaries. But, after his death, his name and Marx's were used as lance and pennant to smite the Social Revolutionaries. Not until the year 1914 did Lenin's old teacher, Plekhanov, seriously propose the unification of the two groups into a single movement. But by then it was too late, for the differences had gained enormous organizational and emotional momentum. As for Lenin himself, he would have no part of such unity.

Both Narodniks and Russian Marxists, then, were critical of capitalism, but with a fundamental difference. The Narodniks hoped that its "pitiless laws" could be avoided for Russia. "We have not yet seen anything good in Western capitalism," wrote Mikhailovsky. But the Marxists not only predicted a capitalist path for Russian development; they even regarded such a devel-opment as "progressive."

"Objectively" you are really apologists for capitalism, charged the Narodniks. You call it progressive, you get enthusiastic over every step in its infiltration of Russia, you celebrate its cruel triumphs. You need it so that you may have your proletariat, and you do not seem to care whether that involves the destruction of the village *mir,* the dispossessing of the peasants, their ruin and proletarianization.

"Objectively" you are no socialists at all, responded the Social Democrats. You glorify Russia's backwardness. You conceal from yourselves the fact that capitalism has already set in and is ruining the *mir* and sowing class differences in the countryside. You base your program upon the real or fancied needs of the peasants, who are not socialists but petty bourgeois. You want to defend the small producer against expropriation. Objectively you are the party of petty-bourgeois democracy and not a socialist party at all.

The socialist ought to break *decisively and finally* with all petty-bourgeois ideas and theories—*that is the most important and useful lesson*—is Lenin's political conclusion from the chain of reasoning we have been outlining—. I ask you to note also that I am speaking of the necessity of a break with the petty-bourgeois ideas of socialism. The petty-bourgeois ideas I have examined are *unconditionally* reactionary *insofar* as they masquerade as socialist theories.

But if we understand that there is really not the least bit of socialism about them, that really all these theories reflect and represent the interest of the small bourgeoisie, then we must have another attitude toward them. Then we ought put the question: *What attitude should the working class take toward the petty bourgeoisie and their program?* . . .

This class is progressive insofar as it makes general democratic demands, i.e. fights against every remnant of medievalism and serfdom. It is reactionary insofar as it fights for the preservation of its position as a petty bourgeoisie, seeking to hold back, even turn backward, the general development of the country in the direction of capitalism. These two sides of the petty-bourgeois program should be sharply distinguished from each other and, while we must deny any socialist character whatsoever to these theories and fight against their reactionary aspects, we must not forget their democratic side . . . The rejection by the Marxists

> of these petty-bourgeois theories does not in the slightest exclude
> democracy from their [the Marxist] program. [Lenin: *Collected
> Works,* Third Russian Edition, Vol. I, pp. 183-4. Emphasis, as
> throughout this book, in the original.]

Thus Ulyanov asserts that he does not want to destroy the
Narodniki at all, only to put them in their proper place and
force them to recognize that they are "not a socialist, but a
petty-bourgeois democratic party." They attack Russian Marxism as he understands it, hence he refutes them. They term
themselves socialist, hence he exposes them. They misjudge the
peasant to be "naively socialist"; he insists that the peasant is a
"naive petty bourgeois." They venture to include the working
class in their general term, *narod,* "the people," hence he fights
them; for only Social Democracy should have any right to appeal
to the proletariat. Any other party seeking to trespass in that exclusive domain should be pitilessly denounced and forcibly ousted
as an interloper. Yet, because the working class, too, needs democratic freedoms for its purposes, he would like to have an alliance with the Narodniki (once he has put them in their proper
place), an alliance in a common struggle for democracy.

> The Social Democrats naturally regard the creation of such a
> democratic party as a useful step forward, and our activity
> against Narodnikism is intended to help in this, to contribute
> to the overcoming of all prejudices and myths, to the gathering
> of the socialists under the banner of Marxism and to the found-
> ing of a democratic party by the remaining groups . . . [It is] the
> direct duty of the working class to separate from this general
> democratic movement in order to organize a socialist labor party
> of its own . . . and then, to fight side by side with the radical de-
> mocracy against absolutism and the reactionary estates.

All the Petersburg Marxists applauded the polemic of the
young Marxist from the Volga. Soon young men and women
of Vladimir's generation, and some who were considerably older,
began to refer to this bald-headed young man of twenty-four as
Starik—"The Old Man." They began to regard him as a *primus
inter pares,* one of the first in a society of equals (there was no

infallible-leader cult in those days), and the shadow he cast lengthened slowly over other parts of Russia. There was as yet no sign of the differences which would one day divide the Social Democrats themselves into angry and hostile factions. All were agreed in disputing with the Narodniki for leadership over the workers, which in practice meant no more than disputing for leadership over the revolutionary intelligentsia; sufficiently to direct the latter's gaze from the peasantry to the working class.

The "peasant socialist" movement did not end with the polemic of the nineties. The police thought they had put an end to it when they destroyed the Narodnaya Volya in 1883. Now the Marxists defeated its attenuated shadow in the nineties in theoretical disputations. Convinced by the continued quiescence in the village, by the giant strides which Russian industry was making in the cities, and by the first big wave of labor strikes, the whole younger generation let itself be persuaded by the arguments of the Marxists. But then, early in the twentieth century, the peasantry began to stir once more: riots, manorhouse burnings, clashes with officials and police—and the ghost of peasant socialism arose from its ashes, mightier than ever, in the shape of the Social Revolutionary Party (founded in 1903). All through the first two decades of the new century—until 1917—the struggle between the "Westernizer" Social Democrats and the "Slavophile" Social Revolutionaries continued. Then suddenly, the same issues took on new and unexpected forms as a conflict between two wings of the Marxist Social Democrats: the Bolsheviks and the Mensheviks. The Social Revolutionary Party, too, split in the year, 1917, the larger branch allying itself with the Menshevik and the smaller with the Bolshevik Social Democrats.

For what was the theory behind Lenin's seizure of power in November, 1917, if not a new version of the theory that Russia (if aided by anticipated revolutions in the West) might leap over capitalism and follow a peculiar non-capitalistic path to industrialization and socialism? The village communal *mir,* too, was still there to build upon; its "naive peasant socialism," its primitive collectivist and corporate ideology, was used by the Bolsheviks to good advantage. The *mir* had not disintegrated as fast as the Marxists had anticipated, because its ancient roots were too deep in the Russian soil and because the tsarist government itself had kept it alive as a convenient unit for exacting collective responsibility for taxes.

If the Narodniki had underestimated the growing importance of the proletariat, the Marxists—deceived by the three decades of miserable quiescence in the countryside—had underestimated the revolutionary potential that was accumulating once more in the Russian village. But Lenin, almost alone of the Social Democrats, was to correct this underestimation early enough and completely enough to utilize that peasant discontent in 1917 for his purposes.

In the polemic we have been discussing Ulyanov assured the Narodniki that as "peasant socialists" they were really only petty-bourgeois democrats. Their views, he told them, "objectively led" to democratic capitalism, and once that was achieved these same views would "inevitably force them" to become opponents of socialism. This to men who sympathized with the lot of all the oppressed and exploited! To men who loved freedom, detested tyranny and bondage, abominated all forms of exploitation, not excluding the capitalist form to which, according to Ulyanov, their view "objectively led." Brashly, Ulyanov insisted that their "subjective desires" could be discounted, that he possessed an infallible science which enabled him to predict whither their wishes "objectively led."

But the discounting of subjective desires is a strange way of apprehending a historical process which is first of all a clash of subjective desires, a conflict of wills. And a clash in which the will of no single man or group ever wins through, be that man or group ever so great, or ever so sure that his will is based upon the most scientific analysis of history's possible or inevitable paths.

"People who imagined that they had made a revolution –

Engels once wrote to Vera Zasulich—always saw next day that they did not know what they had been doing, and that the revolution which they made was nothing like the one they had wanted to make."

Suppose Lenin could look back now upon the subsequent career of the Narodniki and their successors, the Social Revolutionaries. To be sure, he might point out that from their ranks had come a number who would make their peace with capitalism. But so did the ranks of the Marxists beget such men in no less profusion. What he could never have foreseen in the nineties is the startling fact that in 1917 he would find it necessary to part company with all other Marxists groupings, but would form a coalition government precisely with the dissident wing of these "petty-bourgeois peasant revolutionaries"—the Left-Wing Social Revolutionary Party! Clearly, both in the Marxist camp and in the peasant socialist camp, subjective intention, subjective desire and will, in short, revolutionary temperament, would prove far more important than abstract formulae. And the actual formulae Lenin would act upon would turn out to be a peculiar fusion of elements of Narodnikism and Russian Marxism, while Bolshevism itself would take on aspects of Slavophile socialism.

The government Lenin was to set up was to call itself the Dictatorship of the Proletariat. But the leading organizations of the proletariat, the powerful trade unions, would oppose his seizure of power, while the land-hungry peasants, above all the peasant-in-uniform, the peasant-under-arms, would assure victory to his side. So would history turn out differently from that which the most self-assured "scientific analysis" and the most rigorous "objective logic" had predicted.

Was the peasant, as the Narodniks thought, an exploited toiler and a primitive socialist? Was his land-hunger the longing for security and the love of the soil which he must possess and till in order to live?

Or was he, as the Marxists thought, first of all a small proprietor, a petty bourgeois, an owner or would-be owner of property, longing to possess it *in extenso* and to exploit as many workers as possible upon it?

The Marxists in Russia, Bolsheviks as well as Mensheviks, tended to look upon the Russian peasantry with distrust and suspicion. Having set him down as a petty bourgeois, unconsciously the Marxist workingmen looked upon him as a potential enemy. Hence it became easy in Soviet Russia for the Bolshevik workingmen to sanction the use of force against the peasant majority and the use of police overseers over them: first to requisition grain and stop "profiteering" or private trading, then to police the planting and the harvesting and the marketing of the crops, then to marshal them in droves into the collective farms. But this same peasantry was really the overwhelming majority of the Russian people, so that to sanction a police overseership over them would inevitably exclude the possibility of democracy—in the simple sense of government of, for and by the majority of the people.* And a police apparatus huge enough to police the planting and harvesting all over vast, rural Russia, would it not tend to spill over into the very organizations of the advanced city workers who had sanctioned it: into their state, their unions and their party?

But none of this could be foreseen by either side in 1894. No man could know then whither this controversy "objectively led," when such Marxists as Plekhanov, Ulyanov and Struve, of the older and younger generations, joined forces for a victorious counter-offensive against the hitherto dominant, indigenous peasant socialism of the Narodniki.

---

* There are many forms and degrees of democracy but all include control of political and economic apparatus by the people, and not the reverse. Totalitarianism is not "just another form" of democracy any more than kicking over the checker board is "just another way of playing checkers."

CHAPTER SEVEN

LEGAL
MARXISM

Alekseev: If we go and ask for a rise in pay, they accuse us of making a strike, and they banish us to Siberia. That means we are still serfs. If the employers turn us out, and we ask for an account of wages due, they call out the soldiers . . . That means we are still serfs. We can look to no one to help us except the young intellectuals—

Judge: Silence!

Alekseev (shouting): But they will march with us until the day comes when a million sturdy workmen clench their fists—

Judge: Silence, I say. Silence!

Alekseev (shouting still louder): And despotism will be pounded to dust.

The police were by no means displeased by the strife between Marxists and populists. To them it was a simple case of "when thieves fall out." Still shuddering at the memory of the terrorists of the Narodnaya Volya, who had slain one Tsar and besieged another in his palace, the police tended to "sympathize" with the more academic and less dangerous-seeming Marxists.

That very year, 1894, in which Ulyanov's "Little Yellow Books" against the Narodniks were spreading painfully through the underground by hectograph, Peter Struve, another young Marxist of the same age as Ulyanov, tried submitting to the censors an academically phrased treatise against the Narodniks. To the astonishment of author and public, the police gave their approval to Struve's *Critical Notes on the Problem of the Economic Development of Russia.* With that, "legal Marxism" became a reality.

The same year, one Beltov submitted a work more openly Marxist, *Toward the Development of the Monistic Conception of History.* It, too, passed the censor. The writing had a familiar ring:

> "I am a worm," says the idealist.
> "I am a worm," says the materialist dialectician, "so long as I am ignorant. I am a god, when I know. *Tantum possumus, quantum scimus.*"

With great excitement, the Marxists recognized the slashing style of Plekhanov, who had been in exile abroad since 1881. The entire edition sold out in three weeks. It created as much of a sensation as would today the legal publication in Soviet Russia of a book *against* dialectical materialism. With these two works, the police had made Marxism respectable: the honeymoon of "legal Marxist" literature had begun.

Reviews and journals of Marxist trend sprang up in capital and provinces, carefully edited with one eye on Marx and the other asquint at the censor. Students, professors, members of the social elite, who but yesterday had called themselves liberals or humanitarians or Narodniks, began to flaunt the new, fashionable banner. Marx's *Capital* and *The Communist Manifesto* had always enjoyed great popularity among the Narodniks, having received their first Russian translation before they had been done into any other language. But now they were displayed in best-selling editions.

Finding Marxism a salable and distinguished commodity, publishers contracted for translations of the classics and of contemporary German and French Marxist books. They even offered advances for original works. To pass the censor these had to be couched in academic phrases; they had to be fat volumes (no pamphlets were tolerated); they had to avoid using language of battle or practical action. It was easier to get past the censor a whole volume which bombarded the Narodniki with statistics and formulae, than to say a single direct word of praise for their revolutionary struggle against autocracy. One might prove that the old agrarian village commune was destined to extinction, that capitalism was inevitable in Russia, that it was actually developing according to the general laws laid down by Marx, that as against feudalism it was a progressive force, that it brought into being new, progressive classes: the bourgeoisie and the proletariat. But one could not be too explicit on the fact that these new classes could only realize their destinies by uniting in a revolutionary struggle against feudal absolutism.

In common with the other Marxists, Ulyanov was pleased at this sudden break-through into legality. Yet, almost alone among them, he felt more uneasy than pleased. He at once began to work on a "legal Marxist book" and laid plans for a legal journal. But at the same time he began a polemic against the one-sided, non-revolutionary "reflection of Marxism in bourgeois literature," i.e. the dilution of its revolutionary content by its effort to maintain legality and pass the censors. And he redoubled his own efforts to reach the workers with the "illegitimate" portion of the Marxist message, multiplying the leaflets produced by pen and hectograph, casting about for means of acquiring or setting up an underground printing plant, for smuggling publications from abroad, for developing an underground newspaper.

At the end of that same year, with Peter Struve present in a Marxist circle to which they both belonged, Ulyanov entered into a sharp criticism of the latter's new book. He felt that Struve had been too easily carried away by enthusiasm for the expansion of capitalist industry. What angered Ulyanov most, however, was the fact that the book contained a first Russian example of what was later to be known as Marx-revisionism. According to Struve, Marx had "at times" thought of the collapse of capitalism as something abrupt and catastrophic, but "modern Marxists" thought of it not as a sudden revolution but as a gradual transition, through a series of reforms. "Reforms," retorted Ulyanov, "are not to be contrasted to revolution. The struggle for reforms is but a means of marshalling the forces of the proletariat for the struggle for a final revolutionary overthrow." This negative attitude toward improvements in the prevailing system remains to this day a distinguishing feature of all Communist parties.

To satisfy the requirements of the censorship, and to prevent a break between himself and such "legal Marxists" as Struve, Ulyanov softened his critique somewhat when he sought to have it published legally as a lengthy review-article under the title: *The Economic Content of Populism and Its Critique in the Book of Mr. Struve. (The Reflection of Marxism in Bourgeois Literature.) In Reference to "Critical Remarks on the Question of the Economic Development of Russia," by P. Struve, Saint Petersburg, 1894.* Rather a sizable title for a book review! But the review itself is long enough to dwarf the title: it occupies 139 pages in Volume I of the Russian edition of Lenin's *Collected Works.*

It was the longest of a half-dozen or so essays intended for legal publication, as a symposium by leading Marxists, mostly using pseudonyms. The symposium, edited by Potresov, a friend of Lenin's, bore the general title: *Documents Concerning the Problem of the Economic Development of Russia.* Ulyanov signed his critique of Struve with the pen name of *K. Tulin.* Other contributors to the work were Plekhanov, Potresov, and, of course, Struve. Despite all the precautions taken, the police, guided by a spy or by a sensitive nose, detected the odor of brimstone from the Plutonic underground and confiscated the entire edition of two thousand copies. But a few dozen extra copies were "stolen" from the printing plant.

In the spring of 1895, after a severe case of pneumonia, Ulyanov again applied for permission to go abroad "for his health." This time it was granted. He took with him copies of the proscribed book as gifts for the leaders of the Group for the Emancipation of Labor in Switzerland, contact with which was the real object of his trip. Here is the account which Paul Axelrod has written of it in his memoirs:

He introduced himself: "Vladimir Ulyanov. I have just come from Russia. George Valentinovich (Plekhanov), in Geneva, sends his greetings." The young man gave me a rather thick book . . . We talked about the situation in Russia and then the young man got up and said politely, "If you will permit, I shall come tomorrow to continue our conversation."

During the night I looked through the volume . . . My attention was arrested by a long article by Tulin, whose name I was seeing for the first time. The article made an excellent impression . . . It was not very well constructed, perhaps even careless. But one felt in it a temperament and the fire of the spirit of battle; one felt that for the author Marxism was not an absolute doctrine but a weapon in the revolutionary struggle . . . But there were some tendencies in Tulin's article with which I could not agree . . .

Next morning Ulyanov returned: "Have you looked at the symposium?"

"Yes. And I must say I got great pleasure from it. At last there has awakened in Russia real revolutionary social democratic thought. The article by Tulin made a particularly good impression—"

"That is my pseudonym," said the visitor.

Then I explained where I did not agree with him. "You show," I said, "exactly the opposite tendency to the one expressed in the article I had prepared for the same symposium. [Axelrod did not finish it on time because of illness.] You identify your attitude towards the liberals with the attitude of the socialists toward the liberals in the West. And I . . . wanted to show that in the given historic moment the immediate interests of the Russian proletariat coincide with the vital interests of the other progressive elements of society . . . Both face the same urgent problem . . . the overthrow of absolutism . . ."

Ulyanov smiled and observed: "You know, Plekhanov made exactly the same remarks about my articles. He expressed his thought in picturesque fashion: 'You,' he said, 'turn your behind to the liberals, but we our face.' . . ."

Thus early did his two mentors sense a difference in attitude towards liberals, democrats and other "allies" in the struggle against absolutism, in the young man who offered himself as a respectful, even worshipful disciple. Otherwise Axelrod found his visitor "a modest, businesslike, serious young man, without the slightest vanity." He felt sure that he and Plekhanov had instructed their disciple on his error and had convinced him of his need of correcting it. Ulyanov did indeed appear to defer for the next decade to these veteran leaders and their approach, but psychologically he was inclined to be of the same opinion still. Thus, in 1899, in a letter to Potresov, he ventures to criticize Axelrod for having written of "support for and alliance with" the democratic opposition to tsarism. "In my opinion," wrote Ulyanov, "*utilize* is a much more accurate and appropriate word than *support and alliance.*" This attitude toward "allies"—the determination to "utilize" them rather than to give them mutual support and genuine alliance—remained a characteristic Leninist view for the rest of his life. And today, as in the past, it is a distinguishing feature of every united front or alliance entered into by any of the Communist parties.

In the course of the next five years, the "Legal Marxists," with Struve and Tugan-Baranowsky as spokesmen, actually went through the evolution which the young Ulyanov had so brilliantly sensed and foreseen: from demonstration of the inevitability and progressiveness of capitalism in Russia to apologetics and glorification; from a bowdlerized Marxism cut to measure for the censor as a matter of reluctant necessity, to a castrated Marxism robbed of its revolutionary vigor; and finally, to open opposition to Marxism. This early success as a prophet served to confirm the deep self-confidence of this "serious young man." In 1907, when Ulyanov had become Lenin, and was growing used to leading his own faction against all the old veterans at once, he would write:

> The old controversy with Struve furnishes an instructive example of the practical value of being uncompromising in theoretical controversy . . . It was useful to consider the situation as it was ten years ago, from what minor theoretical differences with Struvism as then visible—minor at first glance—the complete political demarcation of the Party has come about . . .

The closing words of Struve's book of 1894 had been: "Let us confess our lack of culture, and turn to capitalism for instruction." At the time, those words had infuriated Lenin. But a quarter-century later, when he was head of the Russian state, striving to combat economic inexperience, incapacity and chaos, he was to use, word for word, exactly the same words!

Vladimir Ilyich spent four months in Western Europe during the spring and summer of 1895. In Germany, he tried out his book-learned German with disastrous results. ("I do not understand even the simplest words—their pronunciation is unusual and they talk so fast. I ask the conductor a question —he answers; I do not understand. He repeats his answer louder. I still do not understand; he gets angry and goes away.") He made the personal acquaintance of Karl Kautsky, editor of *Die Neue Zeit,* and his chief living idol after Plekhanov and the aging Engels. He swam daily in the Spree, took long walks about Berlin, spent as many hours as possible in the *Koenigliche Bibliothek,* yielded to "the temptation to buy too many books" and had to send twice to his mother for additional funds. Among his most cherished purchases was the third volume of Marx's *Capital,* just issued by Engels from Marx's posthumous notes.

In France, as was characteristic of educated nineteenth-century Russians, he understood the spoken language somewhat better. He fell in love with Paris ("wide light streets, many boulevards, much greenery"), piously sought out Marx's son-in-law, the socialist leader Jean Longuet. In Switzerland he held long conversations with Plekhanov, Vera Zasulich, and above all Axelrod, promised to report to them regularly, laid plans for setting up an organization in their name inside Russia, and for smuggling in their writings. He yielded to the charm of the Swiss mountains and lakes, took a cure for "my tiresome stomach trouble"—apparently a species of colitis complicated by a "nervous stomach" whenever he was under great strain—tramped the hills near Zurich with Axelrod, listening, questioning, talking himself out.

"I must say," wrote Axelrod years later, after he had come to detest Lenin, "that these discussions with Ulyanov were like a real festival. Even now I remember them as one of the happiest moments in the life of the Group for the Emancipation of Labor."

Since 1883 these exiles had waited in Geneva in loneliness and isolation; now their long effort promised to bear living fruit inside the land which they longed to serve and transform.

Ulyanov took all manner of precautions, or at least so he thought, but when he returned from abroad with his false-bottomed trunk stuffed with illegal literature, the police rapped on the trunk while his heart rapped at his throat. Then they let it through inviolate and they detailed "shadows" to follow him and his baggage their separate ways. Apparently, Russian spies abroad had reported on his movements.

"Look," a cousin of Nadezhda Konstantinovna's heard a detective boast in the address bureau where she worked, "we've tracked down the important state criminal Ulyanov—

his brother was hanged—he's just come from abroad but he won't escape us now."

Despite these suspicions, the "important state criminal" visited Moscow, Vilna and other nearby towns, to make contacts for the Union for the Emancipation of Labor. For the first time the veteran émigrés received reports from Russia and began to feel that they at last had the beginnings of an organization in the homeland.

The autumn of 1895 saw the first great wave of strikes in Saint Petersburg. Fat Marxist books were one thing to the police, and strikes another. They had not yet come to the idea of "legal" or "police unionism" which might keep the workers' wrath directed at the employers and deflected from the throne. That idea would come later.

Ulyanov, the like-minded Martov—who had learned to work in the labor movement within the Jewish pale—and some of their associates, now tried to inject themselves into the strike movement. They were the "party of the working class" but how could they make these striking workers aware of it? Vladimir's sweetheart, Nadezhda Konstantinovna, was of help to him now, thanks to the workingmen she had taught in the classes of the Committee for Literacy. With a vague feeling that he was being shadowed and working against time, Vladimir Ilyich cross-questioned the few workers he could get to, elicited facts concerning their grievances, drew up leaflets laboriously in his own hand with printed letters on the hectograph, or had them copied by hand in total editions of three or four copies. A few of his and Martov's leaflets were even printed in a secret printing plant of the Narodovoltsi. Apparently these were more friendly to the Marxists and the working class than accorded with Ulyanov's hostile analysis.

Of four copies of a leaflet distributed by the workingman Babushkin in the Semmyanikov works, two were seized by a foreman, but the other two passed surreptitiously from hand to hand. Next the women in the Laferme tobacco factory, the men and women in Thornton's textile works and the metal workers in the Putilov plant learned that there was such a thing as a "Petersburg League of Struggle for the Emancipation of the Working Class" which seemed interested in them, was informed about their needs, knew how to express these in simple leaflets and link them up with a vaguer, grander struggle for socialism and freedom.

At the same time, Ulyanov turned out two simple, repetitive, didactic pamphlets: *On Fines* and *On the New Labor Laws*. Hand in hand with the experienced young Jewish agitator Martov, he sought to link all the dispersed study circles that were reading Marx with the "League of Struggle for the Emancipation of the Working Class," and to gather material for a paper to be called *The Workers' Cause*.

All through the autumn, while these modest plans were maturing, his sense of being spied upon continued to grow. To this problem, too, he turned his businesslike attention. He imparted to his comrades his pitiful store of conspirative technique, which he had acquired by interrogating the veterans of the Narodnaya Volya in Samara. He showed them how to employ secret codes; how to put names and addresses into cipher; how to mix invisible ink; how to send messages in innocent volumes by putting tiny dots inside letters which, sought out and combined, grew into words and sentences; how to paste letters inside the bindings of books; how to use houses with through courtyards as a means of getting rid of one's "shadow." Even to the veteran Axelrod in Zurich he wrote detailed instructions:

> Add a crystal of potassium bichromate—$K_2Cr_2O_7$—to the ink; use thinner paper; use liquid paste, not more than a teaspoonful of starch to a glass of water, and potato flour, the ordinary flour is too strong . . .

All this seemed very wonderful to his associates. Among the most attentive of his auditors was a "Marxist" dentist, Dr.

Mikhailov, who dutifully passed on all he learned to his superiors in the police department.

December found *The Workers' Cause* ready to go to press, with most of its articles written by the indefatigable Ulyanov. It was to be printed by the underground press of his friendly enemies, the Narodovoltsi. Two proofs were pulled, and sent to two different addresses. One was carefully corrected by editor Ulyanov himself. That very night, the police jerked the noose they had been spreading, hauling in both copies; the editor; his chief associate, Martov; the engineer Krzhizhanovsky (one day to become head of the State Planning Commission); Vaneev, who developed tuberculosis and died in prison; Gutsul, who went mad and was released in the custody of his parents; Starkov—in fact, practically all the members of the little, new-born Petersburg League of Struggle for the Emancipation of the Working Class. Of those Ulyanov had seen frequently, only Krupskaya, Potresov and Struve remained at large. The police were to pick the first two up later. Somehow, the workingmen with whom these intellectuals had been in contact discovered that Dr. Mikhailov was an *agent provocateur*. Soon after the big haul, Dr. Mikhailov was found murdered. And *The Workers' Cause* died at the hour of its birth while the entire Petersburg League transferred its domicile to Siberia.

CHAPTER EIGHT

PRISON
AND
EXILE

They make strange and very pleasant reading—these letters of Lenin from Siberia to his family. With the exclusion of but a few sentences they might be the letters of a delightful and indolent country squire of outdoor tastes but of a gentle epicurean philosophy which forbade him even to take such tastes too seriously —one whom wisdom had taught to turn his back upon the press of men and on the folly of affairs. Nor is there any reason to think that Lenin did not genuinely enjoy this quiet life just as he was quite certainly genuinely devoted to his family.

—CHRISTOPHER HOLLIS

Ulyanov's first letter from jail served a double purpose. It was addressed to Mrs. Chebotareva, wife of one of his comrades, and it was approved by the prison authorities because he had taken his midday meal at her home and could pass her off as the mistress of his boarding-house. The letter was long, impersonal, free from any hint of self-pity. It did not read like the message of one who has been newly thrown into jail, or is uncertain of his fate, but like the missive of some medieval scholar who has retired to a cloister and writes to his former housekeeper to send his books. It spoke of "a plan which has been interesting me intensely ever since my arrest—the study of the marketing of goods produced by domestic manufacture." It asked her to send an enormous amount of material. More than three pages (with two precise footnotes!) outlined his plans for research on the development of the internal market; additional pages listed the titles of works he would need immediately.

"Perhaps you will not think it useless to hand this over to someone else to seek advice—while I wait for an answer." Reasonable enough, for how would the mistress of a boarding-house know how to procure all that? Mrs. Chebotareva showed it to the writer's sweetheart, to his sister Anna, and to a few other comrades still at liberty. These, his intimates, privy to every subtle allusion, pored over it for cryptic meanings in each deviation from the expected. They were struck by the fact that this always precise student with a prodigious memory for books and citations seemed uncertain of the titles of some of the volumes.

"As I am working from memory," he wrote, "I think I may have muddled some of the titles, and where I am not certain I have used a question mark."

One so marked was a work by Mayne-Read. Krupskaya perceived in it the anagram of Mynoga (lamprey), his nickname for her.* Mayne-Read, his sister answered, was available. Thus he knew that she was still at large.

---

* The nickname was originally a teasing pet name. Krupskaya had large bulging eyes due, as it developed later, to exophthalmic goiter, which caused her friends to tell her she looked like a fish. Later she adopted Mynoga as her party name. When she was ill, she complained to Vladimir with mock indignation that his sister Anna said she looked like a smoked herring.

In an inquiry whether "some writer or professor" could give him access to the books of the University Library and the library of the Ministry of Finance, they recognized the underground names of Struve ("The Writer") and Potresov ("The Professor"). They answered that a writer and a professor had been found who would help him. (Krupskaya and Potresov were not arrested until some months later. Struve not at all.) Thus the prisoner's theoretical work—for the letter as a whole was seriously meant—and his clandestine correspondence got started together before he had been a month in jail.

He had taken the precaution, as he explained, to discuss his research project with the Public Prosecutor. The latter, impressed by the scholarly interests of his charge, had "confirmed that there would be no limit set on the number of books permitted." He might keep a case of them in his cell with him, might borrow from friends and from libraries in the outside world, and return the books again after he had finished with them. He might buy from publishers and bookstores. Even the prison library, well stocked with the bequests of two generations of "politicals," contained much that was of use.

If, as Tolstoy said, "no one knows what kind of government it is who has never been in prison," the difference between the tsarist and the present Stalinist régimes inspire sombre reflections. The tsarist prisons were administered by educated and often scholarly officials. The jailers themselves ranged from the brutal to the mercifully venal and sometimes even the secretly sympathetic. By hunger strikes, by demonstrative suicides, and by the support of public opinion, a succession of martyrs had won a considerable range of privileges for political prisoners. It is ironical to contemplate that in lands where the dissenter is prosecuted in the name of the people, the category of political prisoner is often not a recognized one. But in autocratic Russia, when the accused was not charged with some specific terrorist act, he was as a rule not sentenced to hard labor but permitted to spend his days, if he had it in him, in scholarly pursuits. Moreover, this was the heyday of "legal Marxism." The criminal seemed academic enough, and it was obvious that he would be a model prisoner. During a little over a year, he worked serenely in his cell. When they sent him to Siberia for three years more, he said to his sister: "It's a pity they let us out so soon. I should have liked to do a little more work on the book. It will prove difficult to get books in Siberia."

But it did not prove so difficult. During his four years as ward of the state, he bought and borrowed many hundreds of journals, wrote articles for the legal press, even procured works which obviously subserved his activities as an opponent of the status quo.

The prisoner's plan for a study of the development of Russia's internal market slowly grew in scope until it became the major theoretical work of his lifetime: *The Development of Capitalism in Russia*. Every bit of research, every line of writing and patient rewriting, all the negotiations for its legal publication (under the pseudonym of V. Ilyin), took place while Vladimir Ilyich was a police ward. The book appeared during the last year of his exile in Siberia (1899) without any interference from the censor. When the archives were opened by the first revolutionary government of 1917, it became clear that the police had known all along who "V. Ilyin" was. It was they who had largely financed the first organ of "legal Marxism," *Nachalo* ("Beginning"), and set up one of their secret agents, a certain M. Gurovich, as "angel" and publisher. His task was to find out the true names of all the Marxists writing under pseudonyms. He reported that Plekhanov, Zasulich, Martov, Potresov and Ulyanov were among those contributing. In the issues of March, 1899, before Ulyanov submitted his big book to the censors, he published in *Nachalo* a part of its third chapter, under the title: "The Displacement of Feudal Economy by Capitalist Economy in Modern Russian Agriculture." The article was signed V. Ilyin, and carried a footnote to the effect that it was "a section of a comprehensive investigation by the author of the development of capitalism in Russia." Thus the police knew that the author was their prisoner and the brother of a man who had conspired to assassinate the father of the reigning Tsar. In 1907—after Russia had gone through the general strikes and uprising of 1905, the government still permitted a second edition to be published. It carried a new introduction with some fairly explicit political remarks. Today, after we have come to accept a legendary conception of how complete tsarist censorship was, it comes rather as a shock to read such passages as this and know they were legally permitted:

> Either the old landed economy connected by a thousand threads with serfdom will continue and gradually transform itself into a Junker economy [said the preface to the 1907 edition], or the revolution will destroy the old large landowning economy, annihilate every remnant of serfdom and, especially of large landownership. . . . Gentlemen like Stolypin work systematically, stubbornly and consistently for the completion of the revolution on the first model. The coup d'état [of Stolypin] of June 3, 1907, signifies the triumph of the counter-revolution which strives to assure to the landowners full predominance in the popular assembly. How long, however, this "triumph" will endure is another matter. The struggle for the second way out continues . . . Where this struggle will end, what outcome finally the first push forward of the Russian Revolution will have—it is still not possible to say. . . .

By actual count "Ilyin's" book makes use of 299 theoretical and statistical works in Russian, and 38 foreign studies in German, French and English, or in Russian translation. All these books, journals and reports Ulyanov purchased, or borrowed by mail from distant libraries, while he lived in prison and in Siberia. Terrible enough in their day, imprisonment and exile under the last Tsar, to some of its former victims, were to seem in retrospect like an intellectual's retreat, compared with the régime which one of their fellow-prisoners would one day set up for them in Soviet Russia.

Those who brought books to the Petersburg prison for Ulyanov were subjected to no interrogation. They could leave their packages of books—or food, or clothing, or other comforts—

in the office any hour of the day up till five o'clock, and even at night with the watchman. No mere police censor or jail warden, but the Supreme Court Prosecutor or his delegate, subjected the packages of books to a superficial examination. The very next day they were in his cell. He received and dispatched such bundles at least twice a week all through 1896 and the first two months of 1897, while he waited for the authorities to decide further steps in his case. Every batch of books he received or sent back contained at least one volume with a letter hidden in the spine of its binding, or written in invisible ink between the lines of one of its pages, or coded by tiny markings within the printed letters. The two-way traffic enabled him to keep in touch with his organization, to write several strike leaflets, to draft and send out a proposed program for the Social Democratic Party, even to communicate with other comrades in jail. All through his stay in Siberia, books continued to come to him and return from him, carrying invisible letters to other exiles, to men and women in Russia, to Plekhanov and Axelrod in Switzerland. His foresight in having instructed his comrades in the lore of underground communication now served him in good stead. He could not secure the cobalt and sulphuric acid solutions such as were used outside. However, prison afforded homelier chemicals like milk and citric acid (lemon juice), which, to a casual inspection, left no marks upon the paper. But when they were heated, they turned a vivid brown. Milk was his chief writing fluid, and for inkwells he molded tiny cups of hard bread. If he heard footsteps, he could swallow ink and well together. "Today I have eaten six inkwells," reads the postscript of one of his secret communications.

Hints told him where to look for the answer. "The report of the Professional Congress in Moscow," he would say in a letter, "is very interesting," and they would know that he had found the letter concealed in the otherwise uninteresting work. Holding a match under the paper was a dangerous procedure, so he invented a new way of developing the invisible writing. He would tear the letter into thin strips, and when they brought him the boiling water for his evening tea, he made a strong infusion and immersed the strips in it; the tea made the milky letters a rich yellow brown.

Prison is a severe test of the will. Some never adapt themselves; their spirits are broken by ineffectual beating against the bars. Others, after the first restless weeks, get lost in a world of daydream, or in endless preoccupation with petty inconveniences. Still others let the hours pass idly like lizards dozing on a rock—but without the pleasant caresses of the sun. Most of the old Bolsheviks I have known seemed to me younger than other men and women of their years. They attributed it to the quiet parentheses of prison sojourn, where the flame of life burned slowly and the years slipped by without seeming to leave their usual mark.

Vladimir Ilyich settled down to the quiet of his prison cell almost with an air of satisfaction. Never was this orderly spirit's gift for planful expenditure of energy more in evidence. He had no labor to perform, beyond the cleaning of his cell, which he carried out with exaggerated meticulousness. He worked out a careful time schedule—so many minutes for physical exercise, so many for language study, so many for research and writing.

"I have everything I need," he wrote to his mother, "and even more than I need." They sent him so many dainties and comforts, that he told them he was playing with the idea of opening a prison store, and driving the official canteen out of business. The letters from prison to his intimates express a quiet, steady and deep affection, and assume sufficient interest on their part to make them carry out any number of burdensome commissions. Almost the only hint of inconvenience comes in the request to Anna that she procure for him a mechanical pencil because the rules will not permit him to keep a knife, while the warder grumbles and takes such an unconscionable time when he is asked to resharpen the prisoner's pencil. The letters to his mother perhaps have the special aim of reassuring her, who had suffered so much in her children. But those to his sisters and brother, and to Krupskaya and others, are no less cheerful. Once only does a note of loneliness creep into one of his messages to Krupskaya. Here is her account of it:

> But no matter how much he mastered himself, even Vladimir Ilyich was affected by prison melancholy. In one of his letters he put forward this plan: when they were taken out for exercise, it was possible through one of the windows in the corridor to catch a fleeting glimpse of the Shpalernaya pavement. So he suggested that at a definite time I (and a friend) should come and stand on this piece of pavement, and then he would see us . . . I went several days and stood a long while on that spot. Something went wrong with the plan, however, though I do not remember what.

Some notion of the routine of his planful prison days we can get from his letters of advice to his younger brother, Dmitri, when the latter landed in jail:

> First of all, is he keeping to a diet in prison? [writes Vladimir to his mother]. I am sure he is not. But in my opinion it is essential to keep to one there. And, second, does he do physical exercises? Again probably not. And yet, again, this is essential. I at least can say from my own experience that I derived great pleasure and benefit from doing exercises *daily* before retiring. They loosened my joints so that I used to get into a glow even on the coldest days, when the cell was icy cold; and one sleeps ever so much better afterward. I can recommend to him this as a fairly easy exercise, though a ridiculous one: fifty reverential prostrations! This is exactly what I made myself do—and I was not in the least disturbed that the warder, on peeping through the little window, would wonder in amazement why this man had suddenly grown so devout when he had not once asked to visit the prison church . . .

When his younger sister, Maria, was imprisoned, and later Anna and her husband as well, he again was detailed and exact in his advice. He especially recommended language study, telling them that his method of working without a teacher was to write out the Russian translation of all the exercises, put them aside until they grew "cold," translate them back into the foreign language and check against the original. "My own experience has born out that this is the most rational way of learning a language."

> I would again advise you to divide up your study periods according to the books on hand in such a way as to vary the subjects. I remember very well that a change of reading or work —from translation to reading, from writing to exercise, from serious reading to fiction—helped me enormously . . .
>
> In the evening, after dinner, for relaxation I remember that I would *regelmaessig* turn to fiction and nowhere did I appreciate it as much as in prison. But the main thing is not to forget your daily exercises, and to make yourself perform each exercise a score of times—without giving in.

Such, more or less, was the actual schedule of this redoubtable mental and physical gymnast, whom no mere imprisonment could break or even swerve from the pursuit of his aims.

Siberia! The name strikes terror into the hearts of lovers of freedom. All through the nineteenth century, the roster of its exiles reads like a Russian *Who's Who,* in literature, thought, and public life. Its marshy taiga, limitless steppes and frozen tundra, its polar and sub-polar winters, its ice-locked river systems which empty only into the Arctic, its successive generations of broken and forgotten men—these were Siberia to the nineteenth century. But as the Transsiberian pushed its track eastward toward Port Arthur, as the exile colonies increased in numbers until they were sufficient to give each other moral sustenance, as the terms of exile shortened and more and more prisoners returned, or, by incredible feats of perilous overland journey, escaped to Western Europe, the picture in men's minds began to change.

When on February 25, 1897, Vladimir Ilyich Ulyanov was conducted from his cell to the Prosecutor's office and informed that two weeks earlier an administrative decree had been issued exiling him to Eastern Siberia for the next three years, he sighed good-humoredly at the interruption of his research. There had been no trial; there rarely was in these political exile cases, just as there rarely is in analogous cases in Soviet Russia today. The political police had the right to give up to five years of administrative exile without trial. Today there is no such limitation. At the request of his mother—and with a little financial aid from her—he was allowed to travel to his remote place of exile at his own expense. Being an official's son and a hereditary nobleman had its advantages. They released him from the House of Preliminary Detention, let him spend almost a week in Saint Petersburg to say his farewells, consult his physician, gather things he would need for the journey, and even—though this was not comprehended in the authorization—hold conferences with the remaining footloose members of the League of Struggle for the Emancipation of the Working Class.

The prisoner journeyed freely to Moscow, spent a few days there with his mother, conferred with some of his comrades, then proceeded in leisurely fashion on the Transsiberian as far as Krasnoyarsk. There he waited for the spring floods to make river travel possible on the Yenissei, and for the authorities to notify him as to the exact spot of his final destination.

At Krasnoyarsk, provincial capital, he spent several weeks of the Siberian spring, walking two versts* out of town each day to visit the magnificent private library of the Siberian merchant and bibliophile Yudin. There he found one of the best collections of eighteenth- and nineteenth-century periodicals in all Russia, and additional sociological works and statistical monographs for his book.†

Freed for the journey on February 26, he did not reach his final destination in the village of Shushenskoye near the headwaters of the Yenissei until May 20. The leisurely trip, the stopovers, the wide horizons, all left him refreshed after the confinement of his cell.

* A verst is about two-thirds of a mile.
† The Yudin library was sold to America in 1907 and forms the basis of the Slavic section of the Library of Congress in Washington.

"I am not at all tired," he wrote his mother from Ob, "which seems strange, for a three-days' journey from Samara to Saint Petersburg used to knock me out. The fact is that without exception I sleep splendidly through each night. . . . The air is good; it's easy to breathe."

To be sure, those who could not afford a trip at their own expense or could not secure the permission did not find it so pleasant travelling under guard and being locked up on the way.

Yenisseisk Province is one of the healthiest and pleasantest regions of Eastern Siberia, far southward in the northern land of cold. Lenin's new home lay not far from Tannu Tuva, secretly annexed by Stalin in 1945 and now the site of Russia's most jealously guarded secret, its "atomic city." They call the region, Lenin wrote, "the Siberian Italy." His comrade Martov, because of official prejudice against a rebellious Jew, was exiled to lonely, frozen Turukhansk, some nine hundred miles farther north on the same Yenissei River, where it enters the Arctic Circle on its long course to the polar sea. Despite repeated petitions, Martov was kept up there during all of his three years of exile under conditions so hard that he found it impossible to do any systematic work. Krzhizhanovsky, Starkov, Vaneev, Lepeshinsky, Silvin, Lengnik, and Shapoval, were all sent to the nearby towns of Minusinsk, Yermakovsk, and Tessinsk, within a radius of less than fifty miles of Vladimir Ilyich. The Governor General of the Province assigned to each of them a monthly stipend of eight rubles (four dollars) for board and lodging, let them seek out their own homes within the prescribed village, wander pretty freely through the province on hunting expeditions, visit each other for as much as a week on end for Christmas and Easter holidays and on the occasion of weddings and funerals. Some brought their mothers out to Siberia to keep house for them, others sent for their wives; three weddings were celebrated among the Minusinsk contingent during Ulyanov's three-year stay. Those who could were allowed to get work to eke out their allowance, while the cost of living in Siberia was so low, and the purchasing power of a ruble so high in those days that even the eight rubles were sufficient for bare necessities, except where the upkeep of a family was involved. During the long visits to each other's villages there were days and nights of political discussion, of singing, of hotly contested chess games—with Vladimir the invariable victor—and long hunting expeditions with dogs and guns in the forests abounding with game.

The village was "not a bad place," although it was a little bare for all its fifteen hundred inhabitants, cold in winter as all Siberia is, torn at by great transcontinental winds in autumn and early spring, infested by clouds of mosquitoes after the melting of the snows. But there was the Yenissei to swim in, the forest for hunting, and, on clear days, the snow-capped Sayan range to lend magnificence to the horizon. Vladimir grew plump and forgot the very name of the mineral water he used to take for his stomach trouble.

Twenty years earlier, Prince Kropotkin, the anarchist leader, had spent his exile in this same "Siberian Italy." And thirty years after Ulyanov's stay, a letter smuggled out of here by anarchist opponents of the Soviet régime revealed that they had been sent there after their health had been broken by other, less healthful places. But they were receiving an allowance of only six inflation-weakened Soviet rubles a month, and were blacklisted against receiving work. Near them, under more comfortable conditions and with a considerably larger stipend, lived Smilga and other opposition communists, from whom the G.P.U. was then hoping to secure a "recantation." Thus does the pattern of Russian administrative exile of political opponents repeat itself under changing régimes, but with differences, especially during the later years of Stalin's rule, that it will not be pleasant to relate.

On his "salary" of eight rubles a month ("we receive the government allowance regularly,") Ulyanov was able to engage a furnished room in a peasant's cottage, get his food, and have his laundry, mending and cleaning done.

> One week they would kill a sheep and feed Vladimir Ilyich with it from day to day until it was all eaten up. When it was all gone they would buy meat for the next week, and the farm girl chopped up his supply in the trough where the cattle fodder was prepared. This mince meat was used for cutlets for Vladimir Ilyich, also for a whole week. And there was plenty of milk for both Vladimir Ilyich and his dog. [Krupskaya's *Memories of Lenin.*]

What he lacked was money for books. He set about to earn it by the translation of *The Theory and Practice of English Trade Unions* by Sidney and Beatrice Webb, by articles on economics and sociology, by book reviews and by the sale of the manuscript of his work on *The Development of Capitalism in Russia*. This he sold to the bookseller and publisher Alexandra Mikhailovna Kalmykova, whom we have already met as "Auntie," for the not inconsiderable sum of fifteen hundred rubles. His articles sometimes fetched him as much as a hundred or two hundred while the least of his book reviews was paid for in the form of books selected for him by the editor of the magazine, his old friend Peter Struve. He never lacked funds for the purchase of a steady stream of publications ordered from Moscow and even abroad, while his mother was ever ready to tide over a temporary shortage.

Life was lonely at Shushenskoye. With a little petitioning, he could easily have been transferred to one of the nearby towns, where his comrades lived in little collectives. But he refused to make the request, for he was afraid of the ingrown exile's squabbles, the endless hours of chess and disputation, the needless drain upon his sleep and working time. Here there were only two workingmen exiles: Prominsky, a Polish Social Democrat, a hatmaker by trade; and Enberg, a striking Finnish workingman from the Putilov works in Saint Petersburg, personally rebellious though lacking a Social Democratic outlook.

Ulyanov tried to cultivate the local schoolmaster but found him interested only in drinking and cards. Then there was Zhuravlev, a consumptive peasant, formerly a clerk; and an old, thick-headed but devoted muzhik, Sosipatych. Through these two, says Krupskaya naively, "Vladimir Ilyich studied the Siberian countryside." The information he pumped out of them he supplemented by running on Sundays an unofficial lawyer's office for the peasants living nearby. The fame of this volunteer jurisconsult spread: muzhiks came from miles around with their quarrels about trespassing cows, unpaid wages, grievances against a brother-in-law who had failed to treat to ceremonial drinks.

For added company, there was a she-dog that the exile tried in vain to train for hunting, a little kitten, and Minka, the little son of an old Lettish feltbootmaker, all the rest of whose fourteen children were dead. When the prisoner left Shushenskoye at the end of his appointed time, writes Krupskaya, "Minka fell ill with grief. Now he is no longer living, and the bootmaker has written asking for a piece of land over by the Yenissei—'for I don't want to go hungry in my old age.'" He got his piece of land from the Soviet Government as a reward for having befriended Vladimir Ilyich when the latter was his neighbor.

Exile had its sorrows, too. Vaneev, who had contracted tuberculosis while in prison, slowly wasted away and died. Prominsky, with a wife and six children, received at first a subsidy of thirty rubles a month, then was cut to nineteen. In vain did he try to make enough by selling hats to the villagers, so that he might return to Poland after his exile was over. Almost a quarter-century he spent there as a "free man," never accumulating enough to transport his numerous family. In 1923 the Soviet Government, under his old friend Lenin, arranged for him to return at last, but he contracted typhus and died on the homeward journey. Efimov, an exiled workingman at Tesinskoe, went mad with persecutory delusions. Julius Martov, in lonely northern exile at Turukhansk, petitioned in vain for transfer; a political prisoner he lived with quarreled with him so that they broke up their collective household. The ever high-strung Martov suffered a nervous breakdown, while his brilliant talents as student, writer and agitator went to seed.

"God preserve us from the exile colonies and the exile conflicts!" commented Ulyanov sadly in a letter to his mother. A bitter quarrel broke out between the older Narodovoltsi and the younger Social Democrats. Political issues, the conflict between generations, contempt of the terrorists for the opponents of individual terror, and finally the escape of a Social Democrat which imperilled the privileges of those who remained, all mingled to exacerbate the quarrel.

> The scandal [writes Krupskaya] grew like a snowball. There is nothing worse than these exile scandals, Vladimir Ilyich said to me. They pull us back terribly. These old men have got bad nerves. Just look what they've been through, the penal sentences they have undergone. But we cannot let ourselves be drawn away by such scandals—all our work lies ahead. And Vladimir Ilyich insisted that we should break with these old people. I remember the meeting at which the rupture took place. The decision as to the break had been made beforehand. It was now a question of carrying it out as painlessly as possible. We made the break because a break was necessary. But we did it without malice, indeed with regret. And we lived afterwards in separation.

Such was Vladimir Ilyich's way. He was no friend of needless fraying of the nerves. Whom he could not work with, he broke with. Then, unless they opposed the things he stood for, he said no more about them. Yet, the exiles' quarrels were to affect his spirit, too. Both in Siberia and abroad in Western Europe, they would work more ravages on the movement than all the persecutions of the police.

But the police seemed to be doing well enough, too. The pitiful stratagems of the few members of the Petersburg League still at large availed them little. The hunt closed in; one by one they went overland to Siberia, or, in milder cases, to provinces in the north of Russia. Though the time seemed ripe for the fusing of the local study circles into a single, all-Russian, social-democratic party, the police appeared to know every secret move. Ulyanov and Martov had been at work on this task when they were picked up. From prison, Ulyanov smuggled out a draft program, but again and again the constituent convention had to be postponed because of fresh raids. By the time the "First Congress" was finally held, in March, 1898, there were only four members left in Saint Petersburg to elect a delegate. Three of these were women, one being Krupskaya, who had already been arrested but temporarily released under police surveillance while they determined her fate. The police seemed to know about the secret congress, too. It gathered in Minsk with representatives from Petersburg, Moscow, Kiev, from the journal *Southern Worker,* and from the Jewish Socialist League or Bund, of which Martov had been a leader before coming to Saint Petersburg. The gathering was poor in numbers and in talents, hurried through its sessions in three days, failed to adopt a constitution or a program. Its sole achievements were the issuance of a manifesto, drafted by Peter Struve, the promulgation of the idea of a nationwide party, and the election of a central committee of three. The manifesto was virtually Struve's last act as a revolutionary, already representing his past rather than his future. It was notable chiefly for the sentence: "The farther east we go in Europe, the weaker, more cowardly and abject does the bourgeoisie become politically, and the more do its cultural and political tasks devolve upon the proletariat." This thought was to have a profound influence upon Leon Trotsky, who was just then becoming a socialist.

Eight of the nine delegates, and two of the three central committee members chosen by the congress, were picked up within a few days of its adjournment. The victory of the police and the rout of the new party seemed complete.

Eight months after Vladimir's arrest, Nadezhda Konstantinovna was arrested. When one of the prisoners in the women's section of the House of Preliminary Detention set fire to her own clothing and perished in flames, the authorities released the other female politicals pending official disposition of their cases. In due course—the wheels of Russian bureaucracy turned very slowly—Krupskaya was notified that she had been sentenced by administrative decree to three years' exile in Ufa in North Russia. She petitioned to be permitted to go to Shushenskoye in Siberia instead, in order to join her "fiancé," and asked that her term be shortened so that she might accompany him back to Russia at the expiration of his.

The authorities agreed to the first part of her petition. Their desire to see the lovers united however was not so strong as to impel them to shorten her term. They allowed her to go to Shushenskoye at her own expense, and to take her mother along. They warned her that if she did not get legally married "immediately," she would be sent to Ufa as originally provided.

Marriage had been unfashionable in certain revolutionary circles—particularly among the nihilists and the anarchists—but among Social Democrats a life-long union, with or without the ceremonial forms, was the rule in those days rather than the exception. It is clear that Nadezhda Konstantinovna and Vladimir Ilyich did not object to the official proviso, and already regarded their union as seriously as the most bourgeois marriage in all Russia. Living in that shifting world of prison, underground and foreign exile, a world in which a "Who with Whom" would have to be altered more frequently than a "Who's Who," their marriage was destined to be a true union for better and for worse until death should part them.

If one looks for it, one can detect the note of joy in Vladimir's unobtrusively affectionate letters when he learned that Nadya was to join him. But the actual words were merely a flood of instructions as to what his future wife should do, and what she should bring with her. She was to see Struve, who had become editor of a learned legal Marxist journal, and arrange with him for further articles and book reviews. She was to contract for a collection of articles by Ulyanov in book form. She was to subscribe to a number of periodicals. She was "to be loaded with as many books as possible," was to bring his straw hat, one of his chess sets (he had been playing with one he had carved himself), a penwiper to protect his coat lapel from further inking, graph paper in a dozen sizes, a pair of scissors for clippings (to replace the sheep shears borrowed from his landlord), picture books for Prominsky's children, new works for translation, grammars and dictionaries, a leather jacket for hunting, mountains of statistical reports. All the while that bureaucratic red tape kept delaying Nadezhda's departure, Vladimir continued to deluge her with additional commissions, so that when she and her mother finally left for Siberia they were loaded with a princely train of bags and boxes.

> At last [he wrote his mother in May, 1899] I have received the so long awaited guests . . . and just that day I got the bright idea of going hunting, so that they did not find me. Nadezhda Konstantinovna does not look well at all and will simply have to take care of her health. As for me, Elizabeth Vasilievna [Krupskaya's mother] said: "Gracious, how you've spread!" . . . Anyuta asks who I am inviting to the wedding. I invite you all . . . As you know, they have put to Nadezhda Konstantinovna the tragi-comic condition: either get married *immediately* (*sic!*) or go back to Ufa. I am not disposed to let her get away, and so have already begun the "moves" . . .

It was the officials themselves, however, who held up the marriage. Though he had lived more than a year now in Siberia, his record had not yet arrived from Petersburg, and without this "the local police chief doesn't know who I am and can't give me a marriage certificate!" Nadya arrived in May, but it was not until July that the wedding was held. By that time they had been living together so long in the calm monotony of a Siberian village that they seem to have forgotten to communicate the news in their letters.

Nadya enriched his life by serving as wife, secretary, housekeeper, and devoted disciple. Her mother helped in the housekeeping, too, remaining a member of their household until her death during World War I. According to Potresov, Vladimir

Ilyich "good-naturedly carried on a daily struggle with his mother-in-law which was not without its comical side. She was the only person in his immediate circle who resisted him and defended her own personality." Krupskaya hints that the "resistance" turned about the clash between her mother's religious observances and Lenin's atheism. But the future leader of the Godless State was quite tolerant in personal relations, limiting himself to sly banter and comically assumed indignation.

The correspondence from Shushenskoye now took on a livelier, more personal tone. The envelope that carried Vladimir's concise communications bore "postscripts" from Nadya three or four times as long. Or she enclosed several sheets of her own, full of personal things and the breath of the Siberian countryside. Knowing his mother's interest in everything concerning Volodya, she rambles on for many pages about his hunting trips, his chats with the local folk, the children and animals, the antics of their "hunting" bitch, the preserves she and her mother put up, the walks they all take together in the woods, what they are reading, what he is writing, how they solve the servant problem (with a girl-of-all-work at two and one-half rubles a month plus shoes), how Volodya was commissioned to buy a blouse for Prominsky's little girl and instead of asking the size, wanted to know "how many pounds?"—all the intimate things that go into a warm and lively personal correspondence and help those far off to envisage the lives their loved ones are leading in an unknown place.

Vladimir was growing restless. While he had still a whole year to go, he had permitted himself to look at a map of Europe, in order that, as he wrote his younger sister, he might locate Brussels, whither she had gone to continue her studies.

> By stretching your hand you can touch London, Paris, Berlin . . . Yes, I envy you. During the earlier period of my deportation, I decided not for anything to look at maps of Europe or of European Russia, so deep was the bitterness I felt at unrolling the maps and seeing the various little black spots on them. But now I am grown calm and can look tranquilly at maps. In fact,

we often devote ourselves to dreaming in which of those spots it would be interesting to land after we leave here. Perhaps it is that in the first half of our exile we were looking backwards, and now we are looking forwards. Ah well, *qui vivra verra* . . .

As his final year crawled its interminable course, Vladimir found it harder and harder to work. His big book was done, except for Nadya's careful recopying. The Webb translation likewise. He was becoming uneasily aware of a change of mood in Russia. In but two years of exile he had lost touch with what was taking place over there. All the revolutionary Marxists of his generation—the *stariki* or "oldsters" they were called despite their youth—were in Siberia. The "youngsters" of all ages who had taken the places they left vacant, were leading the movement in quite another direction.

Even more disquieting was the news that in the very citadel of Marxism, the mighty German Social Democracy, a movement had arisen to "revise" and "modernize" Marxism. The "revision" seemed to Ulyanov a blasphemy, an attempt to cut out of Marxism its orthodox revolutionary heart. The leading Revisionist was no less a personage than Eduard Bernstein, friend of Engels and his literary executor. Engels had died in 1895. The very next year, Bernstein had begun his literary offensive in the pages of the theoretical journal *Neue Zeit*. Now, in 1899, the cautious series of articles had grown into a far from cautious book. In every letter, Vladimir pestered his sisters for a copy. When at last it arrived, he couldn't wait to finish it before he exploded.

"We have already read half of it," he wrote his mother, "and its contents caused us genuine astonishment. Theoretically it is incredibly weak. . . . It is not possible to doubt of his failure. The insinuation of Bernstein that there are many Russians who agree with him has filled us with indignation."

Alas for Ulyanov, he was to prove wrong on both counts. For him "it was not possible to doubt of Bernstein's failure" because Vladimir Ilyich was intellectually and temperamentally incapable of doubting the total soundness of Marxism, and he was no less incapable of doubting the essential health of the German movement, which led the Socialist International.

Contrary to the impression given by Lenin's official biographers, he played no international role in the titanic battle of the books which followed the publication of Bernstein's *Voraussetzungen des Sozialismus*. Never did he dream of making the claim, which since his death has been made for him, that there was a sort of apostolic succession in Marxism: Marx, Engels, Lenin. . . . Nor did he, as his disciples have since done, belittle the great galaxy of Marxists who worked with Marx and Engels in their later years and, after them, continued to lead the Socialist International. Until the World War, Lenin cherished the profoundest respect for such men as Kautsky, Mehring, Bebel, and—though he quarreled with them on Russian matters—for Plekhanov, Parvus and Rosa Luxemburg. Even when he found that only Rosa Luxemburg and Mehring agreed with him on the war, and while he was denouncing the others as "traitors," he did not attempt retroactively to reduce the importance of their earlier achievements in Marxist theory. Nor did he believe, least of all in those humble days, that the Russian movement was capable of dictating to all the others. Or that, until the war, he had ever been right against them all, except on peculiarly Russian matters.

In the great polemic which raged around Bernstein's book, he limited himself to combatting the Russian "Bernsteinians" and to expressing agreement with Kautsky's works on the economic and political aspects, and Plekhanov's and Labriola's on the philosophical aspects of the controversy. When Potresov, from Siberian Vyatka, mailed him a copy of Kautsky's book against Bernstein, he was so enthusiastic that he and Krupskaya dropped all other work and scarcely slept for two weeks until they had completed its translation into Russian.

To all appearances, Bernstein was easily worsted in the debate. Almost every outstanding Marxist entered into the lists against him. The convention of his party expressly voted to condemn his views and stick to "the old victory-crowned tactics." But the defeat of Bernstein proved in the end to have been merely a defeat in words; for his book expressed in plain-spoken language what was increasingly becoming the unconscious practice of his party.

The reason for Bernstein's hidden triumph lay in the changing intellectual climate of Europe. His trivial remarks on economic trends could not stand up against Marx's *Capital.* Though twentieth-century Europe was to assume a different shape from the prophecies of either, it was to resemble far more the catastrophic forecasts of Marx than Bernstein's optimistic predictions of an increasingly crisisless economy, an ever-wider diffusion of wealth and an imperceptible growing of capitalism into socialism, without convulsion or revolution. Yet Bernstein's views exactly suited the prevailing mood of Europe as the nineteenth century set and the twentieth rose bright with promise.

Marxism was the unacknowledged child of the stormy adolescence of capitalism. Politically it represented a series of deductions from the period of revolutions from 1789 to 1848. But Europe had known neither great wars, nor revolutionary upheavals, nor profound economic crises since the early seventies. Bernstein's generation knew of revolution only from the Marxist classics. They reserved their tribute to it for holiday occasions, and in their daily practice moved familiarly in the bustling, prosperous atmosphere of growing trade unions, improved labor legislation, mounting votes, increasing parliamentary representation, enlarging socialist newspaper circulation.

The sudden expansion of Europe overseas, the picking to pieces of the "dark continent" of Africa within a decade, the piling up of armaments, gave Europe a brief period of febrile prosperity. Railroad building, armament and capital export stimulated heavy industry. Monopoly profit and colonial profit seemed to offset Marx's dread law of the falling rate of profit. The capital plethora was taken up in stock speculation, in export to rapidly industrializing lands like Russia, and to colonies overseas. Crises diminished in intensity, recoveries soared to new heights.

In the face of these phenomena, "orthodoxy" held doggedly to Marx. Only Hobson, Parvus, Hilferding and Rosa Luxemburg—and later Lenin—ventured on any real investigation of these new phenomena. Nowhere but in Russia, where there was an absolute Tsar to fight, did a movement arise that was really based on a spirit of revolution. To the superficial observer it was far easier to believe in Bernstein's social meliorism than in grim prophecies of coming wars, social and political and economic breakdown, open struggles as to the nature of the future new order.

Even in Russia, things seemed quiet. The years of Ulyanov's exile were years of boom. The workingmen, largely with a leadership arising from their own ranks, were conducting strikes, many of them successful. The intelligentsia, tending, as is the intellectuals' habit, to elaborate temporary and superficial phenomena into deep and timeless generalizations, developed a new theory to fit the new situation. Because of the new theory's emphasis on economic struggle, rather than political struggle against the Tsar, it acquired the name of "Economism."

All that this new movement required—given the Russian tendency to worship authority—was encouragement from authoritative voices in the leading party of Western Europe. Bernstein was not bluffing when he claimed to have many Russian supporters. Ulyanov's indignation at the claim yielded to white hot fury when he found that he and his fellow-exiles were in the minority in their own movement.

Indeed, a document had already reached remote Shushenskoye which Ulyanov had taken at first to be an individual aberration. The document, baptized by him "the Credo," was drawn up by Mrs. Kuskova. Its mere perusal, as he wrote to his mother, "infuriated" him.

The general law of labor activity, declared the "Credo," was for the movement to follow "the path of least resistance." In the West, where the bourgeoisie had conquered political rights for itself and for the proletariat, the working class had found it easier to go into politics than to build unions. But in Russia, where the Tsar represented a stone wall blocking political action, the path of least resistance was economic action against the employers and the attempt to organize trade unions. The Russian working class was too weak and backward anyhow for politics. All talk of an independent political party of labor was but an importation of alien doctrine based on different conditions. The duty of the socialist intellectuals was to support the workers in their effort to build unions, and support the liberal opposition against tsarism in its effort to democratize Russia. The workers would learn from their experience in strikes the necessity of supporting the liberal opposition on the political field also.

The "Credo" moved like a sword through the movement, dividing it into two quite unequal parts. Paul Axelrod had already warned against it in a pamphlet printed in Zurich and smuggled into Russia. Ulyanov now drafted a sharper and more irate rejoinder. Taking advantage of some festival, he arranged for all the exiles in the province to come together at a "party." He read the "Credo," analyzed it, read his answer. Seventeen exiles, including himself and his wife, the Finnish workingman Enberg, who had been studying Marxism with Krupskaya, Vaneev, who was dying of tuberculosis and had to be carried, bed and all, into the meeting, and the entire little group of the three nearby towns, signed the document. It became known by that fact as "The Protest of the Seventeen." Potresov, Dan and Vorovsky sent a similar document from Vyatka. Ulyanov mailed a copy of the "Protest" to Martov, who secured additional signatures in Turukhansk. It was smuggled out of Siberia for circulation in printed and hectographed versions. Thus began the counter-offensive of the revolutionary Marxist minority against "Economism."

From now on Ulyanov was like a bull that had felt the first thrust. He raged at the distance and the forced inaction, at the slovenliness of Russian thought, and at the slackness of Russian organization, which had landed every revolutionist in exile. He walked through the forest for hours with Krupskaya, or with visitors from the nearby towns, talking, talking, talking, confidentially, didactically, like a schoolmaster with his most advanced pupil, on what must be done. A plan was taking shape in his mind: a plan for an all-Russian underground newspaper, and a chain of secret agents who would smuggle it across frontiers and into cities and factories. The paper would lay the basis for fusing all the local circles into a nationwide organization. It would explain theoretical problems and make known practical tasks. It would educate and organize. It would defeat the "Economists" and take intellectual and organizational guardianship over the movement. Out of its pages would come the ideas, and out of its agents would come the organizational machinery, on which to base a unified, centralized, conspirative party, which the police could not break nor "liberal chatterers" weaken.

> Vladimir Ilyich began to spend sleepless nights—writes Krupskaya—He became terribly thin. It was during these nights that he thought out his plan in every detail, discussed it with Krzhizhanovsky, with me, wrote about it to Martov and Potresov, discussed with them a journey abroad. The more time went on, the more Vladimir Ilyich was overcome with impatience, the more eager he was to get to work.

CHAPTER NINE

LENIN'S ORGANIZATION PLAN

Before we can unite, and in order that we may unite, we must first of all firmly and definitely draw the lines of demarcation between the various groups.

—EDITORIAL STATEMENT OF FIRST
NUMBER OF ISKRA, DRAFTED BY LENIN

Aided by clear, frosty moonlight, the little party pushed on day and night by sled down the frozen Yenissei. Nadya's mother suffered from the intense cold, but the impatient Vladimir rode through the sharp February air without his elkskin coat. He would scarcely permit stops for adequate rest; yet, wherever there was a chance to meet an exile or a little group of them, he halted to talk over his plans for an all-Russian newspaper. He seemed bent on knowing personally every Socialist in Siberia: later that knowledge would be useful to him. Many have left testimony of their sudden sense of the bigness of his simple, practical-sounding plans, and the potency of his concentrated will. As with a Loyola, as with all outstanding organizers of parties of action, the force of Ulyanov's personality, no less than of his ideas, was beginning to bind men to him by ties that resembled those of disciple and master.

His wife, whose term of exile had yet another year to run—this was February, 1900—could not accompany him beyond Ufa in the Urals, where she was to serve her final year. It did not enter into his mind to remain with her there, though the big cities of Russia were forbidden to him. He must get nearer to the capitals and the frontier. He chose Pskov, a rail junction not far from the border.

Ulyanov, Potresov and Martov, of about the same age (Potresov was a year older and Martov three years younger than Ulyanov), tacitly regarded themselves as the *troika:* a three-man team that was to lead their generation and become the editorial board of the paper they were planning. While in exile, they had carried on a lengthy correspondence about it; who should write for it; where it should be published; how be smuggled into the country; what its position should be on a multitude of questions. The three were so close that Ulyanov dubbed their union "the triple alliance" and referred now to one, now the other, in his code letters as "Brother." Martov, his term of exile over, went to Poltava to get contacts in the south of Russia, while Potresov joined Ulyanov in Pskov. What talk there was between them we can guess from the way their host Radchenko's two little daughters used to tease them: "Placing their hands behind their backs the little girls paced solemnly up and down the room side by side, the one saying 'Bernstein' and the other replying 'Kautsky.'"

When the "brothers" applied for permission to go abroad in pursuance of their plan to found a paper, the government readily granted passports.

Before leaving, Ulyanov asked for permission to go to Ufa to see his ailing wife. While he was at it, he went to see his mother and sister in Moscow—and to pick up connections there. Then he made a tour of a number of lesser towns for additional contacts. Only impatience to get started on the paper itself made him give up a wild project of returning secretly to Siberia to see yet other exiles. Scarcely less reckless for police-dogged men was the decision of "Brothers" Martov and Ulyanov to visit Saint Petersburg together, a city forbidden to both. The very day after their arrival, they were arrested. Prisoner Ulyanov had on his person two thousand rubles, just received from "Auntie" (A. M. Kalmykova) to start the paper, a list of addresses, and a letter for Plekhanov. The letter and addresses had been written in invisible ink on old bills and notes. Still, the failure to travel "clean" in a forbidden city did not argue great skill in underground work on the part of the man who was about to become the teacher in such matters of a whole generation. But the police, who caught them easily enough, neither heated the scraps of paper, nor confiscated the considerable treasury of the future newspaper, nor detained more than a few days its would-be editors. Their arrest on this foolhardy mission constituted the first narrow escape for the unborn paper. The second came soon after from an émigrés' quarrel.

When Ulyanov crossed the frontier on July 29, 1900, he found a split situation bordering on hysteria. Potresov, who had preceded him, was plunged in gloom. He reported that Plekhanov and his veterans had quarreled with all the members of a recently founded Union of Social Democrats Abroad, the majority of whom were "Economists," and supporters of Bernstein against

Plekhanov in the great debate then raging on "revisionism." The Union had held a Congress in April, where the scrap had been so bitter that the veterans had walked out and formed their own rival League of Revolutionary Social Democracy Abroad. Ulyanov went at once to Geneva to see Plekhanov.

> My conversation with him—wrote Vladimir Ilyich in a confidential report intended only for the eyes of Krupskaya, Martov, and a few close adherents—did indeed show that he was suspicious, distrustful and *rechthaberisch* to *nec plus ultra*. I tried to be cautious and evaded all the "touchy" points, but the constant restraint I had to place upon myself could not but affect my temper . . .

Plekhanov, he complained, had used "diplomacy" in dealing with his future editorial colleague. But, from the above, we can see that "diplomacy" was used by both. Ulyanov was angry that his old master had split the émigré movement just when he was counting on producing for it a journal which would guide and unite all Social Democrats both abroad and inside Russia. The conversation between master and disciple degenerated into a wrangle. Ulyanov nourished the idea that the unborn journal could be the unswerving champion of the revolutionary, orthodox Marxist viewpoint, which he and his master, Plekhanov, held in common, could polemicize against Liberals, "Economists," "Revisionists," and Populists, and yet at one and the same time be everybody's paper, supported by all, admonishing and instructing everybody, admitting all the warring opinions into its columns—in the form of contributions which would be systematically criticized by the editors in accompanying editorial notes. This peculiar notion, psychologically untenable, Ulyanov derived as a logical corollary of his twin formulae: the "alliance" of all opposition elements, and the "hegemony of the proletariat" in the general struggle against tsarism. But Plekhanov, opposing the admission of such contrary views altogether, "displayed a hatred toward 'allies' which bordered on the indecent—suspecting them of espionage, accusing them of being *Geschaeftsmacher* and scoundrels, and asserting that he would not hesitate to 'shoot' such 'traitors.' "

Strange to hear the future arch-splitter complaining against Plekhanov in the identical terms which would later be used against Lenin by his opponents, including his present comrades-in-arms, Martov, Potresov and this same Plekhanov.

Another and deeper, because less conscious, source of friction was the older man's treatment of an editorial statement for the first issue, which had been prepared by the younger. Plekhanov made no objection to the ideas—which silence Ulyanov interpreted as "intolerable diplomacy"—but condemned the declaration as too commonplace, too lacking in depth, too pedestrian in tone, for a would-be historic document. From his first meeting with Ulyanov, he had conceived an admiration for this eminently businesslike disciple as a future practical organizer of the revolutionary movement but had been unable to take him seriously as a writer and thinker. "This is not 'written,' as the French say," he told the hurt author. "This is not a literary work. This does not look like anything . . ." As one reads Lenin's pedestrian manifesto, one cannot help but feel that Plekhanov's criticism was justified. But style, too, is a matter of temperament. Nor was the situation improved when the old master took the document with the intention of "elevating the tone," and a few days later haughtily returned it unaltered.

In the course of the same week, Plekhanov, Axelrod and Vera Zasulich met with Potresov and Ulyanov to negotiate an agreement between the two "organizations," or rather, the two generations. The strained relations between "master" and "disciple" flared into open conflict:

> Now G.V.'s [Plekhanov's] desire to possess unlimited power became obvious . . . He stated that it was evident that we had differing views . . . he understood and respected our point of view, but could not accept it. It would be better if we were the

editors and he a contributor. We were positively amazed, and began to argue against this . . .

The unstated source of the conflict was the question: whose leadership, Plekhanov's or Ulyanov's, the "older" or the "younger generation"? This was an issue that would never be clearly and consciously formulated, yet one that would never die down. But Ulyanov could not then dream of leading the movement without its most revered leaders, his own teachers. He stifled his indignation, and persuaded Plekhanov to reconsider. Immediately the latter asked pointedly how voting would be conducted among six editors, an even number. (The editors were to be Plekhanov, Axelrod, Zasulich, from the veterans, and Ulyanov, Martov, Potresov, from the younger group.) On Vera Zasulich's motion, that question was decided by giving Plekhanov two votes to break the potential ties, and one apiece to each of the other five!

> On that—Ulyanov's confidential report continues—G.V. took the reins of management into his hands and in a high editorial manner began to apportion tasks . . . We sat there as if we had been ducked . . . we realized that we had been made fools of . . .
>
> My "infatuation" with Plekhanov disappeared as if by magic . . . Never, never in my life have I regarded any other man with such sincere respect and veneration. I have never stood before any man with such "humility" as I stood before him, and never before have I been so brutally "spurned" . . . Since a man with whom we desire to cooperate intimately resorts to chess moves in dealing with comrades, there can be no doubt of the fact that he is a bad man, yes, a bad man, inspired by petty motives of personal vanity and conceit—an insincere man . . .
>
> This discovery struck us both [Ulyanov and Potresov] like a thunderbolt because up to that moment both of us had been enamored with Plekhanov, and, as we do with our beloved, we forgave him everything, closed our eyes to his shortcomings . . . Our indignation knew no bounds. Our ideal was destroyed; gloatingly we trampled it under our feet. There were no bounds to the charges we hurled against him . . . Good-bye journal! We will throw up everything and return to Russia . . . Had we not been in love with him, our conduct toward him would have been

different . . . Young comrades "court" an old comrade out of
the great love they bear for him—and suddenly, he injects into
this love an atmosphere of intrigue . . . An enamored youth re-
ceives from the object of his love a bitter lesson: to regard all
persons "without sentiment"; to keep a stone in one's sling . . .

There are many more pages to this curious document which,
under the title "How the 'Spark' was Nearly Extinguished," occupies fifteen pages of volume four of Lenin's *Collected Works.*
From it we can learn little concerning the political differences
which were to divide these two men in the future, but much concerning differences of temperament. No other document from
Lenin's hand would ever again be as psychologically revealing.
He soon learned well the lesson he here set for himself: "To regard all persons 'without sentiment'; to keep a stone in one's
sling . . ." He taught himself to discipline severely the emotional
side of his nature; to seek for and enlarge the political aspect of
all future quarrels; to play down, even ignore where possible,
the personal. But this document suffices to show us how far this
self-disciplined, inexorably logical man shared the "peculiar
soul" of the Russian intelligentsia whence he sprang. All this
talk of boundless love, humiliation and disillusionment could
well have come from a Russian novel; but it can not be matched
in any political report from the labor movement of any other
country. The historian is forced to the conclusion that, in the
future quarrels, even when all sides are agreed that the issues are
exclusively political, there remains a strong probability that the
personal element has merely been "sublimated" or "rationalized" rather than altogether eliminated.

The quarrel ended, if not with mutual forgiveness and the joy-
ful sobs of a "lovers' reconciliation," at least with a formal
agreement to continue living together and to keep up appearances. The final negotiations were conducted "coolly, quite
coolly." Potresov it was who proposed the compromise "so that
a serious party enterprise might not be ruined by spoiled *personal* relations." (The emphasis, as always, is Lenin's.)

> We agreed among ourselves not to relate what had passed to anyone except our most intimate friends . . . On the surface everything appeared as if nothing had happened . . . But we felt an internal pang: instead of friendly relations, dry businesslike ones . . . We were always to be on our guard, on the principle: *Si vis pacem, para bellum.*

It is not too much to conclude that, from the disillusionment which ended his "youthful love affair," the thirty-year-old Vladimir Ilyich suddenly matured from Ulyanov to Lenin. Indeed, behind the whole "lovers' quarrel" was the fact, never consciously formulated, that Ulyanov was beginning to feel within himself the capacity to lead the movement, if necessary, without his master. When differences in temperament would ripen into differences in approach and formulation, Martov and Potresov, no less than Plekhanov, Axelrod and Zasulich, would remember the sudden anger and stubborn firmness which Ulyanov had displayed on this occasion. And they would find to their dismay that there was more than rhetoric in the conclusions about keeping a stone in one's sling and, while wishing peace, preparing war. Ulyanov immediately saw to it that the paper would be printed in Germany and not in Switzerland, so that Plekhanov would have to vote by mail. And he provided that all the machinery for underground distribution would remain in his hands.

> When I arrived in exile—Krupskaya writes—Vladimir Ilyich told me that he had succeeded in arranging that I should be made secretary of *Iskra* . . . This of course meant that contact with Russia would be carried on under the closest control of Vladimir Ilyich . . . He told me it had been rather awkward for him to have to arrange this, but that he considered it necessary for the good of the cause . . .

Now Vladimir Ilyich stopped using a different pseudonym for each article, and began to sign all of them with the single underground name: Lenin.* He was acquiring a serious view of continuity of leadership and of his own capacity to exercise it. His object was to build for the name Lenin a cumulative reputation, to make it stand for a set of systematic views on theory, politics, and, above all, organization. Whether signed or unsigned, his articles were supposedly an expression of a common view of all the editors, yet with a selfless intellectual self-love and an even profounder self-confidence he fought jealously for every fragment of his special viewpoint, even inserting it, often after shattering quarrels, as an interpolation into articles by the others. Most of his articles were unsigned, yet agents and readers became increasingly aware of the fact that a special set of ideas, presented in an especially stark, insistent, repetitive, unadorned and matter-of-fact way, kept recurring again and again over the same signature, or in the same style, from the same hand. Unlike the other editors, he would constantly refer to his own previous articles, expand them, gloss them, defend them, link the latest onto all the preceding ones in an unbroken chain.

The name Lenin passed from mouth to mouth in the underground. The police made increasing note of it. Exiles going abroad now often asked to meet Lenin as well as Plekhanov. In the obscure unconscious, Vladimir Ilyich was paving the way for its being known in separateness from and even against the fame-hallowed names of the "Oldsters" or the corporate name of *Iskra*. He began to sign it to personal letters to close followers, who looked to him within *Iskra* as they looked to *Iskra* within the less defined world of the labor and socialist

* Sometimes, N. Lenin. Between 1895 and the latter part of 1901, he had used the following names: K. Tulin, K. T—in, K. T—n, S.T.A., T.P., F.P., Petrov, Frey, T. Ch., T. Kh., Karpov, Meyer, Starik (in letters), Ilyin, V. Ilyin, Vl. Ilyin, and Vladimir Ilyin. The story told by Walter Duranty to the effect that he did not use the name Lenin until 1912, when he is supposed to have assumed it in honor of the Gold Strike on the Lena River, has no basis in truth. Beginning in 1901 he used the name Lenin or N. Lenin continuously, and over that signature even commented upon some of his earlier writings signed with his other pen names, thus tying them up with the set of ideas to be associated thenceforward with his continuous signature. Prior to 1901, the name most frequently used had been Ilyin and its variants, V., Vl. and Vladimir Ilyin. Lenin is apparently derived from Ilyin, and Ilyin in turn from Vladimir Ilyich, his first name and patronymic, and from the "Ulyan" of Ulyanov. There is no basis for the American newspaper legend that the N. in N. Lenin stands for Nikolai. In European, and especially in Russian writing, N. or N.N. is a familiar symbol for anonymity, thus a kind of hint that Lenin is but a pseudonym.

underground. Sometimes his letters began with the impersonal "Lenin writing to . . ." or "Lenin speaking." And, despite his mere thirty years or so as against the more venerable ages of Plekhanov, Axelrod, Deutsch, Zasulich, he began some of them with "*Starik* speaking . . ." or ended them with the simple signature, *Starik* (in Russian, "The Old Man"). In a land soaked in patriarchal tradition, it was a nickname expressive of authority and respect, tinged with affectionate admiration. Stalin has since used all the overwhelming machinery of propaganda in vain to attach the nickname to his own person, but in their intimate moments his lieutenants still refer to him as *Khozyain* —"The Boss"—instead of *Starik*—"The Old Man."

It was unforeseen, yet inevitable, that this energetic, precise, schoolmasterly, youngish "Old Man" should dominate the new paper from the outset. It was his brain that had conceived it. He had found for it the name *Iskra*—"The Spark"—and for its masthead the Decembrists' longing, prophetic cry: "Out of the spark shall spring the flame." How could he fail to put his impress upon it when he attributed to it a role so much more ample than the others? To Plekhanov and his friends, and to Lenin's two "Brothers," it was just a revolutionary paper. That was no small thing, to be sure, in a country where all oppositional papers were forbidden. But to him it was more than that. It was to be a crusader against all forms of opportunism, revisionism, unorthodoxy, anti-Marxism. It was to encourage all the other oppositional currents against tsarism, yet criticize and expose them, too, and undermine their influence over the masses. It was not to serve a party but create a party, to unite Russia's scattered, narrow-visioned, short-lived, local circles into an All-Russian Social Democratic Labor Party. Its little band of secret agents, who would smuggle it across frontiers, were to form a close-knit company of schooled conspirators. They would penetrate everywhere, gather news, spy out information, report on moods, carry commands, recruit the best in every factory and locality and bind them closer to the movement. They would acquire influence over the working class and the whole revolutionary opposition; endow all spontaneous strikes and rebellions with socialist consciousness; teach the proletariat to look beyond the merely local to the nationwide and international; raise the workingman's eyes above the limited horizon of working-class concerns to those of all the oppressed and discontented. *Iskra* would be "the collective agitator and collective organizer," it would serve as "an enormous pair of bellows that would blow every spark of class struggle and popular indignation into a general conflagration." Its editors would be the ideological leaders of the future Party. Its agents would be the very framework of the Party, would, indeed, be that Party. And, as the Party, they would lead the proletariat, which in turn would lead all other oppressed, exploited and oppositional classes and strata of the population. Thus this group of *Iskra* editors, contributors, agents and organizers would form the skeletal general staff and officers' corps which tomorrow would mobilize and lead mighty armies into battle, hold them back from premature conflict, teach them to lay efficient, relentless siege to the fortress of autocracy, and, at the right moment, go from siege to storm attack and victory.

There was poetry in this audacious conception of the role of a paper which, if it survived a few issues, might consider itself fortunate, and which at best could hope to appear only irregularly, perhaps once a month or so, in an edition of a few thousand copies, more than two-thirds of which would be confiscated at the border. The other editors did not quite realize what thoughts their colleague was thinking. In the whole history of journalism, no other paper had been assigned quite so vast a role. Even if the careful Lenin had not taken the steps to bind the secret agents to him and get for his wife control of all the connections with Russia, his conception of *Iskra* as he expounded it in article after article and as it gradually filtered into the Russian underground was sufficient to give readers and agents and supporters a sense of their own and the journal's importance, and to rally round the name of Lenin all those attracted to such audacious visions.

In the first number readers found an article, unsigned, bearing the title: "Urgent Tasks of Our Movement." Two ideas in it were momentous for the future history of Russia: (1) that the labor movement, left to itself without the guidance of the self-chosen "socialist vanguard," would "become petty and inevitably bourgeois"; and (2) that the vanguard in question would have to consist of people "who shall devote to the revolution not only their spare evenings, but the whole of their lives."

Only a few years before, Ulyanov had been proving that the peasants were "petty bourgeois" and that the peasant-socialist, Narodnik movement was "inevitably bourgeois," because they did not base themselves solely and exclusively upon the proletariat, "the class which alone can act as an independent fighter for socialism." Now he was taking a big step farther: the proletariat, too, would "become inevitably bourgeois" in its outlook unless it accepted the leadership and teachings of a self-appointed socialist vanguard of professional revolutionaries. If in the first contention was hidden the germ of a minority proletarian dictatorship over the majority of the Russian people, the peasants, in the second contention was hidden the germ of a party dictatorship over the proletariat itself, exercised in its name.

This was a drastic departure from the much-quoted dictum of Marx and Engels: "The emancipation of the working class is the work of the working class itself." But the idea was not a new one in Russia. More than a quarter-century earlier, Lenin's prototype and predecessor, Tkachev, had written:

> Neither in the present nor in the future can the people, left to their own resources, bring into existence the social revolution. Only we revolutionists can accomplish this . . . Social ideals are alien to the people; they belong to the social philosophy of the revolutionary minority.

Lenin's sole change was to strike out the word "people" and substitute "proletariat." The spirit was the same. Questions still hidden in the mists of the future were these: how were the members of the revolutionary vanguard to be selected? how were they to know what was best for the people, or for the proletariat? could they, or would they, arouse it to take control of its own destinies, once they had taken power in its name?

In the fourth number, Lenin returned to the same theme in a longer article entitled "Where to Begin." Unsigned also, it pointedly referred to the first article and promised to elaborate both into a pamphlet. When the pamphlet, almost a year in gestation, finally came out, it was a smallish book (160 pages in the English edition of Lenin's *Collected Works*). It was entitled, after Chernishevsky's famous novel, *What's to Be Done?* It bore the signature, N. Lenin, henceforth to be identified with these views.

Indeed, *What's to Be Done?* contained, some in germ, some fully developed, virtually all of the ideas on politics and party organization which would later be known as "Leninist." It was destined to mark the great divide down the opposing slopes of which would flow separating waters. It was to become the gospel of all the "hards" ("rock-hard" was the word they chose for themselves), to whose only partly sensed ideas on leadership and control of the nascent movement it gave a many-sided and sharply-chiseled formulation. And it was to possess a seductive attraction, too, for all those "tender-minded" ones who mistrusted their own softness. These might begin by opposing Lenin on one question or another, but once they became convinced that they had been wrong and he right in some conflict, they were likely to make complete surrender, and become the most zealous of "Leninists." Thus, from the outset, there were "repentant" Economists among the Bolsheviks. Other penitents would come with each new conflict. Together, these two types, the original "hards" and the "repentant softs" would make up the future Bolshevik leadership. That is why it could simultaneously harbor a Lunacharsky, who would shed tears and resign his commissar's post when he heard that the historic St. Basil's was under bombardment by the Bolsheviks, and a Stalin, whose self-chosen underground name suggested his steely core of hardness. As long as Lenin lived, most of his closest associates would be of the repentant soft type; under Stalin most of them would vanish from leadership altogether.

In intention, *What's to Be Done?* is a work of orthodox Marxism; not a mechanical copy or literal translation, but an attempt to assimilate the experiences of the Western labor and socialist movements and adapt them to the special conditions of Russian backwardness and lack of liberty. The profound respect for authority which characterized Lenin and his milieu caused him to "take counsel with Marx" (the words are his own), whenever some critical problem presented itself. Now as always he found quotations to fit his needs. But, of course, opponents searching so rich and varied a Scripture, could find quotations to fit an opposing viewpoint. In practical politics Lenin was too much a realist to rely on scholastic exegetics for the real outlines of his solutions. Sometimes the citations suggested a fertile line of thought; more often his line of thought suggested relevant quotations to lend authority to his solutions. In any case, to judge the present work by its quotations and professions alone is to miss its essence.

Thus the quotation which adorned its fly-leaf, if not from Marx or Engels, was at least from a letter to them from the hand of Lassalle. "Party struggles give a party strength and life . . . A party becomes stronger by purging itself!" These sentences, so alien to the real course of the unification of the Marxian and Lassallean movements in Germany, will bob up again and again in Russian labor history, taking on ever more sinister meaning with every split and expulsion, until they become the text of the great blood purges of the nineteen thirties. From all the voluminous writings of Marx, Engels and Lassalle, this was a strange choice to strike the keynote on the title page of a book intended to promote the "unification" of the still unformed Russian Social Democratic Party!

But Lenin did not mean the same thing as the others by "unification." His meaning was: the uniting of the autonomous local circles of the Marxist movement into a centrally controlled and ideologically homogeneous All-Russian party. Central control and ideological homogeneity: that was "unification." To secure it he was prepared to exclude all those who would not accept centralized organization; to force the merger of all papers into a single national organ; to exclude the Jewish Socialist Bund unless it was ready to give up its autonomy; to exclude Revisionists and Economists and all who were unready to accept without question the "orthodox" Marxist program, which he and Plekhanov and the other *Iskra* editors would prepare for the coming convention. There were some who thought that the first need of the still unborn party was a prolonged, full and free discussion of first principles. But to Lenin, as to Plekhanov, all that had already been settled, in Western Europe, by the works of Marx and Engels, and anew by Kautsky and Plekhanov in their still-raging controversy with Bernstein.

In Russia, the Bernsteinians, the Economists and Revisionists were already in retreat, defeated not so much by argument as by a deep change in mood. The economic boom which had given easy victory in strikes, had yielded to economic crisis. Storm clouds were gathering that three years later would burst out in revolution. Workers were even then beginning to go from petty economic demands to political demonstrations against the autocracy. Brooding students once more were meditating the assassination of tsarist officials. Manor-house burnings were beginning to illuminate the land. Even the liberal intelligentsia and bourgeoisie were drinking dangerous toasts at banquets, offering financial help to, and expecting political support from, the revolutionary movement, planning to participate in the socialist underground press or create an underground press of their own. All that the retreating Economists now asked before going into a unified party, which would apparently be led by Plekhanov and Lenin, was the right of continuing the discussion of those fundamental problems which they still regarded as unsettled.

But Lenin's conception of unification involved unconditional surrender or exclusion. The first chapter of his little book was one long attack on the very phrase "freedom of criticism":

We are marching in a compact group along a precipitous and difficult path . . . surrounded on all sides by enemies . . . We have combined not to retreat into the marsh but for the express purpose of fighting the enemy. . . .

Oh yes, gentlemen! You are free, not only to invite us, but to go yourselves wherever you will, even into the marsh. In fact, we think that the marsh is your proper place; and we are prepared to render *you* every assistance to get there. Only let go of our hands, don't clutch at us, and don't besmirch the grand word *freedom;* for we too are "free" to go where we please, free also . . . to fight those who are turning towards the marsh.

Abandoning his opponents thus in the swamp, Lenin invites the rest of his readers to scale heights from which is visible a vast panorama. With Marxism as guide, the party can place itself at the head of the proletariat, and the proletariat at the head of the nation. And not only the nation!

History has confronted us with an immediate task that is more revolutionary than all the immediate tasks that confront the proletariat of any other country. The fulfillment of this task, the destruction of the most powerful bulwark, not only of European but no less of Asiatic reaction, places the Russian proletariat in the vanguard of the international revolutionary proletariat.

That is to be vanguard, indeed! Here in germ is the audacious conception that inspired the Bolshevik revolution, of 1917, and the founding of the Communist International.

Having disposed of peasant socialism, Economism and Marx-Revisionism as "bourgeois," Lenin turns his attention to the nascent trade-union movement. No flattery here either! The proletariat, left to its own devices, without the benefit of direction by the Marxist vanguard, becomes "bourgeois" too:

The working class exclusively by its own efforts, is able to develop only trade-union consciousness . . . Modern socialist consciousness can only be brought to them from without . . . can arise only on the basis of profound scientific knowledge.

The bearers of science are not the proletariat but the bourgeois intelligentsia. It is out of the heads of members of this stratum [Marx and Engels—and Lenin might have added himself and Plekhanov] that modern socialism originated . . . Pure and simple trade unionism means the ideological subordination of the workers to the bourgeoisie . . . Our task is to bring the labor movement under the wing of revolutionary Social Democracy . . . Working-class consciousness cannot be genuinely political consciousness unless the workers are trained to respond to all cases of tyranny, oppression, violence and abuse, no matter *what class* is affected . . . To bring political knowledge to the workers, the Social Democrats must *go among all classes of the population,* must dispatch units of their army *in all directions.* The Social Democrat's ideal should not be a trade-union secretary, but *a tribune of the people.*

The multiplying italics suggest the excitement with which Lenin presented his views and the importance he attached to them. Indeed, this vision of the role of Russian socialism brings us to the core of his political theories, and gives us his choice between the diverging crossroads at which the young movement was then standing.

Russian labor might choose to lay its major emphasis on immediate living conditions—wages, hours, dwellings, factory sanitation, social insurance. And it might limit its immediate political objectives, accordingly, to the legalization of the right of assembly, of the right of political party and union organization, and the securing of labor legislation. Or it might subordinate all these issues to the general revolutionary struggle against tsarism.

If the first path were chosen, it might lead to the gradual legalization of the labor movement, to the slow and at first precarious growth of autonomous, self-governing unions, the destinies of which would be directly determined by the workingmen who composed them. Later, it might lead to the development of a socialistic labor party formed on this trade-union foundation and controlled from below by the organized workers. In that case the professional revolutionaries of the intelligentsia, whose whole soul was concentrated on the struggle to overthrow tsarism, would find themselves still conspiring in a social vacuum, without a labor army over which to assume officership. Or this would-be general staff might change its course and offer itself to the labor movement as mere servitors, advisers, specialists, whose ideological views would be accepted only to the extent that they could convince the labor movement to adopt them.

However, if the second course, Lenin's course, were chosen, strikes and unions would be subordinated to the struggle against tsarism. The nascent labor movement would prolong its illegalization. Its transitory organizations would come under the control of the budding party of socialist intellectual conspirators, and these latter would determine labor's direction, its aims and its destiny.

Though it was never so clearly formulated, this was the real issue between "Economists" and Marxists, then between Mensheviks and Bolsheviks, then between Workers Opposition and Lenin, between Tomsky and Stalin, changing forms of the protean battle between Westernizer and Slavophile. One path led closer to the parties and trade unions of the West, which were democratically organized, comfortably adapted to the sizable legality permitted them, and long since devoid of insurrectionary spirit except as a banner for festal occasions. The other led to concentration of conspiracy and insurrection under the leadership of a self-selected, rigidly centralized, secret and conspirative band of revolutionary intellectuals under a self-appointed leader, formed on the pattern of the early "professional revolutionaries" of the Narodnaya Volya.

To be sure, Lenin did not feel the divergence of his path from that of the Western socialist parties and unions. They were right for the West because the West was "democratic, modern and progressive." But Russia was "Asiatic, barbarous, and backward." Into the holiday revolutionary phrases of the Western unions and parties, he read the meanings springing from the immediately revolutionary spirit of Russian life. Politically, Russia was still living in the eighteenth or early nineteenth century, still on the eve of its "1789" or its "1848." This it was that made the *Communist Manifesto,* issued on the eve of the European revolutions of 1848—now little more than a revered, if seminal, document in Western Europe—seem in every sense a contemporary document in Russia. How could Lenin know that the resounding phrases that issued from the tongues and pens of Western leaders on high holidays were but dimming reminiscences? For him, the West, above all Germany, was sweeping steadily toward social revolution. All that had held Western Europe back from successful revolution in 1848 had been tsarist Russia's intervention. Therefore, all that was needed to unleash the overdue revolution in the West, was to remove once and for all the threat of tsarist intervention. The overthrow of tsarism would start a socialist uprising throughout Europe, and even backward Russia might be dragged into socialism in its wake.

On Lenin's side was the newness and backwardness of Russia's working class, little suited as yet to organization in autonomous and democratically self-controlled unions and parties. On his side the narrow obstinacy of the Tsar and his closest advisers, who, while they yielded piecemeal to the demands of the "modern age," yielded too slowly and too little at a time. On his side the dark camarilla around the Tsarina, which was to take ever tighter control over affairs of state and seek the snatching back of every concession made to a slowly awakening people. On his side the conflict between the swiftly changing needs of modern industry and the slowly changing, ancient structure of the land. On his side the tremendous charge of energy which came from the so long overdue "bourgeois revolution," stepped up by the energy created by the modern, post-bourgeois movement for socialism. When a latecomer takes ideas from more advanced lands, it wants the "latest," freed from its origins, counterpoises and complexities. On his side, though he did not suspect it, was a coming crisis in the West itself, that would threaten the very existence of all its hard-won institutions of democracy and freedom. On his side, finally, was the simplicity, the fanatical ardor and fighting *élan* of a new,

million-headed working class, yesterday's peasants in today's
overalls and tomorrow's uniforms, just torn loose from their
village ways of life and thought, open to whoever might present
the simplest, most dramatic and most persuasive outlook to
take the place of that which they had just lost.

On the surface, much of *What's to Be Done?* is an attack
upon the intelligentsia, "careless and sluggish in their habits."
Lenin's consuming "un-Russian" passion for system and order
is largely explainable in terms of his reaction to the slackness of
the human material with which he had to work. His book proposed a rigorously centralized hierarchical structure for the new
party. The center would issue commands, the local organizations would carry them out, "discussing" them mainly in the
sense of discussing how best to execute them. The center could
draw people out of local work for its purposes, and would
have the power to approve or reject the personnel of leading
committees in the localities. The center would safeguard the
purity of doctrine and action of the Party. This system he de-
nominated "proletarian discipline," and castigated the intellectuals for their reluctance to accept it. The factory, Lenin asserted, accustomed the proletarian to such discipline; but it was
alien and distasteful to the self-reliant, individualistic, slippered
ease of the intelligentsia. The latter's opposition was therefore
"petty bourgeois" and constituted "opportunism in the organization question."*
   Despite these strictures upon the intelligentsia, this book of

* It was not some spokesman of the "opportunists" but the leader of the revolutionary wing of the
German Social Democracy, Rosa Luxemburg, who made the classic critique of this Leninist doctrine
of "proletarian discipline":
   "The discipline which Lenin means," she wrote, "is impressed upon the proletariat not only by the
factory, but also by the barracks and by modern bureaucratism, in short, by the entire mechanism of the
centralized bourgeois state. But it is nothing less than the abuse of a general term which at the same
time designates as 'discipline' two such opposing concepts as the willfulness and thoughtlessness of a
many-limbed, many-armed mass of flesh carrying out mechanical movements at the beat of the baton,
and the voluntary coordination of the conscious political action of a social stratum; the corpselike obedience of a dominated class and the organized rebellion of a class struggling for freedom. It is not by
making use of the discipline impressed upon him by the capitalist state, with a mere transfer of the
baton from the hand of the bourgeoisie to that of a Social Democratic Central Committee, but it is only
by breaking through and uprooting this slavish spirit of discipline that the proletariat can be educated
for a new discipline: the voluntary self-discipline of Social Democracy."

Lenin's really assigns to them a larger role than does any other socialist work ever written. What were the "professional revolutionaries" if not revolutionary intellectuals, detached from "orderly society," breaking with family, friends and place in the social structure, and living in the Russian underground exclusively for the struggle against tsarism? All through the nineteenth century young men and women of generous vision had been abandoning other professions for this one of revolutionist, with its outlawry, its brief hide-and-seek with the police, its prison, exile to Siberia, flight abroad, or gallows. Every wing of the Russian revolutionary movement had been made up of such underground "professionals," and would continue to be. But Lenin alone, though he castigated them for their weaknesses, instilled in them a sense of their own importance and made a virtue of what had hitherto been a lonely necessity. Now that the masses were beginning to enter into motion on their own account, Lenin still proposed that the revolutionary party should be made up of professional revolutionists and that the masses and their wider, more elementary organizations should be directed and controlled by this underground party of professionals. As always when expounding his convictions, he was ruthlessly logical and unequivocal:

> I assert: 1. That no movement can be durable without a stable organization of leaders to maintain continuity; 2. that the more widely the masses are drawn into the struggle and form the basis of the movement, the more it is necessary to have such an organization and the more stable it must be; 3. that the organization must consist chiefly of persons engaged in revolution as a profession; 4. that in a country with a despotic government, the more we *restrict* the membership of this organization to those who are engaged in revolution as a profession . . . the more difficult it will be to catch the organization; and 5. the *wider* will be the circle of men and women of the working class or of other classes of society able to join the movement and perform active work in it.

Of course, Lenin did not object to workingmen being recruited into this classless company devoted to "their" class struggle—quite the contrary. But these would be only "exceptional workingmen," carefully selected by the professional revolutionaries, tested and trained for entrance into this élite of professional officers. Because of their lack of general culture, it would be harder for them than for the intellectuals to develop "full social-democratic consciousness" and Marxist theoretical knowledge, though they would possess, in compensation, a closer knowledge of the psychology of the class from which they had come and which they were to lead in the future. But they, too, would have to be declassed, that is, cease to be workingmen, in order to make revolution their profession. Aside from the initial advantages in psychology and disadvantages in culture, no distinction would be made in the revolutionary movement between one who had been a workingman and one who had been an intellectual before he took up this profession. ("The organizations of revolutionists must be comprised first and foremost of people whose profession is that of revolutionist . . . As this is the common feature of the members of such an organization, *all distinctions as between workers and intellectuals* must be dropped.")

In this kind of party, Lenin thought he had found not only the devices for protection against the police, but also a guarantee against theoretical weakness, lack of principle, opportunism, against the dilution of the revolutionary philosophy. Only those who had theoretically assimilated the whole range of Marxist thought and practically mastered the difficult technical arts of conspiracy were fit to make up the organization he envisaged. Such an organization, he thought, could not degenerate and could not fail. Its ideas, programs and decisions, given material force by the working class, and, beyond that, by all other discontented and aggrieved classes in tsarist society, would be able to destroy the old world and build a new. "Give us an organization of revolutionaries," exclaimed Lenin, Archimedes-like, "and we will turn Russia upside-down."

It must be clear that this "professional revolutionary" was

something quite different from the full-time paid official of the Western party or trade union. These latter are chosen by and responsible to the rank and file. Expertness, a "machine," or the passivity and inertia of the rank and file, might give them more or less permanent tenure. But always there remained the possibility of their being overruled, even removed by their membership. Lenin's plan, on the other hand, involved men who were self-chosen, who had chosen themselves as professional revolutionaries and professional leaders of a movement they were to create in their own image. At the top were the self-appointed *Iskra* editors. They, in turn, were to select their agents by careful winnowing and send them into the localities. These, in their turn, would select their local following with equal care. This organization constructed hierarchically from the top downward would set up or seek to control all broader organizations of actual workingmen, and, in the name of the workingmen, would attempt to assume leadership over the activities of other oppositional classes.

Nor were their lives as comfortable, or their "profession" as well-paid, as that of the full-time officials of other European organizations, not to mention the salaries of our American union leaders. Plekhanov, until his wife became a successful physician, earned his poor living by such mean tasks as copying and addressing envelopes; Axelrod by making and selling *kefir* ("yogurt" or "clabber"); Lenin did translations, placed an occasional article in a non-party magazine, got small sums from his mother; Trotsky, always an able journalist, gradually tapered off the receipt of aid from his family and earned his living by writing for non-party papers; Stalin worked as a night clerk in an astronomical laboratory, then lived by sleeping and eating around in the homes of members and sympathizers and collecting small sums from them. Only later did the movement, not through dues but through the donations and bequests of wealthy liberals, and, for a while after 1905, through the revolutionary holdups, acquire enough money to give these "professionals" a wage of anywhere from five or ten rubles to thirty to fifty rubles (fifteen to twenty-five dollars) a month.* Those who could get money from their families or from literary ventures often took nothing from the movement, even, like Potresov, contributing considerable sums to it.

What Lenin's theory of the centralized hierarchical organization of "professional revolutionaries" would mean in practice, what kind of party and general labor and revolutionary movement it would beget, what relations would obtain between the band of self-chosen, dedicated professionals and the still unborn mass organizations—all this was still hidden in the future. The immediate effect of the expression of this theory in *What's to Be Done?* and in the columns of *Iskra*, was to strengthen the latter journal in its feud with rival socialist papers, and to enhance Lenin's own rapidly growing reputation among the little band of professionals that made up the actual movement. The theory was truly Russian in that it was built upon the established tradition of the Narodovoltsi and other terrorists of the past: conspiracy, centralism, hierarchy, life-dedication, arrogant humility. The tiny band of *Iskra* agents were stirred by the vision of themselves as an officers' corps destined to lead mighty armies. Audacious yet detailed, the plan seemed to hold promise of overcoming the feebleness, slackness, local dispersion, transience and amateurishness which afflicted the movement. It gave new "Marxist" justification to the already traditional Russian revolutionary structure evolved by the old terrorist conspiratorial movement; it promised efficiency, uncompromising purity, ultimate victory.

While, in the underground, enthusiasm for *Iskra*, for its famous editors and its network of resolute agents steadily grew, clashes of temperament and unanalyzed differences of viewpoint slowly deepened the rifts among the editors themselves.

---

* "Those members of the Party who gave their entire time to the Party work got very small remuneration, sometimes as low as 3, 5 or 10 rubles, and never exceeding 30 rubles per month." Yaroslavsky: *History of the Communist Party*, English Edition, Moscow, 1927, Vol. V, Chapter X, p. 15.

In the painful vacuum of silence and exile, there was no superior force, no democratic rank-and-file organization to which they could submit their differences. Just because, to use Potresov's words, "we fought over special, individual, partial questions without as yet being able to catch the general sense of the differences which lay at the bottom of all these disputes," their clashes had a sharpness out of all proportion to the issues. Like the Russian intellectuals that they were, they tended to elevate every difference into a matter of principle.

Obsolescence, too, was doing its corrosive work. Not by quarter-centuries, as is the common reckoning, but by half-decades and less, did the revolutionary generations succeed each other. Plekhanov was forty-five when *What's to Be Done?* was written; Axelrod, fifty-one; Vera Zasulich, fifty. Theirs were names to conjure with, but they had been away from Russia for two decades. Lenin was thirty-one; Potresov, thirty-two; Martov, twenty-eight. Inside Russia, these three were already referred to as "the old ones." The Economists were the "youngsters." And from Siberia, a still more youthful Russian was beginning to send articles to *Iskra,* written with sufficient gusto to have earned for him the pseudonym of *Pero* ("The Pen"). This "Pen" was only twenty-two, far younger than the "youngsters"—herald of a new generations that was soon to give the Iskrists the victory over their Economist opponents. Already, Plekhanov with his mere forty-five years and his two decades of activity was alienating such young men when they disagreed with him by snapping: "Your fathers and mothers were still crawling under the table when I—" If Plekhanov was irascible, Axelrod was poor in health. Poverty and exile had taken their toll. The warmth with which Axelrod had first greeted the young Ulyanov back in 1895 had had in it an element of the feeling that at last there was something growing up inside Russia, and someone to hand over the burdens of organization. According to Krupskaya, Axelrod had "lost three-quarters of his working capacity . . . did not sleep for nights at a stretch . . . wrote with extreme intensity for months on end

without being able to finish the article on which he had started."
While Plekhanov was to waver for the next decade between
bolshevism and menshevism, it was upon the ailing Axelrod
that the task fell of working out the basic political and organizational conceptions that came to be known as menshevism.

If Plekhanov was the philosopher and Axelrod the political
thinker of the old guard, the most picturesque and lovable of its
members was Vera Zasulich. At the age of sixteen (that was
back in 1867), she had been arrested for the crime of being acquainted with the conspirator Nechaev. From then on, she
went into and out of prisons, into and out of administrative
exile, until she acquired renown by shooting the Governor General of Saint Petersburg, Trepov, because of the flogging of an
imprisoned fellow-student. Her trial—incautiously the government granted her a jury trial—turned into one long demonstration in her favor. Though her attorney had merely pleaded ex-
tenuating circumstances, the jury acquitted her. The crowd res-
cued her from police bent on her re-arrest. An "underground
railway" smuggled her out of Russia. That was in 1878, when
she was twenty-seven. During all the decades of her faithful
discipleship to Plekhanov and Axelrod, she had longed with
the deep longing of her warmly emotional being for another
sight of her beloved country. Plekhanov and Axelrod had families but she had none. She lived in cheerful penury and bohemian disorder in a tiny, tobacco-dust- and stale-smoke-laden
little room. Krupskaya tells how she used to cook her meat on
an oil stove, clipping off pieces with a pair of shears. When
some English ladies, to make conversation, asked how long she
cooked it, she answered: "If I am hungry, ten minutes; if not,
three hours."

More than once she spoke to Krupskaya of her loneliness. "I
have nobody close to me." And then, to hide the poignancy of
her feelings, "But you love me, I know. And when I die, you'll
say—dear me, we're drinking one cup of tea less—"

Krupskaya did indeed love her, and so did Lenin. ("Wait till
you meet Vera Ivanovna," he had written his wife, "there's a

person as clear as crystal.") Yet, within a couple of years, he would be proposing to oust her and Axelrod from the *Iskra* editorial board so that he might be sure of a dependable majority.

Later a rift would grow up between Lenin and the other two members of his own "triple alliance," Martov and Potresov. But so far he thought of them as "brothers" and of all differences as something arising between the three of them and the older editors. It was his bloc against Plekhanov's. A tiny episode dramatized the growing tension. In 1902, young *Pero,* "The Pen" whose writings had attracted Lenin's attention, escaped from Siberia. He fled to London to drink wisdom at the fount of the famous six, and, having received the address from an underground *Iskra* agent, went straight to Lenin's lodgings. His knock waked the still-sleeping household, and he heard Krupskaya call up to her husband: "Hallo, *Pero* has come!"

Lenin examined the new supporter, took him walking, showed him London, discussed the "Leninist" views with him, decided that the bright but inexperienced young "Pen" must remain abroad for some time to be trained, and must be coopted onto the editorial board of *Iskra* so that a seventh man might break the frequent three-three deadlock. It was an astonishing proposal to add a mere youngster to the famous board of editors. Plekhanov, sensing an eclipse of the veterans by a lineup of four against three, developed an intense dislike for "The Pen," which that young man could not understand, for he had no more idea than the rest of the Russian revolutionaries of the secret antagonisms developing in *Iskra.* The new recruit was brought into the sessions, but without a vote because of Plekhanov's opposition. When he ventured to speak his mind in an insignificant controversy, Plekhanov poured upon his head the vials of his acid irony. Young "Pen" defended himself with spirit, and proved, too, to have an eloquent, ironical tongue, so that Lenin had to call him aside to teach him tact: "You had better leave it to Martov to answer Plekhanov. Martov will cement what you break. It is better for him to cement it." When Lenin submitted to the other

editors an article from the newcomer, Plekhanov sent it back
with the notation: "I don't like the pen of your 'Pen.'"

"The style is a matter of acquisition," Lenin replied, "but
the man is capable of learning and will be useful."

Shortly thereafter, the young journalist abandoned the name
that had given rise to these feeble puns, in favor of the name
under which he was one day to become known throughout the
world: Leon Trotsky.

CHAPTER TEN

LEV DAVIDOVICH BRONSTEIN

During a heated discussion at Karlsruhe in 1903, Medem asked his opponent Trotsky: "When it comes to classifying yourself, you certainly cannot ignore the fact of national allegiance. You consider yourself, I take it, to be either a Russian or a Jew."

"No!" cried Trotsky, "you are mistaken! I am a Social Democrat, and that's all."

—The Biography of Vladimir Medem

Until the eighteenth century, the Ukraine—as its name implies—was a borderland or frontier. Only at the century's end, with the defeat of the Turks, the partition of Poland, and the dissolution of the free Cossack settlements, did Muscovy's power expand securely through the Ukraine to the shores of the Black Sea. The annexation of eastern Poland and Lithuania brought to the Tsars a considerable number of Jewish subjects, the largest and densest concentration of Jews in the world. They were desperately poor for the most part, making their living chiefly as innkeepers, petty merchants and artisans. By *ukaz* in the year 1804, Alexander I forbade his newly acquired subjects to continue in the liquor trade. But the *ukaz* opened to them a new avenue of escape out of the economic noose that had been steadily tightening about them: it offered state lands in the so-called "New Russia," the sparsely settled Ukrainian provinces of Kherson and Ekaterinoslav, for Jewish agricultural colonization. Thereby the course of history, which had been driving the Jews ever more completely out of agriculture since the decline of the Ancient World, gave promise of being reversed. Alexander's brother, Nicholas I, continued the Alexandrine policy, even granting exemption from the 25-year term of forced military service to Jews who would take up new lands and settle new villages in the midst of the steppes. In 1866, Alexander II put an end to the movement his father and his uncle had started. In 1872 much of the land was taken away from them. In 1882, after the assassination of Alexander II, in which several of the participants were Jewish, a new *ukaz* forbade Jews to rent, lease or buy further land. The noose was tightening again.

From one of these Jewish farms in the Province of Kherson, in the spring of the year 1879, a hardy, hard-working, well-built farmer named David Leontievich Bronstein set out with his wife and children to take up a larger farm in the same province, part of a run-down estate of one Colonel Yanovsky, after whom farm and village were known as Yanovka. Bronstein must have been a second, perhaps a third generation farmer, a fact testified to by the non-Jewish form of his patronymic, Leontievich, by his lack of Yiddish and Hebrew, and by his skill in husbandry. Farmer Bronstein had been born in a little Jewish town in the Province of Poltava, from which, as a small boy, his parents had taken him to the open prairie in the Province of Kherson. He spoke a broken mixture of Russian and Ukrainian, in which the latter predominated. Until he was an old man, and wanted to spell out for himself the titles of his famous son's books, he was not able to read. But he was a good judge of people, of hired help, of animals, of tools, of markets and crops. The years of life in the open plains were Russifying such families, ruralizing them, making them less and less of a "peculiar people," more and more like the neighbors around them. In spirit even more than in physical distance, Farmer Bronstein was almost completely outside the invisible ghetto walls that his grandparents had carried with them when they first entered the steppes. As his prosperity grew with the years of his unremitting toil, the small store of his piety and conformity and Jewish heritage continued to diminish. At first he kept up appearances out of habit and under pressure from relatives and Jewish neighbors, continuing to make journeys on high holy days to the synagogue in nearby Gromokley, four versts away. Mrs. Bronstein, being town-bred and a woman, was a little more conservative in such matters. She refrained from sewing on the Jewish Sabbath ("at least," one of her sons would write, "within the sight of others"), and, when that son was dangerously ill and had to be taken to the doctor on a Saturday, she refused to ride with him, sending instead a trusted Christian employee. Was it piety, or because the doctor lived in the midst of a Jewish settlement? As the children grew older, Farmer Bronstein spoke openly in their presence and hers of his disbelief in the existence of God. And even Mrs. Bronstein, though she prayed occasionally in moments of crisis, increasingly neglected ritual prescription and prayer with the increasing tale of her years.

The Bronsteins raised wheat and sheep and pigs, like their neighbors, and lived lives that were scarcely distinguishable from those around them, unless by the fact that they were not so given to drink as most, worked harder, were more foresighted, drove better bargains with the grain merchants, were able to make a go of it during the prolonged crisis of the eighties, when the competition of American, Canadian and Argentine wheat ruined so many farmers of the steppes. But their thrifty German neighbors were as sober in their habits and did every bit as well. One other distinction—perhaps ascribable to their heritage as descendants of "the People of the Book," was the respect of this illiterate farmer and his barely literate wife for book learning, not merely as something practical to be used on the farm, but more as something desirable for their children, and elevating in whoever might possess it.

When the Bronsteins moved to their Yanovka farm from the Province of Kherson, in the spring of 1879, they brought with them two children, a son and a daughter, and left behind them the graves of two others who had died in childhood. In her womb, Mrs. Bronstein carried yet another child. It was to be a lusty manchild, born that same autumn, on October 26 of the Russian calendar, or November 7 on the calendar in use in the West.* They gave him the name of Lev or Lyova, the Russian word for "lion." Many in after years would feel the name's appropriateness. It would be translated into German as Leo, and into English, French and Spanish as Leon, and, coupled with the later pen-name of Trotsky, it would become known around the world.†

* The Russian calendar was twelve days behind that of Western Europe in the nineteenth century and thirteen days behind in the twentieth. On February 1, 1918, the Soviet Government adopted the Western or "New Style" calendar. In the present work, except as otherwise noted, the Western calendar is used throughout. The Bolshevik seizure of power took place on this boy's birthday, i.e. October 25, Old Style, November 7, New Style, 1917. It is referred to in Russian literature as the October Revolution, but, of course, it is now celebrated annually on November 7.

† As the son of David Bronstein, Trotsky's legal name was Lev Davidovich Bronstein. In childhood he was generally called by the diminutive Lyova. The pen-name "Trotsky," originally adopted for underground purposes, finally displaced "Bronstein" altogether, so that in 1917 he signed himself for legal purposes Lev Davidovich Trotsky. His admirers, and even his wife in her memoirs, generally refer to him merely by the initials "L.D.," and I have seen letters of his signed with that signature.

Thirty-eight years later, the boy's birthday would, by coincidence, become the birthday of the Bolshevik Soviet power. "Mystics and Pythagoreans," Trotsky comments in his *Autobiography*, "may draw from this whatever conclusion they like. I myself noticed this odd coincidence only three years after the October uprising."

For non-Pythagoreans it is more instructive to note two other calendar events of the year 1879 which were closely intertwined with young Bronstein's fate. Two months before he was born, the Narodnaya Volya passed its sentence of death upon the reigning Tsar. Two months after his birth was born one Iosif Vissarionovich Djugashvili. The first of these events led to the assassination of Alexander II, with which began the black reaction of the eighties. As part of the reaction there was devious governmental encouragement of the first modern pogroms; the Jews were prohibited from further owning or leasing of land; the *numerus clausus* was introduced into higher education.* The second event, the birth of Iosif Djugashvili in Transcaucasia, was to provide David Bronstein with the chief antagonist of his closing years.

Yanovka was a lonely little village on a dirt road, scarcely distinguishable from the surrounding steppe, lost in sheep runs and wheat fields that spread in all directions to the horizon. The nearest postoffice was fifteen miles away, the railroad twenty-two; to see a doctor meant an overnight journey. Newspapers never reached this home; a letter was a rarity; a telegram, brought on horseback, could only signify calamity. The rest of Russia impinged on the closed life of Yanovka only to purchase wheat, levy taxes and conscripts, supply migratory workers for the harvest. Beyond Russia was a world which seemed to consist principally of two sinister places called Canada and Argentina, which, some years, dumped so much cheap wheat on the market that tight-fisted, hard-working landowner Bronstein could not make his cost of production, and his less thrifty

* A decree of 1887 limiting the number of Jews to be admitted to state schools to 10 per cent of the total number of students.

and energetic neighbors were completely ruined. It seemed
hardly likely that a lad born in this little village would ever acquire a world outlook or become a symbol of internationalism.

In the relentless language of status which his son's success
would later make into a human touchstone, David Bronstein
was a kulak. At the age of seventy, when that son was already
in the seat of power, Old Bronstein was "menaced by the Reds
because he was rich, and the Whites persecuted him because he
was my father" (Trotsky, *Autobiography,* p. 19). By dint of
parsimony and ambition and cruel, unremitting toil—his own
toil and his wife's no less than that of his hired help—by paying
no more wages than was customary or necessary, by adding
kopek to kopek, building to building, animal to animal and
acre to acre, he had come to own outright 250 acres of land and
lease an additional 400. When, by the decrees of 1882 and 1887
the Tsar forbade Jews to buy or lease new land, he was well
enough established and his neighbors friendly enough and sufficiently in need of his rubles so that subterfuge, palm-greasing,
and extra tribute on each leased or purchased acre enabled him
to continue to enlarge his farm. His long, open sheds were filled
with wheat, which he could afford to hold until the harvest
dumping of the more necessitous was over. He had well-stocked
stables, cowsheds, pigsties, chicken coops; a machine shop with
a roof that did not leak like the one which sheltered his family;
a mill with a ten-horse-power engine to grind his grain and, for
10 per cent in kind, that of all his neighbors for miles around.
The mill made him more than the most energetic farmer, it
made him the dominant figure of rural Yanovka.

As befitted an uncultured, middle-class family on the make,
the Bronsteins lived in rude, self-denying simplicity. They knew
no hunger nor want, but little luxury or leisure. Lyova, all his
life an exaggeratedly neat dresser, remembers the agony he felt
at his torn shoes when he was introduced to a revered older city
cousin come on a visit. The barns might be wood with raised
stone foundations to protect the harvest, the machine shop

with its valuable machinery might boast a tiled roof, but all through his boyhood the family lived in a house of mud which they had found on the land when they purchased it from the Tsar's original beneficiary, Colonel Yanovsky. There were deep crevasses in the mud walls, where adders nested; the roof of thatched reed was aflutter with sparrows; the rain came through in summer storms, and pots and pans had to be set in strategic places to prevent the water from making mire of the earthen floors. Only two of the five little, low-ceilinged rooms had flooring of wood: the living room, which was sanded weekly, and the tiny parlor, where the wood was painted. Fleas nested in the earthen floors of the other rooms, as Lyova had cause to remember. In winter, the snow blowing from all the corners of the open prairie walled in the adders sleeping in the crevasses, closed up the cracks, piled up above the dingy windows, making the long winter evenings longer still, keeping the occupants— idle now—snug and warm. Not until Lyova was grown and had left his father's home for good, did David Bronstein take the time and substance necessary to build himself a house of brick with roof of tin. He built it sturdily—as was his wont—so that after the Revolution of 1917 it was taken over by the government and used as a schoolhouse. That was the first time there had ever been a school in Yanovka.

There was little time for display of affection or care in the gray-colored childhood of Lev Davidovich. Both of his parents were busy about the farm, except in mid-winter. The long summer days were spent with an older brother and sister, a younger sister, a visiting aunt or two, and above all with the help: a nurse, a chambermaid, a cook, a steward, a mechanic, a fireman, a shepherd, a stableboy, a number of permanent hired laborers. These were Lyova's principal companions and tutors. When crops were large and prices high there might be scores, even hundreds of temporary workers besides, from whom to pick up scraps of information and instruction, of amusement and discomfiture. His older brother, Sasha, and his older sister, Liza, taught him his first letters. As soon as he had a little additional schooling, he displaced them as his father's "accountant," taking down the sketchy and sporadic notations dictated to him by old Bronstein whenever they came into the farmer's head. The old man could neither read nor figure until his sixtieth year, when he began to wrestle with the mysteries of the alphabet to spell out the titles of his son's books and puzzle over their contents. Mrs. Bronstein could read, albeit with difficulty. When the snow walled in the old house and made work outside impossible, she loved to sit near the great stove in the living room, whispering loudly to herself the words of some Russian novel, which had been borrowed from a library many miles away.

An ink bottle, stoppered with paper, resting on the long, low rafter; a penholder with an old and rusty pen; a copybook to take down the notations dictated by the head of the house to his children; an old number or two of some rural magazine intended for the country gentry, probably acquired with the house; the borrowed novels read by Mrs. Bronstein; the tumbledown spinet bought for sixteen rubles from a bankrupt neighbor and repaired by the versatile mechanic; a bit of schooling and music lessons for the two older children while they lived with relatives near a schoolhouse—these would appear to represent the cultural aspirations of the Bronstein family. If you pressed old Bronstein as to why he worked himself and his wife so hard and why he continued to add to his wealth and cares after he had acquired a sufficiency of both, he might at first be at a loss to answer. But he would doubtless come to it in the end that he hoped to give his children an ampler life than he had known and endow them with that respected something called an "education." The important thing was the male children. Bronstein might be irreligious, but he wanted them to learn to read the Bible in the original Hebrew for that was part of his inherited concept of learning. When his older boy showed little aptitude for studies the farmer set his hopes on his younger son.

There was little in Lyova Bronstein's childhood of the sunny gaiety, the family warmth and closeness, the atmosphere of culture, the outdoor sports, which we noted in the boyhood of Lenin. Lyova never learned to skate or swim, never entered into tests of strength or physical skill. Though he was endowed with a good frame he never developed it until years later; it took Siberia to make him aware of nature and turn him into a passionate fisher and hunter; and it took command of the Red Army to give him his military bearing. Until he learned to read, the center of his world was the farm machine shop, his chief tutor in the ways of things and men being Ivan Vasilevich Grebin, the mechanic who presided there. It was Ivan Vasilevich who cut him out his cardboard train, let him blow the bellows and thread screws and nuts, showed him how to turn wooden croquet balls on the lathe; in later years even made him a home-made bicycle on which he learned to ride. It was from the lips of Ivan Vasilevich that he got his first inkling of the complexity of human conduct. When not with the mechanic, he would play games with his little sister Olya (Olga): "hide-and-seek" in the bins of wheat, or "house" with homemade rag dolls on the torn divan in the living room. Sometimes, of a winter evening, the whole family would play "Old Maid," the father joining in with the rest. As soon as Lyova learned to read and wield a pen, the new pursuits it opened to him crowded out all the others, until even the machine shop seemed to lose its attraction.

His pen became a sort of fetish with a power and will of its own. With the help of a table knife he carved himself a new one, using it to copy pictures of horses from an old magazine. On another occasion its magic powers impelled him to write down forbidden obscenities, heard in barn and fields but never in this puritanic household. He shed copious tears when his sister caught him at it and she and his mother tried to see what was on the secretive paper. Again the mysterious pen drew verses out of him, and his sister told the family, which thought him quite a poet. The boy knew better, somehow, fleeing in shame when his father tried to make him read them aloud to guests.

With the pen's aid, he and his cousin played at editing a magazine. Clutched in his hand, it took down his father's mysterious gains and losses in contest with "Argentina," his debts and those his neighbors owed him, the calculations of the tithe for grinding at the mill, the miserable figures in kopeks and rubles that represented a summer's toil for his laborers—figures which gave the boy his first sense of the hardness of a system which left the rural laborer almost nothing to tide him over the enforced idleness of winter. The pen copied magnificent passages from the poets, eloquent speeches from the dramatists, then began to write original compositions that amazed and thrilled their author. When in later years he chose his first illegal name to throw the police off his track while he contributed articles to revolutionary journals, the name was *Pero*—"The Pen."

To the magic of the pen was closely linked the magic of the book. Books were the Arabian carpet that carried him far from drab Yanovka, lifted him aloft so that he could see great stretches of the world. From books, he learned of Russia's past and grandeur, of other provinces and kingdoms and ways of life more civilized than the rude ones his boyhood had so far known. He used books to show off, too, for he was always fond of displaying his powers. At school he deliberately read history books more advanced than the required text, and asked questions to show that he knew the answers, or to stump his teachers. In time he found that there were forbidden books: one on sexual crimes and perversions which his older brother brought home from the city and tried to hide behind other books out of reach; another by Tolstoy, called *Powers of Darkness*, which the censors had barred from the stage and which his learned cousin refused to read to him because he was "not old enough."

For a long time the world of reality around the village and farm and the world of reason, wonder and passion between the covers of books, were kept sharply separate in his mind. The farm had taught him many things, for he was curious and observant. He watched the hired help climb into the hayloft to make love, heard derisive stories about the gentry they had served, heard them berate his father with especial malice in his presence, spent so much time in kitchen, machine shop, barn and fields that he came to understand the point of view of the help and even take their side in controversies between them and his father. He found life around him hard, crude, occasionally cruel. But in the world of books he found people who were gentle and refined and exalted; they loved without evil words or haylofts or apparent physical basis; they spoke to each other in delicate, even poetic fashion of incorporeal, unterrestrial, inscrutable things. The ambit of his reading extended, his comprehension of the two worlds deepening until at last they began to merge and serve as counterpoint and clarification of each other. Where they differed, the world of books held him more closely.

> In my inner life—he wrote later—, throughout my youth, nature and individuals occupied a lesser place than books and ideas . . . The very word "author" sounded to me as if it was uttered from some unattainable height . . . From early years my love for words had been now losing, now gaining in force, but generally putting down ever firmer roots. In my eyes, authors, journalists, and artists always stood for a world which was more attractive than any other, one open only to the elect.

These words are taken from his autobiography, written in exile in Prinkipo after Stalin had deported him from Russia. In the preface to the same work he wrote:

> A well-written book in which one can find new ideas, and a good pen with which to communicate one's ideas to others, for me have always been and are today the most valuable and intimate products of culture. The desire for study has never left me, and many times in my life I felt the revolution was interfering with my systematic work . . .

In the end, Death would catch him pen in hand.

Allied to the magic of book and pen was that of the theater. During Christmastide of 1886, when Lyova was seven and had barely learned how to write, a troop of mummers descended from nowhere upon the dining room while the family was at tea. The boy was so astonished that he fell on the divan from fright and remained rooted there spellbound while Tsar Maximilian declaimed till the rude living room became a realm of splendor. Imagine his amazement when he found that Tsar Maximilian was one and the same with the hired man Prokhor! Armed with pen and paper he penetrated into the servants' quarters, where Tsar Prokhor was at rest after dinner, and plagued him to dictate his monologue. When old Bronstein interrupted the eager boy and the reluctant Tsar at their "idle" task, Lyova was inconsolable.

His first visit to a real theater took place during his initial year in school in Odessa. "It was like no other experience and beggars description," he could still write fifty years later. "I sat pale as a sheet . . . and was tortured by a joy which was more than I could bear. During the intermissions I did not leave my seat lest—God forbid!—I might miss something." Then he planned, with a boy who had actually taken part in amateur theatricals, that together they would stage Pushkin's *The Niggardly Knight*. But his partner in the enterprise was tubercular and went off somewhere to die before their dream could become reality. An original play which he tried to write with another comrade a few years later also came to naught. After he had been in Odessa a while, he developed a fondness for Italian opera, spending every spare penny and even doing extra tutoring to earn money to go to the theater. He fell in love with a coloratura soprano "bearing the mysterious name of Giuseppina Uget, who seemed to me to have descended from heaven to the stage-boards of the Odessa theater." But since this was his third "love affair," it is clear that we are running a little ahead of our story.

Before we leave the subject of the stage, however, we must note that all his life this ardent follower of the theater retained a strong sense of drama. One could note it in his erect carriage on the public platform, in his scrupulous neatness and liking for being well dressed, in his boyish love of a student uniform, his later military outfit and bearing as War Commissar, his conduct of his own case in a tsarist courtroom in 1906, his blinding eloquence on the rostrum, his skillful dramatization of every role his highly dramatic life provided. His life possessed style no less than his writing, that touch of heightening which, when not carried to excess, makes for a compelling type of attraction and leadership while one has the center of the stage, and emphasizes the tragedy of a fall from high place. In his writings he would become one of the greatest stylists that the socialist movement had produced since the days of Marx. In the dramatization of his life none would equal him since the days of Marx's contemporary, Lassalle.

At the age of seven Lyova began his first schooling. For that purpose he went from Yanovka to nearby Gromokley, two and one-half miles away, to live with his Aunt Rachel and Uncle Abram near a Jewish village school. His teacher, a lean, apologetic, self-effacing man, plagued by a frolicsome wife, instructed him in Russian, arithmetic, and the Bible in the original Hebrew. With the other children Lyova had little to do, for their talk was in Yiddish, a language he did not understand. He became dimly aware here that the Jews were a people apart, held in some inferior status by incomprehensible forces. The village was divided by a ravine, on one side of which were prosperous German farmhouses, most of them with tiled roofs, on the other the dilapidated huts of the Jews. His most vivid memory of Gromokley was of the coercive force of the Ghetto when it turned out to drag a woman of evil repute through its miserable street, shouting at her, cursing, screaming, spitting. Later the community secured from the authorities the deportation of the young woman's father to far-off Siberia as an alleged horse thief. This "biblical" scene made a deeper impression on the boy than all the passages of ill-understood Hebrew shouted in chorus with his fellows. But, had his schooling ended with this meager year at Gromokley, as did that of most of his schoolmates, it would have left little mark upon him.

The peculiarities of that "peculiar people," the Jews, are largely a product of their centuries of intensive urbanization. Two or three generations of rustication had almost wiped out the influence of the city on the Bronstein family, but when the city came to Yanovka, adorned with gentleness and learning, in the shape of a scholarly cousin from Odessa, its appeal to young Lyova was instantaneous. Moisey Filippovich Shpentser was a man of book and pen, hence this unlettered family treated him with deference. He had come to the farm to drink fresh milk, eat fresh eggs, breathe fresh air, and fight off incipient tuberculosis. A *gymnazia* graduate, he had been excluded from the university for a minor political peccadillo. He made his modest living by free-lance journalism, writing children's books, preparing history texts, translating and annotating Greek classics, doing statistical work. He was shortly to open a little publishing house, which in later years would prosper. He was engaged to be married to the principal of a state school for Jewish girls, a fact which inspired even more awe in the Bronsteins than did his own learning. Finding no one else in Yanovka on whom to exercise his intellectual powers, he set to work on Lyova Bronstein, read to him, answered his incessant questions, taught him how to speak grammatically, how to hold a clean glass with the fingers outside, not inside, how to distinguish the Ukrainian part of his vocabulary from the Russian, and—more by example than by words—to feel a sense of revulsion at some of the cruelties and barbarities of the rude life of Yanovka.

In the spring of the next year, 1888, the Shpentser marriage having duly taken place, Lyova left his home in Yanovka to go to live with the Shpentsers in populous Odessa. He was fitted out with a new suit, a large trunk containing butter, jam and other rustic gifts for city relatives, and such clothing as the country might furnish to a future city-dweller. Though his autobiography complains of the "grayness" of the childhood years he was leaving behind him and the lack of attention and affection, when he left Yanovka he suddenly felt that it was very dear to him. His mother and sisters wept. He wept long and loud with them, continued sobbing all the way across the steppe until the cart came to the main road. Then he straightened up as befits a lad who is going to the big city to seek wisdom.

CHAPTER ELEVEN

LYOVA BECOMES A POPULIST

A shudder passes over us when we hear the terrible story of what happened in the theater. How do we Jews, who are likened to a little worm—the worm of Jacob—come to get messed up in such matters? How do we Jews, who, according to all sense and reason, are always obligated to pray for the well-being of the sovereign power, without whom we would long since have been swallowed alive—how do we Jews dare to climb to such high places and meddle in politics? Oh, beware, Jewish children! Look well what you are doing! God only knows what you may bring upon our unfortunate nation, upon yourselves, and upon your families. Our people always were proud of one thing—that they never had any rebels among them; and now you desire to wipe out this virtue too. We hope you will think well about all this and you will not wish to place in jeopardy the happiness of our whole nation, your own fate and the fate of your parents and your families.

—SERMON OF THE CHIEF RABBI OF MINSK
IN 1902 AFTER HIRSCH LECKERT ATTEMPTED TO
ASSASSINATE THE GOVERNOR OF VILNA.

oisy, colorful, many-tongued Odessa was founded as a free port in 1794 by émigré Frenchmen. When Lyova Bronstein went there nearly a century later, it had great wharves and harbors and a turbulent waterfront, behind which rose on terraces a busy city, overlooking Odessa Bay and the Black Sea. It was a place where a boy could get the foundations of cosmopolitanism if not internationalism. Ukrainians, Great Russians, Jews, Italians, Germans, Frenchmen, Englishmen, Greeks, Armenians, Persians, Syrians, Turks, Tartars, rubbed elbows, drove bargains, exchanged currencies, goods, vocabularies, ideas, on the easy principle of live and let live. The Jews were the largest single group in Odessa, 30 per cent of the total population. Among so many urban, mercantile peoples from the Near East, they had not stood out especially nor felt any unusual discrimination. But, one year before Lyova's arrival, the *numerus clausus* decree limited Jewish students to 10 per cent of the student body despite the fact that Jews formed 30 per cent of the city's population. The nine-year-old candidate for learning was one of the first victims.

The Shpentsers chose for their ward the Saint Paul *Realschule,* founded by the local German colony for the education of its own children on the "progressive" and "practical" principle of mathematics, sciences and modern languages, rather than the classics. Shpentser chose it not out of admiration for the curriculum but out of consideration for the fact that the *Realschule* would be easier for a poorly trained rural Jewish boy to get into than the more crowded classical *gymnazia.* The entrance examinations, however, laid bare the gaps in the boy's training. A "4" in Arithmetic and a "3" in Russian—"3" being a bare passing mark under a system in which 5 equals 100—were not enough to win Bronstein a place among the top 10 per cent of Jewish applicants.

Thereupon, the Shpentsers, wise in the ways of the Odessa educational system, enrolled him in the Saint Paul preparatory class, thus giving him preference over outside Jewish applicants for the ensuing year. He was, after all, very young, his parents having falsified his age by a year to expedite his eligibility. Thus, despite the lost time, he actually entered the *Realschule* at the minimum age of ten. Nor was the year wasted, either. The low marks were a spur, so that the mediocre arithmetician of the year before became top man in mathematics and dreamed of taking up pure mathematics as a career. The year's training in discrimination between the Ukrainian and Russian elements in his vocabulary, and the increment of maturity in the ideas expressed in his compositions, helped to make him top man in the Russian class also. His teacher made a point of reading his compositions aloud to the class and rating them with the prideful mark of "5 plus." Thus the career of author continued to exert its rival attraction to the new dream of mathematician, while old David Bronstein hoped that his promising son would become an engineer.

There are those who would interpret the subsequent stormy life of this boy in terms of the Jewish rebel whose rebellion arises out of racial persecution, or compensation for enforced inferiority. For this view, the year lost because of the *numerus clausus* is virtually the only point of support. In Yanovka, where David Bronstein was the leading farmer, respected by all his neighbors, the lad had known no discrimination. In Odessa, the growing trend to Russification which began with the accession of Alexander III (1881-94) weighed heavily upon Saint Paul's. But it was the Germans, who had founded and directed the school and made up the largest group of its pupils, that were the chief victims. Next in order came the Ukrainians, for whose land Odessa was the chief seaport. To guarantee the Russification of those who had gone through so German a school, the government obliged the students to spend their final year in a Russian state institution. The German Lutheran director, the German chaplain, and many of the teachers of German origin, were forced out during Lyova's seven years there. The Orthodox Russian priest who gave instruction in religion was patronizing to the boys who had to leave the room for other mentors, but his derogatory remarks were addressed to German Protestants and Roman Catholic Poles no less than to Jewish boys. The history teacher directed caddish questions concerning the reverses and "crimes" of their respective peoples at Polish and Ukrainian pupils. Bronstein, however, he treated with unfailing correctness as the star history student, even with a little fear, because Lyova would wade through the advanced books in Shpentser's personal library and use his extra knowledge to ask questions to which the instructor did not know the answers.

In this matter of nationality, like most of the Jews of the large urban centers of the Ukraine, the boy and his guardian unconsciously sided with the Great-Russian administrators and the superior Great-Russian culture as against the Ukrainian peasants and the handful of Ukrainian intellectuals who were striving to create a Ukrainian language and literature, and beginning to aspire to autonomy for their culture and their land. To Lyova Bronstein, all his life, as is revealed in his autobiography written in 1929, the Ukrainian tongue was no language, but a peasant "dialect" or "jargon." Insensibly, this would color his attitude towards the independent Ukrainian Republic which his armies would crush in 1919.

Far from giving him a sense of inferiority, his school triumph made the little lad from Yanovka vain and sure of himself. He never doubted for a moment in those days that he would get ahead in a world which he imagined to be very much like a greater classroom, where his compositions would always be good enough to be read aloud, where in the competitive struggle for marks his would always be "5" and "5 plus" and his place would always be at the "head of the class." Whatever the forces were that drove him during his sixteenth to eighteenth years to abandon thoughts of a career as mathematician or engineer—but never that of author—in favor of the profession of revolutionary, they were in the main the same forces that drove his entire generation of student youth in the same direction.

Important as the role of the Jew has been in the Russian revolutionary movement (there was no *numerus clausus* for intellectuals there), it has been much exaggerated and misinterpreted by Russian monarchist and German Nazi writers. In their zeal to expound the thesis of "Jewish bolshevism," they have passed over in silence the role of Jews like Martov and Axelrod, the two leading ideologists of menshevism, and made all they could and more out of the prominent place of Zinoviev (Radomysl-ski), Kamenev (Rosenfeld), and, above all, Trotsky, among the Bolsheviks. Actually there were many more intellectuals of Jew-ish origin among the Mensheviks than among the Bolsheviks and the few who were associates of Lenin, like Trotsky and his Russian Orthodox-born brother-in-law, Kamenev-Rosenfeld, were likely to be "unjewish Jews": non-professing, Russified, brought up outside the pale. The bulk of the Jewish masses, insofar as they were politically organized, were to be found in neither wing, but in specifically Jewish movements like the Jewish General Workers Union or Bund, and the Zionist or-ganizations. In 1917, in the hour of Bolshevik triumph, there was not one among Lenin's associates with sufficient knowl-edge of the language of the mass of Jews, or sufficient under-standing of their outlook, to start a paper in Yiddish. Only aft-er a section of the Bund joined the Bolsheviks could that task be undertaken.

To understand the role of the Jew in the Russian labor move-ment we must bear in mind a few facts concerning his position in old Russia. There were more Jews there after the partition of the Kingdom of Poland and Lithuania, than in any other land on earth. In the course of the nineteenth century their numbers had grown by natural increase from a little less than a million to a round five million, while bit by bit the noose of closed areas of settlement and forbidden occupations was tightening around them. Herded into the teeming ghettos of the Jewish pale, they were reduced largely to trading with, and working for, each oth-er under increasingly miserable conditions, like the legendary Chinese who lived by taking in each other's washing. Cultur-ally, they tended to hold themselves superior to the Polish, Lithuanian and Latvian peasants around them, continuing to speak their German dialect—which developed into Yiddish—

or adopting the superior, dominant culture of ruling Great-Russia. Thus, almost unconsciously, most of the Jews of the cities of Poland, Lithuania and the Ukraine tended to become opponents of the national separation movements that arose during the breakup of the Empire in 1917.

More urban by far than the general population of Russia, they produced more than their proportionate share of the men and women of the professions, those who lived by ideas and ideals, those who engaged in that most urban of activities: politics. There was not a liberal, radical or revolutionary movement in Russia, from the Constitutional Democrats to the "peasant socialism" of the Social Revolutionists, that did not have some Jewish intellectuals among its leadership. This was due to the double yoke of oppression which weighed upon them, and to the passion with which they delivered themselves to ideas. Doubtless their inherited background of urbanism, their wandering past, their sense of kinship with the fate of Jews dispersed through many lands, tended to promote cosmopolitanism and internationalism among them, an internationalism which sometimes took a socialist, sometimes a liberal-humanitarian and pacifist, sometimes a Zionist form. For, paradoxical as it sounds, Zionism, too, is a peculiar international nationalism.

Never numerous in absolute terms, or in comparison with the number of Great-Russians that figured in such leaderships, Jews nevertheless were to be found in the leadership of all Russian oppositional movements in larger numbers than the proportion their people bore to the total population. Five Jewish names among the doughty band that besieged and assassinated Alexander II were sufficient to cause Alexander III to visit the fury of his fright on "all their kindred," whence the first pogroms of modern times (1882), the *numerus clausus,* and the land exclusion law, which affected the lives of farmer Bronstein and his son.

If about 50 per cent of the Jewish population lived by small business and trade, about 30 per cent, more than is generally realized, were artisans and mechanics. More compact, more proletarianized, more influenced by Western socialist ideas than was the great peasant Russian mass, these Jewish artisans gave the first strong impulse to labor organization, in their own ranks, and then among the Russian workingmen. While the revolutionary movement of the Empire as a whole was still made up almost completely of intellectuals, the Jewish General Workers Union of Poland and Lithuania (the Bund) was not only working class in composition, but even in leadership. Of the Bund's thirteen founders, only five were intellectuals, at a time when in the leadership of the *Iskra* group there were no workingmen at all.

Deutsch and Axelrod, Russified Jewish intellectuals, were among the founders of Russian Marxism along with Plekhanov and Zasulich. Martov (Tsederbaum), after a brief period as a member of the Jewish Bund, broke with it to become Lenin's chief collaborator in the Petersburg League. Martov and Axelrod were two of the six editors of *Iskra,* and, when the Iskrists split into Mensheviks and Bolsheviks, they became the theoreticians of menshevism. Indeed, despite the Nazi-fostered legend of "Jewish bolshevism," Jews always played a much larger role in the "Westernizing" Menshevik wing than in the much more specifically Russian Bolshevik wing of the Party.

What is perhaps more surprising is that even the "peasant socialist" Social Revolutionary Party had a much higher proportion of Jews in its leadership than did the Bolsheviks: Gershuni, Mikhail and Abram Gotz, Fundaminsky, Rubanovich, Vishniak, Azev, Minor, Zhitlovsky, the two Rappaports, and later Kamkov, Natanson, and Steinberg, the Internationalist Left Social Revolutionaries who were to cooperate with the Bolsheviks in their dictatorship. Of course, as we survey the total list of leaders, the Jewish names prove to be no more than a minor fraction. But the propagandists of reaction, striving to create an abyss between the peasant-worker masses and the revolutionary intellectuals and to channel discontent into the by-pass of antisemitism, did their best to stress every Jewish name and make it appear as if all these opposition movements were "Jewish" and alien to Russia.

Outside the mass of artisans and workingmen who formed the Bund and the sprinklings of Jews that took part in other oppositional movements, there was a solid body of conservative Jewry. The bulk of the rabbinate and of the orthodox religious Hebrews, the bulk of those engaged in trade, the privileged whose privileges depended upon the favors of the government, the timid and conformist of all classes, that 2 to 3 per cent of Jewish farmers, most of those who were permitted to live outside the pale of settlement, were inclined to be conservative and to doubt, if not deplore, the activities of their oppositional brethren.

"Lyova," said Farmer Bronstein to his son, "this thing will not come to pass even in three hundred years." And when that son, as resident of the Kremlin, reminded his father of the prophecy, there was paternal pride and a core of still unbroken stubbornness in the old man's answer: "This time, let your truth prevail!" Having known persecution from his son's comrades for his wealth, and from his son's enemies for his paternity of the stormy petrel of revolution, he spent his last few years as a bewildered and unregenerate employee of the state his boy had helped to found: directing a little government-owned grinding mill near Moscow until typhus carried him off in 1922. As he lay dying, his son, at the height of his prestige and power, was delivering a report on the world situation at the Fourth Congress of the Communist International. Some of the bitterest opponents of what Trotsky stood for at that moment were to be found among Jewish intellectuals, Jewish organized workers, Jewish merchants. Hundreds of thousands of them had fled abroad rather than make their peace with bolshevism, while the latter had outlawed in Russia both the more largely Jewish Menshevik and Social Revolutionary Parties and the wholly Jewish Zionist movement and Bund. Later, Trotsky, Zinoviev, Kamenev, the few names that had been used to give a semblance of support to the legend of "Jewish bolshevism," were to disappear in the purges. The Bund lived on as a mass movement of Jewish labor in Poland, to give a heroic account of itself in the tragic Warsaw insurrections of World War II. The scattered remnant of menshevism abroad still has a fairly high proportion of Jewish names among its leaders. But in the immediate entourage of Stalin, only one, Kaganovich, is to be found whose parents accounted themselves Jews.

The boy from Yanovka slept behind a curtain in the dining room of the Shpentser home. He was held to an agreeable discipline, so different from the random life on the farm and so much more divorced from concrete physical things: homework, reading, being read aloud to, early bedding and early rising, proper language, elimination of "Ukrainian jargon" words from his speech, personal cleanliness, common courtesy, urbane social forms, humane and literate conversation, enthusiasm for fine sentiments, good books, and large ideas. Only the problem of getting the lad to bed with page or chapter unfinished, or the next one unread, required any exercise of constraint. In all other matters, example was more potent than prescript. Self-regard, vanity, the attractiveness of the things of the mind and the social graces which Yanovka had denied to him, made the boy a ready imitator of the superior models before him. Insensibly, too, the high examples of conversation, thought and conduct in the great classics of Russian literature sank into his soul. In after-years he would go from prison to prison, storm the heights of power, rush from front to front in the hard years of famine and civil war, but always he would care for his personal appearance, remain scrupulous to the point of prudery in his vocabulary, cherish the world of culture and books to which the Shpentsers were now introducing him. Shortly before his fall from power he would write a little brochure such as no other of his comrades could have composed, a series of homely lay sermons called *Problems of Life* (1923). In it he would urge upon the victorious proletariat, with its deep-rooted tradition of cursing and obscenity, the use of "cultured speech," the employment of "civility and politeness as a necessary lubricant in daily relationships," a "fight against bad language as part of the struggle for the purity, clearness and beauty of Russian speech."

Then, even as the ways were being greased for his disappearance from public life, he switched from homely sermons to some of the most audacious flights of fancy that socialist writing had offered since the days of Marx and Lassalle. The closing passages of his *Literature and Revolution* (1924) envisaged a future world where

> . . . the imperceptible antlike piling up of quarters and streets, brick by brick, from generation to generation, will give way to titanic construction of city-villages, with map and compass in hand. Around this compass will be formed . . . the parties of the future . . . Architecture will again be filled with the spirit of mass feeling and moods . . . Mankind will educate itself plastically, will become accustomed to looking at the world as submissive clay for sculpting the most perfect forms of life . . . Man will occupy himself with re-registering mountains and rivers . . . rebuilding the earth, if not in his own image, then at least according to his own taste . . . More than that, man at last will begin to harmonize himself in earnest. He will make it his business to achieve beauty by giving the movement of his own limbs the utmost precision, purposefulness and economy in his work, his walk, his play. He will try to master first the semiconscious and then the subconscious processes in his own organism. Social construction and psychophysical self-education will become two aspects of one and the same process. All the arts—literature, drama, painting, music and architecture—will lend this process beautiful form . . . Man will become immeasurably stronger, wiser and subtler; his body will become more harmonized, his movements more rhythmic, his voice more musical. The forms of life will become dynamically dramatic. The average human type will rise to the heights of an Aristotle, a Goethe, or a Marx. And above this ridge new peaks will rise.

It is not too far-fetched to see the elevating influence of the Shpentsers, the prophetic extremism of the Russian classics, the violence of the farm boy's reaction to the crudeness and spiritual poverty of life at Yanovka, still at work in this little series of Red sermons and in this audacious vision of the future. Our hardest task will be to keep in mind this side of his nature and to trace in the combative and often difficult personality of Leon Trotsky the subterranean line which leads from the boy who slept behind the curtain in the Shpentser home in Odessa to that rebel who could leave such a luminescent trail behind him in his fall.

Like every big seaport, Odessa had its rough and seamy side: its taverns, waterfront dives, sailors trying to crowd into a few brief days of shore leave all the things the land offers and the sea denies. But that side of the great port never entered into Lyova Bronstein's life. Though the sea danced and beckoned at the city's edge, he never learned to swim, nor went rowing or fishing as the other students did. No image of the sea ever seems to have figured in his writings. Taverns were "out of bounds" for the students, and Lyova, at least, did not enter one until it became part of the defiant routine of the day after graduation. It was as if mighty Odessa were some little inland town, made up of a school, a library, a theater, an opera house, a few friendly homes and familiar connecting streets. "The street" as such did not exist for him. Brawls, so common among the students, he detested. When a bully from another school tried to pick a fight about some of the meaningless things on which growing boys feed their combativeness, he disarmed the challenger by politely inquiring: "What is it you want of me?" so that the quarrel died in mutual bewilderment.

Athletic competitions and physical games held no attraction either. In recompense, he entered with a will into a different type of rivalry: to excel, to surprise the teacher, to lead the class, to talk well, to write well—these were his ambitions and in these he found his triumphs and pleasures. He would comb through books, fragmentarily for the most part, to garner a few elegant phrases and sparkling ideas to embed in his own compositions. He would read works intended for older heads than his in order to surprise his teachers with abstruse and difficult questions. He picked up easily viewpoints, attitudes, pieces of information, from the conversation of the Shpentsers and their guests or from random browsing through books. He possessed the gift of employing, combining, displaying his smallish acquisitions in the show window so that people would get the idea that behind it was a well-stocked store. But he was capable of a feeling of shame afterward and of fierce self-depreciation when he found that there were others who had really mastered the books he but pretended to know. The desire to shine was not altogether cut loose from the desire to know, to be able, and to excel. Yet it took many years before the latter dominated the former.

The infant publishing house which Shpentser founded about the time Lyova came to live with him, and which in later years grew to be the largest editorial enterprise in Southern Russia, took the place which the machine shop at Yanovka had earlier held in his affections. Here he learned type, make-up, layout, printing, paging, binding, made a pastime of the correction of proofs. This was his nearest connection in Odessa to actual, physical things. To happy hours spent thus he attributes his life-long love of the freshly printed page. In the years of the Civil War, one of his few pleasures was the printing press he carried with him on his armored train and the military newspaper and resounding proclamations he issued as he hurried from front to front. In the last years of his exile in Mexico, though he was surrounded by secretaries who would gladly have relieved him of such cares, he still insisted on going personally over the proofs of the articles, pamphlets and books which came from his pen.

His actual schooling, as distinguished from the cultural guidance of the Shpentsers and the personal adventuring in the world of books, left upon him a residual impression of grayness. The courses were routine and heavy with formalism and taboo, the texts dull and lifeless, the teachers petty, uninspiring and uninspired. The boy was not one to make personal attachments. At Yanovka only his younger sister Olga had been close to him, she who was afterward to become a revolutionary like her more celebrated brother and end up as the wife of the Bolshevik leader Leo Kamenev. At school there was not one outstanding teacher whom he could regard with gratitude and affection, or whose teaching he could carry with him consciously through a lifetime. Nor was there a single schoolmate whose friendship he would cherish after graduation. In his inner life, to use his own apt phrase, "nature and individuals occupied a lesser place than books and ideas . . . people passed through my mind like random shadows . . ." He was talking of his youth, but with rare and counted exceptions this was true of him all his life.

The "star pupil" was never late, did his homework assiduously, was quiet at his desk; listened attentively, learned quickly and precisely, answered—with invariable attention to what was expected—all the questions put to him; wrote well, recited well, easily led his class; was respectful to his teachers in the classroom, bowed deferentially when he met them on the street. Yet even so proper and bright a boy came into conflict with the régime.

The conflict arose out of a combination of accidental things with his own dawning sense of justice. The teacher of French, a man named Burnande, hated all German boys with a cold fury, and delighted in torturing the backward for their backwardness. His chief butt was one Wacker, a dullard and fawner for whom Lyova felt no liking. Yet he, along with many of his classmates, thought that Burnande was unjust to Wacker; with that rude sense of solidarity so common in schoolboys, they decided to teach the teacher a lesson. They planned a "concert," which consisted of "music" made by howling with shut mouth, to avoid detection, while the teacher was departing from the classroom. Inquisition yielded ten or twelve culprits for detention after school, though Lyova was not among them and felt no call to confess his complicity. During their detention, some of the worst and most backward boys, the ungrateful Wacker included, accused Bronstein of being a participant, even the ringleader. One added the terrifying information that Bronstein had proposed the writing of a joint letter to the Inspector General asking for Burnande's dismissal. In the petition—a neat conspirative detail that really suggested the head of the "star pupil"—each boy was to write a single character so that no one could be held responsible.

In vain did the Shpentsers intervene, urging their own experience as teachers, the boy's youth and record. A solemn trial was held by the faculty council, which considered three degrees of penalty: permanent expulsion from the school system, expulsion from Saint Paul's with no right of reinstatement, and expulsion with the right of reentry a year later if he could pass the requisite examinations. They adopted the mildest of the three measures. When Shpentser brought home to the waiting boy the fateful verdict of expulsion, he turned green, so that they thought he was going to faint. They were scarcely less frightened themselves, for Shpentser remembered his own blasted educational career. Nor did they know how to apprise old Bronstein.

Lyova stayed out the term in Odessa as if nothing had happened, then went on a visit to a friend's home while his older sister, tearful and frightened, was entrusted with the task of informing the stern old man. The boy returned to his home at last, to be greeted by stony silence. For three days not a word, then, in a moment of family reunion, Farmer Bronstein broke into hearty laughter, crying: "Show me how you whistled at your headmaster. Like this? With two fingers in the mouth?" Lyova tried to assure him that it was not whistling and not the headmaster. The mother burst into tears. The old man, as if the episode tickled his vanity, laughed harder than ever. Then he paid for a private tutor so that Lyova might make the next grade along with his classmates.

Even before the episode, the star pupil from Yanovka had

based his friendships among the students on their acknowledgment of his own leadership. On reentering the class, to quote a self-revealing passage from his autobiography:

> ... I met most of the boys who had either betrayed me, or defended me, or had remained neutral. This determined my personal relations for a long time ... Such, one might say, was the first political test I underwent. These were the groups that resulted from that episode: the tale-bearers and the envious at one pole, the frank, courageous boys at the other, and the neutral, vacillating mass in the middle. These three groups never quite disappeared during the years that followed. I met them again and again in my life, in the most varied circumstances.

The reader will do well to bear this passage in mind when he comes to Leon Trotsky's subsequent "political tests." It will help us to understand the vicissitudes in the latter's relations with the men and women he met in the revolutionary movement, above all the astonishing ruptures and feuds that characterized Trotsky's closing years in his personally led "Fourth International."

The episode of the "concert" for the French teacher was followed by a conflict of lesser scope with a new Russian teacher, who failed to read and mark the themes he exacted from his pupils. Both incidents suggest that in Lyova Bronstein there was growing up a feeling of indignation at injustice. Imperceptibly this feeling had been nourished by a whole series of childhood experiences at Yanovka, experiences which were evaluated increasingly with the criteria supplied by the attitude of the Shpentsers and the ideals of the masterpieces of Russian literature. His contact with the servants and laborers at Yanovka had made them aware of their humble viewpoint. He remembered a woman's walking seven versts and sitting submissively a whole day on his father's doorstep to collect a ruble; the arrest of two peasants for their failure to renew their passports; a sitdown strike of the farm help—no worse treated than most—because they did not get enough to eat; a man pleading with his father for the release of a cow that had trespassed on the Bronstein field; the shame he felt when old Bronstein failed to tip a porter adequately and the latter cursed at him; the spectacle of an overseer striking a shepherd with a knout because he had kept the horses out late, with Shpentser standing by, face pale, hissing between clenched teeth, "how shameful!"

He began to contrast the more shameful things around him with an ideal, imaginary world of Western Europe and America. In that world there was literacy, culture, democracy, freedom of speech and press, parliamentarism. Bit by bit he built up his picture of it from conversations and fragmentary remarks in books, from the prevailing "Westernism" of the liberal intelligentsia. If they were not permitted to criticize the Russian institutions, they could still describe—and idealize—those which were found elsewhere. The boy from Yanovka was becoming, without knowing the terms, a "Westernizer" and a rationalist. His inexorable rationalism made him believe that consistency prevailed everywhere but in Russia, that whatever was agreed to in principle was universally applied in practice. Later he was astonished to learn that in Western Europe "people could have superstitions and the Church exercise a great influence," that in the democratic United States there was race discrimination against the Negro, that throughout the West there were whole areas of culture and well-being closed to millions. The same rationalism made him indignant when, on vacation in Yanovka, he could not persuade his old hero, the mechanic, that perpetual-motion machines were theoretically impossible, or could not convince the local peasants that his methods of mathematical mensuration of their fields were superior to their old, inaccurate rule-of-thumb methods. He was indignant, too, when his classmates walked out of the science class talking of the unlucky number thirteen. Every such inconsistency made him feel as if human reason were being degraded and his own intelligence personally outraged. He felt capable of doing any mad thing to convince those around him to be consistent.

It was largely via this abstract intellectual route of critical rationalism that he arrived at his ultimate revolutionary position. Through all his writings runs the guiding thread of worship of reason: sometimes it takes the form of doctrinaire pedantry; sometimes vitriolic scorn of all waverings, half-measures, middle positions and inconsistencies; at its worst it degenerates into abstract, diagrammatic sectarianism, impotent to obtain any purchase upon the changing and complicated reality of a given moment; at its best it gives his writing a tremendous intellectual sweep and eloquence, enables him to grasp the most varied and random facts on the wing and link them to the unifying thread of brilliant generalization. Unlike Lenin, whose long-run objective was the physical one of taking power, and who, never losing that end from view, was a flexible tactician, a steersman changing the course of his skiff with every hidden rock and every twist and turn in the rapids, Trotsky early elaborated a single, unchanging, intellectual direction-principle (that of "permanent revolution") and stuck to it, applying it well or ill on a national and a world scale, from 1905 to the day of his murder. Other men might lose their vision of their distant goal in concentration on the next step of their march route; he would be more likely to lose his sense of the next step with too-fixed gazing on the distant goal to perceive the broken nature of the terrain he was treading. "Without a broad political view of the future," he would write, "I cannot conceive either of political activity or of intellectual life in general." Socialism itself he was to envisage as an "effort to rationalize life, i.e. transform it according to the dictates of reason. . . . It is only socialism that has set itself the task of embracing reason and subjecting all the activities of man to it." During the leisure hours of his exile in Siberia, he would try to reorganize his personal life and attitudes, "to consider from the new viewpoint [of Marxism], the so-called 'eternal' problems of life: love, death, friendship, optimism, pessimism . . ." In a backward glance over his career up to his exile in Prinkipo in 1929 he would write:

> . . . the feeling of the supremacy of the general over the particular became an integral part of my literary and political work. The dull empiricism, the unashamed, cringing worship of the fact, which is so often only imaginary and falsely interpreted at that, were odious to me. Beyond the facts I looked for laws. Naturally, this led me more than once into hasty and incorrect generalizations, especially in my younger years when my knowledge, book-acquired, and my experience in life, were still inadequate. But in every sphere, barring none, I felt that I could move and act only when I held in my hand the thread of the general. The social-revolutionary radicalism which has become the permanent pivot for my whole inner life grew out of this intellectual enmity toward the striving for petty ends, toward out-and-out pragmatism, and toward all that is ideologically without form and theoretically ungeneralized.

That is Leon Trotsky's own conception of how he became a revolutionary.

It is instructive to compare the respective approaches of Lenin and Trotsky to this problem of the relation of the particular to the general. Both acknowledged the theoretical Marxist conception in which the general is derived from the particular and in turn applied to, tested by, and modified by further intercourse with the particular. But, in all his writing and thinking, Trotsky's emphasis is on "the supremacy of the general over the particular," whereas Lenin again and again emphasizes the view that "the truth is always and everywhere concrete." This difference in emphasis is in large measure the key to a difference in style, approach and political method.

The year 1896, at the end of which Lyova turned seventeen, marked a sharp break in his life. It was a year of important textile strikes and social agitation. (Lenin, Martov, and their associates spent it in jail, waiting for deportation to Siberia.) The strikes caused the intelligentsia, young and old, to become aware of the nascent labor movement and to go over in great numbers from theoretical populism to "legal Marxism."

At the year's opening, Bronstein completed his course at Saint Paul's. He left it without regret, to take his final year of secondary education elsewhere. Neither he nor the school authorities could imagine then that one day his stay there might be regarded as its chief glory, and that Saint Paul's name would be hauled down in order to put over it the name of L. D. Trotsky.

At home that summer he was especially restless and ill at ease. His book learning, which had given him all the little successes that fed his vanity, did not seem to impress anyone about his father's farm. More than ever he shrank from the crudeness with which social relations and the forces of life seemed to be laid bare. There was more than one useless argument between father and son on his still vague oppositionist and liberal leanings. The seven years in Odessa had made Lyova a stranger in the home where he had spent the first nine years of his childhood. Sensing the change, shrewd David Bronstein sought to keep a closer watch on his son by arranging for his last academic year to be spent at Nikolaev instead of Odessa.

Nikolaev was smaller and closer, a lesser seaport, also with a large Jewish population. The change meant that the lad had to board at a stranger's instead of with the Shpentsers. It meant separating him from his classmates and thrusting him, at a critical age, into an entirely new environment. Important in that environment was something old Bronstein had not reckoned with: as a smaller town, Nikolaev was a permitted residence for some of the old exiles of the Narodnaya Volya, who had completed their terms in Siberia. Radical talk—there was no such thing as organization—was more fashionable here than in Odessa. The mistress of Lyova's own boarding-house turned out to have several children, older than he, who professed to be socialists.

With the cocksureness of ignorance, the new boarder picked arguments with them, assuring them that their "utopias" were old stuff for him and that he, with his mellow seventeen years of wisdom, had long outgrown such childishness. A model for her own children, thought the mistress of the boarding-house! A dangerous model he proved to be, however, for the next few months found him fighting an unequal battle against being carried away by the overwhelming current of opposition which was once more taking possession of the student youth. Yet a few months more, and he would be swimming vigorously with the current, dragging her children after him.

Now the "star student" from Saint Paul's seemed to deteriorate. He neglected his homework, stayed up late, failed to hand in assignments, played truant, got by on his past study. The transition from dutiful, neutral-minded grind to thinking person often manifests such contradictory forms. The chewed-out straw of the textbooks, the daily minuscule pellets of unrelated fact and information, lost all savor. He hungered for stronger fare: for culture and wisdom rather than rules and facts, for understanding, rather than definitions. He wanted to begin his education—which is always self-education—but he found himself in an intellectual forest: so many promising titles, so many false trails, so many alluring perspectives. He did not come from a cultured home as Vladimir Ilyich had; nor did he possess the same plodding persistence and thoroughness, the same unwillingness to talk until he knew what he was talking about. Was there not some one work, or at least some one subject, which would be the key to everything? He wanted to become wise overnight, find answers to questions which he could not even formulate, grasp great systems of thought by violence, by an impetuous effort of the will.

He tackled Mill's *Logic,* lured by the promise of its title until its cool formalism disillusioned him. In like fashion he dipped into Lippert's *Evolution of Culture* and Mignet's *French Revolution,* only to abandon each of them unfinished. For several weeks on end he was a follower of Jeremy Bentham, assuring all who would listen that the utilitarian calculus of pain and pleasure—which he would later refer to as a philosophy of social cookbook recipes—was the last word in human wisdom and the formula for all of man's problems. Before he could make a single convert, he himself had abandoned Bentham for an equally brief discipleship to Chernishevski. Each book was tasted rather than digested; each had a disparate existence for him. He strove, as thoughtful adolescents have done before him and since, to reduce his thought to a system. But Marxism—of which he knew nothing but the name—repelled him because its adherents alleged that it was systematic.

Looking for people to talk these things out with, Lev Davidovich found his way to the garden of Franz Shvigovsky, a Czech vegetable gardener, whose hut was the provincial "salon" of Nikolaev's radical intelligentsia. In it foregathered the students who had no taste for cards and drinking, a few young professional men, a few rusting old political exiles. From Shvigovsky one could get forbidden books, foreign newspapers, anecdotes about the great and near-great of the vanished Narodnaya Volya. He had read some of the Marxist classics in German, and reassured Lyova Bronstein by proclaiming his own opposition to Marxism. The older visitors talked of Zhelyabov, Sophia Perovskaya, Vera Figner, not as heroic legendary figures but as familiar personages. Bronstein now felt that he was himself a populist, a "tiny link in a great chain." He talked populism with no more knowledge of it than of the previous *isms* he had adhered to. His quick mind, his skill in argument, his scornful tongue and ready wit, his facile assimilation of ideas, his fiery condemnation of Marxism, made him the immediate leader of the coterie of students there. All the frequenters of the "salon" were populists except one. "Wait till you meet Lev Davidovich," Ilya and Gregory Sokolovsky told their sister Alexandra, the lone Marxist. "Such brilliance, such logic. No one can get the better of him in an argument."

Alexandra Lvovna Sokolovskaya went to the Shvigovsky garden from time to time because there was nowhere else to go in Nikolaev for serious discussion. She was older than most of the frequenters—she was twenty-two—simple, emotional, warm-hearted, single-minded in her devotion to socialism. During vacation times she was supported in her views by a medical student named Ziv, who was studying at the University of Kazan, and who counted himself a Marxist too, after having read Beltov's (Plekhanov's) *Monistic Conception of History.* The rest of the time she held the fort alone against the banter and onslaughts of her two brothers, of Shvigovsky himself, and all his company. Lev Davidovich prepared for his arguments with her and Ziv much as he had previously prepared for his recitations and compositions. He browsed around in legal populist magazines and books, of which there were quite a number, picking up fragments concerning Russia's "noncapitalist destiny," and random, fine-sounding strictures on Marxism. He memorized strong, well-turned sentences, aphorisms, crushing arguments, covering up his uncertainties as sophomoric debaters are apt to do, by a variety of rhetorical tricks. If we think of Vladimir Ilyich, patiently plodding for years through stacks of statistical reports and the major works of populism and Marxism before he could bring himself to utter a word, we see at once the difference between the two generations and, no less, between the two temperaments. Ulyanov worked out his whole chess game in theory before he moved his first piece; Bronstein improvised his game impulsively, even thoughtlessly, changing it for a while with each fresh move. With Ulyanov the hard thing had been to go over from study to public exposition and activity, and then from elaborate theoretical propaganda to simple, piecemeal agitation; with Bronstein both populism and Marxism were adopted impulsively and he began to agitate others before he had thought through whither he was going. He learned not so much from meditation and study as from contact with the people, the movements and the ideas that were swirling around him. For him the difficult feat was to continue to deepen his knowledge and revise his views, when in this garden of schoolboy debaters he so easily won first place and scored debater's triumphs without serious study. Both his populism and his early Marxism were superficial acceptance of what was in the air. As the atmosphere became more heavily charged, he would grow in stature—in 1905 and in 1917 to titanic proportions. Again and again we shall have to note the difference in the two "styles" that are two men.

Alexandra Sokolovskaya came to the garden to meet the new master of logical swordplay. She was astonished at the ignorance no less than at the self-assurance of the dynamic blue-eyed youth with the great shock of black hair, who was so confident that he could slay Marxism. All their meetings were combats, cheered on by a lively, one-sided audience. "I can't imagine how a young girl like you can stand that dry, narrow, impractical stuff," was his summing up at their first meeting —as she remembered it when interviewed many years later by Max Eastman. And, "I can't imagine how a person who thinks he is logical can be contented with a headful of vague, idealistic emotions," was her rejoinder. Between them arose a magnetic field of mutual antagonism.

The school inspector visited Lyova's boarding house to find out why he was so frequently absent. Next his father appeared. He stormed and threatened. The boy struck attitudes, talked incoherent mixtures of sense and nonsense, defended his right to intellectual independence, asserted the insignificance of university training and engineering in comparison with what he was doing.

But what was he doing, besides talking and groping? How could they understand each other, these two Bronsteins, when all they had in common was the strong will which separated them? David Bronstein presented an ultimatum. Lyova dramatized his defiance by refusing to accept further support. He abandoned the lodgings his father had been paying for, and went to live—with six other students—in a populist "commune" in the midst of Shvigovsky's garden.

At first the seven "communards" aspired to little more than

plain living and high talk. They all slept without bed linen, wore blue workmen's blouses, carried mysterious black canes, lived on stews made from the garden's vegetables reinforced with chunks of cheap meat. Lyova, having managed to get his high-school diploma, applied his education to giving private lessons. The other students picked up the small amount of cash needed by similar devices. They read copiously and unsystematically, made the Shvigovsky "salon" more lively than ever, attracted the attention of the neighbors and the authorities by their "meetings," believed that they had seceded from the present and were already living in the future.

Before long, chiefly on Bronstein's impulsive prodding, they decided on "action." When the local library association raised the membership fee from five to six rubles annually, they flooded the library association with new members, captured the board of directors at the annual meeting, and restored the old fee. On the new board they elected the gardener Shvigovsky, the Russian novelist Osipovich, who had done time in Siberia, and other "persons of evil repute." Then the youthful Marx-slayer Bronstein circulated a petition to have the library cancel its subscription to the former populist magazine *Novoye Slovo,* because the "legal" Marxists had gotten control of it.

His impatience and brashness next inspired an attempt on the part of the "commune" to give Nikolaev society the benefit of their wisdom. With great fanfare, they announced public courses of lectures in which they were to be the lecturers, modestly titling the venture "The Universal Knowledge Association." Lev Davidovich's department was "sociology." He prepared for his course with all his powers, but his slender store of universal sociological knowledge petered out by the second lecture. Some of the other courses did not even get that far.

They formed a society to "distribute useful books among the people," collected funds, chipped in from their own meager earnings, reduced the already crowded space in their communal hut by acquiring bundles of paper-backed volumes. But where to go to find "the people"? Marxism would have suggested the workmen of Nikolaev, who were many of them literate and knowledge-hungry. But their superficial understanding of populism suggested that "people" meant peasants. Where, then, should they look for peasants to take their volumes? Thus, on a diminutive, ridiculous scale, they were recapitulating all the tragic experiences of the generations of the seventies and eighties, acquiring by their own efforts some smattering of the knowledge which censorship, deportation and the gallows had prevented from being handed down to them. During the vacations, returning university students brought to the vegetable garden the first news of the great wave of strikes among the weavers, not one word of which had been permitted to appear in the papers. Unconsciously, Lev Davidovich began to turn his face from "the people" in the villages to the workers in the towns.

Shvigovsky now hired a garden laborer and an apprentice, the better to devote himself to the activities of the "commune." At last, here were two people who might be viewed alternatively as workers or peasants. Upon them Shvigovsky and the six students fell with unrestrained ardor. What was their delight to find that the elder of the two was full of questions: about tactics, violence, terror, conspiracy, revolution. While the boys cudgeled their innocent brains, raced through their unresponsive books, talked the nights away in quest of answers, their interlocutor gave detailed, if confusing reports to the police chief of Nikolaev. It was this spy who made the first real recruit in the garden, for he succeeded before long in enlisting the apprentice into the police service also.

Lev Davidovich made a brief last visit to Yanovka. There he met with nothing but useless argument, and a lack of a common tongue for discussion. The father stormed, the mother and sisters wept, the boy held his uncertain ground. Everybody went around depressed. It was a relief to accept an invitation of an uncle in business near the University of Odessa, where, if so minded, Lyova might take courses in engineering or prepare for the career of mathematician. The uncle, a repentant liberal, hinted that he could bring the boy to his senses. Like many another oldster, he thought that radicalism was a mere infantile disorder, like teething, measles, growing pains, adolescent sexual turmoil. But Lyova could not find what he was looking for in Odessa. By the end of the year he was back in Nikolaev, in the communal garden once more and looking forward to fresh arguments with Alexandra Lvovna Sokolovskaya.

The crowded year 1896 ended with a New Year's Eve party at the garden. Shvigovsky had gone personally to invite Alexandra. "Congratulations," he said, "did you know that Lev Davidovich is back from Odessa and has become a Marxist?" She was sceptical, fearing to rejoice, but her two brothers assured her that the leading light of their circle had indeed been converted.

Her arrival was greeted with friendly raillery, suppressed gaiety, fresh congratulations, grave courtesy on the part of Lev Davidovich. At midnight, he arose from his place, a mocking smile on his lips, and proposed a toast:

"A curse on all Marxists, and on all those who want to bring into all the relations of life, hardness and dryness."

Laughter died as Alexandra Lvovna rose and walked out of the hut. Shvigovsky ran after her, assuring her that it was all a joke. "Some things are too sacred to joke about," she told him, "and as for Bronstein, you can tell him that I never want to see him again as long as I live."

CHAPTER TWELVE

FROM POPULISM TO MARXISM

The delegate from Nikolaev was Kalafati. Vladimir Ilyich questioned me in detail about him . . . and then he added, with a sly smile: 'He says he knew you as a kind of Tolstoyan.'
'What nonsense that is!' I said almost angrily.
'What is the matter?' Lenin replied, half to calm me, half to tease me. 'You were then probably eighteen years old, and men are certainly not born Marxists.'

—LEON TROTSKY

It was the spring of 1897. Lev Bronstein and Gregory Sokolovsky, each aged seventeen, were walking solemnly along a Nikolaev street. The whispering gallery had brought to them the news that, in the fortress of Saint Peter and Saint Paul, a girl student, Vetrova, had committed suicide by burning herself to death.

"We must find some workers," said Bronstein.

"I used to know a workman," Sokolovsky answered. "He belonged to some Bible sect. Let's go look him up."

The Bible sectary no longer lived in his old lodgings, but a woman there told them the address of one of his co-religionists. That very evening the two boys met the electrician Ivan Andreevich Mukhin.

Their "find" introduced them to other sectarians. All were touched with opposition to the régime, an opposition which, in harmony with the unripeness of Russian political life, expressed itself as a religious dissent. They were primitive evangelical Christians, communing over the heads of the princes of state and Church, directly with their God. For the most part they were skilled workers, earning good wages, feeling no special trade grievances, only a thirst for knowledge, righteousness, and justice. They showed no surprise when the students came, for they possessed a simplicity of spirit which mated well with the naïveté of the young revolutionaries. The two explorers returned to the vegetable garden proud and excited. Reinforcements were called up from Nikolaev's radical society: Alexandra, the Marxist girl; her brother, Ilya, and younger sister, Maria; the medical student Ziv; the garden communards. Out of this innocent fusion of students and dissenting Christian workingmen was born the South Russian Workers' Union!

The large name was Bronstein's doing, but with unparalleled energy and a flair for public activity, he set about to justify it. Each week he took the night boat to Odessa, sleeping out on deck to save money, and the night boat back the next evening, so that no days were lost in travel. Before long he made contacts for the new organization there, and in Ekaterinoslav and other Southern cities, found his way to the experienced organizer of an underground printing plant in Kiev, even returned from one triumphant trip to Odessa with some literature that had been smuggled into Russia from abroad. The grudging Doctor Ziv, whose subsequent memoir is one long stricture on the mind and personality of Leon Trotsky, concedes that "the lion's share of the success of the new organization we owed unquestionably to Bronstein, whose inexhaustible energy, skill in plans and contrivances of all sorts and resistance to fatigue, had no limits."

Alexandra Sokolovskaya welcomed Lyova's tacit acceptance of Social Democratic methods without a word: her gentle heart was no refuge for grudges, least of all against her attractive and valued antagonist. To celebrate the foundation of the new movement, four of its youthful leaders went to a Nikolaev photographer and had taken for history (and the police) a collective photograph. Young Bronstein is there, magnetic and proud, eyes slightly crossed because he has taken his glasses off, bushy haired and shaggy browed, large featured, with thick, full lips and a strong jaw, despite the suggestion of a dimple in the chin, later to be hidden by his beard.

Alexandra is next to him, with an air of dedication about her; then her brother, Ilya, who later became editor of the *Odessa News;* and the medical student Ziv, in European dress, collar and tie, a stiff and solemn dress which Bronstein regarded as a lapse from revolutionary purity. They autographed each other's copies with appropriate sentiments. Because Ziv was soon to leave for Kazan once more to complete his final year in the medical school, Bronstein wrote on Ziv's copy words of implied scorn: "Faith without works is death." Alexandra, gentle and compassionate, insisted on its erasure. Ziv treasured it along with other grievances, to merge it later with his opposition to bolshevism.

The success of the amateurish organization was instantaneous. The times, the reawakening public life, the longing of the sectaries for greater human dignity, contributed more than the zeal of these inexperienced youths. Even before their "unionization," most of the dissenters were already on the road to a more secular opposition. Mukhin, their leader, had come to regard religion as a useful cover. A cabinetmaker whom Bronstein enrolled in the library filled out his faith in the application blank as *Ratiolist*—explained, it turned out to be *Rationalist*. The influence of the non-believing students and of young workers who had been trained in the technical school connected with the shipyards, pushed religious language, ritual and outlook more and more into the background, until even the aged evangelist member whom everyone called "grandpa" became apologetic in his references to the catacombs and the secret meetings of the primitive Christians.

The grievances which the South Russian Workers' Union publicized were in the main offenses against human dignity. On the positive side, their meetings were much concerned with the culture of the members. At the secret gatherings in the woods they would have talks on sciences; readings from a badly mutilated mimeographed copy of the *Communist Manifesto,* which Bronstein had obtained in Odessa; recitations, songs and poems, often of their own composition. The "ratiolist" cabinetmaker composed a "Proletarian March" in which his past found expression in such lines as "We are the alphas and omegas, we are the beginnings and the endings." Nesterenko, a red-headed carpenter, wrote a song in Ukrainian about Karl Marx, "Lo, a Great Prophet Comes." Out on the sand dunes, they sang it softly together.

In a closed room with blinds down and fire lit to burn the telltale evidence, or in Mukhin's home, specially rigged up with electric buzzers to warn of the police, Bronstein mixed gelatine and glycerine on a tin tray to make a hectograph pad for offset reproduction. It was a point of honor with Lev Davidovich to pen every letter personally in clear printed characters so that even the semiliterate should have no difficulty reading the leaflets. Two hours it took him—bent back never straightening for an instant—to pen a single page for the hectograph. Then they pulled two hundred or so beautiful copies in purple ink, more legible than the pallid, misprint-laden sheets being turned out by underground printing presses elsewhere in Russia.

To the workmen and the "public" of Nikolaev, the new leaflets were a sensation. Their neatness, their simple but eloquent language—the future "Pen" was learning fast—their mysterious air of knowing each foreman's rudeness, each act of outrage, what went on inside each factory, gave public and police the idea that there was behind them a mighty and experienced organization. Workmen did not have to be sought, they sought out the Union, offering help, information, enlistment. Lev Davidovich knew from his reading what a thanksgiving it had been to the older revolutionaries when, after prolonged effort, they recruited one or two solitary workmen. Yet here they soon found themselves at the head of a loose organization of some two hundred! He was in a constant state of exaltation and excitement. The Nikolaev police chief himself went from plant to plant in Nikolaev personally remedying abuses complained of in the leaflets, so as to rob the mysterious South Russian Workers' Union of its issues. This only increased the organization's prestige.

The success of the leaflets led to a hectographed newspaper, *Our Cause,* with Bronstein as editor. Now his aching back did not unbend for days together. He wrote most of the articles, penned every letter himself for the hectograph, ransacked the newspapers in the public library for cartoons, which he copied, combined into new composites, adapted with new legends. Nikolaev was proud of its underground socialist organ. Even in Odessa and other towns there was talk of it.

The police redoubled their efforts. Spies multiplied. Shrentzel, a mechanic who claimed to be an engineer, appeared from nowhere, unprepossessing, furtive, inquisitive. (Later Lyova learned that he had been driven out of Odessa as an exposed spy. Mukhin and Bronstein staged a little comedy in the Café Russia to throw a scare into him; he disappeared once more—until he was needed at the police hearings.) Nesterenko, the red-headed carpenter who had sung of Marx the Great Prophet, met Bronstein one winter midnight, near the end of 1897, in a graveyard to receive a roll of proclamations. Out of the darkness loomed another figure, walked past them, scrutinizing Lev Davidovich closely. Nesterenko, too, had become a police spy.

Still the police withheld their blow, unwilling to believe that in these boys and girls and simple religious dissenters they had found the real leaders of the organization.

Not until January, 1898—when the Union was nearly a year old and the third number of *Our Cause* had appeared, did the police close in upon it. By then their information was detailed, their dragnet thorough. Bronstein had gone out of town to visit Shvigovsky where he was working as a gardener, and to leave some papers with him. A detective trailed Maria Sokolovskaya, Alexandra's younger sister, who had come to warn him, so that all three were arrested together. Alexandra was in Ekaterinoslav. With the abnegation that characterized her, she came in to surrender so that the workers should not think their leaders had deserted them, and that the trial might be hastened when the police had all those they were looking for. Later such idealism in the conduct of political leaders would yield to more practical considerations of the continuing struggle. The medical student Ziv, identified from the collective photograph, was arrested when he returned from Kazan with his doctor's degree. All the papers which Shvigovsky had hastily hidden in the snow when the police came, turned up in the spring thaws, detailed, incriminating, so that Bronstein spent a good part of his time at the hearings accepting responsibility to exonerate the gardener. Virtually every workman who had had any contact with the organization was identified by the spies in their midst. All in all, there were some two hundred prisoners of varying degrees of complicity crowded into the moldering, foul, cold Nikolaev jail, never intended to house so many and with no tradition or resources for the special treatment of "politicals." One attempted suicide. Another went insane. Some were released without apology. Most held their tongues and took their punishment, or quixotically gave the police excessive evidence against themselves in the hope that they would thus shield others. There was no trial, no confrontation with accusers or with each other, no opportunity for counsel, only secret administrative hearings. Even these attentions were so rare that they were welcomed as a relief from solitary confinement.

This first prison, and its successor a few weeks later in Kherson, inured Lyova Bronstein, spending his nineteenth birthday in jail, against a lifetime in twenty prisons in a half-dozen countries. Prison, too, settled the question of engineering and mathematics, gave him time to think through the unthinking actions of the past year, took the place of the Tsar's universities. His father and mother were heartbroken when they learned of it, but to the boy, still held incommunicado, imprisonment was no disgrace, rather a badge of honor linking him up with the great names he had already learned to cherish. From the days of Nicholas I, the list of prisoners and exiles had read like a *Who's Who* of Russia's great men and women. It would continue to be so through all the years of tsardom. With the Tsar's fall, the prison and exile lists would empty for a brief season of their men of distinction, only to become a partial roster of anti-Bolshevik intellectuals a little later, and the completest *Who's Who* in Russian history during the high tide of the purges of the nineteen thirties. To the young prisoner, the consciousness of forming part of a distinguished company robbed imprisonment of one of its terrors, that of moral obloquy.

Cut off from contact with the outside world, unaware of who else had been arrested, housed in a large, cold reception room big enough for thirty prisoners, with only himself and a young Jewish bookbinder named Yavich as occupants, the lad had need of all his store of health and pride and idealism. The two boys slept on a straw mattress which, at six in the morning, was taken from them. Then they would sit on the bare floor—there were no furnishings—in hats, coats, galoshes, huddled close for animal warmth, hugging a stove which was barely warmer than they. There they dreamed away the timeless days, speculating on their future and their fate.

Three weeks slid by. He was transferred, alone this time, to solitary in Kherson. Still no word from the outside world, no parcels of food or clothing. For three months, no soap, no opportunity to bathe, or to wash clothes, no change of underwear. His body was consumed by vermin. He recorded later that he was able to judge the foulness of the air only by the grimace the warder made when he brought in the chunk of of bread which had to serve for both breakfast and supper, and the prison stew which was his dinner. No pencil, no paper, no books, not enough bread to make him forget his continuous hunger. To distract his spirit he would pace the cell meditating on the problems of Marxism versus populism, trying to construct for himself a Marxian system of thought out of his own meager resources, composing verses and memorizing them for future commitment to paper. During the recent months before his arrest, he already knew that he was on the road from populism to Marxism, but he had been unwilling to give Alexandra the satisfaction of admitting it. Now, as a sign of his conversion he turned the peasant song "Dubinushka" into a proletarian "Machinushka" in exaltation of the machine. The verses, mediocre enough but "ideologically improving," lived to find their way into Soviet songbooks.

At the end of three months, the jailer entered one day with a clean pillow, a warm blanket, soap, a package of tea, sugar, cookies. Lev Davidovich may have renounced his father's aid, but father and mother were not so easily put off as an old suit or outgrown ideas. They had caught up with his whereabouts and had come to "save" and to help him. In fact, not until Lev Davidovich's fame had spread far in the Revolution of 1905 and the boy had become a man in his late twenties did stubborn old David Bronstein renounce the idea of someday winning him for respectability and engineering. Whenever the impecunious Lev Davidovich or his wife and children of a later date needed money, the Bronsteins were ready to help. But the connection was largely onesided; there was never the intellectual understanding or the filial affection that we have seen in the relations of Vladimir Ilyich Ulyanov to his mother. Detachment from all but followers and friends-in-the-cause was a striking aspect of this boy's character.

Soon after the parental visit, Lev Davidovich was transferred to the so-called model prison—all steel and stone—at Odessa. Here the Tsar's government recognized the "political" as a special class of prisoner not to be grouped with common criminals. Bronstein was allowed books from the prison library, and from outside, was permitted to have paper and pencil, to make notes and write. He was kept in a section with other politicals, could tap out messages to cellmates which would be passed on to their destination, learned how to code messages by little dots under letters in agreed books in the prison library, even to circulate manuscripts of his own composition written in microscopic letters, then passed through a drain or left in a matchbox in the toilet, to which the prisoners were taken in a fixed order every morning. But this last method drove him to desperation because the recipient could never comment on the document or respond to it. Successive generations of political prisoners had developed a whole technique of communication and common life in prison.

He located one of the Sokolovsky boys, then Ziv, and Shvigovsky. To each he announced his conversion to Marxism. Sokolovsky agreed, Ziv was triumphant, Shvigovsky was cold and indignant. Alexandra, when the news finally got to her by the grapevine telegraph, found in it cause for a deeper rejoicing.

With so much time on his hands, so many busy thoughts in his head, Bronstein's pen could not long remain idle. The prison library, being a prison library, was made up of edifying works on theology, back files of a conservative historical journal and of the *Orthodox Review*. He waded through them all, learned the lives of the Saints, the ways of Satan and his devils, what was known of the plan and structure of paradise, the Orthodox arguments against Catholicism, Protestantism, Darwinism and the heresies of Tolstoy, and Archbishop Nikanor's scientific proofs of such miracles as that of Balaam's ass.

Then his sister Olga and the Shpentsers began bringing him books: the New Testament in five languages, which enabled him to study German, French, English and Italian; histories; Beltov (Plekhanov) on the *Monistic Conception of History;* Antonio Labriola's *Essays on Historical Materialism;* Darwin's *Origin of Species* and *Autobiography.*

> Darwin stood for me—he wrote later to Max Eastman—like a mighty doorkeeper at the entrance to the temple of the universe. I was intoxicated with his minute, precise, conscientious, and at the same time powerful thought. I was the more astonished when I read that he had preserved his belief in God. I absolutely declined to understand how a theory of the origin of species by way of natural and sexual selection and a belief in God, could find room in one and the same head.

Much of Labriola's simple-seeming, gnomic observations on Marxian philosophy still escaped him. He determined to master historical materialism and test his mastery by an independent study of an obscure phenomenon which had begun to intrigue him: the social meaning of the strange history of Free-Masonry. He took notes on the history of Masonry in a fat notebook of a thousand numbered pages, writing with almost microscopic minuteness, interspersing the notes with his comments. When any part of it seemed complete, he copied it out on thin paper and smuggled it to the other prisoners. Later he carried the fat notebook with him to Siberia and had Alexandra Lvovna forward it to him in Switzerland, where it got lost, a loss he always regretted.

All through 1898 and most of 1899, he remained in the Odessa prison, waiting for administrative disposition of his case. In November, 1899, he was informed that he had been condemned to four years in Far Eastern Siberia. Alexandra and her two brothers were also given four years, Dr. Ziv three, others lesser punishments. Now the long monotony was relieved by preparations for the journey. Those who had lovers proceeded to marry; those who had none arranged fictitious engagements because fiancées and wives were allowed special visiting privileges. Lyova Bronstein sent a proposal of marriage to fellow-prisoner Alexandra Lvovna Sokolovskaya. But as the would-be bridegroom was still a minor, having just turned twenty in October, his father's permission had to be secured. Old Bronstein was not minded to let his wayward son marry another state criminal, who, he felt, had been the cause of his son's undoing. Moreover, he thought the girl too old (six years older, according to Max Eastman, who interviewed her, "at least ten years older," according to Dr. Ziv's memoirs) and the boy too young. The rage of Lev Davidovich at this indignity to his independence knew no bounds. But his father was armed with legal authority, backed by a well-lined purse to convince any official inclined to sentimental indulgence of the young lovers.

The prisoners were taken from Odessa to the transfer prison of Butyrki in Moscow, to wait there until a big enough batch should accumulate for shipment to Siberia. A group had just left, so that the prison was nearly empty. Once more the weeks passed into months while they waited. Now, however, their life changed completely. In place of solitary cells, the men were all kept together in the great clock tower, the women in another tower of the prison. There was company, talk, collective discussion. Here Bronstein first heard the name of Lenin as the prisoners read together his impressive economic work (published legally under the pseudonym of Vladimir Ilyin) *The Development of Capitalism in Russia.* They read and discussed Bernstein's revisionist critique of Marxism and decided for Marxist orthodoxy against revisionism. Lev Davidovich gave expression to his overflowing energies by leading a hunger strike; by writing and smuggling out of the prison a pamphlet on the labor movement in Nikolaev, which was published in Geneva; by beginning work on a Marxist propaganda novel, never destined to see the light of day.

Twice a week the prisoners were visited by their wives or fiancées, received books and packages, exchanged messages rather freely, held long interviews in a common room under the eyes of a single indulgent guard. Lyova gave Alexandra's name as his fiancée and she was conducted to the visiting room at the same time as the women from the outside world. "During those interviews," Ziv writes, "he showed a touching tenderness not only to his fiancée but also to all the other ladies who came to meet their husbands, brothers, etc., and charmed everyone by his chivalrous bearing." Old David Bronstein being far away now, Lyova soon succeeded in persuading the Butyrki prison authorities to allow the rabbi-chaplain to perform a marriage ceremony. His *Autobiography*, which is extremely reticent and dry in its few references to his relations with women, limits its account of his marriage to the following:

> There—in the village of Ust-Kut in northeastern Siberia—I was put ashore with one of the woman prisoners, a close associate of mine from Nikolaev. Alexandra Lvovna had one of the most important positions in the South Russian Workers' Union. Her utter loyalty to socialism and her complete lack of any personal ambition gave her an unquestioned moral authority. The work that we were doing bound us closely together, and so, to avoid being separated, we had been married in the transfer prison in Moscow.

One would never suspect the transports of a lover in this almost unfeeling suggestion of a party marriage of convenience. But Alexandra's own account (as told to Max Eastman), and Ziv's no less, carry the conviction that he ardently reciprocated the love which Alexandra Lvovna had long felt for him. In Siberia she was to bear him two daughters.

Not until May, 1900, after more than two years and three months in Russian prisons, did the Nikolaev criminal begin the journey to eastern Siberia. On the train to Irkutsk, "Bronstein," according to Ziv, "did not seem to interest himself in anything. He was entirely absorbed by A. Sokolovskaya." After a brief stay in the prison at Irkutsk on the edge of Mongolia, he and his bride, separated from their comrades, began a voyage in a convict barge down the Lena River to their final destination.

Ust-Kut was a solitary, vermin-ridden village of about a hundred peasant huts lying between the forest and the river. At night the cockroaches "filled the house with their rustling"; in the summer they were tormented by great swarms of midges. The beautiful countryside had no attraction for Lev Davidovich, wrapped up in his wife, his books, his writings, his plans for the future. "I lived between the woods and the river," he wrote later, "and I almost never noticed them . . ." With the passion for logic and consistency which we have already noted, he set out to revise his point of view on the personal problems of life: love, death, friendship, optimism, pessimism, in the light of his new-found Marxist *Weltanschauung*. Alexandra appears to have subordinated her life to his, following with anxious joy his excursions into the universal application of the philosophy she had urged upon him.

A daughter was born and named Zina, then a second, Nina, both destined to have a tragic end, as all those whose lives were linked with his. The Bronsteins' stipend from the government was raised to nineteen rubles a month, enough to pay for cooking, cleaning, rent and food. Books were another matter. To add to their income, Lev Davidovich got a job as a clerk for an illiterate but wealthy trader of Irkutsk. His heart, however, was not in his work. The billing of 40 pounds of red lead as 40 poods (i.e. 1600 pounds) caused him to lose his job. The family was sent back to lonely, frozen Ust-Kut once more.

Next he became local correspondent for the *Eastern Review,* a legal journal started by the older populist exiles in the Siberian provincial capital. At this work he was happy. His "local correspondence" developed into the familiar Russian essay type known as the *feuilleton* analogous to the "column" that has become so popular in recent American journalism. All the exiles of the Province of Irkutsk read the paper and many of them contributed. His column was well liked; before long his pay jumped from two kopeks a line to four. The peculiar pen-name he had chosen, Antid Oto—the Italian for "antidote"—achieved some local reputation.

The young columnist from Ust-Kut was proud of his first experience in non-political literature. He was to have recourse to this method of making a livelihood again and again in his troubled career. Still as *Antid Oto*—that slightly arrogant pen-name which seemed to suggest that his writings might be an antidote to the poison distilled by the rest of the paper—he wrote for many years for the liberal democratic *Kievskaya Mysl* ("Kievan Thought"), first from Vienna, then as war correspondent in the Balkans during the "Little War" of 1912, and then in France during the "Great War" of 1914. When the Soviet Government published both series of *Antid Oto* essays in his collected works, he looked them over and found them good. "Of course, I couldn't say all that I wanted to . . . but I never wrote what I did not want to say." Many an émigré revolutionary sought to eke out his living abroad by placing less partisan writings in the general press, but none with such genuine vocation for the writer's trade as he.

The Bronsteins received permission to move to Verkholensk, where there were other exiles. In company with them, or in argument with them, Lev Davidovich settled accounts to his own satisfaction, with Revisionism, "legal Marxism," anarchism. His first contact with an anarchist was with that romantic Russian type which glorified banditry, a man who wounded a local police chief "not that he had anything against him personally, but that he wanted, through him, to strike at the tyranny of the state." A little later two lengthy hectographed essays from

the pen of their fellow-exile Makhaisky reached the colony of
Verkholensk politicals. The first essay was a sharp critique of
the political opportunism of the German Social Democracy.
Coinciding as it did with their own opinions of the opportunistic tactics being advocated in the book of Bernstein's they
were then reading and discussing, the Makhaisky pamphlet
made a profound impression. Then the second hectographed
volume arrived from the same pen, criticizing Marxism itself
and evaluating the socialist movement as one which would lead
to a social order in which the intellectuals (managers, technicians, bureaucrats, politicians, professional men) would be substituted for the capitalists as a new privileged class of exploiters
of the proletariat. For months the exiles discussed nothing but
Makhaisky. To Bronstein, this second essay was sufficient to
"tear away the mask" from Makhaisky's face, and to inject into
the young Marxist a "powerful inoculation" against anarchism,
syndicalism and all related theories. Even in 1929—and to the
day of his death—though Trotsky increasingly concerned himself with the bureaucratization of the Russian state, it never
occurred to him to re-examine Makhaisky's views; he always
cited them as self-evidently monstrous. But we cannot dispose
of them quite so easily, and shall have to return to them again
for further examination.

Word came from Russia of Tolstoy's excommunication; then
of the assassination of the Minister of Education, Bogolepov,
by a student, and the Minister of the Interior, Sipyagin, by another. Obviously, the political cauldron was beginning to sim-
mer. "All the exiles were as much aroused as if they had heard
the bugle-call of alarm." They had heated discussions once
more of the vexed question of terror as a revolutionary tactic,
Bronstein siding with those who were against it.

Social Democratic organizations began to spring up among
the railwaymen along the Transsiberian. He wrote leaflets and
proclamations for them. Smuggled in the binding of books,

arrived Lenin's pamphlet, *What's to Be Done?* and several numbers of *Iskra*. To Bronstein they were a summons. The mounting restlessness among the exiles who sensed the growing movement in Russia (the Revolution of 1905 was but three years away), was causing a veritable epidemic of escapes. The numbers who wanted to risk the long flight were so great that they had to draw lots and take turns. Lev Davidovich consulted his wife. That devoted woman, though her younger daughter was less than four months old, did not hesitate for a moment. She met his objections with the two words: "You must."

His turn came. With another fugitive, a woman, buried in a pile of hay at the bottom of a peasant cart, he left Verkholensk. For four days the local inspection was staved off by Alexandra by means of a dummy lying upstairs in his bed, "too sick to be disturbed." In those trackless wastes, four days' headstart was enough. The underground railway was run by peasants whom the old populists had converted into sympathizers. Later, in starched shirt, collar, necktie, and European suit, and with a copy of the *Iliad* in Russian, he boarded a train. In his pocket was a forged passport, which he himself had filled out in the name of *Trotsky*. It was the name of the chief jailer in the model prison of Odessa! Once on the passport, he was to use it, with occasional breaks, for the rest of his life.

In Samara he reported to someone using the name of "Claire" (or "Kler"). It turned out to be Lenin's old friend of the Samara days, the engineer Krzhizhanovsky, chief *Iskra* agent in Russia. The escaped convict from Siberia made an excellent impression on all the Samara comrades. "Claire" wrote a letter on him to Krupskaya, secretary of *Iskra* abroad, in which he nicknamed him *Pero*—"Pen"—pronounced him a fervent supporter of *Iskra* and a young man of brilliant talents. "He is a real young eagle," the report concluded. The "young eagle" was sent around by Krzhizhanovsky on organizing trips to Kharkov, Poltava, Kiev, but the connections were unreliable;

as organizer he did not distinguish himself. However, a brief negotiation on behalf of *Iskra* with the local illegal paper, *The Southern Worker,* elicited such a precise report on the possibilities of joint work and the obstacles and grounds of possible difference, that Lenin was deeply impressed with the new recruit's political acumen. Before long, a summons came to him to leave for Western Europe and put his pen at *Iskra*'s service. Krzhizhanovsky supplied the necessary funds, and addresses for smuggling across the Austrian-Polish border. As he approached the frontier, a police official asked to see his passport. To the genuine astonishment of the newly christened Trotsky, the official found nothing wrong with it.

At the border, the usual smuggling difficulties, hiding in peasant huts, crossing a shallow river at night on another man's back so as to be dry on arrival, traveling hidden in a two-wheel cart with chickens as fellow-passengers, were varied only by the fact that the smugglers overcharged their inexperienced and spendthrift patron. Reacting against the hateful niggardliness of his father's household, he overtipped right and left, so that the money which was to carry him to London was gone by the time he reached Vienna.

Undaunted, this self-important young man who believed that the great parties of Western Europe were waiting breathless to welcome and to assist escaped Russian revolutionaries, demanded to see none other than the outstanding figure in the Austrian Social Democratic Party, Victor Adler. The good "Comrade Doctor" had a Russian daughter-in-law, and a sympathetic sense of humor, so that the impecunious young Russian refugee who disturbed his Sunday rest received better treatment than was to be expected. By the time he reached Zurich, he was broke again. In the same "uncivilized" fashion he woke Axelrod at 3 A.M., instead of waiting until dawn, and made him pay for the cab. It was almost the same story in London, where he knocked loudly at Lenin's door while the latter, always an early riser, was still asleep. Krupskaya, in dressing gown, hastened to answer the triple knock, an agreed sign, before the house should be roused by the knocking. "Hallo," she called up the stairs, "*Pero* has arrived." "The kindly expression of Lenin's face was tinged with a justifiable amazement," but he began forthwith to question the newcomer. Krupskaya had to pay for the cab.

CHAPTER THIRTEEN

LENIN
PREPARES

. . . The fact that all his powers and energies are concentrated
upon one thing makes it easy for him to appear extraordinary
in the eyes of the masses and become a leader, in the same way
that those who really concentrate on God become saints and
those who live only for money become millionaires.

—IGNAZIO SILONE

In London young Trotsky, to use his own words, "fell in love with *Iskra*." Not with this shading or that, but with the whole board of editors, all the back numbers, viewpoints, formulations. When Lenin asked what he thought of the draft program which they had published for the consideration of the coming Party congress, his answer was wholesale endorsement. How could he dream that there were differences among those titans of orthodox Marxism, that the draft had been a product of bitter, dragging controversy, versions, counter-versions, ruptured relations, go-betweens, peacemakers, compromises? The newcomer was given a tryout as lecturer to the émigrés in London. His theme, derived from study in prison and Siberia, was a defense of historical materialism against the strictures of the Russian subjectivist school. The title was: "What is Historical Materialism and How Do the Social Revolutionaries Comprehend It?" The patriarch of Russian populist exiles, the venerable Chaikovsky, took the floor against him in the discussion period, as did the scarcely less venerable and distinguished anarchist leader Cherkesov. The young lecturer disposed of these great men so easily—to his own and most of the audience's satisfaction—that he returned to his lodgings "walking on air." Lenin fed his pride by suggesting that he write up the lecture notes as an article for the theoretical organ *Zarya* ("Dawn"), alongside of which even *Iskra* was but a "popular journal." But, as he wrote later, "I didn't have the courage to appear by the side of Plekhanov and the others with a strictly theoretical essay." He submitted instead a lesser article for *Iskra,* which Lenin, jesting the while, pruned of some of its literary adornments.

Next he was sent on a tour of the émigré colonies in Brussels, Liège, and Paris, to repeat the same lecture for a small admission fee and thus raise money for *Iskra.* In the diary of a young Russian girl, Natalia Ivanovna Sedova, who served in Paris as a sort of receptionist for visiting revolutionaries, his arrival merited a number of entries. She found a room for him in the cheap lodging house where she herself lived. She marveled at the youth of the theoretician (he was twenty-two). She reported anxiously that when she passed his door he was whistling instead of working on his lecture. Blushing, she brought a message to him from an older woman comrade that he was to work hard and not to whistle. "The lecture," she recorded, "went off well and the colony was delighted, as the young follower of *Iskra* exceeded all expectations."

That ordeal over, she presented herself as guide to the glories of Paris, its boulevards in constant movement, its history-haunted buildings, its galleries, museums, river banks, green gardens. But the young man, resistant to being absorbed by anything that was not politics or Marxism, fought against the contagion of her enthusiasm. "Paris resembles Odessa"—she reports his verdict in her diary—"but Odessa is better."

Natalia Ivanovna was one of those devoted girls of the "repentant privileged classes," cultured, emotional, self-sacrificing, who had early dedicated herself to righting the immemorial wrongs of Russia. While still in a young ladies' boarding school she had been a ringleader in introducing forbidden books. In the university, first in Moscow, then in Geneva, she had joined rebel student circles. As "post-graduate" work, she unhesitatingly embraced exile and the self-denying, anonymous role of a subordinate professional revolutionist. All her thoughts were selfless, unless we except her young girl's dream of finding some male comrade whom she could love and learn from, and at whose side she could enrich her service to the movement. To the self-assured, brilliant young visiting lecturer, she made no secret of her admiration. With his usual reticence in affairs of the heart, he has left no record of his own feelings except to note in his *Autobiography:* "I was much more interested in learning about Paris than I had been about London . . . because of the influence of N. I. Sedova."

In Siberia, while Trotsky as a new-baked Marxist was "considering from the viewpoint of Marxism the so-called 'eternal' problems of life: love, death, friendship," he had consciously rejected any remnants of prejudice in favor of monogamy. Sex and family life, like all things personal, would have to be subordinated to the comings and goings required of him by the revolutionary movement. When his wife Alexandra had urged him to flee, she knew that the task of supporting their two girls would devolve upon her, that his escape to Western Europe would separate him from her for an indefinite period. For years they did not see each other. When her children were in need, his old father helped. Toward the man she had married in prison, her loyalty never faltered. When she was over sixty, Stalin sent her to Siberia as part of the vengeance which cost Trotsky both his daughters and both his sons.

Though he set the demands of the movement above love or friendship, there was nothing of the puritan or ascetic about Leon Trotsky. In every period of his life—as young wandering revolutionary, as victorious War Commissar, as exile fallen from high station—this man was attractive to many women. He had little time for wooing; indeed, he would have fitted ill into the role of conventional suitor or ladies' man; but a number of "affairs," temporary and not engaging his spirit very deeply, came his way without much expenditure of effort.

His legal marriage to Alexandra, however, was different from these. And still more so his Paris idyll with Natalia Ivanovna Sedova. Natalia's affections clung to him, her admiration and comradeship were to sustain him all his life. She it was who would share the days of triumph in the Kremlin and follow him into exile into Soviet Asiatic Russia, then to Prinkipo, France, Norway, Mexico. Her love, like Alexandra's, was all giving and no demanding. Two children were born to her, too, both boys. Like the two daughters of Alexandra, they would know the bitter lot of having sprung from so ill-starred a father. Natalia Ivanovna was at his side when he died in a Mexican hospital. One of his last deathbed thoughts was of her lonely, uncertain future. She is today his literary executor and a revered symbol to the devoted remnant of his followers. Alexandra Lvovna retained the legal name of Bronstein, but Natalia Ivanovna is properly known today as "Mrs. Trotsky."

I suggested to all the members of the Editorial Board—wrote Lenin on March 2, 1903—that they coopt "Pero" as a member of the Board . . . We *very much need* a seventh member, both as a convenience in voting (six being an even number), and as an addition to our forces. "Pero" has been contributing to every issue for several months now, works most energetically . . . gives lectures in which he has been very successful . . . Unquestionably a man of rare abilities, he will go much farther . . . Possible objections: (1) His youth; (2) his leaving for Russia possibly in a short time; (3) his pen [*pero*], this time without quotation marks, which shows traces of a *feuilleton* style and is excessively florid.

Lenin took up each of these possible objections. His youth? Time would remedy that, and already he was "a party man, a man of faction." He might leave for Russia? So much the better, for organized connection with the Board would be a plus for *Iskra*. The defects of style? He would outgrow them; in the meanwhile he accepted corrections, albeit reluctantly; if necessary, corrections could be made by majority vote of the editors.

The letter ended with a pointed postscript:

I consider that it would be most inconvenient and awkward to put off cooptation, as it has become clear to me that *Pero is considerably* annoyed—though of course he does not show it openly—about being treated as a "youth." If we do not take *Pero* at once, he will slip away...

Far from resenting any alleged hesitancy to promote him to a full editorship, the innocent subject of this letter would have been flattered, and astonished, to learn that such a move was being proposed. The fiction had an element of verisimilitude, however, for Lenin, quick to size up the character of those he sought to utilize, had sensed the component of vanity in the young man's makeup. But why the fiction? Whose resistance was it designed to overcome? Not Martov's certainly, for the latter had answered that the proposed Board member showed "undeniable talent, is quite 'ours' in thought, wields considerable influence thanks to his exceptional eloquence . . ." Axelrod liked the newcomer sufficiently to spend long hours talking to and enlightening him. Potresov agreed with Martov and Lenin. Vera Zasulich, as women of all ages are likely to be, was enthusiastic about the proud and promising youth. But Plekhanov opposed Lenin's motion with ill-dissimulated fury. What, then, had happened to his dual vote which was to be exercised whenever there should be a three-three tie? Against what, if not his own leadership, would future four-to-three decisions be directed? What did Lenin mean by proposing a mere boy of twenty-two on the Editorial Board of *Iskra?* What could his object be if not to strengthen the "youngsters" against the "oldsters," and his own influence above all by the vote of an unconditional follower? Plekhanov countered with a proposal to wait with the reorganizing of the Editorial Board until the coming congress. A fateful motion it turned out to be!

Since coopting could only be done by unanimous agreement, Lenin's proposal to break the vexatious tie votes was blocked. To save face, he moved to invite young *Pero* to editorial meetings without vote. This elicited from Plekhanov a flood of sarcastic persiflage about the young candidate's "pen" and manners, until even the faithful Vera Zasulich was moved to declare, "I'll bring him, no matter what you say, to the next meeting." And to the next meeting she actually did bring him, proud and unaware of the atmosphere surrounding his invitation. But all his life he would remember "the studied coldness" with which Plekhanov shook hands with him.

From the worshipful distance of the Russian underground, or even from the closer vantage point of the new contributing editor, *Iskra* presented a solid front in political and organizational matters, a steadily advancing front that seemed to drive liberals, Revisionists, "Economists," anarchists, renascent populists (of the new Social Revolutionary Party), and all other rival opposition groups, triumphantly before it. Plekhanov expounded the major generalizations of Marxist doctrine, applying them particularly to the field of culture; Lenin discussed agriculture, cherished and enlarged upon every strike and riot, sharpened the edge of polemic against "Economists" and Social Revolutionaries, above all, laid down organization precepts; Martov, the most productive and speculative of the editors, wrote absorbingly on a wide range of happenings and problems. Potresov did not contribute much because he was going through an illness, and his few writings seemed to differ little as yet from Lenin's and Martov's. As he grew older, he was to reveal a political personality which would seem an anachronism in this new atmosphere of storm: a Marxist in ideas with the temperament of an intellectual of the Enlightenment of the eighteen-forties. Axelrod did not write often, but his fundamental political articles had a quality of durable solidity about them. Their full implications, like those of Lenin's articles, were to become clear only after the break between menshevism and bolshevism. Vera Zasulich contributed, as a woman, something lacking in the other editors: emotional expression, a lively psychological intuition, a capacity for seeing persons and programs in human, sentimental terms, and not as mere embodiments of political positions. To the Russian emigration and the Russian underground, the Editorial Board of *Iskra* seemed a closely knit team of champions, linking up the celebrated older generation with fresh blood and new energies for organization and combat.

Lenin, for his part, had displaced Axelrod as the organization theorist and organization agent for the group. Axelrod had yielded willingly, knowing that for the practical work of organization Lenin had both more talent and vastly more concern and energy. Vladimir Ilyich was the only man of high theoretical capacity which the Russian Marxist movement produced, who possessed at the same time the ability and the will to concern himself with detail organization work. This was at all times to represent his particular strength and the strength of any faction he would build around himself. This systematic attention to detail was the only un-Russian feature in a political temperament that in all other respects was to think and feel in more peculiarly Russian terms and traditions than his more Europeanized associates.

He sent *Iskra* representatives hither and thither, made sure that the corresponding secretary was always a person of his choice and confidence, personally read every bit of mail and generally answered it in person or through his wife, Krupskaya. He invited released Siberian exiles and escaped prisoners to come to stay a while abroad, received them, gave them "inside information" on all the groups and controversies, bound them firmly to him. He drew promising men and women out of local work to use them nationally; planted his agents in *Iskra's* name in cities where opponent views prevailed in the local committees; gradually weakened localism of outlook and local initiative and autonomy, thus paving the way for all-Russian organization under the centralized domination of *Iskra*. Until such a foundation should be securely laid, he was opposed to the holding of a convention, which would adopt a program, name a leadership (or rather confirm a self-constituted leadership), and organize a national party. Thus the big battle for the convention was planned as the culmination of innumerable obscure skirmishes, both locally and—though this was less apparent to the contenders—within the self-appointed general staff of the projected party.

Rabochee Delo ("The Workers' Cause"), organ of the "Economists" and chief rival of *Iskra* for ideological leadership, tried to head off the latter's growing domination by itself starting a drive for unification. It, too, was published abroad, and was older than *Iskra*. As late as 1902, it still had behind it more supporters both in emigration and inside Russia. But it lacked the power instincts and driving force of a Lenin and the prestige of a Plekhanov. When it convoked a unification congress, the *Iskra* editors were as one in opposing this threat to their hegemony. In view of the longing for unity prevailing in the Russian underground, they dared not take upon themselves the onus of rejecting *Rabochee Delo's* invitation. So they all journeyed to Zurich together, to lay down what they hoped would prove unacceptable "conditions."

> Akimov, Krichevsky, and the rest of the *Rabochee Delo* people argued until they were blue in the face—records Krupskaya—Martov became terribly heated . . . and tore his tie from his throat . . . Plekhanov bristled with wit. A resolution was drawn up (by the *Iskra* group) recording the impossibility of unity. It was read out at the conference by Dan in a wooden voice, accompanied by shouts of 'Papal nuncio!' . . . Plekhanov was in a very good mood, for he had dealt a knockout blow to an opponent he had fought so much. Plekhanov was both jolly and communicative. . .

Next the Jewish Socialist Bund, the best organized workingmen's body inside Russia, tried its hand at summoning a convention to unite the party. As was the case with the ill-fated first congress it had called at Minsk, this too was to be held secretly inside Russia at Bialystok. The Iskrists, knowing that they could not dominate there either, sent Theodor Dan once more as "papal nuncio" to read a statement pronouncing the convention premature, improperly prepared, insufficiently representative (which last the Iskrists made sure of by keeping away the representatives of all the committees under their leadership). The statement ended with a demand that the Bialystok convention declare itself a mere "provisional conference" and limit itself to appointing delegates to serve on a wider committee to organize a real party congress. The Bialystok meeting did not feel equal to rejecting the ultimatum.

Meanwhile Lenin continued to work unceasingly to set up regular connections with the Russian local committees. His correspondence with them, and with the traveling and resident *Iskra* agents, was full of exhortations to write regularly and send detailed reports. The amateurishness of his letters from the standpoint of conspirative technique was equaled only by the amateurishness of the still inexperienced secret police. The letters spoke of "handkerchiefs" (passports), "barrels of beer" (shipments of *Iskra*), "warm fur" (illegal literature). It used Christian names beginning with the same initial letter to designate places (Ossip for Odessa, Petya for Poltava, Terenty for Tver); substituted women's names for men's and vice versa when dealing with persons; contained an amazing lot of nature-faking nonsense about animals like "the Snail," for Zinaida Krzhizhanovsky; "the Young Bear," for Lenin's sister; "the Horse," for Krassin, etc. It might seem plausible when "Papasha" (Pop) was used for Meyer Wallach, better known to history as Maxim Litvinov; but what censor could be so obtuse as not to see through a letter giving instructions to "Absolute" or "the Residue," both code names for Elena Stassova?

Small "barrels of beer" were sent through Stockholm destined for Saint Petersburg; through some misunderstanding they piled up in the cellar of the Stockholm People's House, where Lenin found them all several years later when he passed through bound for Russia. Other "beer" went through Marseilles, where a ship's cook carried it to Batum and threw it overboard at agreed spots at night in waterproof tarpaulin. Or through Alexandria and Persia, or through Galicia. "Probably not more than one-tenth of the literature dispatched," writes Krupskaya, "arrived at its destination." But "the Horse" (Krassin) and some local Georgians set up a secret printing plant at Baku, of which we shall hear more later, so that if a matrix or even a single copy of *Iskra* or some pamphlet got through, they could reprint it and spread it more widely.

Correspondence with Russia had a devastating effect on Lenin's nerves. He had to wait weeks and months for a reply, never sure whether a given matter had fallen through or whether the silence was due to shiftlessness, inertia, "the cursed Russian disorganization." His letters overflowed with scoldings and beseechings, fulsome praise for the slightest information, insults intended to prick a laggard into activity. He would spend sleepless nights waiting for answers, and still stormier nights when return letters did not carry the requested information. "Those sleepless nights," writes Krupskaya, "remain engraved on my memory." They preyed on Vladimir Ilyich's health, especially when they happened to coincide with periods of disagreement with the other *Iskra* editors.

As the long-awaited convention of the party finally drew nearer, he was so overwrought that he "developed a nervous illness called 'holy fire' [apparently shingles], which consists in inflammation of the nerve terminals of back and chest." Krupskaya looked it up in a medical handbook and consulted a Russian medical student. "We could not think of going to an English doctor, which would have cost a guinea . . . I painted Vladimir with iodine, which caused him agonizing pain." When he reached Geneva, a few months before the scheduled congress, he was in complete collapse and had to lie in bed for two weeks before resuming activity.

In April, 1903, the Editorial Board of *Iskra* was officially moved to Geneva. Lenin had been striving to keep the headquarters elsewhere, since he feared that Plekhanov would dominate the Board completely if it met in the city in which he resided. Vladimir Ilyich had gotten the paper out first in Munich, then in London. But early in 1903, by a vote of five to one, the paper was transferred to Geneva. Lenin's was the one negative vote!

He went to Geneva with mixed feelings. He had just gone through a second tremendous "lovers' quarrel" with his master, a quarrel which had raged in unabating fury all through 1902. At one point he had been moved to write:

I have received my article—(on the *Agrarian Program of the Russian Social Democracy*)—with your remarks upon it. You have a fine idea of tact with regard to your colleagues on the Editorial Board . . . You do not hesitate to use the most contemptuous expressions, not to mention the matter of voting on suggestions which you did not even take the trouble to formulate, and voting even on style. I should like to know what you would say if I were to answer your article on the Program in the same way! If your aim was to make mutual work impossible —then the way you have chosen should help you to succeed very quickly. As for our personal, as distinguished from our business relations, you have finally spoiled them, or, more exactly, you have achieved their complete cessation. [Letter of May, 1902.]

The quarrel had begun early in January, 1902, and really, it was Lenin who had been the aggressor. It was he who had begun the motions on fine points of style and formulation, proposing to amend the draft program prepared by Plekhanov for the consideration of the coming party congress.

To everyone but Lenin, it had always seemed self-evident that Plekhanov must be the author of the program of the nascent party. From the day that he founded the Group for the Emancipation of Labor in 1883 until the congress now to be held in Geneva two decades later, he had been esteemed by all revolutionary Marxists as the founder, the outstanding leader, thinker and teacher of their movement. The men of Lenin's and Trotsky's generations alike acknowledged him as their master. His was a wide-ranging mind, at home in philosophy, esthetics, literature, as well as history, sociology, economics, and all the specialized subjects that went under the head of Marxism. His works were known and admired abroad, translated into French and German, formed part of the general treasure of Marxist theoretical writings. All Russian socialists admired him, and, when they had occasion to oppose him, were in awe of his flashing brilliance, his sharp, irrepressible wit, his habit of making sarcastic jests and quips at the expense of unclear or dull-witted opponents. As he had shown in his polemics first with the Narodniks and then with the émigré "Economists," he was, like Lenin, quick to split with those who could not be made to accept his ideas.

For more than six months of 1901, Plekhanov had labored on the program which was to serve as the permanent theoretical foundation for the coming party. When he completed it and it seemed good in his eyes, he submitted it as a matter of form for the ratification of the other editors of *Iskra,* in the name of which it was to be offered. Lenin took his copy and marked it full of underlinings, doubled and trebled question marks, exclamation points, suggestions as to style, proposed alterations at retail and wholesale. Not a sentence, not a clause escaped criticism. The elegant, compact and highly theoretical outlines of Plekhanov's program were dissolved and buried in a rain of specific, detailed counter-proposals. Some emendations dealt with scholastic trivia, anxious splitting of the finest of hairs. Others revealed unconscious differences of temperament, of attitude toward the movement and its doctrine, of approach to Russia's peculiar problems. Plekhanov's was the more European mind, Lenin's the more Russian. Plekhanov's draft sought first of all to teach Russia the theoretical generalizations of Marxism, and only in the tenth of twelve sections did it come to grips with special Russian peculiarities. Yet the real problem of Marxist politics lay in applying its brilliant generalizations concretely to concrete circumstance in each land and at each shifting moment. Plekhanov was all things the movement might require save only a politician, while Lenin's mind was political before aught else, and dipped into the body of Marxist generalizations only occasionally for guidance or for polemics.

Lenin now went so far as to draw up his own draft in rivalry to Plekhanov's. Viewed from the standpoint of intellectual esthetics it was a homely, inelegant thing. But it opened with the word Russia in the very first line, and determinedly if clumsily got down to practical business. The general Marxist description of capitalism it took for granted, focussing all its bare, clear light on the peculiarities of the Russian scene. And if Plekhanov's draft had more elegance, Lenin's had more pathos. Where Plekhanov had written of the "dissatisfaction" of the proletariat, Lenin wrote in the margin: "Instead of dissatisfaction—indignation!" Where Plekhanov wrote "labor," Lenin wrote "the laborer." Next to Plekhanov's "worsening of the lot," Lenin queried: "Would it not be better to indicate directly: unemployment, poverty?" These differences were characteristic. The inclination to analytical logic marked the teacher, the inclination to pathos marked the would-be agitator, the practical politician.

Finally, Lenin in his criticisms, and in his own counter-draft, insisted on his two favorite dogmas: (1) that the discontent of the workers would grow with the growth of capitalism, but not its socialist consciousness, "which must be brought in by us"; and (2) that Social Democracy aims "to create *an organization of revolutionaries,* which leads the struggle of the proletariat."

Latter-day Stalinist historians have stated that Plekhanov omitted the dictatorship of the proletariat from his draft program. This is not so, as an inspection of his draft will reveal. As a matter of fact, from the standpoint of "theoretical orthodoxy," there was no reason why either man could not accept the program of the other. Yet each produced a number of successive drafts and marked up the margins of his rival's with ironic and angry criticisms. Feelings became so outraged that an arbitration committee of the other *Iskra* Board members had to be set up to iron out differences and soothe ruffled feelings. In the end, Plekhanov's version, and not Lenin's, became the basis of the draft submitted by *Iskra* to the congress. Again the vote was five to one against Lenin! Yet, once he had cooled off, Vladimir Ilyich was quite pleased with Plekhanov's program and ready to defend it against all its critics. As a matter of course, Plekhanov reported on it at the congress. It actually remained the officially recognized program of the Bolshevik Party until after the Revolution of November, 1917!

Only in one respect had Lenin succeeded in amending it materially: he had added, and gotten accepted, a specifically Russian plank on the problem of the land and the peasants. When that codicil was later changed, the change, too, would be drafted and proposed by Lenin. Among the Marxists, he was almost alone in his sensitivity to the peasant question, and constantly engaged in thinking about it. It would be one of the secrets of his strength in 1917.

Before setting out for Geneva, Lenin once more sought to restore peace with Plekhanov. It seemed impossible to face

Revisionists, "Economists," Bundists, and other assorted opponents at a congress without the agreement and support of the chief teacher and leader of revolutionary Marxism. Lenin wrote urging Plekhanov, who was on his way to an International Socialist Congress at Brussels, to cross over to London and visit him:

> Your report would be most useful here . . . But the main reason is that we have a number of things which need discussion . . . the measures to be taken for uniting the party . . . the agenda for the Congress, what reports are to be delivered *by our people*, etc. . . . You know, I think it would be a good idea if we were to begin (informally) to be more friendly to the *Rabochee Delo* people . . . With a firm handclasp, Your Lenin.

Yet, even as he was asking Plekhanov's opinion on the agenda and related matters, he had already settled everything clearly in his own mind, and had actually sent explicit instructions to his *Iskra* agents in Russia. Thus, about the same time as the above note, he had sent a letter to E. Y. Levin in Kharkov, urging that the question of the attitude of the party toward the Jewish Bund should be made "the first order of business," so that, if the latter refused to yield its autonomy to a centralized party, it might be ousted from the congress and not permitted to vote on other closely contested matters. ("It is necessary to prepare everyone's mind for this.")

The second order of business should be the program, to divide the orthodox from the unorthodox on basic matters of principle. The third order should be the question of a central organ, which Lenin was convinced must be *Iskra*. It should have "ideological leadership" over the party and should continue to be published abroad. With this Editorial Board should be coupled a central committee, meeting inside Russia, to conduct the practical struggle. "Then: as much centralization as possible. Autonomy of local committees in local matters, with the right of veto by the Central Committee . . . District organization only with the agreement and approval (of its personnel) by the Central Committee."

The letter admitted that his proposed order of business, running on through eleven points, was subject to change. But "I consider it important from the beginning to decide point 3, in order immediately to give battle to all opponents on a basic and broad question of principle and to get a clear picture of the entire Congress: to separate on a serious issue."

"To separate on a serious issue!" It is doubtful that Lenin actually anticipated a split, though the word he used, *razoitis,* literally means to go apart; separate; sunder; each go his own way. Yet this insistence on the readiness to oust the Bund, on the readiness to "separate on a serious issue," is revealing as to the state of mind and psychology of Lenin, and goes far to explain the air of fatality with which a split did develop at the "unification" congress. (Incidentally, though Plekhanov's interests and insistences did not turn so much around organization questions as did Lenin's, Plekhanov's mood and temperament were otherwise similar. He too would be ready to split with the Bund if it did not accept his views on the "national question" and with the *Rabochee Delo* people and all and sundry, if they were opposed to his program.)

These letters are interesting, too, for the light they throw on Lenin's method of work, and how he prepared himself for battle. Most men would come to the congress filled with a vague exhilaration, prepared to trust much to its collective wisdom, to last-minute inspiration and exchange of opinion, to proposals that would come out of discussion and out of the spontaneous bright ideas of so many devoted people. Plekhanov, too, was ready to do that on everything but his pet project, the party program. But not so Lenin. He was never one to leave anything to chance when he expected a fight. He had little faith in collective discussion and spontaneous improvisation. His days and nights were spent in trying to prepare everything, anticipate everything, work out everything to the last detail. "Do not fail to obtain from *each* Local Committee and group," he admonished Levin with his usual underscorings, "an official and *written* answer as to whether it recognizes the Organization Committee."

The Organization Committee, of which Lenin was a member, was his, too. Not, to be sure, at the outset, when its members had been named by the abortive Bialystok Conference. But, as luck would have it, there had been a police spy at Bialystok, and when the first committee was arrested, Lenin was quick to take advantage by having *Iskra* agents named to replace them. To his old friend, agent F. V. Lengnik in Samara, he had written:

> And so your task now is to create from *your own selves* a committee to prepare the Congress, to admit a Bundist into the Committee (after sizing him up *from all sides*—note this well), and to push your own people on to as many committees as possible, guarding yourselves and your people more closely than the apple of your eye [against arrest] until the Congress. This is most important! Keep it in mind. Be in this bolder, more impudent and more ingenious, and in the rest quieter and more careful.
>
> Wise as serpents—and as gentle (with the committees, the Bund, and Peter[sburg])—as doves.
>
> All yours
>
> THE OLD MAN

Petersburg is mentioned because the anti-*Iskra* tendency had a majority there; the Bund because the Iskrists were determined to put an end to its autonomy; the Local Committees because they would elect most of the delegates. The letter is dated May 23, 1902, which shows how far back Lenin had been preparing for a congress that would not take place until the summer of 1903. There was not another man on the *Iskra* Board that could conceivably have written such letters. Nor was there any among his opponents. The injunction to be wise as serpents and gentle as doves had no sinister import in Lenin's mind, for he did not think of himself as a person looking for personal advantage or personal power, but as the selfless embodiment of a political line which was the only conceivably correct one. That unconscious conception of himself was as much a part of his strength as was the care with which he prepared the strategy, the tactics, the detailed deployment of forces and the general plan of every anticipated battle.

After taking care of the Russian Organization Committee and the Bund and the packing of the local committees in Russia with *Iskra* agents, Lenin turned his attention to the émigré colonies, where the opponents of *Iskra,* the *Rabochee Delo* supporters outnumbered the Iskrists. To Martov, who had gone to Paris because he could not stand the London climate, he wrote:

> The section of the Organization Committee abroad should be a section of the Russian Organization Committee—which should adopt an arch-important and an arch-severe attitude . . . either recognition of the Organization Committee and subjection to it, *or war. Tertium non datur.*

These prosaic preparations, this unblinking attention to organization detail, this predetermination of the selection of delegates and precalculation of the putative number of votes at the congress would be far more decisive than the debates, once the delegates should come together.

At the same time, Lenin did not neglect the preparation of his arguments either. He was already at work on the documents and resolutions he intended to present to the congress, the reports and speeches he intended to make there, even the refutation of anticipated objections. Night after night he paced the floor while poor Krupskaya tossed in their sleepless bed, whispering to himself, composing articles, resolutions, clauses, arguments, rehearsing reports, formulating precise phrases. When the parts of something had at last fallen into place in his mind, he would go for a walk with his wife and tell her about it.

Fearful lest the modest and laconic plank he had written as the agrarian section of the program might prove too difficult of understanding for the peasants, he was at the same time at work on one of the best pieces of popularization he ever did in his life, a pamphlet entitled *To the Village Poor.* In strikingly simple language it explained not only the immediate and long-range programs of the socialists for agriculture, but all the social, political and economic aims of socialism. The writing of this homely work was Lenin's diversion from the inexorable business of the preparation of the congress: it rested his torn nerves and restored his shattered health.

No sooner did he get out of the sickbed in Geneva than the delegates began to arrive. He greeted, sounded, walked, talked with each one personally. Martov was continually at the Ulyanovs now, and never tired of talking to the delegates either. They discussed program, party structure, theories, the role of the Bund. Martov's talk had the ampler sweep, but Lenin's was more sharply directed to the precise points that might become issues in the voting. When a doubtful delegate arrived from hostile Saint Petersburg, Lenin saw to it that he roomed with his young admirer, Trotsky, "for purposes of training."

"How Vladimir Ilyich longed for this Congress!" wrote Krupskaya a quarter of a century after it had taken place. "Longed for" . . . and prepared for it. "The general view was that there were no real differences and that everything would go swimmingly . . ." When it was too late, when the Congress had passed into history, one of the leaders of one of the defeated factions, Axelrod, would pay this reluctant tribute to the man who had tried to anticipate every eventuality:

> There is no other man who is absorbed by the revolution twenty-four hours a day, who has no other thoughts but the thought of revolution, and who, even when he sleeps, dreams of nothing but the revolution.

CHAPTER FOURTEEN

UNIFICATION CONGRESS

Vladimir Ilyich and I recalled a simile that L. Tolstoy used somewhere. Once when walking, he spotted in the distance the figure of a man squatting on his haunches and moving his hands about in an absurd way. *A madman*! he thought. But on drawing nearer, he saw that it was a man sharpening his knife on the paving-stone.

—KRUPSKAYA

lose to sixty revolutionaries, some from the underground and others, the majority, from émigré colonies, gathered in Brussels for a conclave that was to be kept secret from the Belgian police. Four of the delegates were, or had once been, workingmen. The rest were typical members of the intelligentsia, something we must keep in mind if we are to understand the length, breadth, depth, fanatical stubbornness and Byzantine subtlety of debates so heated that they must have awakened policemen sleeping in the cemetery. The injured self-love of men who identified self with their ideas combined with a feeling of selflessness to make every defeat on the minutest question a banner of conflict.

Those unfamiliar with Brussels were instructed to report to the home of Koltzov, where they would be given connection with the secret committee in charge of the Congress. After the first four Russians had rung Koltzov's bell at odd hours, and engaged him in intense and enthusiastic discussion, the landlady issued an ultimatum: "If one more Russian comes here, you will have to move!" Poor old Koltzov and his wife took turns on the street corner, to head off visitors and bid them go to the Coq d'Or. The first arrivals became restless while weeks dragged in waiting for the representatives from underground Russia. Some of these did not arrive until the Congress was over. Delegates overran the hotel in noisy bands. "Gusev, glass of cognac clutched in his hand," remembers Krupskaya, "sang operatic arias every evening in such loud tones that crowds gathered beneath the windows. Vladimir Ilyich loved to hear Gusev sing: 'We Were Wedded Out of Church'. . ."

By the time the sessions got underway all Brussels was aware of the fact that some mysterious Russians were assembling for a secret gathering that could bode no good for Belgium's foreign relations. But what could be more secret than a Congress on whose organizing committee Lenin had named Dr. Zhitomirsky, Okhrana agent delegated to shadow him, from 1902 to 1917? When the Congress split, naturally Zhitomirsky sided with Lenin. In the scandals over Bolshevik holdups and illicit funds (see Chapter XXII), Lenin named this "man of confidence" to serve on a joint Bolshevik-Menshevik investigating committee, and to block the inquiry "lest it reach the police." The most secret of Lenin's secret committees, that on finance, consisted of Lenin, Bogdanov and Krassin. When he ousted the last two, he promoted Dr. Zhitomirsky to a place on it!

According to Lenin's account, probably the most accurate, for he was always one to check such things, there were forty-three delegates with fifty-one votes. Some of these, including Lenin and Martov, were "two-handed" delegates with two votes apiece because they had secured mandates from both a Russian underground and an émigré organization. In addition there were fourteen "consultative votes," that is, fraternal delegates with voice but no vote. These included Axelrod, Zasulich and Potresov of the *Iskra* Board (Lenin and Martov had the two votes to which the Board was entitled); Arkadi Kremer of the Bund; Noah Zhordania, founder and outstanding leader of the Georgian Social Democracy and future president of Georgia's short-lived democratic republic; Hanecki and Warski of the Polish Social Democracy; and others whose names need not detain us, since they will not play an important role in our story.

Of the fifty-one official votes, thirty-three, or a clear majority, belonged to adherents of the *Iskra* faction. Lenin's careful preparations had made that certain. Among them were his younger brother, Dmitri Ulyanov, some old friends from Samara and Siberian exile, and a number of *Iskra* agents that he had personally sent to Russia. This did not necessarily mean that the local organizations which had sent them knew what issues might arise or what Lenin stood for. Often an agent had been chosen because he had demonstrated his ability to get in and out of the country, was possessed of the necessary funds and willing to undertake the hazardous journey, whereas the local people lacked means and were bound to the spot by employment and family ties. Thus, unwittingly, was begun a fateful system in which a central body (or a leader) first chose the local leadership and then the latter were designated as convention delegates to choose the central body, that is, to confirm the very men who had appointed them in the first place.

Iskra's chief rival, *Rabochee Delo,* possessed only three votes at the Congress, two as a journal, and one, a delegate elected from Petersburg! Yet they had the support of a good part of the emigration, and a decisive majority in Saint Petersburg, which Local Committee the Iskrists had just split so that the Congress might be made to seat one from each faction. From *Rabochee Delo* itself came the "Economists" Martynov (A. C. Piker), and Akimov (Vladimir Makhnovets), and from Saint Petersburg his sister Lydia Makhnovets. Even the powerful Jewish Bund, numerically the largest and best organized body of workmen in Russia, possessed only five votes, by no means representative of its actual strength in the total Russian movement. Six of the remaining delegates were faceless men and women who had not lined up on the anticipated issues, but had come to see and learn. These earned from Plekhanov and Lenin the derisive appellation of "the Swamp" because they voted now with one faction and now with the other. If the thirty-three Iskrists, most of whom had been conveniently planted by Lenin as local delegates, should stick, all the others might talk themselves blue in the face, as they likely would, but *Iskra* would have its way.

The Congress opened at last on July 30, 1903, in a big flour warehouse festively draped with red cloth. The old edifice was infested with rats and fleas, while representatives of the Russian and Belgian police swarmed around nearby alleys and courts.

Georgii Valentinovich Plekhanov, who had waited twenty years for this occasion, delivered a moving opening address. There were tears in many eyes as the delegates, standing, sang with muted voices "The International." Out of respect for the still-born Minsk Convention of 1898, they called this the "Second Congress"; but really it was the first. They were coming together at last to found a party, adopt a program, draw up a constitution, unite the local committees, rival factions, warring papers and national and émigré groups, into a single, united, All-Russian Social Democratic Labor Party.

The exaltation soon gave way to wrangling over credentials. "The composition of the Party Congress," as Lenin put it bluntly, "was settled in advance by the Organization Committee." Still, if only as a matter of form, the convention had to set up a committee to pass on credentials. The committee included a Bundist whom Lenin denounced for "applying the strategy of tiring out the other members of the Commission, holding firm until 3 A.M., and still remaining in every question with his own 'special opinion.' " It is not hard to guess that his opinion was that the Congress was "packed" by the *Iskra*-controlled Organization Committee. Of course, the "pack" itself voted down all his protests.

Then briefly, the first puff of wind before a storm, Lenin and Martov clashed. It was a seemingly small matter, taking place not on the floor of the convention but in the "private" and "secret" (but of course quite generally talked about) sessions of the *Iskra* caucus. They were discussing the presidium of the convention, a directing body similar to an American steering or ways and means committee, plus the standing officers. If this were representative of all factions it could, and usually did, settle a great many matters by negotiation, without taking up the time of general sessions. Martov proposed such a representative presidium of nine members including one spokesman each for the Bund and *Rabochee Delo*. But Lenin was for a narrow presidium of three, Iskrists all, which should rule "with a firm hand, if necessary with an iron fist." Some uncomplimentary words about "hardness" and "softness" were exchanged. Lenin's steam-roller proposal won in the caucus; the caucus won in the convention. The presidium was Plekhanov, chairman, Lenin and Krasikov, vice-chairmen, all three Iskrists!

Exactly as Lenin had planned, the first full-dress debate took place on the question of the relationship of the Jewish Socialist

Bund to the Party. The Bund was a product of the active awakening of the Jewish Pale in Russian Poland, Lithuania and White Russia, an awakening at once cultural, social and political. It is symbolic of this awakening that the Zionist movement and the Socialist Bund were born in the same year as rivals for the leadership of the masses in this, the largest concentration of Jews in the world. For a few years the Bundists, in their zeal to fight nascent Jewish nationalism, looked only to the Russian workers to lead in the solution of their special Jewish problems, and "forgot to maintain contact with the Jewish masses who understand no Russian." (It is from Martov, who was briefly a Bundist before he joined Lenin in Saint Petersburg, that these words are quoted.) But the Bundists soon discovered that the Jewish workers were far ahead of the Russian in organization and in consciousness. At the same time, their war with Zionism for the awakening Jewish communities compelled them not only to adopt Yiddish as their language but to recognize that "the growth of national consciousness and class consciousness must go hand in hand." Thus they came to this unification congress determined to demand continued autonomy in the handling of specifically Jewish problems, and to assert the claim to represent all Jewish socialists, not merely in the territorially compact pale of settlement, but in Southern Russia (where the Jews were more Russified), and wherever in the vast empire men might be found who suffered disadvantages as Jews or who, by reason of cultural or other considerations, classified themselves as Jews.

Behind this demand were both a theory of party structure and a theory of national self-determination. Its acceptance implied that, as the rest of the minority nationalities of the Empire awakened, they too would require similar arrangements of autonomy. Thus the Social Democratic Party would eventually become a federated party rather than a centralized one, with each nationality having its autonomous federation. And, if it should ever triumph, the state that would issue out of its victory would have to be a federalist rather than a centralized state. Lenin for his part held to the idea of a strictly centralized party in which national subdivisions would be no more than agencies for translating into their respective languages the slogans, program, decisions and will of the all-powerful Central Committee. And his conception of national self-determination was based upon territorial rather than cultural nationality, a difference which would become clear only a decade later.

Martov, the ex-Bundist, Trotsky and Axelrod, assimilated Jews, and the more or less Russified Jews of Southern Russia present at the Congress all lined up with Lenin and Plekhanov against the Bund. They were supported by the general desire for a centralized party, by the fear of fostering nationalistic separatism in this conglomerate of peoples, by socialist distrust of nationalism in the name of a supra-national internationalism, by the unconscious Great-Russianism of many of the delegates. "The Bund," wrote Krupskaya, "were brought to their knees." If they were, they found their feet again before the end of the Congress, and suddenly walked out, with unexpected results for the whole future of the Russian Social Democratic Party. Only Lenin, as we have seen from his letter to *Iskra* agent Levin (in the preceding chapter), was not taken by surprise but had actually based his calculations upon this secession.

Next the acknowledged founder of Russian Marxism, Plekhanov, rose to report on the projected party program. In 1929, Trotsky still remembered:

> With a clear, scientifically exact outline of the program in his mind, sure of himself, of his knowledge and of his superiority, with a gay, ironic sparkle in his eyes . . . with slightly theatrical but lively and expressive gestures, Plekhanov illumined the entire large gathering with a living fireworks of wit and erudition.

Given the composition of the Congress and the prestige of the reporter, adoption was a foregone conclusion. Yet a small determined minority, led by the "Economists" Akimov and Martynov, conducted a stubborn rearguard action. Every formulation was examined with subtlety. The debate raged through endless, round-the-clock sessions of a special Program Commission, and nearly twenty full sessions of the Congress itself! Akimov proposed no less than twenty-two separate amendments, every one of which was eventually defeated. He attacked the program wholesale and retail for its spirit of tutelage over the proletariat:

> The concepts Party and Proletariat are set in opposition to each other, the first as an active, causative, collective being, the second as a passive medium on which the Party operates. The name of the Party is used throughout as subject, in the nominative case, the name of the Proletariat as object, in the genitive case. (Laughter.)*

Some of those who laughed loudest at this "grammatical critique" of the program would live to wonder whether it had not touched on something symbolic, not of grammar, but of underlying sense.

But the main fire of the opposition was concentrated on a single sentence:

> The essential condition for the social revolution is the dictatorship of the proletariat, i.e., the conquest of such power by the proletariat as will allow it to suppress all attempts at resistance on the part of the exploiters.

How do you reconcile your endorsement of dictatorship, Akimov asked, with that part of your draft which comes out for a democratic republic? How do you square it with your demands for a constituent assembly elected by free, equal, direct, secret and universal suffrage? With your demand for freedom of speech, press, parties, organization, conscience, movement, occupation? for equality of all citizens regardless of status, sex, race, religion, nationality? Is not democracy an absolute good?

---

* In Russian, masculine personal objects have the same form in the genitive as in the accusative.

Is it not a matter of principle? One of the desiderata for which we are fighting in every field? Shall we, representatives of those who suffer from dictatorship, countenance its use ourselves?

Trotsky rose to the defense of the program with a paraphrase from the *Communist Manifesto:*

> The rule of the working class was inconceivable until the great mass of them were united in desiring it. Then they would be an overwhelming majority. This would not be the dictator-ship of a little band of conspirators or a minority party, but of the immense majority in the interests of the immense majority, to prevent counter-revolution. In short, it would represent the victory of true democracy.*

Later, Stalinist historians would hold this speech against Trotsky, as a "repudiation of the principle of dictatorship." And he himself would abandon it in practice in 1917 . . .

Plekhanov brushed his unwelcome young defender aside. Akimov, Martynov and their supporters, he said, were confus-ing two distinct things: one was the immediate program of overthrowing tsarism and establishing a democratic republic; the other was the longer range struggle for socialism, which would not properly begin until the democratic republic had been achieved.

> Of course, we place universal suffrage in the foreground of our demands [he continued] but as revolutionaries we must say openly that we do not want to convert it into a fetish. It is not hard to imagine a situation in which the victorious working class may take away for a time the right of suffrage from its opponent, the bourgeoisie . . .
>
> The fundamental principle of democracy is this: *salus populi, suprema lex.* Translated into revolutionary language that means: *the health of the revolution is the supreme law* . . . If the safety of the revolution should demand the temporary limitation of one or another of the democratic principles, it would be a crime to hesitate . . .

---

* The minutes are not as a rule verbatim but represent summaries approved by an editorial committee and by the delegates themselves.

Some delegate has proposed that we amend our democratic demand for a parliament that meets at least every two years. He asks: Would not *every year* be even more democratic? But you must bear in mind, comrades, that the question of the term of parliament is for us revolutionaries a secondary one. If the people, in a moment of revolutionary enthusiasm, should elect a very favorable parliament, naturally we would try to make of it a Long Parliament. But if the elections should turn out badly for the working class, we might try to dissolve it, not at the end of two years, but in two weeks if possible . . .

Lenin said nothing in this debate, but his head must have nodded vigorous agreement, and the words of his master were a treasure in his memory. Fifteen years later he would quote them as he ordered the Constituent Assembly, elected by free, equal, direct and universal suffrage, to be dispersed!

Plekhanov's remarks on the subordination of democratic principles to the needs of the revolution were interrupted by demonstrative applause. But there were hisses, too. Lenin, who was in the chair, called the hissers to order. Rozanov cried out: "When in the congress of a labor party such unheard-of words are spoken, it is my duty to hiss!" Years later, still hissing these same ideas when Lenin was putting them into practice, this same Rozanov would be falsely accused of setting up a conspirative "National Center" to "help Denikin overthrow the Soviet Government."* Sentenced to death, he would be pardoned by Lenin's order and given employment in the Commissariat of Health . . .

"Abolition of the death penalty?"—Plekhanov continued imperturbably. "Very good! Still I am of the opinion that a few reservations are necessary. What do you think? Should Nicholas II be permitted to live? I think we should reserve for him a death penalty."

Martov was listening, too, with painful tension. One day he

* The "National Center" in question was that of the *Soyuz Vozrozhdenia* ("Union of Rebirth"), which aimed to unite the Right Wing of the Mensheviks and Social Revolutionaries with the Left Bourgeois Liberals to reconstruct a democratic Russia after the anticipated collapse of the Bolshevik dictatorship. Perhaps this loose "union" included one of the ubiquitous Chekist "Denikin officers." In any case, Rozanov's group did not.

would write a burning indictment of the Bolsheviks for restoring the death penalty after the Revolution had abolished it. Listening, he agreed with the general tenor of Plekhanov's remarks, but thought them unnecessarily "hard."

Plekhanov could have avoided arousing indignation—he said —if he had added that one could not imagine such a tragic situation in which the proletariat would have to trample on such political rights as freedom of the press in order to consolidate its victory . . .

To which Plekhanov responded by shouting an ironical "*Merci.*"

The convention was bringing Plekhanov and Lenin closer. The master dominated the public sessions, the disciple the private caucuses of the *Iskra* faction; the one marshaled the arguments, the other the votes. When the program was finally adopted, everyone present voted for it except Akimov, who abstained. It seemed that a united party must be assured since all had accepted a common foundation of principle.

Yet there was an ambiguity in this common program, a program which would serve Bolsheviks and Mensheviks alike until 1919. It aimed at two successive revolutions: a "bourgeois democratic" and a "proletarian socialist"—the overthrow of tsarism and the overthrow of capitalism. What was the relation between them? Would the bourgeoisie, supported by the proletariat, make the first revolution? Would the proletariat make the "bourgeois" revolution, then hand over power to the bourgeoisie in order to go over into opposition? Or would the professional revolutionaries acting in the name of the proletariat take power and hold it in trust until both revolutions were completed? Would the one revolution flow over into the other, or would there be years, perhaps decades, between them? It would take the experiences of 1905 even to raise these questions. Meanwhile, the delegates voted unanimously, some of them with eyes fastened on the democratic republic, while proletarian dictatorship and socialism appeared some remote vision of the future; others strained in their thoughts, beyond an unsatisfying revolution that had not yet begun, toward another that was to follow after.

To no one present did it occur to ask the crucial question that the French socialist Charles Peguy had already asked in 1900: "I should like to know who will actually be the persons who will exercise the dictatorship of the proletariat." Nor to raise his corollary questions as to how the proletariat might dictate to its dictators, how determine the extent or duration of dictatorial powers, how liberate itself, if need be, from its liberators . . .

Thus far, the differences were more matters of temperament than doctrine. They were obscurely felt, rather than thought, which explains the passion that charged subtle debates and technical divergencies on all sorts of secondary things. Martov could only plead that "one could not imagine such a tragic situation in which the proletariat would have to trample on such political rights as freedom of the press." And the tougher-minded, more impatient delegates could only express their attitude and expectations by being ultra-orthodox in matters of theory and ultra-hard in matters of organization. In their hearts they unconsciously knew the answer to Peguy's crucial question. It was: "Such as we . . ." They were ready to give expression to that conviction by building a rigidly centralized, highly conspiratorial party to dictate, if not yet to an "enemy class," then to the "softs" in their own ranks. Repentant "softs" turned "hards" could only satisfy their own self-doubt by being hardest of all. Plekhanov's remarks on two revolutions, one for democracy and a second for socialism, Martov's plea to "imagine" or hope for the best, Akimov's opposition on principle to dictatorship, Rozanov's hiss—these lifted for a little moment a corner of the veil that hid future conflicts. But Marx himself had used the term *proletarian dictatorship* (in the sense that young Trotsky had rightly explained: "Not the dictatorship of a minority party, but of the immense majority in the interests of the immense majority, to prevent counter-revolution"). Who but Akimov wanted to be counted as not an orthodox Marxist?

Unanimity, except for his vote, drew the veil down once more.

It is interesting to note how little part Lenin took in this great programmatic debate: only to explain and defend his small plank on agrarian matters, and to make one other brief, apparently insignificant remark. There was a sentence in the program which said that, as the contradictions inherent in capitalism continued to grow, with them would grow "the dissatisfaction, the solidarity and the numbers of the proletariat." The Program Commission brought in an amendment to add: "and the consciousness" before "proletariat." On this Lenin was moved to take the floor:

> This amendment would be a worsening—he declared. It would give the idea that the development of consciousness is a spontaneous thing . . . Aside from the influence of the Social Democracy, there is no *conscious* activity of the workers.

Here was something he could not leave to Plekhanov to say. Was it mere pedantry? This dogma, obscure as yet in its implications, was at the very core of "Leninism." From it flowed an attitude toward the working class, toward its ability to think for itself, to learn from experience, toward its capacities and potentialities for self-rule, toward its "spontaneous" movements such as might take place without orders and control from the party of socialist theoreticians and professional revolutionaries. From it would spring a special attitude toward trade unions, toward the impromptu strikers' councils or soviets, even toward two revolutions—in 1905 and the spring of 1917—that would come not on order but by surprise.

As one continues with the minutes of the Congress one gets a growing impression of watching a congregation of somnambulists. The treasury—contributed by well-to-do ("bourgeois") sympathizers—dwindles to exhaustion. Agreement on fundamental principle seems virtually unanimous, yet nerves grow frayed with sleepless nights, endless wrangles, summer heat.

Men squabble unceasingly over procedure. The discussions get tied up in knots. The delegates grow inordinately angry, gesticulate with inexplicable violence, lacerate each other's spirits.

In Russia at this very moment events are moving without the intervention of these men toward some unforeseen outcome. Here in an obscure chapel in working-class London, somnambulists are contending with each other impotently, as in a dream. All Russia's socialist leaders are here—prideful, strong-willed men, each sure that he is in the right, all comrades in a common cause with a common program and doctrine, contending endlessly over rules of procedure and niceties of formulation that seem infinitely remote from the first general strike in her history, at this very moment sweeping over south Russia and the Caucasus. The least of the somnambulists will be away for months; the leaders for years, decades . . .

The Russian and Belgian police swarm around the convention. They stick like autumn flies. They follow the delegates to their lodgings, sit at tables near them in the Coq d'Or, trail them into the park and along the lake shore, where, after midnight, discussions spill over in loud voices. They search rooms and baggage, rob the delegates' briefcases, intercept their correspondence. Finally, they seize pedantic-looking, tight-lipped Rosa Zemlyachka, an *Iskra* agent and one of Lenin's "hards," and deport her. They give several other delegates twenty-four hours' notice to leave the country. At this, the entire Congress packs up and takes train and boat for the freer atmosphere of London. All the way on the train, and on the boat over the Channel, the excited discussion never ceases. In London, they continue to meet, in a "socialist church," day and night in the midsummer heat, from August 11 to August 23.

The debate on the Party constitution began quietly enough. But now the Iskrists themselves were divided: Lenin and Martov had rival drafts. Lenin proposed that Article I should define a party member as one "who recognizes the Party's program and supports it by material means *and by personal participation in one of the party organizations."* Martov proposed a substitute with the identical language, except that the final italicized phrase read: *"and by regular personal assistance under the direction of one of the party organizations."*

The delegates were puzzled. Both formulations seemed substantially the same. Even Plekhanov, so close to Lenin now, was puzzled by the latter's excited insistence on the enormity of the difference.

Lenin explained his formulation. He took the floor again and again and again. Time would clarify the difference in approach, but for the present, all the delegates could make of it was that he wanted a "narrow" party of selected revolutionists, every one of them subject to control by the center, surrounded by broad circles of workers who obeyed the party without belonging to it.

> My formula restricts the conception of party member while Martov's broadens it . . . It is better that ten who actually work should not call themselves members (real workers don't hunt for titles!) than that one who just talks should have the right to be a party member . . .

Martov, too, took the floor again and again. He was for a centralized party but not one whose members "abdicated their right to think." He wanted a broad party, not a party of professional revolutionists alone, but one open to all workers and intellectuals who believed in its program and were willing to work under its direction. Party membership was not merely a "title" but the right to a voice in the party's affairs. Those who carried out its directions should have the right to influence its decisions, even if they did not work for it full time. But how? Martov's formulation provided no definite answer. He did not yet realize whither his divergence with Lenin was tending, nor did he have the latter's skill in giving organizational form to his approach. The delegates continued to be puzzled.

Trotsky surprised Lenin by siding with Martov:

> I do not believe that you can put a statutory exorcism on
> opportunism. I do not give the statutes any sort of mystical
> interpretation.

Axelrod joined in:

> Is not Lenin dreaming of the administrative subordination of
> an entire party to a few guardians of doctrine?

Plekhanov in turn rallied to Lenin, who seemed to be losing
out:

> I have no preconceived idea, but the more I reflect on what
> has been said, the stronger is my conviction that the truth lies
> with Lenin ... Intellectuals may hesitate for individualistic rea-
> sons to join the party, so much the better, for they are generally
> opportunists . . . for this reason if for no other, the opponents
> of opportunism should vote for his draft.

Two full sessions, many votes on procedure, and two time-
consuming roll-calls on Article I alone! The vote: for Martov's
formulation twenty-eight, for Lenin's twenty-two! Lenin was
beside himself. Then and there he determined to split the *Iskra*
caucus and build up a "hard" faction of his own, to try to make
every other article in the Constitution ultra-centralist, "to bind
up"—as he wrote later—"the broken cask with double hoops
. . . to load our weapons with a double charge . . . to propose
the limitation of the rights of the majority" in the interests of
his minority. In short, he prepared on the spot for a long, irreconcilable war against the Congress decision, that had just been
taken after a full and free debate.

The Iskrists gathered for what turned out to be their last caucus or faction meeting. The tension can be deduced from what
Lenin wrote months later when he had cooled off:

> Lenin conducted himself like a madman. Right. He banged
> the door, that is correct. But with what result? . . . Only this,

that out of the sixteen members of the *Iskra* organization present, after all, nine were with me . . . If there had been no "rudeness" perhaps more than nine would have been on my side . . .

Perhaps. But with four members of the old editorial board against his two, himself and Plekhanov, and with nine members of the larger caucus on his side against Martov's seven, Lenin called a new meeting of the "firm" Iskrists and posted guards outside the door with orders not to admit Martov, Axelrod, Zasulich, Potresov, or any of the other close comrades-in-arms who had voted against him. The excluded sent in a written demand to be admitted but it was denied. Vladimir Ilyich ceased to sleep at all by now, and, according to Krupskaya, was unable even to eat, which left him most of the twenty-four hours of the day to go after every delegate in person. Here is the account of one who up to that day had been known as "Lenin's cudgel"—his young disciple Trotsky:

> Lenin lost no opportunity to win me over to his side. He, Krasikov and I had a long walk together, during which they both tried to persuade me that Martov and I could not follow the same road, for Martov was a "soft" one. Krasikov's descriptions of the other editors of *Iskra* were so unceremonious that they made Lenin frown, while I shivered. My attitude towards the editors of *Iskra* was still touched with the sentimentality of youth. The conversation repelled me . . . Lenin made another attempt to win me over by sending a woman delegate, Z., as well as his younger brother Dmitri . . . The emissaries would not let me go. "We have orders," they said, "to bring you with us at any cost." In the end, I flatly refused to follow them.

And here is Lenin's own account of his talk with one of the delegates of the so-called "Swamp":

> "What a depressing atmosphere . . ."—he complained to me. "All this fierce fighting, this agitation one against the other, these sharp polemics, this uncomradely attitude!"
>
> "What a fine thing our Congress is,"—I replied to him. "Opportunity for open fighting. Opinions expressed. Tendencies revealed. Groups defined. Hands raised. A decision taken. A stage

passed through. Forward! That's what I like! That's life! It is something different from the endless, wearying intellectual discussions which finish, not because people have solved the problem, but simply because they have got tired of talking."

The comrade of the "Center" looked on me as though perplexed, and shrugged his shoulders. We had spoken different languages.

While Lenin was battling day and night for the soul of every delegate, the giddy wheel of fortune took an unexpected turn. The Bund delegates, who had been nursing their wounds apart since the blow dealt them on the question of autonomy, announced their withdrawal from the Congress—five solid votes that had been cast for the proposition of Martov! Following up this advantage, Lenin proposed a motion calculated to drive out another group of his opponents: he moved to dissolve the *Rabochee Delo* and give exclusive recognition to *Iskra* and its foreign organization as the only émigré body. Martov, as a loyal Iskrist, fell into the trap and voted in favor of the motion. Thereupon, two more delegates who had supported his draft of Article I of the Constitution withdrew from the Congress in a huff. Lenin's bloc was converted from a minority of five or six to a majority of two votes!

> It is incomprehensible to me why the *Bund* left the Congress under such circumstances—Lenin wrote later. It showed itself master of the situation and could have put through many things.

Since, all his life, Lenin attached a feeling of moral baseness to "opportunism," he found it hard to understand that these men of the Bund and *Rabochee Delo* could have firm convictions, principles of their own, and, defeated on them, would not content themselves with "putting through" what he regarded as opportunistic measures.

Now his keen sense of organization and power taught him that, with the aid of the slender majority handed to him by their withdrawal, he himself could "put through many things." The first of these was a moral advantage: the adoption of a name for his new caucus: *Bolshinstvo* ("Majority") or *Bolsheviki* ("Majorityites"). Though but yesterday he had been in a minority, and, more often than not would be in the minority in the future, he would never relinquish the psychological advantage of that name. A name, he knew, was a program, a distilled essence, more powerful in its impact upon the untutored mind than any propaganda slogan. What pride it could give to his caucus, no matter how it might dwindle, always to call itself "Majorityites." What conviction, what an air of legality, of democratic, majority sanction, it would give in appealing to the rank and file and the non-party masses. If he had remained in a minority, he would have chosen some other banner name—like "True Iskrists" or "Orthodox Marxists" or "Revolutionary Wing of Russian Social Democracy." But it is characteristic of the ineptness of his opponents that they permanently accepted the designation of *Mensheviki* ("Minorityites") for their group.

His next move was to make sure that the new Central Committee should be small, and contain a firm majority of "hards." He knew that arrests and escapes might make it necessary for such a committee to add to its number by coopting, so he provided an elaborate machinery which would enable him to veto the coopting of any unwelcome persons. Experience had taught him that the police can break up Central Committees and that new men may have other views. So, despite his predilection for centralism, which should have subordinated a mere group of editors of a party paper to the Central Committee in Russia, he put into the Constitution a provision making the Central Organ, published abroad, dominant over the Central Committee itself! The Board of Editors, which he would control, should in turn control the Central Committee. Trotsky had an argument with him on the matter:

> "The Central Organ should be subordinate to the Central Committee."

"That won't do," Vladimir Ilyich replied. "That is contrary to the relative strength. How can they direct us from Russia? It won't do . . . We are the stable center and shall direct from here..."

"But doesn't that mean complete dictatorship by the Central Organ?" I asked.

"What is there bad about that?" Lenin answered. "In the present situation, it cannot be otherwise."

This was typical of Lenin. For all his dogmatic preaching of organization principles, he always subordinated them to the pragmatic realities of the specific power situation, and to his unalterable conviction that his views were good for the Party and must, at all costs, be made to prevail. If he was unsure of the Central Committee, he would give power to the Central Organ. If he lost the latter (as he soon did), then he would give power to the Central Committee. If he lost both (as he would within the year), he would defy both and set up his own caucus committee of the "hards" for whom he would still claim the suggestive name "Majority." Having managed to hammer out a majority of two for the final days after the Bund and *Rabochee Delo* delegates withdrew from the Congress, he would continue to claim that any caucus he might form, however small, represented the "true majority" of the Congress, even on issues which the Congress itself had not considered. While he himself had control of the leading committees, however, he was remorseless in his denunciation of those who defied their discipline. This flexible inflexibility, which made his own views the test of when it was a crime to break discipline and when it was a crime not to, did not spring from hypocrisy or arrogance or lust for power. It sprang from his unshakable conviction of his own rightness. It was selfless in the sense that for Lenin the distinction between self and the movement had become completely obliterated. It never occurred to him to say: *I am right* but only: *We are the stable center and shall direct from here.* As Plekhanov said to Axelrod in an aside of half-fearful admiration: "Of this dough, Robespierres are made."

Lenin's next move with his exiguous majority stretched the bent bow to the breaking point. He proposed that the old Editorial Board of *Iskra* should be dismissed, and in its place should be set up a new Board of three members, "with power to add to their number." His candidates were Plekhanov, Lenin, Martov. When the delegates realized that the veteran political thinker and organizer Axelrod, and the movement's heroine, Vera Zasulich, were being thrown out, a storm broke about Lenin's balding head. He wasted many words, then and later, in trying to prove that he had not sprung his proposal as a surprise, that he had discussed it in advance with all the editors and that the victims had agreed to their demise. Against this we have not only the testimony of the other editors, but that of Lenin's own wife:

> This was a very painful problem and nothing was said to the delegates about it. The fact that the *Iskra* Editorial Board as formerly constituted was no longer fit to carry on the work was too depressing to talk about.

And, in one of his innumerable polemics on the convention, Lenin himself let slip the fact that his original plan, as revealed to Martov and perhaps to a few other close cronies prior to the Congress, had been more moderate: to set up an Editorial Board of the old six plus one other—seven in all—and have them elect out of their own number a small working sub-committee of three. "But," wrote Lenin:

> beaten in the question of Article I of the Statutes, I could not help but try to get even in all the other questions which were left for me and the Congress. I could not help but try in the first place for a "strict" Iskrist Central Committee, and in the second for an Editorial Committee of three . . .

Finally, we have the evidence of Krupskaya's psychological insight into the spirits of the two members of the Old Guard who were being thus unceremoniously dismissed:

P. B. Axelrod was particularly pained by the fact that *Iskra*
was not published in Switzerland, and that the stream of communications with Russia did not pass through him. That is why
he took up such an angry attitude at the Second Congress towards the question of the editorial triumvirate. *Iskra* was to be
the organizing center, and *he* removed from the editorial board!
And this when, more than at any other time, the breath of Russia could be felt . . .

To her—Vera Zasulich—leaving *Iskra* would mean once more
becoming isolated from Russia, once more beginning to sink in
the dead sea of émigré life, that drags one to the bottom. It
was for this reason that, when the question of the editorship
of *Iskra* was brought up at the Second Congress, she revolted.
For her it was not a question of self-love, but a question of
life and death . . .

No, these two could not have accepted in advance their sentence of extinction.

The air of the quiet Brotherhood Church rang with cries of
"autocrat," "dictator," "martial law," "state of siege," "in-
sult," "execution," "coup d'état." Delegates reminded Lenin
that only a few days back, they had voted unanimously—all
but Akimov, who had abstained—to endorse *Iskra,* which had
meant to them not merely a body of doctrine but its human in-
corporation in an editorial board. Martov, who had learned to
love and revere the veterans Axelrod and Zasulich, threatened
and pleaded, then served notice that he would not make up
part of any editorial board from which they were absent. "In
place of a period, put a tear in the minutes!" shouted one of
Lenin's "hards" after Martov's plea. When a motion to reelect
the old board was defeated, the outraged minority refused
thenceforward to vote on any question. Plekhanov, Lenin and
Martov were elected editors of the Central Organ, regardless of
declination of the last named. Noskov, Krzhizhanovsky and
Lengnik, "Leninists" all three, were elected as the Central Committee. Each of these bodies was to name two men to a Party
Council of five, for which the Congress chose a chairman, Plekhanov. But the vote? Seven had already walked out of the Congress. Twenty more refused to participate in the balloting. In

the voting for Plekhanov, who but yesterday had been the honored master of them all, twenty-two wrote his name on their ballots, two deposited blanks, twenty refused to vote! Twenty-two out of forty-four with twenty-two abstentions, and that after seven others had walked out—such was the celebrated "Majority" *(Bolshinstvo)* out of which the Bolsheviks were born!

And even before the Congress was dispersed, a swing away from Lenin began to be perceptible once more. Topuridze, the "hard" delegate from Georgia, turned "soft" and joined the "Minority" as soon as the Congress adjourned. Plekhanov switched within less than six months, making Lenin a minority in the Editorial Board of three (which Martov had never consented to attend). Before a year was out, the hand-picked Central Committee and the hand-picked Party Council, too, had turned against Lenin. Yet he never ceased to claim that he spoke for the "Majority" of the Party as expressed at the Congress, and that those who turned against him were revolting against the majority will.*

On Saturday, August 23, at five o'clock in the afternoon, the nightmare battle about the personnel of the leading committees, simply petered out. It had not been settled, since Martov had already announced that he would refuse to serve on the three-man Editorial Board to which he had been elected. It petered out more from exhaustion than from the conviction on any one's part that a workable conclusion had been reached. The exhaustion was general: funds, nerves, energies, throats, capacity to sit or listen. Lenin himself had spoken, according to the careful count of the Marx-Engels-Lenin Institute, approximately one hundred and twenty times, including reports, declarations, statements, interpolations, motions, etc. Of twenty-four points

---

* The official Party History of Emilian Yaroslavsky has this to say on Lenin's majority:

"The majority of the Congress (by 2 or 3 votes) upheld the Mensheviks. This should be borne in mind by those who believe that it was on this question (Article 1 of the Party Constitution) that we gained a majority at the Congress. No, Lenin gained a majority in the elections of the Central Committee and the Central Organ of the Party, when the most reactionary Economists and the Bundists had quit the Congress." (English Edition, Moscow, 1927, Vol. I, p. 87.)

on the order of business, the delegates had thus far handled but
four. After 5 P.M. on the last day, they began a desultory discussion of some of the resolutions on tactical questions: important matters like attitude toward the liberals, toward the new,
legally permitted, police-controlled "Zubatov" labor unions;
toward the Social Revolutionary Party. In two hours they
pushed through a half dozen or more resolutions, some of them
(as in the case of two on the Liberals) even contradicting each
other. Not even Lenin had the energy left to fight to a finish for
the exclusive adoption of one or the other.

Feeling himself in control of the Party machine, he permitted
his hopes to rise at the listless unanimity:

> The attitude toward the resolutions was so unanimous that
> we got the impression that a mood of conciliation had arisen
> ... All resolutions were adopted in a peaceful and friendly fash-
> ion. [From Lenin's Report on the Congress.]

But the convention, which, after two decades of longing and
two and one-half years of intensive planning, had been called
for the purpose of unifying the movement, adjourned that
same night *sine die,* hopelessly divided. It had been assembled
to constitute a party. It would take at least ten years to realize
that it had really constituted not one party but two.

CHAPTER FIFTEEN

TAKEN
BY
SURPRISE

Member of the International Socialist Bureau: Do you mean to say that all these splits and quarrels and scandals are the work of one man? But how can one man be so effective and so dangerous?

Axelrod: Because there is not another man who for twenty-four hours of the day is taken up with the revolution, who has no other thoughts but thoughts of revolution, and who, even in his sleep dreams of nothing but revolution. Just try and handle such a fellow.

—DIALOGUE AT THE INTERNATIONAL SOCIALIST CONFERENCE, COPENHAGEN 1910

The fight was the more bitter because it was rooted in differences that had not yet become explicit. In time the two factions would really diverge widely: in their estimates of the nature of the Russian Revolution and in consequent conceptions of grand strategy and detailed tactics. Then the rupture and the sharpness of the fratricidal struggle might be rationalized and systematized, or made to appear acceptable to rational men. Moreover, factionalism has a law of momentum of its own which tends to incubate difference, exaggerate and systematically enlarge it, and minimize or ignore agreement. But at the moment of this first split, springing thus unexpectedly out of a long labor for unification, all these divergencies of the future existed merely in germ: incompatibilities of temperament ("softs" and "hards"), differences on personnel, and on questions of organization. Since organization itself seemed but ancillary to common aims, a split on such secondary grounds could not be accepted as natural. Agreed on Marxism, on socialism, on opposition to tsarism, disagreeing only on a definition in the Party Statutes, and on the personnel of a committee—even to the combatants themselves it was altogether incredible that they should actually be drifting toward irreparable estrangement.

Bolshevik historians have since sought to portray the split as a brilliant anticipation on Lenin's part of all the subsequently engendered disagreements between bolshevism and menshevism. There is a sense in which this is so, for politics is one of the arts, and many of its profoundest decisions spring from deep, unconscious sources. But the actual outcome of the Congress— particularly the rupture with Martov—had been as unexpected for Lenin as for any others, and his first efforts were directed to minimizing the conflicts. For several years thereafter, his writings were filled with assertions of the unnecessariness of the split. More than once, before their final divorce, the two factions would resume uneasy cohabitation in a common party.

No sooner had the Congress adjourned than Lenin sent

the following personal appeal to Potresov, intending it for
Martov's and Axelrod's eyes:

> And now I ask myself: why should we separate as enemies for
> the rest of our lives? I admit that I often acted and behaved
> with frightful irritation and rage. I am quite ready *to acknowl-
> edge to any comrade whatsoever this my fault* . . . But when I
> consider without any rage the results arrived at . . . I cannot see
> in the outcome anything, absolutely anything, harmful for the
> Party or hurtful or insulting to the Minority . . .

Of course, the letter may be interpreted as the calculated gen-
erosity of a victor, aware of his responsibility for the function-
ing of the Party, and eager to get all valuable forces to work
once more. But this is something quite distinct from a sense of
irreconcilable split. And how shall we explain, if not in terms
of indecision, that Lenin's *Collected Works* for this period contain an unprecedented number of unmailed letters, undelivered
statements and declarations, articles drafted and left unpublished? A month after the Congress he wrote to Central Committee Member Krzhizhanovsky:

> . . . write to Martov, appealing for the last time to rea-
> son . . . Act formally and prepare for a definite war with
> the Martovites . . . Let Krzhizhanovsky not look upon Mar-
> tov as before. The friendship is at an end. Down with all
> soft-heartedness!

But after Krupskaya had taken down the letter and coded its
names, he told her not to send it. It was not easy to decide to
break with the comrade who had been closest to him.

Julius Martov (Tsederbaum) was three years younger than
Lenin. Between them there had been a closer political partnership and intimacy than Lenin was ever to form with any man
again, even with Trotsky in the crucial year of their common
assault on the heights of power. Lenin had regarded Martov
as a gifted younger brother. Together they had formed the

Petersburg League of Struggle, together gone to prison, together planned *Iskra* (Potresov was less important in their "triple alliance"). Together they toured the underground on *Iskra's* behalf, together edited it abroad, and together resisted the prestige and overbearing attitude of Plekhanov. Martov was unmarried, gregarious, bohemian in temperament, possessed of the Russian intellectual's hunger for impassioned talk. Like Lenin he was wholly devoted to the movement, to the exclusion of all other matters, ever ready to take upon himself the most ungrateful tasks and carry them out conscientiously. He read, wrote, conversed, speculated ceaselessly, kept up with all the news and all the latest ideas, combined a far-ranging independence of thought with an exceptional talent for taking the slightest hint from Lenin or Axelrod, from his reading or from events, and giving it a rich application and development of his own. This stoop-shouldered Jewish intellectual, with the thin, ascetic face, the unkempt curly hair and pointed beard, the slightly soiled and misted glasses through which shone the dreamer's eyes of a ghetto seer . . . and this stocky, bald-headed, solid, practical-looking Great-Russian, with the high cheekbones and the twinkling little Tartar eyes: these two had seemed till now to complement each other as the most splendid of working teams. In the first forty-five numbers of *Iskra,* Martov had written thirty-nine articles and Lenin thirty-two; while Plekhanov had done twenty-four, Potresov only eight, Zasulich six, and Axelrod four. The rest had been written by occasional contributors like Rosa Luxemburg, Parvus and Trotsky. Lenin and Martov had done all the technical editorial work. Though their emphases and approaches had been distinct, there had been no shadow of political difference. To Potresov, the third member of the "triple alliance," Lenin, so little inclined to sentiment, "spoke of Martov with the unconcealed admiration of one who was quite carried away by his feelings."

Yet, even before the break, in the rootless isolation and ingrown intercourse of émigré life, they occasionally got on each other's nerves. Martov became critical of the Lenin he admired when a casual squabble about an *Iskra* agent "opened his eyes to the amoralism in Lenin's makeup." He discovered that Vladimir Ilyich was "uncompromisingly severe with 'strangers' " but was "prepared to defend 'his own' agents with characteristic stubbornness, consciously closing his eyes to their personal misconduct." This conflict had occurred, according to the memoirs of Potresov, a half year before the 1903 Congress, as Lenin stubbornly opposed the investigation by the Editorial Board of an accusation made by a victim against one of his appointees.

During the same period, Krupskaya notes that Martov's love of endless talk and too eager readiness to seize on new theories were making Lenin "quite ill and incapable of working." He even asked Martov to stop dropping in at all odd hours of the day and night, and arranged for Krupskaya to go over mail and manuscripts with his co-editor, to save wear and tear on his own nerves.

Might it have been that in a movement less ingrown and less torn up from its roots, these two could have continued to collaborate indefinitely despite differences of viewpoint and temperament? Certainly, in other parties that did not live under émigré conditions, parties in which all quarrels and differences had ultimately to be submitted to decision of the membership, such cohabitation was possible. Moreover, Lenin always retained in his own faction men who differed from him on critical occasions far more than Martov did, while the latter, for his part, was often in deepest conflict with his fellow-Mensheviks. Thus, in the crucial test of the World War, Martov remained, like Lenin, an internationalist, though many of Lenin's Bolshevik associates deserted him. After the seizure of power by the Bolshevik Party, which Martov naturally opposed, he nevertheless remained active in the congresses of the Soviets and defended the new government against all attempts at reactionary counter-revolution and foreign intervention. Indeed, so important did his support seem to Lenin in 1920 that he had Martov's speech in the Soviet Congress against the

Polish attack on Kiev printed by the government, first in Russian and Polish, and then in German by the German publishing house of the Communist International.

When Martov at last could no longer stand the ever-growing terror and narrowing dictatorship and applied for a passport to go abroad, it was freely granted to him on Lenin's personal order. The days when even Bolsheviks would be executed *en masse* were still more than a decade and a half away. Before those days could come, death would long have removed Lenin from the scene. For, despite all his professed "rock-hardness," there was about him something of the inherited humane tradition of the Russian revolutionary intelligentsia, which he never wholly lost.

> It was exceedingly difficult for him to break with Martov—writes Krupskaya. Afterwards, Vladimir Ilyich fought the Mensheviks, but every time that Martov, even in the slightest degree, took the correct line, his old attitude towards him revived. Such was the case for example in Paris in 1910, when Martov and Vladimir Ilyich worked together on the editorial board of the *Social Democrat*. Coming home from the office, Vladimir Ilyich used to relate in joyful tones that Martov was taking a correct line . . . Later, back in Russia, how pleased Vladimir Ilyich was with Martov's position in the July 1917 days; not because it was of any advantage to the Bolsheviks, but because Martov was acting worthily—as behooved a revolutionary. When Vladimir Ilyich was already seriously ill he said to me somewhat sadly, "Martov, they say, is dying too . . ."

With the shift in relationships attendant upon the split, all the persons were revealed in a new light. Martov, not yet grown to the full stature of independent leadership, fell for some years under the sway of Axelrod and Martynov. Plekhanov, separated from his associates of a lifetime, was clearly uneasy in the new partnership with Lenin. Trotsky, too, seemed out of his natural element. By temperament an imperious "hard," all his political instincts lay at the opposite extreme of the spectrum from Martov and Axelrod and Martynov, with whom he now found himself associated. From his acid-dipped pen issued two sharp attacks on Lenin, the *Report of the Siberian Delegation* and *Our Political Tasks,* the latter significantly dedicated "To My Dear Teacher, Pavel Borisovich Axelrod." In them, he portrayed Lenin as a caricature Robespierre, talking socialism but modeling himself on the dictatorial bourgeois revolutionary, setting up a pseudo-Jacobin dictatorship over the masses, installing a committee of public safety over the Party, using the "guillotine" to eliminate those he could not control, forming local organizations on the Cartesian principle: "I am confirmed by the Central Committee, therefore I am." Lenin's celebrated centralism, he said, was in reality "egocentralism" and one day it would lead to a state of affairs in which:

> The organization of the Party takes the place of the Party itself; the Central Committee takes the place of the organization; and finally the dictator takes the place of the Central Committee . . .

In 1917, when Trotsky and Lenin had "amnestied" each other for all their past political and organizational differences and Trotsky was voluntarily assuming the unaccustomed role of disciple once more, he would do his best to have these polemics against Lenin forgotten. But how many times must he have thought of the above prophetic words during the later stages of his struggle with Stalin!

"How did I come to be with the 'softs,' " he asks himself in his *Autobiography:*

> In 1903 the whole point at issue was nothing more than Lenin's desire to get Axelrod and Zasulich off the editorial board . . . My whole being seemed to protest against this merciless cutting off of the older ones . . . I did not fully realize what an intense and imperious centralism the revolutionary party would need to lead millions in a war against the old order . . . It is not without significance that the words "irreconcilable" and "relentless" are among Lenin's favorites . . .

Even more were those words to be among Trotsky's "favorites." No, assuredly, his imperious spirit was not at home among the "softs." His sojourn in their camp was one continuous quarrel. Before a year went by, not Axelrod nor Martov, but the brilliant and gargantuan Parvus had become his guide; 1905 would find him and Parvus deflecting menshevism politically in Lenin's direction, then breaking with it and steering a course of their own.

Party quarrels have a momentum of their own. While Lenin was still hesitating, it became his obligation to report on the Party Congress to the League of Revolutionary Social Democrats Abroad, the foreign organization of *Iskra* which had elected him as its delegate to the Congress. He sensed that he would be outnumbered there, that spirits would be exacerbated and the split needlessly deepened, so he vainly tried to prevent the meeting. Immersed in gloomy thoughts as he bicycled to this undesired conference, he ran into the rear of a trolley car and was badly injured. In what ways might the fate of his party and his country have been altered if the crash had taken place with a few foot-pounds more of force?

He put in his appearance pale and swathed in bandages, but it cannot be said that for this reason his opponents held their fire. Who was this man, they asked, that he thought he could run the Party without the rest of the historically developed leadership? The debate was frenzied, people stood up, shouted with empurpled faces, hurled epithets, came close to blows. Lenin made three separate attempts to dynamite the conference by staging walkouts of his followers. When it approved resolutions supporting the Congress Minority and adopted a constitution intended to safeguard its independence of the Central Committee, he had Central Committeeman Lengnik summarily proclaim its dissolution. It refused to be dissolved.

That very night, at a meeting of the Bolshevik caucus to consider further strategy, Plekhanov broke down. "I cannot fire at my own comrades," he declared, thinking of his lifelong association with Axelrod and Zasulich. "Better a bullet in the head than a split. There are moments when even the Autocracy has to compromise . . ."

"Then it is said to be wavering," interjected the voice of a "hard."

Plekhanov was within his legal rights. The Congress, on Lenin's motion, had named a board of three editors, Plekhanov, Lenin and Martov, and empowered them to coopt additional editors. They had not done so merely because Martov stubbornly refused to attend any meetings of the Editorial Board until it should agree to coopt Axelrod, Zasulich and Potresov, thus restoring the original six. For three months after the Congress an appearance of continuity had been maintained, by the cooperation of Plekhanov of the older generation with Lenin of the younger, to get out the paper between them. Now that Plekhanov demanded that the internecine war be ended by coopting the old editors *in toto,* Lenin stood utterly and nakedly alone. True, Plekhanov offered "to step out" but Lenin knew only too well that if Martov should be invited to attend a single editorial meeting under the new circumstances, Plekhanov's proposal would have a majority. Hence, he "stepped out" himself, to "give Plekhanov a free hand"—and to regain his own freedom from an impossible position. It was the only time in his life that he voluntarily relinquished a captured post.

From No. 53 on, the paper became to him the "new *Iskra,*" an empty shell from which he, and with him the old spirit, had departed. He refused to serve now, as Martov had refused to serve before, but with the difference that he stood alone without any of the old guard in the camp of the sulkers along with him. All the guns of the "new *Iskra*" were trained upon its solitary ex-editor, exposed in no man's land, and upon his organization views, which formerly it had appeared to sponsor. Martov wrote on "the state of siege" in the Party; Trotsky on caricature Jacobinism; Vera Zasulich on the necessity of safeguarding the Party against the impatience of people who try to get rid of those who disagree. Plekhanov attacked Lenin's basic postulates in *What Should Not Be Done* (a take-off on *What's to Be Done?*); *Centralism or Bonapartism; The Working Class and the Social Democratic Intelligentsia; A New Attempt to Bring to their Senses the Frogs Who Ask for a King.*

But the main theoretical attacks were made by two people of extreme opposite temperaments and, in most other respects, of opposing political conceptions: Paul Axelrod and Rosa Luxemburg.

Axelrod as usual, though unyielding in content, was gentle and impersonal in manner. In two articles, he sought to deepen the controversy from personalities to principles. Lenin's much-abused name did not even figure. The Russian Social Democratic Labor Party, he warned, did not yet consist of workers, but only of intellectuals who were "adherents in principle" of the working class. Russia faced not a proletarian but a bourgeois revolution. Unless these intellectuals sought to develop the initiative and self-activity of the masses, there was danger that the revolutionary intelligentsia would draw the workers into the coming revolution as a mere physical force—cannon fodder—as in so many revolutions of the past. Therein lay the danger of the traditional Russian conspirative organization forms: excessive centralism, hierarchical structure, ideological tutelage, the curbing of the self-activity of the masses, the discouraging of independent judgment and initiative.

Rosa Luxemburg's two articles for *Iskra* started where Axelrod's left off. Politically and temperamentally she was to stand at the extreme opposite pole from him and all the Mensheviks. A living flame of revolution, her frail body and mighty spirit were a force in three parties, the German, Polish and Russian, and in the leadership of the Socialist International. Where other "orthodox" Marxists were inclined to be mere scholasts, expounders of a closed system of thought, she was of that little band of original thinkers who would use the methods of Marx to tackle new problems in economics and politics. She was even then beginning her fight on bureaucracy and excessive centralism in the German Social Democracy, a fight which was to make her the outstanding advocate of revolutionary policy and the outstanding defender of democracy within the labor movement. Lenin, identifying his centralism with that of the leaders of the German Party, would side with them against her, and live to regret it, one day, with all his heart. Her entry into the lists was the more embarrassing to him since her temperament and her political views on the Russian Revolution were so far from Axelrod's and so close to his. Thus she represented a stumbling-block to his desire to identify menshevism symmetrically as "opportunism in the organization question" linked up with "opportunism in politics." Moreover, she was a harder hitter than Axelrod, while her belief in the creative initiative of the masses went far deeper than Axelrod's or that of any other recognized leader among the Marxists. It was, with her, a fundamental article of faith.

> Socialism—she wrote in *Iskra*—is the first movement in history to base its entire course on the organization and independent action of the masses. The ultracentralism advocated by Lenin is not something born of a positive creative spirit but of the negative sterile spirit of the watchman. His line of thought is cut to the control of party activity, not to its fructifying; to its narrowing, not its unleashing; to the role of taskmaster, not of gatherer and unifier. The Social Democracy stands on the eve of great revolutionary struggles [this was written in 1904] . . . in the midst of a period of the most intensive, creative activity in the field of tactics. The most important and fruitful tactical turns of the last decade in Russia were not invented by certain leaders but were the spontaneous product of the uncontrolled movement itself. At such a time, to put hobbles on the initiative of the party's thought and to wall in its capacity for expansion within a barbed wire fence would be to make the Social Democracy unfit for the great tasks before it.

Even when Kautsky and Bebel, the two living socialists he most admired, took sides against him, Lenin was singularly unable to doubt the rightness of his views. He did not question their authority on anything else, but decided that they "did not understand the Russian question." That capacity to stand alone against the entire world of his peers, and that incapacity to think himself wrong on any idea he cherished as fundamental, were to be two well-springs of his strength in 1914 and 1917. To his opponents, he seemed "organically incapable of assimilating opinions that differed from his own," so that every difference of opinion tended to become the *casus belli* of a minor or major civil war. With him the belief in a centralized, military form of organization had now become as much a touchstone and article of faith or principle as with Rosa Luxemburg her belief in the creative power of the masses. Moreover, his organizational creed, if it was not in the general tradition of European Marxism, drew strength from being in the tradition of Russian revolutionary centralism and secret conspiracy.

> The magnificent organization that the revolutionaries had in the seventies—he had written—should serve us all as a model ... To regard it as something specifically Narodovolist is absurd both historically and logically, because no revolutionary tendency, if it seriously thinks of fighting, can dispense with such an organization ... The spontaneous struggle of the proletariat will not become a genuine class struggle, until it is led by a strong organization of revolutionaries.

Thus, though he stood alone, he had a better than even chance to win a substantial following among the professional revolutionaries of Russia against all his former co-leaders, for his views were in the direct line of the Russian conspiratorial heritage which could not but seem natural to that body of self-constituted "professionals" or "functionaries" on whom the fate of the underground party was most likely to rest. This almost unconscious Russianism was another well-spring of Lenin's strength. And with it went something, harder to put into words, which his bitterest enemies sensed and paid grudging tribute to. Potresov, after ten years of exile from the land in which Lenin had taken power, would write of him:

Neither Plekhanov nor Martov nor anyone else possessed the secret of the directly hypnotic influence exercised on people by Lenin, I should say, his power to dominate them. Plekhanov was respected, Martov was loved, but only Lenin was followed unquestioningly as if he were the sole undisputed leader. For only Lenin represented that rare phenomenon, rare especially for Russia: that of being a man of iron will, of indomitable energy, who combined a fanatical faith in the movement and the cause with no less faith in himself . . . Without wasting any superfluous words on it, Lenin always felt that the Party was he, that he was the will of the movement concentrated in one man, and he acted accordingly . . .

Deprived of his control of the Central Organ and the collaboration of all his old associates in leadership, Vladimir Ilyich displayed amazing energy in the throwing up of new defenses and in the improvisation of new methods of warfare. "Open letters" to *Iskra,* confidential letters to his followers, detailed pamphlets, leaflets, public lectures, plans for a faction journal which would defy, if necessary, the Central Committee, the Party Council, and the Central Organ all at once, private discussions and public arguments, flowed from him in an unending torrent. A whole volume of his *Collected Works,* one of the stoutest, is all but filled with his writings on the Congress and the split. One "pamphlet" alone, *One Step Forward, Two Steps Backward,* constitutes a book of 250 pages, 75 of them devoted to the single question of Article I of the Party Constitution adopted at the Second Congress! Tsarism, absolutism, capitalism, democracy, socialism, are forgotten or pushed into the remote background. Now what is important is not the goal nor even the road to be followed but the precise direction of the next step and the nature of the military formation to be kept on the march. The serene good humor, the confident sweep of thought that had characterized most of his work from *The Development of Capitalism in Russia* to *What's to Be Done?* are gone now. The polemic is arid, irritable, nagging, and sags under a weight of detail which nearly obscures the outlines of its doctrine. It is written, so to speak, with a voice made hoarse by endless, fruitless argument.

The compulsive logic of factionalism now began to drive both groups toward ever greater one-sidedness. Martov, it was driving into a life-long association with some of the opportunists, like the "Economist" Martynov, whom but yesterday he had been fighting. Lenin, it impelled to the obdurate exaggeration of his centralism which had been suddenly called in question. No longer does that authoritarian centralism appear as one of the harsh compulsions of "our Asiatic and barbarous land." No longer does he clothe it in the merely practical justification that the police state and the hard necessities of underground conspiracy were what made it necessary and justified it despite the lack of democracy involved. Now centralism becomes a revolutionary virtue *per se* for all lands and all circumstances of struggle. One looks in vain in *One Step Forward, Two Steps Backward* for what was in the preceding works: some tribute to the desirability and corrective and educative force of democracy. On the contrary:

> Burocratism versus democratism, i.e. precisely centralism versus autonomy, such is the organization principle of revolutionary social democracy as against that of the opportunists. The latter principle strives to go from below upward, and therefore defends as far as possible and wherever possible autonomy and democracy . . . But the organization principle of revolutionary social democracy strives to go from the top downward, and defends the enlargement of the rights and plenary powers of the central body against the parts.

This is the most naked expression of faith in hierarchy and distrust of democracy to be found in all of Lenin's writings. Only the isolation from the criticism of equals and the stubborn tendency to cherish most what was most under attack could have wrung from him such an extreme statement. Later, under the fire of his opponents' arguments and the impact of the activity of great and uncontrollable masses, he would modify his doctrine from bare centralism to the more ambiguous "democratic centralism." But when we seek to understand the Russian state after Lenin came to power, and when we watch the formation of the Communist International, we shall have to keep this one-sided utterance in mind, for it takes an authoritarian party to make an authoritarian state.

Moreover, though Lenin might admit, as later he did, that he had exaggerated the value of centralism in this work in order to overcome the "anarchy" then prevailing in the leading circles of the Party, his followers would make this one-sided and embittered pamphlet the very gospel of their views on the organization question. Stalin, in his *Short History of the Communist Party,* published after the purges to replace all the other official party histories, would devote more space to it than to the ground-breaking, far richer and more balanced *What's to Be Done?* That is one of the difficulties presented by the varied works of any man whose every sentence becomes a canon of authority. Any partial polemical utterance of a moment can easily become the tangent of departure from the original curve.

For the moment, the most painful thing to Lenin was the lack of an organ in which to continue the unequal combat. Having lost control of *Iskra,* he had transferred all his forces to the Central Committee inside Russia. Forgotten was his few-months-old contention that only *Iskra,* because it was published abroad, could be trusted to provide a firm ideological leadership. The suppressed premise in that argument should have read: "because it is published abroad, and *because I am in control of it.*" Now he tried to turn the Central Committee inside Russia into a fortress for blasting back at the paper. Though he was not in Russia, he asked them to coopt him, and several other dependables, onto the Committee, which they did.

But experience had taught him that it would be hard to control any committee from such a distance, and that arrests would sooner or later change its composition, weaken or destroy it. So, while the bewildered Russian members and local

organizations were still trying to find out what had happened
at the recent Congress, he made the following astonishing proposal to the Committee that had just coopted him:

> If we miss the opportunity and the right slogan for a fight,
> then *complete* defeat is inevitable . . . *The only salvation is a
> Congress. Its slogan: war with the disorganizers.* Only this slogan
> will be able to get the best of the Martovites, attract the broad
> masses and save the situation . . . not a word *for the present* to
> anyone . . . *Move all our forces into the Committees and the
> Districts* . . . Resolutions of the Local Committees must fly to
> the Central Organ . . . we must push our people onto the shaky
> Committees in the name of the slogan: against disorganization
> . . . *A Congress is essential not later than January* . . . The worst
> would be *if the Central Organ would be theirs and the Council
> ours.* I repeat: either complete defeat (the Central Organ will
> hunt us down) or *immediate preparations for a Congress. It must
> be prepared secretly at first,* taking a month at the most, *then
> three weeks to collect the demands of half the Committees and
> to call a Congress.* Again and again I repeat: this is the only
> salvation.

The letter was written less than four months after the "unification" Congress had adjourned! And a few days later, he added by way of argument:

> Arrest is inevitable, and will come fairly soon—it would be
> childish to ignore it. And what will there be for us after your
> arrest?
> . . . Do you think over the whole political situation, take a
> wider view, tear yourselves away from the petty everyday fussing
> over pennies and passports . . .

But Lenin was in for a rude shock. This habit of his of powerful concentration on what at a given moment he deemed the
main chance, had carried him far from his followers. All the
iterations and underlinings were powerless to impress his will
upon them. They felt, as he did not, the loneliness of the isolation of his faction from all the other leaders whom the Party
had looked up to. They were in Russia, where the confusion, the

longing for unity, the impatience with the ill-understood controversy, were indescribable. Wealthy sympathizers began to
despair of this feud-torn Party's ever leading a successful assault
on tsarism. The "Bucket," the funds gathered and contributed
by Mrs. Kalmykova, became suddenly empty. The "California
Gold Mine," a mysterious source of funds which to this day
Party historians have not cared to elucidate, ceased to produce.
The millionaire manufacturer Morozov was secretly contributing two thousand rubles (a thousand dollars) a month to the
Social Democratic Party through Lenin's close follower, the
engineer Leonid Krassin, whom he hired to take charge of one
of his factories. But Krassin was soon to become a "conciliator," i.e. an advocate of Party unity, and Lenin would lose that
source of funds also.

Great numbers of intellectuals, who had thought of themselves as Social Democrats, were alienated or discouraged, or
switched to the rapidly growing Social Revolutionary Party.
Workers, too, lost heart, or became bitter "anti-intellectuals"
determined to ignore a movement that did nothing but "split
hairs" and to look elsewhere to organization and leadership.
Within the land was felt the ground swell of great events, while
the Party that should be leading and strengthening the revolutionary upsurge lay helpless, tearing at its own vitals.

Lenin's summons to his Central Committee to wage a fight
to the finish fell on deaf ears. His demand for yet another convention—which might well mean a formal consolidation of the
split—seemed to them monstrous. From a distance, with slow-
traveling underground letters, Lenin pleaded, argued, urged,
abused. Then he tried to stampede them by introducing his own
resolution for a new congress into the Council meeting in Geneva. To his indignation, the Central Committee he had felt
so sure of answered his action by a vote of censure of him, as
its representative in the Council! And, under the leadership
of the hitherto ever-dependable Krassin, the Committee opened
negotiations with the Mensheviks for the cooptation of the latter and a conciliator's peace in the Party.

That splendid working and fighting machine, Vladimir Ilyich Ulyanov, seemed to have reached the end of its resources. "Do not bother me about leaflets—he wrote to them now—I am not a machine and cannot work in the present disgraceful situation." He resigned from all committees. He and Krupskaya took their knapsacks and went tramping in the mountains of Switzerland. They "selected the wildest paths and got far away from human beings." They tramped all day and slept each night where evening found them, too blessedly tired for thought. They subsisted on country bread, eggs, cheese, wine, spring-water. If they came to an inn, they dined cheaply and well at the servants' table. The fat French book and dictionary they carried with them for translation remained unopened during the entire journey. "After passing the time in this way for a month, Vladimir Ilyich's nerves became normal again," writes Krupskaya. Refreshed, he returned to the fray.

Unexpectedly at this juncture, fresh forces rallied to him, men of leadership caliber to take the place of those he had lost: Bogdanov, the able, independent philosopher; Lunacharsky, critic, writer, and future Commissar of Education; Bazarov, Olminsky, Vorovsky. As in the beginning of his struggle with "Economism," he called together the remnant of the faithful. A pitiful twenty-two men and women, out of the whole active emigration, signed their names to a fighting platform drafted by him. In it this centralist denounced all three Central Bodies as having ceased to represent the will of the "Majority" of the Party, as expressed by the "Majority" which had elected them at the Party Congress. It branded Lenin's selectees of yesterday, the "conciliators" on the Central Committee, as worse than the "Minority" with whom they were trying to reconcile themselves. It appealed against the Central Bodies to the Local Committees, urging these to adopt resolutions in favor of the calling of a new congress. And it asked the Local Committees to elect delegates to a new, extra-legal, or illegal body, a "Bureau of Committees of the Majority," which Lenin now planned to set up in opposition to all the existing governing

organisms. What then was left of his centralism if he fought all
the Central Bodies? Only the political conception of how a party should be structured whenever its central bodies were acting
in the way which seemed appropriate to him.

Most of the names of the little band of twenty-two who
signed the document in emigration, and of the subsequent
signatures secured in Moscow and Petersburg, are worth remembering, for out of them largely grew the general staff of the
future Bolshevik Party. The signers included Lenin, his wife
and his sister; Vorovsky, the future Soviet diplomat; Bonch-
Bruevich, who opened a publishing house for Lenin; Krasikov,
who was to be a member of the Soviet Commissariat of Justice; Lyadov; Zemlyachka; Lepeshinsky and his wife; Olminsky; Lengnik; Knuniyants and his wife; Essen; Baumann, who
would be killed in the Revolution of 1905; Stasova, who would
succeed Krupskaya as Party Secretary; Gusev (Drapkin); Litvinov (Wallach), who would one day be Commissar of Foreign
Affairs; and Rykov, the youngest man to be put on the new
Bureau, who would succeed Lenin as President of the Council
of Commissars. With a few others who showed their mettle
a bit later, most of these would make up a more or less permanent Bolshevik staff which would stick with Lenin through
thick and thin and go with him into places of power in the
Soviet Government.

By Christmas, operating through this extra-legal body, Lenin
had succeeded in founding a new paper which should serve as
organ of his faction in its fight to wrest the Party from the control of its leading committees. On Christmas Eve, 1904, cheerful
once more, he wrote to Essen:

> An announcement about the publication of our newspaper,
> *Vpered* ("Forward"), came out yesterday. All the Bolsheviks
> are rejoicing . . . At last we have broken up the cursed dissension
> and are working harmoniously with those who want to work
> and not to create scandals! A good group of contributors has
> been got together; there are fresh forces . . . The Central Com-
> mittee which betrayed us has lost all credit . . . The Bolshevik

Committees are joining together; they have already chosen a
Bureau and now the organ will completely unite them. Hurrah!
Do not lose heart. We are all reviving now and will continue to
revive . . . Above all be cheerful. Remember, you and I are not
so old yet . . . everything is still before us.

Almost at that very moment, much to the astonishment of
both Bolsheviks and Mensheviks and without paying attention
to the prescriptions of either, revolution broke out in Russia!

CHAPTER SIXTEEN

POLICE
SOCIALISM

The air is heavy with ominous things; every day we see the glare of fires on the horizon; a bloody mist crawls over the ground; breathing and living have become difficult as before a storm. The muzhik is sullenly silent, and if he opens his mouth it is in such a way that one feels creepy all over.

—Letter of a Landowner of Voronezh, 1901

Four efforts were started simultaneously to inject some organization into inchoate Russian public life. The same years, 1901 to 1903, that had witnessed Lenin's attempt to constitute and "unify" an All-Russian Social Democratic Party for the proletariat, were the years in which were formed a Social Revolutionary Party, to give leadership to the peasantry; a Constitutional Democratic Party, to organize the liberal and democratic intelligentsia; and an amazing series of experiments in police unionism and police "socialism." All these were so many minor eddies in a swiftly rising freshet—signs that the whole, long-frozen political structure of Russia was about to go into a thaw. But none of the new organizations would prove equal to the task it had set itself: to channelize the rapidly rising flood.

In the countryside, sullenly silent since the flareup over Emancipation, the peasants began to harvest forbidden hay, cut forbidden timber in the woods. Owners who resisted were found murdered on the paths; mysterious fires destroyed their crops and manor houses; they were driven from their estates by a foreboding fear.

In the cities, where there was as yet no organized labor movement (unions were not legalized until 1906), strikes became more frequent, assuming unusual stubbornness. Demonstrations ceased to be little, fugitive affairs manned only by intellectuals. They became great presses of excitable workingmen, who jammed the squares, protected the speakers, hurled missiles and imprecations at the police, re-formed after troops had passed through, held their ground when blanks were fired, dispersed when the police shot to kill—only to reassemble the next day in processions ten times as mighty, to honor and bury the dead.

There was sudden talkativeness and courage and organization among lawyers, doctors, agronomists, teachers, progressive landowners and civil servants of the zemstvos. The long-silent university halls rang again with speeches and the tumult of student strikes. As in the seventies, once more the students supplied their quota of "human bullets" for a direct critique of the bureaucracy by means of the terror. Student Karpovich murdered Minister of Education Bogolepov in 1901; Balmashev shot Minister of the Interior Sipyagin in 1902; Sazonov laid low Minister of the Interior Plehve with a bomb in 1904; Kalyaev killed Grand Duke Sergei of the Royal House in 1905. From Minister of Education, who had direct power over students, to Minister of the Interior, who commanded the police, to the Tsar's own uncle, a Grand Duke of the Royal House—the terror rose in an ascending scale, to lap at the very feet of the throne. These were only the most startling of a series of such deeds which no longer seemed to alienate public opinion as in the past, but rather stirred it to its depths. All the survivors of these attacks, and all the young persons attracted by them, joined the "Fighting Section" of the new Social Revolutionary Party, in which Director of The Moscow Okhrana Zubatov, with Minister Plehve's approval, had recruited one of the most remarkable of his agents, Yevno Azev. To put a police agent in charge of the socialist terror organization, this was one aspect of the rash of experiments in police socialism, an aspect which, as we have already noted, cost Minister Plehve his life!

Even at the summits of society, there was self-doubt and dissent. The celebrated Count Leo Tolstoy, so long a troublesome critic, was now excommunicated by the Church. Two princes of the House of Trubetskoi and two of the House of Dolgoruki made public profession of liberalism. Prince Obolenski became one of the contributors to the columns of *Iskra* and then a founder of the new Constitutional Democratic Party. Millionaire industrialists like Morozov contributed regular and substantial sums to the underground. His own contribution from early 1904 until his death was two thousand rubles (one thousand dollars) a month, through his employee, the engineer Krassin. Was this contribution to bolshevism by one of Russia's richest industrialists a death wish for his class or for himself? Two days before he committed suicide in Cannes in

1905, he handed over a large sum in cash to Krassin for the Social Democratic Party. And the student Schmitt, heir to another branch of the Morozov fortunes, joined the movement directly. Dying in jail either of torture or as a suicide, he willed his estate to the Social Democratic Party. Bank directors and high state officials, writes Krassin in his memoirs, were among the regular contributors of monthly sums to the Party treasury. And once more, as in the middle of the nineteenth century, distinguished writers put pen and prestige at the service of the revolutionary movement.

At Court appeared would-be Neckers, Turgots, Calonnes: Bunge, Vyshnegradsky, Witte, Stolypin, who, given a wiser and stronger sovereign and a more peaceful international situation, might have succeeded in renovating the crumbling structure of the "Asiatic" state, with sounder finances, better and more honest administration and more scope to public opinion and the public will. Most important of these innovators at the turn of the century was Sergei Yulievich Witte. From his modest beginnings as a railway-station master Witte rose to the Directorship of the Southwestern railway lines, then to Minister of Communications, Minister of Finance, and in 1905, to Presidency of the Council of Ministers and architect of the Constitutional Manifesto, with the title of Count.

He introduced the gold standard, secured foreign loans and investors, strengthened both private and state industry, set up Russo-Persian and Russo-Chinese Banks. Under him Russia's railways grew faster than those of any other country in Europe, faster than the Bolsheviks would ever build. Thus stimulated, Russian industry grew at a greater rate per annum than that of Germany, France, or England, and, during many years, than that of the United States. But he was more successful at modernizing industry than the regime. Working, as he had to, through favorites, subsidies, and ancient "Byzantine" intrigues, in these arts he was no match for his arch rival, Plehve. Witte's Transsiberian and Chinese-Eastern Railways, and his Russo-Chinese Bank, all of them in his mind projects for peaceful expansion and penetration of the Far East, actually put into his rival's hand that trump card of a "short, successful war" with Japan which was supposed to "unify the nation."

On all levels of the great bureaucratic structure, along with the corrupt, the complaisant and the brutalized there appeared civil servants and officials who led devoted and abnegated lives, sought to introduce local and departmental reforms, drew up illuminating reports, which, under the guise of warning and alarm, suggested the necessity of change. Contrary to the general impression, a reading of their reports suggests that no set of governing officials in history has ever given a clearer account of the situation facing it.

But at the very apex of the pyramid there existed a dangerous vacuity: a despotism-in-principle wielded by a man who lacked the strength and ruthlessness and understanding required for that exacting trade. Until the very year of his accession, Nicholas Romanov had been ruled like a child by his stern and atrabilious father. Upon the latter's death, Nicholas entered, with ever-increasing completeness, under the sway of the petty German princess who had become his wife. Her victorian prudery, sickly mysticism, narrow obstinacy, her incapacity to believe evil of those who played on her weaknesses or good of those who opposed her desires, were poor equipment indeed for her constantly enlarging dominion over the man who ruled the greatest land empire on earth. All her virtues, like his, were cut to a small domestic pattern. Her chief ambition was to provide the Tsar with a male heir. As buxom daughter succeeded buxom daughter, she put herself in the hands of a succession of thaumaturges, charlatans and mystics, in the hope that they would aid her to bear a son. When at last a Tsarevich was born, she believed, thanks to the intervention of one of them, that "miracle" served to confirm her in her superstitions. The boy proved to be a victim of hemophilia, a weakness which does not show up in females but has been transmitted through the female line to so many males of Europe's royal houses. She blamed and reproached herself and saw the visitation of hemophilia as some fault in her. To do proper penance, and at every critical moment, to keep the precious heir from bleeding to death, she put herself and her weak-willed husband still more completely under the sway of her dark camarilla, until the dissolute holy man Rasputin and the narrow-minded Empress came to rule the Empire in the sovereign's name. The demand for renovation, rising to the very feet of the throne, but made her maternal will grow fiercer, narrower, more fanatical, more concentrated on the single objective of transmitting to the sickly heir the imperial power undiminished by a single iota.

> At the beginning of the nineties—writes an official popular history of the Russian Revolution—there were in Russia 27,229 versts of railway lines, and at the beginning of 1900, 41,714 versts . . . The production of pig iron between 1890 and 1899 increased in England by 18%, in the U.S.A. by 50%, in Germany by 72%, in France by 31%, in Belgium by 32%, and in Russia by 108% . . . The increase in the production of iron and steel during the same period, 1890 to 1899, was as follows: England 80%, U.S.A. 63%, Germany 73%, France 67%, Belgium 48% and Russia 116%. Changes in the production of coal for the same period are as follows: in England an increase of 22%, in America of 61%, in Germany of 52%, in France of 26% . . . in Russia of 131%. In the production of oil Russia had only one competitor, the United States . . . The Russian cotton industry at the beginning of the twentieth century was second only to that of England and America. [*Illustrated History of the Russian Revolution,* English-Language edition, International Publishers, 1928, pp.4-6.]

And in Popov's *History of the Communist Party,* printed in Moscow in many languages in 1934, we read:

> The output of pig iron during the period 1890 to 1900 increased by 220%, of iron ore by 272%, and of oil by 179%. [16th Edition, English, International Publishers, p.33.]

These staggering figures, when checked against the statistical reports compiled at the beginning of the century or more recently, prove not to err on the side of overstatement. The startling difference between the first and the second is due to the fact that the year 1900 was one of tremendous upsurge. They are analogous to the ebbs and flows in increase during the Five-Year Plans and show that Russia at the turn of the century was a sprawling giant, just rising in its might, still a backward, but surely not a stagnant, land. It was this tremendous expansion of Russian life, and not stagnation, which made the Revolutions of 1905 and 1917 possible. Today, such reminders of former bounding growth are no longer to be found in government propaganda. We now have to dig them out of heavier, more scholarly tomes like P. E. Lashchenko's *History of the People's Economy of the U.S.S.R.* But precisely because they come from official histories they serve to give the reader a perspective from which to view the present-day Five-Year Plans.

Then as now, islands of heavy industry thrust up everywhere out of the vast peasant sea. Ancient "Asiatic" centers of bureaucratic administration and marketing were transformed into modern European industrial cities. New metropolises sprouted on the steppes or in the Urals, where there had not even been towns before. The new-born industries exhibited a fantastic elephantiasis: giant factories succeeded by super-giants, as if to match the sweep of the Russian plain and the reach of the Russian imagination.

The working class grew at a stormy and unprecedented pace. As during the Five-Year Plans of the thirties, there was a shortage of "living space" for the influx of new workers. Overcrowding and slums increased; men lived in barracks erected by the enterprises, dined in factory dining rooms, used communal kitchens. Whole families and groups of unrelated persons of both sexes and all ages crowded into single rooms. For the most part they were yesterday's peasants, their families often remaining in the village, themselves returning to it in periods of unemployment. Their outlook was a maze of their crumbling rural traditions and the unsettling experiences of their new city life.

As a land entering late into the current of modern industry,

Russia found its capital ready accumulated in Western Europe, and in the taxing power of its own state. More important, it found its technique ready made. Frequently technicians, managers, funds, investors, owners were imported. Entire factory setups were shipped from Germany, or overseas from America, needing little more than a floor to be fastened down to, a roof to cover them and a labor force to operate them. The Girauds, Thorntons, Nobels, Maxwells, Urquharts, Rothschilds—the great oil, mining, metallurgical and textile companies of foreign ownership—would be at a special disadvantage once the native working class went into action against "foreign" exploitation.

When we examine the actual figures, we are astonished to find that this backward land with its hundreds of thousands of wooden villages now possessed if not the largest, yet the most highly concentrated industrial working class in Europe. In Germany at the turn of the century, only 14 per cent of the factories had a force of more than five hundred men; in Russia the corresponding figure was 34 per cent. Only 8 per cent of all German workers worked in factories employing over a thousand workingmen each. Twenty-four per cent, nearly a quarter, of all Russian industrial workers worked in factories of that size. These giant enterprises forced the new working class into close association. There arose an insatiable hunger for organization, which the huge state machine sought in vain to direct or hold in check.

In the bureaucracy there were striking differences of opinion on the attitude to be taken toward the nascent labor movement and the embryonic political parties. To Plehve, who as Minister of the Interior had charge of the secret police and public order, it seemed that the zemstvo liberals and Constitutional Democrats were the most dangerous, the Social Revolutionaries next, and the Social Democrats only in third place. His chief bugbear was the zemstvos, with their urge for local autonomy, their remonstrances and petitions reminiscent of the French Revolution's *cahiers de doléances,* their demand for a national council of zemstvo delegates or *zemski sobor,* that might easily become the germ of a parliament, another *Etats Généraux.* He feared and detested them because they represented socially the most exalted demand for constitutionalism, a species of treason to the autocracy amongst the landowners themselves.

Next came the manufacturers and financiers with their demands for subsidies, new tariff and taxation structures, a limited state budget, the transformation of the feudal-bureaucratic state in the image of modern capitalism. These, and the moderate zemstvo elements were the more dangerous because in the person of Witte they had their own advocate in the very Council of Ministers.

If the Social Revolutionaries came second in the order of Minister Plehve's attention, it was not by reason of their socialism nor their peasant committees, but because of their use of terror. Socialism never worried Plehve. With an inverted *narodnichestvo* common to many reactionaries in Russia, he looked on rural socialism as a kind of peasant communal village arrangement, not at all incompatible with the tasks of tax collecting, military levies, and absolutist dictatorship. The peasants he regarded as an unshakable rock of loyalty to the throne. Urban socialism he dismissed as a remote and impossible utopian dream, while Witte's projects for state ownership of railways and banks and the vodka traffic naturally troubled him not at all. The real problem was the owners of private industry whom Witte represented so ably at Court.

Plehve pondered much over a report made by the conservative Police Chief of Moscow, General Trepov, in 1898:

> In order to disarm the agitators—General Trepov had written—it is necessary to open and point out to the worker a legal solution of his difficulty, for we must bear in mind that the agitator will be followed by the youngest and boldest part of the crowd, while the average worker will prefer the less spectacular and quiet legal way. Thus split up, the crowd will lose its power.

The suggestion intrigued the Minister of the Interior. What were these restless workingmen, he asked himself, if not the same loyal peasants of yesterday, bewildered by the new industrialism, angered by the greed of the industrialists, led astray by revolutionary agitators from the intelligentsia? Why might the state not shepherd them and watch over them a bit more, weed out the hotheads, give the mass a chance to organize under the most dependable auspices, protect them by social legislation against the greedy and doubtfully loyal bourgeoisie, act as benevolent and impartial arbitrator in industrial disputes, avert strikes and disorders by friendly arbitration, bind them more closely to the paternal state and Tsar? Would it not be a masterstroke of statesmanship to set the workingmen against the factory owners instead of against the government? And as a by-product, might not even a little carefully directed labor disorder be a useful weapon on occasion to show whither Finance Minister Witte's industrialization and liberal flirtations were leading?

The real architect of police-regimented unions in a policecontrolled paternal state was Sergei Vasilievich Zubatov, who now became chief lieutenant of General Trepov in Moscow. It was Zubatov, and not Plehve or Trepov, to whose name would be attached the honor of the great experiment in police unionism, destined to go down in history as the *zubatovshchina*. As a *gymnazia* student he had entered the Narodnaya Volya, enlisting with the police almost simultaneously as a secret agent. Thereafter he had risen rapidly in the service, being the sponsor of many progressive innovations: photography, fingerprinting, and a superior system of secret espionage on a scale hitherto unknown in Russia or in the world. "You must look upon your colleague, the secret agent," he once told the police, "as you would upon a woman with whom you are conducting a secret love intrigue: one rash step and you have dishonored her in the eyes of the world." Clearly a man of sentiment and imagination!

His biggest achievement so far had been the nationwide simultaneous raids that smashed the beginnings of the Social Democratic Party in 1897, rendering nugatory the efforts of their First Congress at Minsk. Now he had risen to the headship of the Moscow Okhrana or Secret Security Police, his only superiors being General Trepov, in charge of all the police services of the Moscow Province, and Minister of the Interior Plehve. This, his most ambitious plan, was really the police counterpart of the general urge for organization that was beginning to take possession of all classes in Russia. Against zemstvo intellectuals, students, Social Democrats and Social Revolutionaries, he would offer his police unionism and police "socialism."

In May 1901, he founded the Moscow *Society for Mutual Aid for Workingmen in the Mechanical Industries.* As an experienced secret agent, he tried to keep his guiding hand as unobtrusive as possible, but his less subtle superiors, Trepov and Plehve, insisted on tying up the Society with all sorts of rigid and too obvious safeguards. The by-laws and financial expenditures had to be approved by General Trepov. The secret agents who were leaders of the union were supplemented by uniformed police openly present at each meeting.

But the Moscow workingmen, heirs to the ancient patriarchal tradition and hungering now for organization, were more trustful of the Tsar and his officials than either Zubatov or the revolutionaries had believed possible. Assured that a paternal government was with them, they rushed into the strange union. Before it was a year old, it was able to lead a procession of fifty thousand workers into the Kremlin for solemn prayer before the tomb of the Emancipator Tsar, Alexander II.

Intellectuals were barred from the organization, and "hotheads" and "troublemakers" among the workingmen were arrested and silently deported. Hence purists among the Social Democrats wanted to limit their activity to denunciation and exposure. The workers were too class-conscious, they contended, to continue to have anything to do with such a monstrosity, once it was exposed to them. But the more realistic knew that denunciation was not enough.

> We must understand—Lenin wrote in *Iskra*—how to develop the struggle of the workers against every shameful intrigue and spy's trick . . . This struggle will develop the political consciousness of all who take part in the police-gendarme-and-spy "labor organization" . . . In the long run the legalization of the working-class movement will be to our advantage and not to that of the Zubatovs. . . .

This freedom from sectarian aversion to working wherever work was needful, was not limited to Lenin. At the Second Congress, one of the resolutions passed unanimously during the last session provided that Social Democratic workingmen should join these unions where possible, and try to defend and enlighten their members against the police. The startling successes even then being achieved by police unionism made any other attitude impossible.

The Moscow Society for Mutual Aid began, with Zubatov's encouragement, by discussing economic and cultural questions and formulating wage proposals. They chose as the first object of their attentions a "foreign exploiter"—a French factory owner. But he went crying to his ambassador, who in turn protested to Plehve concerning this quasi-governmental action against one of his nationals. The demands had to be dropped.

Zubatov's next idea was to help the union draw up proposals for wages and working conditions, impartially for the whole of Moscow industry. As head of the Okhrana he even went so far as to convoke a meeting of the manufacturers, berate them a little, and insist upon concessions. With these first successes, the movement began to spread rapidly, from industry to industry, and then, on the wings of rumor and report, from town to town, until the newly industrialized factory centers of southern Russia were honeycombed with police unions.

While Zubatov supported labor legislation and repeatedly took the part of the workers against the employers, he simultaneously dispatched provocateurs into the rival revolutionary movements with an idea of "provoking you to acts of terror and then crushing you" as he said once in a moment of frankness. Chief of these agents was Yevno Azev, son of a poor Jewish tailor, who became a student spy, then, with Zubatov's aid, a Moscow engineer and one of the founders and the eventual leader of the Terror Section of the Social Revolutionary Party.

In Odessa a Doctor Shaevich appeared to start things moving. Colonel of Gendarmes Vasiliev, assisted by two Jewish women agents, even formed a "Jewish Independent Labor Party" in Kiev. A police-sponsored priest, George Gapon, offered himself as a leader of the working-class movement in Saint Petersburg. Police socialism was booming all over Russia.

In the spring of 1903, the new industrial regions exploded in a series of little strikes, that set each other off, merged with each other, began to grow into something too big for a police official to manipulate in comfort. In July, 1903, at the very moment when the Social Democrats at their Congress in London were adopting a resolution to send socialist workingmen into the police unions, Dr. Shaevich lost control of the Odessa movement. A general strike flared up there, then spread all over southern Russia and into the Caucasus, a dress rehearsal for the greater strikes of 1905. Zubatov, Vasiliev and Shaevich fell from grace, and were banished to their birthplaces, Zubatov was restored to the service in 1905, then dismissed again. But so loyal was he to the Tsar that when Nicholas abdicated in 1917, Zubatov committed suicide.

With the Odessa general strike ended the first phase of the experiment in police unionism. But in the capital, Father Gapon had not gotten started yet, nor was he under the Moscow jurisdiction of the disgraced Zubatov. Minister Plehve did not interfere with the priest's plan for a further experiment in clerical-police unionism.

Meanwhile, the border lands of the Empire, many of them economically more advanced than the Great-Russian central

area, were also astir. The rapid industrialization of the nineties
and the policy of Russification of the last two Tsars were
rousing these non-Russian nationalities to fever heat. Here the
Russian state had little opportunity to insinuate its control.
The labor movement tended rather to submerge itself into a
general nationalist struggle for independence. Where the working class was strongest and best organized, the nationalist movement in turn tended to take on a labor and socialist tinge. In
Russian Poland, for example, the Bund became a labor movement with special views on Jewish nationality, while strong
protagonists like Joseph Pilsudski and Rosa Luxemburg waged
a war over the soul of the Polish proletariat, Pilsudski's nationalism tinged with socialism competing with Luxemburg's
antinationalist or internationalist socialism.

The rise of the nationalist revolutionary movements in all the
border regions suggested to the fertile mind of Plehve another
experiment in "police socialism" of quite a different order. He
would try playing the Mohammedan Tartar masses in Transcaucasia against the Christian Armenians, and, wherever there
were Jewish settlements—most of them were in the borderlands
—he would try playing Russians, Poles and other peoples against
the Jews. His propaganda, spread by secret agents and government printing presses, emphasized the "socialistic" character of
the enterprise. It sought to direct the existing mass anger not
against landlords and capitalists in general, but against Jewish
and Armenian merchants, Jewish estate managers and money-
lenders. Like the "National Socialism" of Germany which later derived from it, the pogrom incitations simultaneously
charged the Jews with being the moneyed and exploiting classes,
and with being disloyal revolutionaries who would destroy Russia's unity and undermine her greatness. This experiment was
more successful than the *zubatovshchina,* surviving its author,
Plehve. Yet it too was to have unlooked-for results. In 1905 and
1906 it would provide the workingmen with one of their best
reasons for demanding and bearing arms. In some of the affected regions, zemstvos, municipal councils, and even entire

provinces of Transcaucasia would vote funds to arm workers' defense corps against the pogroms which a section of the government was secretly organizing.

On the night of February 8-9, 1904, Plehve's third dream bore fruit. Without prior warning, Japanese submarines attacked the Russian fleet in the harbor of Port Arthur, thereby overnight changing the relation of forces in the Far East. Plehve's "little successful war with Japan" opened up before him.

Witte's memoirs seek to put all the blame for the war upon the shoulders of Plehve and a little clique of Far Eastern speculators and adventurers who had the ear of the Tsar. But closer scrutiny reveals Witte as one of those statesmen who do not want war, yet want those things which lead to ever-sharpening conflict with the similarly "peace-minded" statesmen of other countries. His financial and railroad-building schemes for the penetration of China and Korea merit a closer examination for they present a startling parallel with the actions of the Soviet Government in the same regions in 1945. Indeed, they laid the foundations on which Soviet claims in Manchuria, Mongolia, Northwest China and Korea (and Iran, too) are based today.

Early in the nineties, Witte directed the attention of his government to Persia (Iran) and set up a Russo-Persian Bank under the control of the Russian Government. In 1894, when Japan defeated China in war and seized the Liao-Tung peninsula—on which Port Arthur stands—the main attention of the Russian state shifted to the Far East. Nicholas II, backed by Germany and France, forced Japan to relinquish the fruits of its victory and withdraw from the Chinese mainland. Witte negotiated a secret treaty of "friendship and non-aggression" with China, guaranteeing its territorial integrity and arranging to build a railroad through Manchuria to Port Arthur "to protect China from the aggressions of Japan." So deeply did the old Dowager Empress of China cherish this treaty of friendship that she hung the text (for a few years) in her bedroom.

Now Witte was able to extend his pet project, the Transsiberian Railroad, through China (Manchuria) to the sea. This "Chinese Eastern Railroad," as the extension was called, was nominally the property of a mixed company. But the controlling interest was in the hands of a Russian bank created by Witte for the purpose, and the Tsar's government got the right to "protect" and "police" the line. The railroad company soon entered into other industries (also claimed by Stalin today) and the economic penetration of Manchuria began to assume vast proportions.

The next move, made against Witte's advice, caused the Chinese Dowager Empress to tear up the framed document hanging in her bedroom. Still protesting friendship and giving as its purpose the protection of China's integrity, the Russian Navy steamed into Port Arthur, set up a naval base there, and, by a combination of bribery and coercion, forced the Chinese to agree to a twenty-five-year "lease" of the port and base. Simultaneously, the British moved in to take Weh-Hai-Wei, the Germans Kiao-Chow, the French Kwang-Chow, thus slicing off the choicest parts of the Chinese coast. Only Japan, which had softened up the resistance of China by its attack, was left out in the cold. When the Kaiser used the murder of two German missionaries to extort a ninety-nine-year lease to Kiao-Chow from China, the Tsar, not to be outdone by his cousin, forced China to change his lease on Port Arthur to ninety-nine years also.

Now an aroused China attempted to drive out all the foreigners who were cutting her land to pieces (the Boxer Rebellion), whereupon all the Powers moved in with armies of occupation, the Russian Army occupying Manchuria. When the rebellion had been crushed, Russia pledged itself to withdraw its troops but continued to keep them there. It is on these foundations that the Soviet Government in 1945 based its claims to a naval base once more in Port Arthur, the right to police the Chinese Eastern Railway in Manchuria, and its other demands.

Meanwhile Japan was trying to get its share of the spoils by penetrating Korea, but here, too, the Tsar's government sent "police troops," arranged for a Russian gauge railroad, provided military and financial advisers. Korea negotiated anxiously with both countries in an effort to preserve its independence, while Japan tried to come to a peaceful agreement with Russia on the basis of a Japanese sphere in Korea and a Russian in Manchuria. This mutual penetration of Korea is the basis for Russia's present occupation of the northern half of that unhappy country. After several years of vain efforts at negotiation, the Japanese withdrew their envoys from Moscow, and three days later, without a declaration of war, smashed the Russian fleet off Port Arthur by a surprise attack. The date was February 9, 1904.

The internal struggle in Russia died down as Minister Plehve had calculated, submerged in a great wave of patriotic exaltation. But not for long. The Transsiberian, begun by Witte in 1891, had as yet but a single track, and at Lake Baikal there was a big gap which had to be covered by ferry in summer and sledge in winter. Yet this was the slender lane through which Russia's mighty resources would have to pass if they were to be brought to bear upon the far weaker but on-the-spot Japan. General Kuropatkin was for retreating inland into Siberia until Russia's slow-moving might could be brought up to crush his lesser adversary, but generals close to the Tsar disobeyed his orders and had them overruled in Court. For eight months the great Port Arthur fortress held out, falling at last to starvation, indiscipline and siege. As the Russian armies met reverse after reverse and the Court clique proved impotent to mobilize effectively Russia's vast resources for war, anger and shame and open defeatism took the place of the first patriotic fervor. By the time the Russian war machine was really getting under way and the slender resources of Japan were showing signs of exhaustion, the threat of revolution had grown so great in Russia that the Tsar preferred to recall Witte to office (he had been dismissed for his wearisome admonitions against military adventures in the Far East, in 1903), and to send him to the United States to negotiate a humiliating compromise peace with Japan, so that the government's hands might be freed for the mounting war with its own people.

All through 1904, while millions of Russian workers and peasants were called upon to fight and die in the Far East for Port Arthur and Dairen, northern Korea and Sakhalin, and the Transsiberian Railroad, the faction strife between Lenin and his opponents so consumed their energies that they had little left over for reacting to the war, or even defining their position toward it. Incredible as it sounds, during the entire year 1904 there are only three sparse mentions of the war in Lenin's writings! The rest are concerned with his war on the Central Committee, the Council, the Editorial Board of *Iskra*. And the writings of his opponents show similar proportions. No wonder the revolution that began in January, 1905, caught them napping.

The few utterances on the subject made by all these leaders abroad are little more than passing references and casual slogans. There were differences of approach, but they did not achieve clear formulation. Trotsky and Martov regarded the war as an evil, and called for an immediate peace. Lenin, however, was inclined to regard the conflict with Japan as something positive since it would show up the weakness of the monarchy. He expected Japan to win, and thought that this would be an aid to the progressive forces in Russia in their own war with the Russian Government. When, in January, 1905, the Japanese finally took Port Arthur, he wrote one of his few pronouncements on the conflict. Entitled "The Fall of Port Arthur," it is a scarce-concealed cry of exultation that "progressive Japan" had defeated "backward and reactionary Europe," and not merely Russian absolutism. His words are worth pondering, both because they contain within them the germ of his future "revolutionary defeatism" in World War I, and because they contrast so strangely with utterances on the same subject by his self-proclaimed "best disciple." Said Lenin:

> The proletariat has every reason to rejoice . . . The military goal of Japan is in the main attained. Progressive, advanced Asia has dealt backward and reactionary Europe an irreparable blow. Ten years earlier this reactionary Europe, with Russia at the head, was made uneasy by the crushing of China by Japan, and

it united to deprive Japan of the best fruits of its victory. Europe defended its prior and primal right, sanctified by centuries, to the exploitation of the Asiatic peoples. The reconquest of Port Arthur by Japan is a blow against the whole of reactionary Europe . . .

The war of a progressive land with a backward one has this time as so often in the past played a great revolutionary role . . . The proletariat is opposed to every bourgeoisie and every expression of the bourgeois order, but this opposition does not relieve it of the duty of distinguishing between the historically progressive and the reactionary representatives of the bourgeoisie. It is therefore entirely understandable that the most consistent and determined representatives of revolutionary international Social Democracy, Jules Guesde in France and Hyndman in England, have given expression without evasion to their sympathy for Japan, which is giving a beating to Russian absolutism . . .

Not the Russian people but Absolutism has suffered a shameful defeat. The Russian people has won by the defeat of Absolutism. The capitulation of Port Arthur is the prologue to the capitulation of Tsarism. The war is far from ended, but in its continuation every step strengthens the immeasurable ferment and indignation in the Russian people and brings us nearer to the moment of a great new war, the people's war against absolutism, the war of the proletariat for freedom. [*Vpered,* January 14, 1905.]

That "great new war" which Lenin spoke of, was actually to break out within a week, before even that issue of *Vpered* had reached Russia!

"The proletariat has every reason to rejoice . . ." Clearly, Joseph Stalin, if we are to credit his words of 1945, must have felt differently. In his "Victory Address" on the unconditional surrender of Japan, September 2, 1945, we read:

The defeat of the Russian troops in 1904 in the period of the Russo-Japanese War left grave memories in the minds of our peoples. It was a dark stain on our country. Our people trusted and awaited the day when Japan would be routed and the stain wiped out. For forty years have we, men of the older generation, waited for this day. And now this day has come!

Nothing could more sharply mark the contrast between the "master" and the "best disciple" than these two utterances on the fall of Port Arthur, the naval base which first the Tsar and then Stalin was to wrest from China.

The Japanese Government, for its part, felt that it might find interests in common with Russian "progressive forces." With admirable impartiality it offered money and arms to all shades and factions. Pilsudski journeyed to Japan to secure substantial help for his Polish Socialist Party. The Georgian Federal Socialists and the Finnish Activists accepted assistance. Rosa Luxemburg's Polish Social Democracy, however, rejected aid from such a source, as did Mensheviks, Bolsheviks, and Constitutional Democrats. It is characteristic of the Russian intelligentsia, from Lenin to Miliukov, that they thought it shameful to accept such support, and the fact of that rejection should effectively dispose of the slanderous view that Lenin's "revolutionary defeatism" converted him into an enemy agent of the government warring with his.

Since the Social Democrats, especially their foreign "general staffs," were too busy with their faction war, it was the liberals and democrats who first made their voices heard in opposition as misery mounted and the military reverses multiplied:

> Whose fault is it?—wrote Prince Trubetskoi in the Law Journal, *Pravo,* on the occasion of the defeat at Lao Yang—Is it Russian society's? Russian society was asleep, by order of the authorities. For years every measure has been taken to prevent its waking. If now and then someone tried to get up and stand on his two feet and say a human word, it was regarded as a disturbance of order and security. It called forth only a threatening snarl: *Mouth shut! Keep down there!* and a powerful hand would push down the lifted head. In recent years Russia has been like a dormitory in a police station . . .

On July 24, the already shaken bureaucracy was thrown into utter confusion by a bomb, thrown by Sazonov, in a plot directed by police-agent Azev, which tore the recently promoted

Interior Minister Plehve to pieces. Without a strong adviser now, the frightened Tsar appointed a moderate liberal in Plehve's place with a program of "showing more confidence in society."

At that the liberal democratic movement found its tongue and burst into speech like a forest of birds at daybreak. Zemstvos adopted declarations of grievances and made open plans for a national conference of zemstvo delegates. Lawyers, doctors, architects, authors, journalists, engineers, economists, scientists, professors held public banquets, made speeches, memorialized, resolved, protested, demanded and respectfully suggested innumerable changes. Their staid professional conferences turned into political meetings and their professional societies into "unions." Then, under Professor Miliukov's leadership, these unions united into a *Union of Unions*. So powerful was the impression that these intellectual unions made upon the as yet unorganized workingmen that to this day the labor organizations of Russia are called "professional unions," generally shortened to *profsoyuzy,* "profunions."

The Social Democrats, as far as their faction quarrels permitted, followed these liberal oppositional activities with the deepest interest. But how to behave toward them? On this, as on other matters, Lenin and his erstwhile associates were of two minds. As Plekhanov had predicted, the Mensheviks were in favor of "turning their face; you your behind" toward the liberal democratic opposition.

Since we're all agreed that the coming revolution is to be a "bourgeois democratic revolution," reasoned the Mensheviks, such men as these are destined to lead it and form the future government. Let us give them courage and mass support. Let us call upon the workers to demonstrate in front of their zemstvo meetings, banquet halls, political demonstrations. And, in return for helping them win, let us exact promises from them for our own class: a truly democratic régime, universal suffrage, freedom of speech, press, organization, enlightened social legislation. After tsarism is overthrown, begins our fight with them. In the meanwhile, let us not burst into their meetings

in disorderly fashion, make demands that will frighten them
away, or split the opposition to tsarism before it has won its
fight. "Before you divide the skin, first you catch the bear."

Lenin, for his part, waxed ironical at these proposals. True,
he shared with the Mensheviks the common formulae: "alliance
of all opposition forces"; "a bourgeois democratic revolution."
But in his heart he was convinced that the bourgeoisie was too
weak and cowardly to carry out its own historical tasks, that it
was ready to "make a deal with the Tsar," that it was too crafty
and Machiavellian to keep any promises made to the masses.
"Promises," wrote Lenin in English, quoting one of his favorite
English proverbs, "promises are like pie-crust—made to be broken." As for frightening away the bourgeoisie, you can count
upon their being frightened away, all except the peasantry and
the "radical urban petty bourgeoisie." The way to give these
timid heroes courage is to set them an example of irreconcilable
struggle yourself. If that frightens them off, so much the better:
we shall know that we cannot count on them, and shall go on
without them. You call upon the masses to demonstrate before
their banquet halls and zemstvo meetings, to give them courage.
But I call upon the masses to demonstrate before governmental
buildings, palaces, prisons, police stations . . .

But the masses listened neither to Bolsheviks nor Mensheviks.
Many of them followed the liberals directly. Even some of Lenin's Local Committees in Russia ignored his instructions, and
gathered in liberal and democratic meetings, to cheer and support the most vocal opposition that had yet arisen. However, the
bulk of the workingmen of the capital followed neither Bolsheviks, nor Mensheviks, nor Liberal Democrats, but swarmed into
the organizations headed by the police.

Trotsky, who had joined the Mensheviks on the organization
question, now fought them on what he contemptuously called
their "banquet campaign." Alone of Russian Marxists, Trotsky
was trying to break out of the hobbling circle of the formula
that the coming revolution must be a "bourgeois revolution."
The bourgeoisie, he asserted, will never carry their fight from the

banquet hall into the streets, where alone revolutions are fought and won. Once the police and the Tsar snarl a firm *no* at them, their flow of words will come to a stop. Before the end of 1904 this prediction at least was verified.

"What next?" asked Trotsky in a pamphlet written near the year's end. His answer:

> A political general strike . . . A political strike of the proletariat, which ought to be turned into a political demonstration of the entire population . . . Not a local, but a general political strike all over Russia, with a general political slogan. This slogan: To stop the war, and to call a National Constituent Assembly . . . And the peasants ought to come together on the day of the strike . . . We ought to carry on the most intensive propaganda in the Army, in order that, on the day of the strike, each soldier should know that he is facing the people—who are demanding a National Constituent Assembly.*

Of all the formulae, plans, suggestions, slogans, and immediate proposals and analyses made in the year 1904, this one of Trotsky's on a general political strike was to come closest to realization in 1905. But history, as usual, was to prove sly and tricky, and reality was to turn out richer, more bizarre, more complicated than any formula derived from it and meant to describe it and prescribe for it. Not Marxian socialism but one of the experiments in "police socialism" became the bizarre starting point for a general strike. Or perhaps we should say "clerical socialism," for its leader was a priest of the Russian Orthodox Church!

Father George Gapon is one of the most interesting figures thrown up by the Revolution of 1905, and one of the most peculiarly Russian. Son of a Ukrainian peasant, at the time we

---

* *Do Devyatago Yanvarya* ("Before the Ninth of January"). With an introduction by Parvus. Geneva, 1905. The pamphlet failed to get printed until after the stirring events of January 22, 1905 (January 9, Old Style), whence the title. Parvus's introduction contains the first exposition of the theory of "permanent revolution" (the proletariat begins by making a bourgeois revolution and continues it "in permanence" until it becomes a proletarian revolution), a doctrine which was to play such a central role in Trotsky's subsequent, life-long views.

meet him he was only thirty-two. He is described as intelligent, serious, meditative, energetic, strikingly handsome, an impressive orator and inspired leader of men. In his youth, one of his teachers, a Tolstoyan, had given him a clandestinely circulated manuscript tract by Tolstoy. The other main source of his inspiration was Zubatov and his experiment with police-directed unionism. The Saint Petersburg workers, more advanced than those of Moscow, had proved more suspicious of police direction. Father Gapon, who had already convinced his superiors of his ability to handle men as a prison chaplain, now suggested that the Petersburg workingmen could be better led in the direction of wholesome organization under "spiritual supervision" than under police control. His project for a "Union of Russian Factory Workers" with himself as leader and spiritual adviser received Plehve's ministerial approval shortly before the latter's violent death. The new Union's aims included "the sober and rational passing of leisure time," the elimination of drunkenness and gambling, the inculcation of religious and patriotic ideas, the development of a "prudent view of the duties and the rights of workers," and organized "self-activity for the legal improvement of the conditions of labor and life of the workers."

At first the workingmen kept away. The puzzled Gapon, torn between his Tolstoyan views and his moral and social ambitions on the one hand and his police instructions on the other, sought to increase the confidence of ordinary workers by getting active support and advice from the more advanced. After a few secret conferences with such people, he found his society flooded with applications for membership. More effective than their advice was the wartime rise in the cost of living. Before the year 1904 was over, his Union included practically all eligible workers engaged in the mechanical trades in Saint Petersburg, together with a sizable sprinkling of police spies and a few men under the influence of socialist ideas. There were no intellectuals. More successfully than Zubatov, he seemed to be deflecting hostility from the régime to the employers. The great meeting sang "God Save the Tsar" with deep and genuine fervor, for had he not overruled his wicked officials and given them this sympathetic priest to guide their legitimate hope for organization and improvement?

In gauging the patriarchal backwardness of the Russian masses in the dawn years of the twentieth century, we must keep this picture clear in our minds. Nor was it only the unskilled workers, yesterday's peasants, who followed a priest and sang thus fervently, "God Save the Tsar." Actually, the main scene of our drama is the huge Putilov locomotive works and machine shops, the oldest and largest heavy industry factory in advanced Saint Petersburg, containing the largest number of skilled metal workers. Here Father Gapon had his greatest organization. Under his guidance, they formulated some moderate demands upon the enterprise. In December, the latter answered by firing the leading members of Gapon's committee. Thereupon, the entire force of the Putilov locomotive works walked out and urged Father Gapon to take them directly to the "Dear Father Tsar" that they might humbly lay their troubles at his feet.

Priest Gapon was scarcely less naive than the men he had brought together. He was influenced by the mass spirit quite as much as he influenced it. At first he was hesitant at the audacious idea of going directly to the "Father of the Russian people." Then he sanctioned it, finally was carried away by it. The movement was getting too big for its founder to control; its illusions, assuming independent life, were taking control of him. He began to avoid his superiors, the officials of the Police Department and the Ministry of the Interior. Like his followers, he too now sought to go over their heads and seek direct contact with Tsar Nicholas. On January 21 (January 8, Old Style), the eve of the projected procession to the palace, he wrote the following confidential message to the Tsar:

> Sire!
> Do not believe the Ministers. They are cheating Thee in regard to the real state of affairs. The people believe in Thee. They have made up their minds to gather at the Winter Palace tomorrow, at 2 P.M., to lay their needs before Thee. If Thou wilt not stand

before them, Thou wilt break that spiritual connection which
unites Thee with them . . . Do not fear anything. Stand tomorrow before the people and accept our humblest petition. I, the
representative of the workingmen, and my comrades, guarantee
the inviolability of Thy person.   (*signed*)   GAPON.

Next morning, according to the common estimate, more than
two hundred thousand men, women and children, workers and
their families, gathered at many concentration points to con-
verge in procession upon the Winter Palace. They were unarmed in keeping with Gapon's guarantee; the few terrorists,
hot-heads, or police agents who had brought arms were searched
by his ushers and their weapons taken from them. Their intention was pacific, even reverential. It was Sunday. Many bore
ikons and pictures of the Tsar. This carrying of images of the
ruler in procession is an ancient Russian custom that flourishes
still today. As they marched, they sang as only Russian multitudes can sing, and over and over again their song was "God
Save the Tsar."

At the head marched Priest Gapon with a scroll, a reflection
of the medley in his mind and the variegated nature of his
following:

> Sire—We workingmen and inhabitants of Saint Petersburg
> . . . our wives and our children and our helpless old parents come
> to Thee, Sire, to seek for truth and protection. We have become
> beggars; we have been oppressed; we are breathless . . . There
> has arrived for us that great moment when death is better than
> the continuation of intolerable tortures. We have left off work-
> ing, and we have declared to our masters that we shall not begin
> to work until they comply with our demands. We ask but lit-
> tle . . . to diminish the working day to eight hours . . . minimum
> daily wage should be one ruble per day. To abolish overtime . . .
>
> The officials have brought the country to complete destruc-
> tion, have involved it in a detestable war . . . We working-
> men have no voice in the expenditure of the enormous amounts
> raised from us in taxes . . .
>
> These things are before us, Sire, and they have brought us to
> the walls of Thy Palace. We are seeking here the last salvation.
> Do not refuse assistance to Thy people. Give their destiny into

their own hands. Cast away from them the intolerable oppression of the officials. Destroy the wall between Thyself and Thy people, and let them rule the country together with Thyself . . . Order immediately the convocation of a *zemski sobor* . . . order that the elections to the Constituent Assembly be carried on under the condition of universal, equal, secret voting. This is the most capital of our requests . . . the principal and only plaster for our painful wounds . . .

Order and take an oath to comply with these requests and Thou wilt make Russia happy and famous and Thou wilt impress Thy name in our hearts and the hearts of our posterity forever.

If Thou wilt not order and wilt not answer our prayer, we shall die here on this Square before Thy Palace . . .

So the people, finding their voice through a priest who had picked up scraps of demands and slogans that were in the air, marched to the palace of their Tsar, to lay their troubles at his feet. But the Tsar was not in his palace. He had left the city hastily, taking with him wife and daughters. In his stead he had left his officials: generals, police chiefs, and his uncle, the Grand Duke Vladimir.

Troops fully armed descended upon the marchers, surrounded their separate detachments, fired at close range. Men, women, children fell. The crowds melted away. Crimson stains appeared on the white snow. How many fell, no one knows, for the wounded were treated in secret and the dead were withdrawn by their kin. The common labor estimate is 500 killed, 3000 wounded. A public commission of the Bar Association set the figures at 150 and 200 respectively. In any case, enough blood was shed to baptize the day as "Bloody Sunday."

With it an epoch came to an end. It had been sufficient for the masses to get the fearful idea of acting on a cherished fairytale for it to be exploded forever. That day millions of primitive minds took the leap from the Middle Ages to the Twentieth Century. In love and reverence their best had come to lay their troubles at the feet of the Dear Father Tsar. The bullets and the shed blood swept away all vestiges of love and credulity. Now they knew themselves fatherless and knew that they would have to solve their problems themselves. Now their minds were opened at last to the teachings of the republican and socialist intellectuals. Constituent Assembly and Democratic Republic, General Strike and Armed Uprising ceased to be phrases comprehensible only to the educated and the specialists in revolution. They took possession of millions and thereby became a material force for the transformation of Russia.

Father Gapon fled. With the aid of Social Revolutionaries he escaped abroad. From hiding, he dispatched one more note to his Tsar, this time without salutation or respectful capitals:

> The innocent blood of workers, their wives and children, lies forever between thee, oh soul destroyer, and the Russian people. Moral connection between thee and them may never more be . . . Let all the blood which has to be shed, hangman, fall upon thee and thy kindred!

CHAPTER SEVENTEEN

1905 IN EXILE

Zhelyabov: History moves too slowly. It needs a push . . .
Semenyuta: What about a constitution?
Zhelyabov: All to the good.
Semenyuta: Well, what do you want—to work for a constitution or to give history a push?
Zhelyabov: Just now we want to give history a push.

The morning after Bloody Sunday, the Ulyanovs were on their way to the Geneva Library when they were stopped by the Lunacharskys, who were hurrying to visit them. Mrs. Lunacharsky was so moved that she could not speak, only helplessly wave her muff. The four went to Lepeshinsky's restaurant, where they found other Bolsheviks, drawn to the familiar hangout as by a magnet. "The people gathered there hardly spoke a word to one another, they were so excited. With tense faces they sang the Revolutionary Funeral March. Everyone was overwhelmed with the thought that the Revolution had commenced."

Thence forward, they would live in a dreamlike state, suspended between issue and issue of the daily papers. An irresistible force drew them one by one back to the land of their birth. With that controlled impatience which characterized him, Lenin alone resumed his daily trips to the library, until such time as it seemed possible for him to come out in the open in Russia. To his comrades on the scene of struggle he wrote ardent letters, full of suggestions, insistent yet tactfully tentative, because "from the cursed distance naturally one does not trust himself to take a definite position." Statistics began to gather dust once more on the peaceful shelves of the Geneva Library, for Lenin was disturbing other sections. He began to translate into Russian: *On Street Fighting, Advice of a General of the Commune.* Its author, General Cluseret, had first won distinction by the energy with which he had suppressed the revolt of the Paris workingmen in June, 1848. Later he had served with Garibaldi in Italy, then with the North in our own Civil War (where he acquired his generalship). Returning to France he had joined the anarchist, then the socialist movement, becoming a socialist representative in the Chamber of Deputies, and finally a military leader in the defense of Paris during the Commune.

Vladimir Ilyich read everything he could find on military science in peaceful Geneva. He was the only exile who reacted thus to the news of Bloody Sunday. Besides Cluseret, there was Von

Clausewitz *On War,* always the favorite authority on strategy in Russia. He "consulted" with Marx and Engels, as was his wont in each new situation, rereading and annotating everything they had written on military matters and on insurrection as an art.

The night-owl Martov had gotten the news earlier than Lenin. He had stayed up all night with his cronies, discussing meager dispatches, waiting for the morning papers. Trotsky, returning from a lecture and a sleepless night on a train, found them at dawn near the *Iskra* office. Their news convinced him that he must leave for Russia at once. More ardent and venturesome and younger than the others (he was now twenty-five), Trotsky was the first to go. In general, the émigrés were slower to recross the frontier in proportion to their age, the length of time they had been settled abroad, and the ardor of their temperaments. Lenin and Martov did not get back until the October amnesty, near the end of the year. Rosa Luxemburg, whose temperament was no less ardent than Trotsky's, was held back by her multiple activities in the German Social Democracy, so that she did not smuggle herself into her native Russian Poland until December. The death of Axelrod's wife detained him so long that by the time he set out, reaction was once more in full sway; he got as far as Finland, whither the others were already fleeing from Saint Petersburg. Significantly, all through the stormy years 1905 and 1906, Plekhanov did not return to his native land at all.

Natalia Ivanovna Sedova had just made the journey from Russia to Geneva in order to join Trotsky there, but the very next morning after the news came she accompanied him to Munich, and then went back to Russia to prepare things so that he might live clandestinely in Saint Petersburg. Her round trip was typical of her lifelong devotion to him as revolutionist and as man. While she went ahead to make arrangements for him Lev

Davidovich stayed in Munich with Parvus and they talked themselves into agreement in what was to prove a fruitful partnership for the years 1905 to 1907. Parvus (Alexander L. Gelfand) was ten years Trotsky's senior and enjoyed an enormous reputation as a Marxist writer and political thinker. It fortified the young man's self-confidence, if that were needful, that Parvus should be greatly impressed by his still-unpublished pamphlet, even moved by it to fresh thought on Russia. "Why, events have confirmed your analysis," Parvus told Trotsky. "The twenty-second of January (Bloody Sunday) was that political general strike for which you have been calling, even if it was disguised under a priest's frock . . . All that is necessary now is to add that revolution in Russia may place a workers' government in power."

May place a workers' government in power! thus was outlined Parvus' introduction to Trotsky's pamphlet, and thus conceived the germ of the doctrine of "permanent revolution" which was destined to play such an important part in Trotsky's views and to sway Lenin's actions in 1917.

For the next decade, there would be three more or less clearly defined competing outlooks among Russian Marxists as to the nature and prospects of the coming revolution.

1. *That of the Mensheviks:* The coming revolution was a bourgeois democratic revolution. It would abolish feudalism, clear the ground for the free growth of capitalism, establish a democratic republic, bring the bourgeoisie to power. Under the republic there would be open political life, freedom to propagate socialist ideas, to organize the working class politically and economically and develop in it the culture, experience, self-consciousness and power necessary to prepare, at some future date, a second revolution, a socialist revolution. That revolution could be democratic only when the proletariat should become a majority of the population. But the proletariat in its present condition in this backward land could not dream of taking power, nor should the Social Democratic Party entertain the idea of entering into the provisional government. Since it

could not secure the enactment of its own program in so backward a country, it would only compromise its program and itself by taking responsibility for the actions of a bourgeois government. To be revolutionary now meant to fight tsarism, to support the bourgeoisie in its struggle for power, to encourage it and push it and exact from it the promise of a maximum of freedom for the working class.

2. *The view of Parvus and Trotsky:* The first tasks facing the revolutionists were, to be sure, "bourgeois democratic" tasks, i.e. such tasks as had been accomplished in the West by the bourgeois revolutions. But the Russian revolution was taking place "too late" in history to be a bourgeois revolution: the proletariat was already on the scene as an independent force, so that the two revolutions, the bourgeois democratic and the proletarian socialist, would tend to be "combined" or telescoped into one. Moreover, the Russian middle class was weak and cowardly. Equipped with the theoretical achievements and experiences of its Western socialist brothers and supported by the simultaneously developing peasant rebellion, the proletariat would have to do the job which the bourgeoisie was incapable of doing. "In Russia," wrote Parvus, in his introduction to Trotsky's pamphlet, "only workers can accomplish a revolutionary insurrection. . . . The revolutionary provisional government will be a government of the *workers' democracy.*" Thus the "bourgeois revolution" made by the proletariat, would tend to flow over into a proletarian revolution. "Once the revolution is victorious"—the words now are Trotsky's—"political power necessarily passes over into the hands of the class that has played the leading role in the struggle, the working class." And once in power? They would have to act like representatives of the class for whom they professed to speak: they would have to adopt, even if only in fragments, a working-class governmental policy. The line between their minimum democratic demands and their final socialist program would dissolve. Even if they started with the most modest working-class measures, say the enforcement of an eight-hour day or the obligation of the

employers to support the unemployed, the latter would resist
and shut down their factories. Would not the government then
have to take over the factories? And would this not be a big step
toward socialism? In short, wrote Trotsky, "the political supremacy of the proletariat is incompatible with its economic
slavery." Similarly, in the rural areas, the proletariat in power
would soon be impelled to undertake the collectivization of agriculture. There would be resistance to all these measures, from
the enraged bourgeoisie, from the property-minded peasant
masses, perhaps foreign intervention. But to offset this last, there
was the hope that the Russian revolution would tend to spread
to the West, already ripe and overripe, as everyone knew, for a
socialist revolution. Thus the proletariat, once in power, might
hold onto it and keep the revolution going "in permanence,"
transforming it from a brief upheaval into a whole epoch of revolution at home and abroad, combining the bourgeois and proletarian revolutions into a single, continuous process, dominated
throughout by the proletariat. This "law of combined development," as Trotsky was to call it in his subsequent *History of
the Russian Revolution,* he and Parvus now baptized with the
name of "the permanent revolution."

3. *Lenin's position* which moved between these two polar
extremes. In formulae, Lenin sounded much like the Mensheviks;
in spirit he was forever attracted to the Trotskyist pole. With the
Mensheviks, Lenin held that the economic level of a country
determined whether or not it was ripe for socialist revolution.
With the Mensheviks he asserted categorically that economically, politically, and culturally, Russia was ripe only for a bour-
geois-democratic revolution. But with Trotsky and Parvus he
held that the bourgeoisie was too weak and cowardly to be
trusted to accomplish their own revolution, so that the leading
role would likely fall to the proletariat. With Trotsky, too—
and here we come to the dividing line in practical conduct—
Lenin held that the Social Democratic Party must strive directly for a share in the political power, must strive to enter any
provisional revolutionary government that might arise in the

course of the struggle, and must strive to determine the policy of that government.

But how then could the revolution be kept democratic? For Lenin, in those days, was a convinced democrat, and the problem of political freedom concerned him deeply. Not only in those days, but until he seized power in 1917. "Not a single socialist," he wrote for instance in 1914, "unless he decides to pronounce the questions of political freedom and democracy as of no consequence to him, in which case, of course, he ceases to be a socialist . . ." His writings are full of such earnest avowals, and there can be no doubt of their sincerity. Even in 1917, he countenanced a "temporary" minority dictatorship in Russia only because he was convinced that the Russian example in the midst of war would end the war on all fronts by worldwide revolution, thereby solving the problems of Russia's backwardness by a solution on a world scale.

"But how then could the revolution be kept democratic?" Lenin asked anxiously in 1905. If the Social Democratic Party must strive directly to share in the power, to enter into any provisional revolutionary government that might arise in the course of the struggle, how could that government be prevented from degenerating into a minority dictatorship of the proletariat in a country where the proletariat itself was a hopeless minority? Here is where he differed sharply from Trotsky and Parvus. He answered his question to his own satisfaction by categorically rejecting the Trotsky-Parvus formula of a "labor government" or a "socialist government" or a "dictatorship of the proletariat." No, he was in favor of a democratic government by the vast majority of the Russian people. To insure this he advocated not a labor government but a two-class, or more than two-class, government, constituted by two parties or more than two parties. For this he coined the formula: "the democratic dictatorship of the proletariat and the peasantry." This was to be a coalition government of proletariat (through the Social Democracy), peasantry (through some peasant party, perhaps the Social Revolutionaries) and of the democratic sections of the bourgeoisie (through some bourgeois democratic party like the Constitutional Democrats). He regarded the peasantry as a "petty bourgeois class," the most revolutionary, though not necessarily the only revolutionary, section of the bourgeoisie. If a coalition government could be formed with them, with or without the collaboration of the "urban, democratic, petty bourgeoisie," such a government would be a temporary dictatorship against the Tsar's supporters, but only in the sense that every revolutionary government in history has been such. It would be a "democratic dictatorship" because it would represent the will of the overwhelming majority of the population, and could give rise to a genuine democracy as soon as the emergencies of civil war were over and the provisional government had given way to a constituent assembly which would draft a new constitution and create a new constitutional democratic government.

Hence, when Parvus wrote on behalf of himself and Trotsky: "The provisional revolutionary government will be a Social Democratic one . . . with a Social Democratic majority," Lenin answered sharply:

> That cannot be! It cannot be because a revolutionary dictatorship can endure for a time only if it rests on the enormous majority of the people . . . The proletariat constitutes a minority. It can only command a mighty overwhelming majority if it unites with the mass of the semi-proletarians, the semi-property owners . . . Such a composition will naturally reflect itself in the composition of the revolutionary government . . . It would be extremely harmful to yield to any illusions in this regard . . . Anyone who attempts to achieve socialism by any other route will inevitably arrive at the most absurd and reactionary conclusions, both economic and political.

Later that same year, Lenin returned to the attack on Trotsky and Parvus in almost identical language. He spoke of their view as

> . . . the absurd, semi-anarchist view that the maximum program, the conquest of power for a socialist revolution, can be

achieved immediately. The present degree of economic development of Russia—an objective condition—and the degree of class consciousness and organization of the broad masses of the proletariat—a subjective condition indissolubly connected with the objective condition—make the immediate, complete emancipation of the working class impossible. Only the most ignorant people can ignore the bourgeois character of the present democratic revolution. Only the most naive optimists can forget how little as yet the masses of the workers are informed of the aims of socialism and of the methods of achieving it. And we are all convinced that the emancipation of the workers can only be brought about by the workers themselves; a socialist revolution is out of the question unless the masses become class-conscious, organized, trained and educated by open class struggle against the entire bourgeoisie. In answer to the anarchist objections that we are delaying the socialist revolution, we shall say: we are not delaying it, but are taking the first steps in its direction, using the only means that are possible along the only right path, namely the path of a democratic republic. Whoever wants to approach socialism by any other path than that of political democracy will inevitably arrive at absurd and reactionary conclusions both economic and political.

"Whoever wants to approach socialism by any other path than that of political democracy will inevitably arrive at the most absurd and reactionary conclusions . . ."

Fateful, prophetic warning!

Ineluctably, it calls to mind that other prophetic warning which Trotsky had leveled at Lenin the year before. Indeed, the two warnings have an organic connection with each other, for Trotsky's had been a prevision of the dangers of minority dictatorship within the Party, while Lenin's was a prevision of the dangers of minority dictatorship within the State. To perceive the organic connection between the two prophecies, we need only ask the question: *what if the Party should become synonymous with the State?* With such a party ruling such a state, would not the two dangers reinforce each other and become one?

To perceive that connection in all its rigor, let us restate the pregnant syllogism, with the missing link in its place:

Trotsky's Warning: "The organization of the Party will take the place of the Party itself; the Central Committee will take the place of the organization; and finally, the Dictator will take the place of the Central Committee."

Connecting Link: "The Party will take the place of the government."

Lenin's Warning: "Whoever wants to approach socialism by any other path than that of political democracy will inevitably arrive at the most absurd and reactionary conclusions, political and economic."

Thus, in 1904 and 1905, did the two future collaborators solemnly admonish each other of the dangers of minority dictatorship in the Party and the State. Who can doubt in the light of subsequent events that each of them at that moment had a brilliant prophetic vision of the dangers in the other's approach? But when they joined forces in 1917, each withdrew his warning against the other. Trotsky accepted Lenin's party machine; Lenin accepted Trotsky's "absurd, semi-anarchist view that the conquest of power for a socialist revolution can be achieved immediately," and Trotsky's conception of a minority "proletarian dictatorship," or more accurately, a single-party dictatorship. This fusion was the most natural in the world, for there is an indubitable structural and psychological connection between minority dictatorship in the Party and minority dictatorship in the State. Both are based upon the same assumption: namely, that a self-selected élite or vanguard, properly armed with expert knowledge (Marxism), and properly credentialed by a lifetime of experience and devotion, can dispense with the toilsome and hazardous democratic process, and still avoid the "absurd and reactionary conclusions," the dangers of "personal dictatorship," the pitfalls of totalitarianism, and the corrupting potentials of absolute power.

Thus, from 1905 to 1917, while there were two conceptions of party organization: Lenin's on the one hand, and that of Trotsky and the Mensheviks on the other, there were three conceptions of the nature of the coming revolution: the Menshevik at the one extreme; the Trotsky-Parvus or Trotskyist at the other; with the Leninist moving between them. The two extremes had a tidy air of logical consistency that was lacking to Lenin's intermediate view. The latter's apparent inconsistency was due to the conflict between his inherited Marxist formulae, which he shared with the Mensheviks, and the power-centered, self-confident, revolutionary will which he possessed in common with Trotsky.

But there was yet another reason for the lack of logical completeness in Lenin's formula: he was deliberately leaving one question open and unanswered. His whole conception was provisional in character. The "democratic dictatorship of the proletariat and the peasantry" of which he spoke was not a formula for a post-revolutionary government, but a formula for a "provisional revolutionary government." Its mission was to conduct the revolution, call a constituent assembly into being, and then let the constituent assembly decide upon a constitution and form of government. Once that was done, the provisional revolutionary dictatorship would hand over power to the new constitutional government.

When the Mensheviks reproached him with treason to Marxist orthodoxy by his proposal that a Marxist party should enter into a coalition government with the bourgeoisie, he answered: I am not talking of the permanent government of the new bourgeois democratic republic, but of the *provisional revolutionary government* of the period of revolution itself:

> The constituent assembly has to be convened by someone, he explained to the Mensheviks in his major work for 1905, *Two Tactics:* Someone must guarantee the freedom and fairness of the elections. Someone must invest such an assembly with full power and force. Only a revolutionary government which is the organ of an uprising can in all sincerity desire this and be capable of doing everything to achieve this . . .

However—he adds, approaching closely to the Mensheviks once more, and giving a severe glance in the direction of Trotsky—the evaluation of the importance of the provisional government would be incomplete and erroneous if the class nature of the democratic revolution were lost sight of . . . This democratic revolution in Russia will not weaken, but will strengthen the domination of the bourgeoisie.

The last sentence seems to promise quite unequivocally that once the constituent assembly has done its work and the new, bourgeois democratic constitution is adopted, the Social Democratic Party will step out of power and go over to the position of an opposition struggling for the preparation of the next revolution, its own socialist revolution.

But on this point, the usually so precise Lenin grows indefinite. His forecast changes from page to page and from article to article, becomes a restless spark leaping up and back between the fixed points of his dogmas and his will. It is no longer a formula but a series of rival hypotheses, competing *perhapses:*

Perhaps "bourgeois domination" will indeed be strengthened, as he has just so categorically said, and there will be nothing to do but to go over to opposition.

Or perhaps the "provisional revolutionary government" will achieve such miracles—are not revolutions the locomotives of history?— that another path may open out before it. Perhaps from the seats of power it may so transform the countryside, so expedite the organization and consciousness of the proletariat, release such revolutionary energies in the West, that the revolution in Russia may become the starting point of a whole era of revolution. (Now he is not frowning at Trotsky any more!)

The first "perhaps," part of his common heritage with the Mensheviks, is generally uppermost in *Two Tactics* and in all Lenin's writings between 1905 and 1917. But the second "perhaps," part of that charge of revolutionary will which he possesses in common with Trotsky, and in higher measure than Trotsky or any other man in Russia, pops out sometimes in language that is indistinguishable from that of Trotsky and Parvus:

> From the democratic revolution—Lenin wrote in *Proletarii* on September 14, 1905—we shall at once, according to the degree of our strength, the strength of the class-conscious and organized proletariat, begin to pass over to the socialist revolution. We stand for permanent revolution. We shall not stop halfway.

Recent translations by the Marx-Engels-Lenin Institute of this passage have attempted to conceal the identity of terminology with that of Trotsky and Parvus by substituting for the technical Marxian term "permanent revolution" the words "continuous revolution." (*Selected Works,* Vol. III, p. 145, and the Institute's *Lenin: A Political Biography,* p. 84.) Much as if some translator of Einstein would try to conceal his relation to Newton by substituting for the technical term "force of gravity" the words "force of heaviness"!

In short, Lenin's real answer to the question: what happens after we get power? is *Let's take power and then we'll see.* This readiness to "take power and then see" is the real core of "Leninism," separating him by an abyss from the Mensheviks, and blurring to the vanishing point the dogmatic line which divided him from Trotsky. "The seizure of power," he would write in 1917, "is the point of the uprising. Its political task will be clarified after the seizure." No one but Lenin among the Marxists could have written such a sentence. So, too, the last theoretical article he would ever write in his life would take as its text his favorite adage from Napoleon: *On s'engage, et puis . . . on voit.* Published in January, 1923, when he was already near death's door, it was his final attempt to answer the Menshevik reproach that he had seized power in a country unripe for socialism and in the name of a class insufficiently advanced in culture and organization to exercise power.

To Marx it might have seemed that "the forms of the state are rooted in the material conditions of life," that "the economic structure of society . . . independent of men's will . . . determines the general character of the social, political and spiritual processes," and that "no social order ever disappears before all the productive forces for which there are room in it have been developed." But to Lenin's political-power-centered mind, for all his Marxist orthodoxy, such formulae were intolerable fetters unless subject to the proper exegesis. And the exegesis literally turned Marx on his head until the Marxist view that "in the last analysis economics determines politics" became the Leninist view that, with enough determination, power itself, naked political power, might succeed wholly in determining economics.

In practice, the Menshevik view tended to fix Marxist formulae into dogmatic fatality, paralyzing the will to power and the very capacity to appeal to the masses when they were in an insurrectionary mood. In theory, Lenin's whole Marxist training and body of doctrine led him to accept the same formulae as Martov and Axelrod. He was as ready as they to give honest, unblinking recognition to the backwardness of Russia's economy, to the possibilities of its continued rapid expansion under a freer capitalism. He warned even more forcefully than they of "the absurd and reactionary" consequences inherent in minority dictatorship. And yet . . . And yet, the formula so piously repeated sat ill in his soul. It was modified by the concentration on power which had led him to form his hierarchical, power-centered organization. It was modified by the concentration on conspiracy and armed insurrection that had set him to studying Cluseret and von Clausewitz. It was modified by his Russian heritage of voluntarism from Pestel, Tkachev, Bakunin, Nechaev, the *Zemlya i Volya* and *Narodnaya Volya*. It was modified by his revolutionary impatience and longing, by his life-long absorption in the machinery of power, and the seizure of power. He did not expect to live to see the day when power would fall into his eager hands, but if that day should come to him, there could be no doubt but that he would repeat with Napoleon: *On s'engage, et puis . . . on voit.*

Thus when Trotskyists and Stalinists, after Lenin's death, would contest the heritage of the Master and comb his writings for confirmatory texts, it would be as possible to find scriptural authority for the one view as for the other. The Mensheviks, too, would be able to find ground for reproaching him for having abandoned what "once he so well knew" and so categorically asserted in common with them.

What actually happened would not fully justify any one of the three positions. History, a sly and capricious wench, would show that she had yet other tricks up her sleeve. The unity of all oppositional forces would indeed suffice to overthrow the Tsar and set up a democratic republic (the formula of the Mensheviks plus Lenin). But Lenin, who in 1905 had been in favor of entering a "provisional revolutionary government," would refuse to enter: and the Mensheviks, who had regarded such a coalition with the bourgeois parties as impermissible "ministerialism" or opportunism, would take a leading part in the Provisional Government. Further, revolutionary will and a power-centered party organization would suffice to overthrow the republic and set up a minority dictatorship (the formula of Trotsky). But it would not suffice to bring into being a world revolution and a socialist society (the further expressed calculation of Trotsky and Parvus, and the unformulated hope of Lenin). In short, History—with that capital *H* which these men who knew her every intention were prone to use—would decide neither for Axelrod-Martov, nor for Trotsky-Parvus, nor for Lenin-Trotsky, but for yet another variant, undreamed of by any, the chief embodiment of which would be that third one of our protagonists, Joseph Stalin, whom we are shortly to introduce into our story.

And Parvus in 1917? His strange destiny by then will have carried him far from the others. A Russian Jew of the generation of Lenin—he was born a year earlier—A. L. Gelfand (Helfand) was a cosmopolitan internationalist, at home wherever fortune drew him. He had emigrated from Russia at the beginning of the nineties, soon abandoning the ingrown Russian émigré colony to acquire fame under the pen-name of Parvus in the German Social Democracy. There, at the side of Rosa Luxemburg, he fought for a left-wing revolutionary position against the growing bureaucratic stiffening, centralism and opportunism of the German official leadership. He wrote articles for *Neue Zeit*, edited the *Saechsische Arbeiterzeitung*, founded a paper of his own, characteristically called *Aus der Weltpolitik*. His most important writings—*On the World Market and the Agrarian Crisis, General Strike, Russia and the Revolution, Colonial Policy, Socialism and the Banks*—show the scope and bent of his interests. He dreamed constantly of turning his knowledge of economics and world affairs to "practical account" in some colossal speculation which might make him a fortune to found a "great daily of revolutionary Marxism to be published in three languages." In 1904, as agent for the performance of Gorky's "Lower Depths" in Germany, Parvus made 60,000 marks "for the movement," but did not turn over a cent. Bebel and Kautsky hushed the scandal. (See report of Ladyshnikov, summarized in 3d Rn. ed. Lenin, VIII, p. 494.)

The year 1905 revived Parvus's interest in Russia and he hastened to follow Trotsky there. Together they edited the Menshevik legal organ, *Nachalo*, deflecting the Menshevik schemata in the direction of their views. Parvus took over the tiny *Russkaya Gazeta*, turning it into a journal with hundreds of thousands of readers. Both Parvus-Trotsky papers gained much larger circulations than the legal Bolshevik organ, *Novaya Zhizn*, founded by Minsky and Gorky, then taken over by Lenin. The low price of their paper, one kopek, the business skill and journalistic flair of Parvus, the extremism of Parvus and Trotsky ("down with the Tsar, up with a Labor Government," "permanent revolution"), the mounting personal prestige of Trotsky, made theirs the most popular of legal revolutionary journals.

Banished to Siberia in 1906, Parvus, like Trotsky, soon escaped to Western Europe. From 1910 to 1914 he was in the

*Stalin, Rykov, Kamenev and Zinoviev
in 1925 when they were "The Big Four" ruling Russia*

Police pictures of Zinoviev at age twenty-four when first arrested

Police pictures of Kamenev. Date uncertain

Police pictures of Bogdanov
taken shortly before he became a member of Lenin's "troika"

Police pictures of A. V. Lunacharsky

Police pictures of Lenin taken after his first arrest

Police pictures of Kamo, hero of the Tiflis holdup

Police pictures of Litvinov at the age of twenty-five (1901)

*Molotov
at thirty-five*

*Police picture of
Krassin at age twenty-five*

*Police picture of
Dzierzinski, founder of
the Soviet secret police*

Police pictures of Roman Malinovsky, Bolshevik leader and agent provocateur

Tomsky as Soviet Union leader   *Rykov as Premier*

Police pictures of Trotsky at time of first arrest at age nineteen

Police picture of Sverdlov in 1910   *Kalinin as "Head" of Government*

Balkans as correspondent for the German Socialist press. Here he became interested in the "Young Turk" movement and wrote for its paper. In that world of tangled intrigue, Parvus's knowledge of affairs made him the adviser of diplomats, politicians, businessmen, government officials—a role he hugely enjoyed and profited from. One day, a tip picked up from a Turkish official in a Constantinople café and turned over by him a few minutes later to a speculator at another table in the same café, started Parvus on the road to wealth. The "Little Balkan War" of 1912 found him trafficking in war supplies. The Great War of 1914 expanded his traffic, his wealth and his flare for intrigue in proportion. In 1915, he went from Constantinople to Stockholm, where he made money in coal and steel and other supplies needed by wartime Germany. He tried to renew his collaboration with Lenin, Trotsky and Rosa Luxemburg, but all three refused to have anything to do with him. The paper which he founded, *Die Glocke,* combined the criticism of opportunism and reformism with "revolutionary" support of German arms. This he justified after his fashion by asserting that the German armies would shatter tsarism, unleashing a revolution in Russia which would in turn make possible a revolution in Germany and the birth of a democratic, socialist German republic. Thus he completed the swing from Left Wing conscience jogger to that of a most subtle revolutionary apologist for the Right Wing of the German Social Democracy in its support of the war.

When, in 1917, the charge was made that Lenin had been sent back to Russia as a German agent, the enigmatic figure of Parvus loomed in the background as the alleged go-between. It is almost the last we hear of A. L. Helfand-Parvus, except that, after Lenin's rise to power, this revolutionary speculator made one more attempt to act as "broker," for an alliance between the German Social Democracy ruling in Germany and the Communist Party ruling in Russia. When that "deal" fell through, he applied to the Soviet Government for repatriation to Russia, stating that he was willing to accept the judgment of its tribunals on his career and to take any work assigned to him.

His grown son, who applied at the same time, was admitted to Russia but he was refused. Thereafter he stuck pretty closely to his business affairs, taking time out to advise Social Democrat Ebert, who had become president of the German Weimar Republic, and to make generous donations to German socialist papers. In 1924, the year of Lenin's death, he too died of the same cause, the bursting of a blood vessel in the brain.

But we must return to Leon Trotsky. In February, 1905, he crossed the frontier into the region he knew best, the Ukraine, where he took up a hunted existence in Kiev. As a "retired corporal," as an "eye patient" in a hospital directed by a sympathetic doctor, and under various other guises from various hiding places, he wrote articles, issued leaflets, sought contact with such strikers and revolutionists as he could find. One of the latter turned out to be the engineer, Leonid Krassin, of the Bolshevik Central Committee, a man of organizing genius who continued to work as a first-rate technician and factory director while he founded and supervised a clandestine printing plant in the Caucasus, collected funds from wealthy liberals, arranged meetings of secret committees in the most elegant and improbable homes, organized the smuggling of literature and later of arms, and worked in his own laboratory on bombs. One of Krassin's dreams was to perfect a pocket bomb "the size of a walnut" with the explosive power necessary to become a real weapon in street fighting. His other dream was to reunite Mensheviks and Bolsheviks, and such footloose revolutionaries as Trotsky, into a single organization. Despite Lenin's indignation at such "conciliationism," the latter valued this indefatigable, efficient, noiseless organizer most highly.

Now Krassin came to Trotsky's assistance, printed his leaflets in a clandestine printing plant, facilitated his journey to Saint Petersburg, absorbed some of his doctrine of "permanent revolution," and helped introduce it into Bolshevik theses. When scandalized Leninists heard of this, they complained to their chief. But Lenin had already become aware of a new voice in Russia. In his articles, he publicly praised the writings of Parvus. When there were objections to offer, Lenin advanced them with the greatest respect. ("We don't stress these little errors out of a desire to nag but because from one to whom much is given, much is also demanded.") Trotsky he was slower to forgive because of the latter's defection in 1903 and the stinging phrases of his blast against Leninist organization views. But Vladimir Ilyich was never one to let resentment stand in the way of recognition of a capable comrade-in-arms. To a complaining Bolshevik he wrote:

"So they are printing Trotsky's leaflets . . . Dear me! There's nothing wrong in that, provided the leaflets are tolerable and have been corrected. I shall also advise the Saint Petersburg Committee to reprint his writings after they have been edited, let's say by you." (Letter of September 14, 1905.)

After Lenin got to Saint Petersburg and could watch Trotsky at work, in mass meetings and in the Council of Workingmen's Delegates, he was ungrudging in his recognition that his erstwhile disciple had grown up and could now teach him as well as be taught by him. Indeed, in 1905 the master would learn more from the former disciple than the disciple from the master, for 1905 would be Trotsky's year.

In Saint Petersburg, Trotsky lived with the passport of a landowner, working under the name of "Peter Petrovich." "Peter Petrovich" found the local movement fighting under second-string leaders and nameless rank-and-filers, while the top leadership of both Social Democratic factions still continued to remain abroad. In increasing demand as a swift, clear-headed thinker, a writer of short, trenchant leaflets with a spark of fire in them, an amazingly eloquent speaker, he enjoyed the advantages of his interfactional position in the midst of a newly awakening mass of workingmen. These knew nothing of the old controversies and cooperated with each other—regardless of the faction they chanced to enter into, regardless, too, of the continuing émigré feuds and long-distance paper instructions. Working through Krassin with the Bolsheviks, Trotsky at the same time assumed leadership of the local Menshevik group. Thus the Petersburg Mensheviks began noticeably to follow policies which set them into opposition to the views of Axelrod, Martov and Martynov, and which elicited Lenin's praise.

There was the inevitable police agent among them, one Dobroskok, nicknamed "Gold-spectacled Nikolai." Natalia Ivanovna was soon arrested at a secret May Day meeting in the woods. One by one other active workers were picked up. "Peter Petrovich," known by sight to the gold-spectacled spy, left for the comparative peace and safety of a summer resort in nearby Finland. There he spent several peaceful, solitary months, reading, writing, thinking through his views, watching the course of events. The September-October strike brought him back to Saint Petersburg, this time under the name of "Yanovsky," reminiscent of the Yanovka in which he was born.

While unknown men of the masses inside Russia were leading strike waves, peasant insurrections, mutinies in the armed forces, in closest cooperation between adherents of menshevism, bolshevism and the Social Revolutionary Party, the leaders in exile continued their battle of factions. When Father Gapon reached Geneva, he tried to use his prestige to unite all revolutionary parties.

Being first of all a revolutionist and a man of action—he wrote in an "open letter"—I summon all the socialist parties to enter immediately into agreement and to begin the business of armed uprising against tsarism . . . Bombs and dynamite, terror by individuals and by masses—everything which may contribute to the national uprising. The first aim is the overthrow of the autocracy. The provisional revolutionary government will immediately proclaim amnesty for all fighters for political and religious freedom, immediately arm the people, and immediately convoke a constituent assembly on the basis of universal, equal, secret and direct suffrage . . . Every delay or dispute is a crime against the people whose interests you are defending . . .

A Social Revolutionary woman came to Lenin to tell him Gapon wanted to see him. The interview was arranged for late at night in a café—"neutral territory." Unlike Plekhanov, who was cold to Gapon, saying, "No good can come of a priest," Lenin was excited. To him Gapon promised more instruction than thousands of letters from backward workers; he was a part of the living revolution, expressing the million-headed illusions, the new-found enlightenment and wrath.

The interview left Lenin with no doubt as to the priest's sincerity. "I said to him," he told Krupskaya on his return, "don't you listen to flattery, little father; study, or that's where you'll find yourself—and I pointed under the table." That was typical for Lenin: in that sentence was his faith in the power of the classics to illumine, his dislike of flattery, his eagerness to utilize and train all those who showed promise. Father Gapon dutifully took up the works of Plekhanov, which—despite his differences with the latter—Lenin had recommended. The ex-priest tried to penetrate the mysteries of dialectical materialism, revolutionary disputations and feuds, but they seemed to him utterly alien to the force which had caught him up and flung him into the camp of uprising. He spent more time learning to ride and shoot. Distinguished gentlemen and ladies lionized him; famous world newspapers sent representatives to interview him and buy articles from him; funds poured into his hands for the purchase of arms.

On April 2, representatives of eighteen socialistic parties were summoned together by his "open letter." The list will serve to give us some notion of the state of the revolutionary movement at that moment. There were Social Revolutionaries, Bolshevik and Menshevik Social Democrats, the Polish Socialist Party, the Social Democratic Party of Poland and Lithuania, the Polish Socialist Party "Proletariat," the Jewish Socialist Bund, Armenian Social Democracy, Armenian Revolutionary Federalists (Dashnakists), White-Russian Socialist *Hromada,* Lettish Social Democratic League, Lettish Social Democratic Labor Party, Finnish Labor Party, Finnish Party of Active Resistance,

Georgian Socialist Federal Revolutionaries, Ukrainian Socialist Party, Ukrainian Revolutionary Party, Lithuanian Social Democratic Party.

Gapon came to the meeting with an exalted conception of his role as a leader. He was to be a channel to unite all these rivulets into one mighty torrent to overwhelm the Tsar. But the Social Democratic delegates came full of suspicions concerning the language of his call with his mention of "dynamite and bombs." The Lettish Social Democratic Labor Party entered the hall only to deliver an ultimatum. The Lettish Social Democratic League, they said, was non-existent in their land and its so-called representative must be excluded or they themselves would withdraw. When, after an interminable wrangle, their demand was rejected, they walked out and with them walked out the Jewish Bund, the Bolsheviks, and the Armenian Social Democrats, all before the conference had so much as begun. Poor Gapon! This was quite another matter from simple indignation and the calling down of God's curse on the head of the Tsar.

Gapon's role dwindled steadily. Not at home in the emigration, this "revolutionist and man of action" engaged in gun-running, chartering in England the ship *John Grafton*, with a load of arms. Gapon found that Lenin had the best smuggling apparatus and it was the Bolsheviks, through either Litvinov or Krassin, who supplied him with a passport and addresses in Petersburg. But the *John Grafton*, which was to land its arms on a frontier island, ran aground, then blew up near the Finnish coast. The former mass leader was lost as an isolated, hidden and hunted man of the underground. Without the stimulus of crowds, he was reduced to nullity. Returning to Russia, he reentered the service of the police. In April 1906, his body was found hanging from the rafters of a little cottage at Ozerky. The masses who still revered him believed that the police had murdered him. Years later it came out that Pincus Rutenberg, the Social Revolutionary who, together with Gapon, had led the fateful January march and then helped him to escape and flee Russia, had been solicited by him to become a police spy.

Aided by workers who had marched with Gapon, Rutenberg had personally directed his execution. Rutenberg's subsequent career included an official post under Kerensky, prison under the Bolsheviks, voluntary exile, service with a British electric company in Palestine, and a number of years as a leading Zionist. Gapon's life and Rutenberg's and Parvus's are alike symbols of the bizarre complexity of the pattern through which we are trying to follow a few guiding threads.

As the archaeologist attempts to reconstruct from a few shards the whole of a vanished civilization, so Lenin was forever on the lookout for the slightest clues that might lead him to an understanding of the Russian peasant. Knowing that Father Gapon was of peasant origin and had retained much of the mentality of a muzhik, Lenin observed him most attentively. Almost accidentally, as Krupskaya reports it, Vladimir Ilyich made his first real discovery of the peasant as a concrete revolutionary force through this intercourse with Gapon. Not that the most Russian of Russian Marxists had ever left the peasantry out of his calculations: more than any other Social Democratic leader he had kept them steadily in mind. But he had thought of them up till now as a class, essentially conservative in character, which would have to be set in motion by extremely moderate slogans, which he and his fellow-revolutionaries would have to invent and indoctrinate into them. As in dealing with workingmen he had found it fitting to go from such petty beginnings as fines and hot water for tea to the larger general ideas of class struggle and socialism, so by analogy he conceived that the peasant could only be moved in the beginning by some petty, elementary demand. For this purpose he hit upon the *otrezki,* lands formerly worked by the serfs but kept by the landlords during the Emancipation. Since no other Marxists had any definite ideas on the question, Lenin had succeeded in getting the demand for the return of the *otrezki* written into the program adopted by the Second Congress. The trouble with this was that the Russian peasant was by nature an extremist. The very rhythms of his life were determined by the severe alternations of the Russian climate, which for many months of the year prevents any useful outdoor work at all, then calls for prolonged bursts of extraordinary effort. So too his social history was a record of long periods of abject passivity alternating with extreme attempts to turn the world upside down.

One day Father Gapon came to the Ulyanovs to read the text of his latest manifesto. "We do not need a Tsar," it said. "Let there be but one master on earth: God. And you will all be His tenants." Vladimir Ilyich laughed heartily, much to the priest's discomfiture. But beneath the unfamiliar veil of religious formulary, he recognized the authentic voice of the Russian peasant. It was but a variant of that age-old subversive utterance: "The land is God's and the Tsar's," a saying which left the landowners out of the picture. Only now the Tsar was excluded also.

While Lenin was still pondering this he chanced to come upon Matushenko (a sailor of peasant origin who had escaped from the mutiny of the battleship *Potemkin*), when the sailor was engaged in an apparently heated discussion with Father Gapon. Overhearing their angry voices, Lenin paused to listen. He discovered that they were not arguing but agreeing with each other in a heated denunciation of the Social Democrats for the miserable character of their agrarian program. They were denouncing one of Lenin's proudest contrivances: the demand for the return of the *otrezki*. "No!" he heard them shouting, "not the cut-off pieces, but *all* of the land to the muzhiks!" With only such pitifully meager evidence to go by, this man who lived so far away from his country but was so close to it in spirit, humbly recognized that his pet peasant plank was hopelessly inadequate. He decided to seize the first opportunity to change the program so as to include in it a demand for the nationalization of all the land, and its renting out by the state or its distribution integrally to the peasants. That same summer he called a congress abroad, which was attended only by the Bolsheviks. He had no trouble in getting them to drop his *otrezki* in favor of "all the land." A year later, in a united congress of both Bolsheviks and Mensheviks, he fought in vain to put through the same program.

Lenin had been learning, too, from the merciless bombardment to which his organization views had been subjected by Plekhanov, Trotsky, Parvus, Rosa Luxemburg, Axelrod and Martov. His resolute and tidy mind, reacting as always against the slackness and disorganization of the Russian intellectual, was still attracted to centralism and direction from above. He was still sure that the top leadership was somehow guaranteed to be the most devoted, the most skilled in Marxian science, the most fitted to decide issues and pick subordinates. He still insisted as before that the Central Committee should have the power to select or add to the Local Committees and confirm or reject all local selections. But the mass stirrings in Russia, no less than the bitter debate, had schooled him in the necessity of giving ground on the questions of democracy, the elective principle, the safeguarding of some measure of local autonomy, the right of opposition, the protection of a minority. He felt now that his rigid organization must be loosened up to admit thousands and tens of thousands without such close scrutiny as in the past. In short, his one-sided emphasis on centralism was now reformulated as the bifurcated term: "democratic centralism." How much of democracy and how much of centralism would go into the compound was a question which would be answered differently in differing periods. The time would come when democracy would be once more swallowed up in centralism, but for the moment his problem was to re-educate the "hards" and authoritarian centralists he had indoctrinated and gathered around him, and to persuade them to accept some measure of democracy.

Once more he had recourse to a Party congress, that is, a convention of his own faction posing as the leadership of the entire Party. There he could convince and reorient his own followers, correct the agrarian program, amend the Party constitution to correct the error Martov had written into it as *Article I* at the

Second Congress, renew his contact with Russia, put the idea of armed insurrection on the order of business, rearm his faction and the Party for the new day of open mass activity of millions.

"The Congress," Lenin wrote, "must be simple—like a war council—and small in numbers—like a war council. It is a Congress to organize war." Whatever his followers may have thought, he did not mean war against the Mensheviks. It took place in London from April 25 to May 10, 1905, with only Bolsheviks, conciliators and neutrals present. The Mensheviks held a simultaneous "conference" in Geneva.

Lenin prepared for his Bolshevik convention with his characteristic thoroughness, as indeed, he had need. The "Leninists" he himself had trained in centralism, professional revolutionism and "hardness" had learned his dinned-in formulae by rote. Many of them had been attracted by the very authoritarian rigidity of those formulae. Now, in the name of "the traditions of Bolshevism" and "true Leninism," they resisted all his sweeping proposals for change. Lenin would have to refight this ominous battle again and again at every critical juncture in the history of his party, for, while it was easy to teach definite formulae, it was not easy to impart the spirit of realistic flexibility with which he himself approached the changing world. What would happen to a party thus nurtured when its authoritative leader was not present, or when his voice should be stilled forever? But since, as Freud has put it, "in the unconscious every one of us is convinced of his immortality," it never occurred to Lenin to pose such a question.

To him, the organization changes he now advocated were important not so much to meet the Menshevik criticisms half way as to prepare the Party for open public life and imminent revolution. For months he had been firing away at the premature sclerosis which seemed to have taken possession of the Bolsheviks in Russia.

Really, I often think that nine-tenths of the Bolsheviks are really formalists—reads a typical letter—. . . One must recruit among the youth more magnanimously and boldly, more boldly and more magnanimously and still more magnanimously and still more boldly, without fearing them. Forget all the old cumbersome ways, the respect for titles, etc. . . . Give every subordinate committee the right, without many conditions, to write leaflets and distribute them (it is no great misfortune if they make breaks: we will "gently" correct them in *Vpered*) . . . The events themselves will teach *in our spirit* . . . Organize, organize and once again organize, hundreds of circles, push the usual hierarchical committee follies entirely into the background. It is wartime . . . Else you will perish with the honors of Komitetchiki ["Committeemen"—the word of scorn in later years would become *Aparatchiki*, "Apparatus Men"] with the official seal imprinted upon you . . . [Letter of February 4, 1905.]

At the Congress his forebodings turned out to be more than justified. He stormed at his erstwhile followers, took the floor again and again and again, employed irony, ridicule, indignation, interrupted others while they were speaking, made a general nuisance of himself.

I could not sit still—he explodes at one point—and hear it said that there are no workers available who are fit to be committee members. The question is being postponed. Plainly there is a sickness in the Party . . .

At another point:

The Party does not exist for the Party Council, but the Party Council for the Party . . . In all constitutional lands the citizens have the right to express lack of confidence in this or that official or official body. This right cannot be taken from them . . . Who is the judge in the handling of a dispute between the Party Council and the Local Committees . . . Under free political conditions our Party can and will be built completely on the principle of election . . . Even under absolutism the application of the electoral system in much greater measure than at present would have been possible . . .

His old followers could not recognize him! Almost single-handed he succeeded in introducing a number of sweeping changes into the Party Constitution. The first was of course the repeal of Section 1, the celebrated "loose" definition of membership which Martov had succeeded in putting through at the Second Congress. But the others were all in the spirit of those who had been his critics at that Congress: the safeguarding of the autonomy of the locals against Central Committee alteration of their composition; approval of the widespread introduction of the electoral principle; the protection of minorities; their right to oppose and criticize the Central Committee; their right to issue oppositional literature and have it circulated by the Party smuggling apparatus, provided one-sixth of the locals requested it.

But when Lenin pointed out that at this Congress of the "party of the proletariat" there was only one delegate who had ever worked in industry, and he proposed to pump fresh blood into the local organizations by making mandatory a majority of workingmen on each local committee ("I would greatly favor a rule that in our committees for every two intellectuals there should be eight workingmen") his astonished following of professional revolutionaries or *komitetchiki* voted down his proposal as impractical, and likely to dilute the revolutionary clarity of the Bolshevik organization. Vladimir Ilyich was in a towering rage, which diminished only after a few days of reflection had persuaded him that the bubbling, overflowing life that was churning up the stagnation of ages would likely wash this incrustation away also.

The Mensheviks, too, were almost wholly professional revolutionary intellectuals, but their theory predisposed them to look upon the new period as one which would bring millions into "public life" and lead to the formation of a "broad, non-partisan or supra-partisan organization of the working masses," out of which a new and broad and truly working class socialist party might grow, to replace the narrow conspirative organization of intellectuals. It was this predisposition of the Mensheviks which gave them a decisive leadership in the Soviet of 1905 and in the new trade unions which sprang up.

On the other subject close to Lenin's heart: the technical preparations for an armed uprising, his followers gave him no trouble. Lunacharsky made the report, but the thought that went into it was largely Lenin's. ("Vladimir Ilyich provided all the essential theses for my report. Further, he insisted that I should write down my entire speech and give it to him to read in advance.")

Why then, it might be asked, did he not make the report himself? Unlike his successor in the leadership of his party, Lenin was ever anxious to avoid the appearance of one-man rule of personal dictatorship. With more moral authority and less opposition than Stalin would ever know (until the latter had executed all who might challenge him) Lenin sought to maintain the appearance and as far as possible the reality of a collective leadership in his party. When he could prepare a Lunacharsky to give the report on armed insurrection or a Stalin to write on the national question, it seemed to him to be a positive gain in the broadening of the circle of leadership. Even when someone opposed Lenin and was defeated by him in debate, he often arranged for his defeated opponent to report on the very thing which the latter had opposed. Thus the man's prestige was preserved after defeat, for Lenin knew from bitter experience how hard it was to gather together and build up this handful of persons to the stature of revolutionary leadership, and how easy to tear down and destroy them.

Lenin's other proposals: the new and more sweeping agrarian program; the question of participation in a revolutionary provisional government, like the resolution on armed uprising, went through without serious opposition. For these were measures congenial to the temperament of the men he had been welding together into a faction.

At the Congress, Lenin had to agree to considerable relaxation of control from abroad. The new Central Committee was made up of Lenin, Krassin, Bogdanov, Rykov, Postalovski, with Essen, Rumyantzev and Gusev as alternates. Of all these, only Lenin remained in Geneva as "Foreign Representative" and editor of the official organ, *Proletarii.* Two secretaries were chosen, Krupskaya for the Foreign Center and Stasova for the Russian.

If we are to believe the official Bolshevik biographer Kerzhentsev:

> The small apartment of the Ulyanovs in sleepy petty-bourgeois Geneva was the headquarters of the Russian revolution . . . Each day, Lenin viewed, as it were, the map of military operations of the revolution and gave instructions directing the struggle of the different detachments.

But in actual fact, events were moving so rapidly, and Lenin's knowledge of them, based on Swiss and other West European news dispatches, was so meager and inaccurate, that any attempt to guide things from Geneva with the aid of belated letters and smuggled copies of *Proletarii* had become impossible. Lenin could not even get reports from the busy, self-confident Central Committee members in Russia. On events in the homeland he now exerted no influence at all. Even they, on the spot, were finding it easier to follow the mass upsurge than to direct it. "Ilyich," writes Krupskaya, "became very nervy" (i.e., irritable). He made futile attempts to convince his Central Committee to cross the frontier for a conference with him. Then, the same autumn strike wave that had brought Trotsky back from Finland to Saint Petersburg convinced him that he, too, should and could go to Russia.

Krupskaya followed him and Elena Stasova left Russia for Geneva to keep the "foreign office" open, virtually alone. Before Lenin left, he wrote a friendly, flattering letter to Plekhanov, telling him how essential he was, how the Bolsheviks admired him, how small all past differences were in the face of the great events now transpiring, urging him to return also and become one of the editors of the new "legal" paper which the Bolsheviks were founding. Plekhanov did not answer. By the time Lenin reached Saint Petersburg, the Tsar had been forced to issue a pledge of liberties, a promise of a constitution and a parliament, and an amnesty. It was late November. The great Russian cauldron was boiling over.

CHAPTER EIGHTEEN

1905 IN THE CAPITALS

I would delay the uprising until next Spring. But we shan't be asked.

—LENIN

Lenin failed to get to Russia while the great October general strike was on. The agent who was to meet him in Stockholm with a forged passport did not show up. Storms delayed the steamer on which he wanted to sail to Finland. During the two fateful weeks, while he fumed and fretted in enforced idleness with even the post and telegraph on strike so that he could neither send nor receive word from his followers, the strike wave was spreading over the entire country; Saint Petersburg was setting up its "Soviet" and forging its leadership in the struggle; critical questions were being settled without so much as a by-your-leave. Worst of all, his comrades on the scene were committing blunders in the name of what they conceived to be his teachings, blunders which would deprive his faction of the hoped-for post of leadership at this most crucial moment in the country's history.

The farther we get from the original documents (and from the comparatively reliable party histories written while Lenin was still alive), the more difficult it is to make head or tail out of the famed Soviet of 1905 and the relations of the Bolsheviks to it. Thus in Stalin's history of his party (1939) we read:

> As we know, Lenin had not yet arrived in Saint Petersburg; he was still abroad. The Mensheviks took advantage of Lenin's absence to make their way into the Saint Petersburg Soviet and to seize hold of its leadership.

If the expression "took advantage of Lenin's absence" reveals the habits of thought fostered by the Stalin cult of personal dictatorship and one-man factotumship, the phrase concerning the Mensheviks' making their way into the Soviet is contrived to conceal completely the fact that it was the Mensheviks who gave the initial impulse to the Soviet's formation, while the Bolsheviks at first opposed it as an unreliable and uncontrollable substitute for the Party. In fact, during the first few sessions, the Bolshevik Petersburg Committee went so far as to advocate its boycott!

To understand why the Mensheviks favored, and the Bolsheviks in Russia opposed, the formation of such a general Council of Workingmen's Representatives (the word *Soviet* is merely the Russian word for "Council"), we shall have to go back to a series of theoretical disputes between the two factions that had been going on since their respective conferences of the spring of that year.

Since spring, the Mensheviks under Axelrod's leadership had been groping their way toward two new and related formulations for broader public life in a time of growing revolution. One was a call to Russian workingmen to form a "broad non-partisan labor organization"; the other a call to the entire people to set up in the course of their struggle "local and municipal revolutionary self-governments."

To Axelrod, in whose mind these ideas were born, the underground Social Democratic Party as it had developed in Russia was no labor party in the West European sense at all, but a conspiratorial circle of intellectuals who in principle espoused the cause of the still-unorganized working class, a conspiratorial circle which professed to act in labor's name. The new freedom that was being won in the course of the present struggle, he thought, would at last give the workingmen a chance to come together, form their own trade unions and their own party, select their own leadership, draft their own program, become aware of their own existence and interests as a class. This genuine workingmen's party could then supplant and absorb the narrow, conspirative cadres of professional revolutionary intellectuals, who had hitherto acted in its name and who, *faute de mieux*, had passed themselves off as "the party of the proletariat."

Parallel with Axelrod's advocacy of this "broad labor organization" ran his agitation for the creation of "broad democratic organizations" of the people as a whole. These were to assume the powers of local autonomy and local self-government, seek to displace and challenge the local bureaucratic apparatus, and, in due time, send delegates to an all-Russian congress which would convoke a constituent assembly, or perhaps act as one. Axelrod conceived these by analogy with what had happened in previous revolutions: the Jacobin clubs and Communes of France; the Committees of Correspondence and Continental Congresses in America. For a people without organs of self-expression these "village and municipal revolutionary self-governments" would become means of organizing and expressing the popular will.

While Axelrod was developing these ideas in *Iskra,* Lenin kept subjecting them to ceaseless criticism. He was a Party Man in the strictest sense of that expression. These formulations seemed to him to displace "*the* Party" and abdicate its superior knowledge, its right and duty of assuming a leading role. To him Axelrod's formulations were a mixture of utopian nonsense and downright treason. To the notion of "local revolutionary self-governments" gradually growing into a national congress, he opposed the concept of a centrally led and directed uprising which would call into being a national revolutionary provisional government. This would be made up not of representatives of the unorganized masses and local communes, but of representatives of the already organized revolutionary parties. Under the armed shield of this centralized leading body the constituent assembly would be convoked and the local governments of the future created. Thus Lenin's conception was that of a centralized revolution, which would seize power in the capitals, then create the new local administration from above, while Axelrod's was that of a movement starting from below and culminating in a national representation. For Lenin the Party as it already existed was the leader and directing force and nucleus of rule; to Axelrod it was but a group of volunteers who would now put themselves at the service of broader organizations more truly representative of the working class and the Russian people as a whole.

In Axelrod's "broad, non-partisan, democratic organizations" Lenin scented the heresy of subordinating the Social Democratic Party to the democratic bourgeoisie. And his "broad labor congress" or "labor party" was both senseless and dangerous. Senseless, since no broad organization of labor could be formed until after the autocracy had been overthrown. Dangerous, since to advocate a "non-partisan" (i.e. a multi-partisan or supra-partisan) labor organization was to call in question the fact that the Social Democratic Party had already worked out the true program for the working class. If the Party itself set up broader organizations, these should serve only as a wider sphere for its own operations, a recruiting ground and preparatory school, more muscle behind itself as fist. And if broader organizations should spring up without party initiative, it was the Party's duty to penetrate them, control them, get its program and leadership accepted by them. If it could not win control of the broader organization, then it should destroy the latter as harmful to the true interests and true program of the proletariat.

In this theoretical dispute, neither side foresaw the speedy emergence of the Petersburg General Strike Committee or Soviet of Workingmen's Representatives. They were straining their eyes to see into the future with the aid of the past. But each based himself on a different past. Axelrod kept his eyes fixed on the West: England, Germany and France. His thinking was predicated on the expectation that Russia, too, would go through a democratic capitalist stage after a successful bourgeois revolution, and that all its local communities and its labor movement would eventually develop the tradition of self-government, so far lacking in Russian public life. But Lenin thought rather in terms of the historic Russian revolutionary conspiracy in a land which had been so long centralized that every impulse was wont to come from above. His views were in the tradition of all past Russian movements for reform from the palace coup d'état to the conspiracies of the Narodnaya Volya. All his hopes were concentrated on the speedy victory of a centralized uprising and then the organization and education of the working class and peasantry afterwards, from above, from the vantage point of the summits of power.

Since Axelrod's "Westernizer" views required a long period

of development in the tradition of self-government, a tradition which was lacking in Russia, the advantage lay in Lenin's traditional Russianism. It was this that made his simple slogans and proposals so accessible at critical moments to vast numbers of backward but aroused workingmen and—more important for the immediate party struggle—it was this that attracted to his banner the more "Russian" of the Russian revolutionary intellectuals.

If we call the roll of Menshevik and Bolshevik leaders, this "national" difference is immediately revealed. The core of the Bolshevik leadership in 1905 was Lenin himself, a Great-Russian from the heart of the Volga; Rykov, Bogdanov, Krassin, Postalovski—Great-Russians all. But the Menshevik camp was led by Axelrod, Martynov (Piker), Martov (Tsederbaum), Dan (Gurvich), all four of them Russian Jews of Westernized thought. Only Plekhanov and Potresov in the Menshevik top leadership were Great-Russians, and it was the fate of the first to vacillate for years between bolshevism and menshevism, and the second to be forever seeking an alliance between the Social Democracy and Russian liberalism. Indeed, Potresov was a strange anachronism: in temperament a liberal Westernizer of the eighteen forties with a Marxist theoretical equipment.

On the other hand, Trotsky, Parvus and Rosa Luxemburg—all three of them Jewish, and the last two with years of experience and activity in the West European movement—combined a revolutionary temperament with a Westernizing outlook, vacillating between criticism of Lenin's organizational centralism and attraction to his organic Russian revolutionism. In the light of these personal backgrounds, how fallacious appears the Nazi legend of "Jewish bolshevism." Indeed, the virtues and defects of bolshevism alike come from its deep roots in the national heritage of Russia, and—despite all international and Western modification and theoretical embroidery—bolshevism expresses fundamentally the national peculiarities of the Russian revolutionary tradition.

That centralizing tradition possesses both advantages and dangers. It tends to concentrate initiative and power in a top leadership, even in a single leader, and requires from the rank and file not so much initiative and understanding and democratic control over the leadership as loyalty and energy in executing the latter's decisions. To understand enough to grasp the leadership's understanding and expound and act on it, is understanding enough. This gives the multiplied fighting power of a disciplined army capable of carrying out orders swiftly and with a minimum of disputation; it relieves the common man of the painful duty of thinking out difficult problems; but it leaves the rank and file at the mercy of an error of the leader, and makes them less capable of reacting with new appreciations to sudden turns of history, if the leader happens to be mistaken, or cut off from them.

The Council of Workingmen's Representatives of Saint Petersburg was the child of an unforeseen and unprecedented general strike. Though its nucleus was formed by Petersburg Mensheviks and its appearance was in harmony with the idea of initiative from below that Axelrod had been groping toward, the Soviet was not called forth by anybody's theoretical formulations, nor could it be conjured away by boycott or theoretical exorcism. With the flexibility and realism which characterized Lenin whenever he was faced by important new phenomena, he was quick to realize that the general strike and the general strike committee it called into being represented something new and magnificent in Russian life. But he was cooling his heels in Stockholm, while the distrust he had inculcated toward broad organizations not controlled by the Party seemed to his followers to be directed against just such bodies as this creation of the Mensheviks and non-party masses. Lenin's last attack on "broad non-partisan labor organizations" and "local revolutionary self-government" had appeared in the *Proletarii* of October 17—at the very moment when the Soviet was coming into being! On the other hand, all the recent articles of Axelrod,

Dan, Martov and Martynov had predisposed the local Mensheviks to welcome the Soviet as something which seemed to fit to perfection their two favorite formulae of the moment.

Trotsky, too, hastening back from Finland to participate in the general strike, had brought with him a plan for a representative labor body to run the strike, with one delegate for every thousand workers. When he got off the train at the Finland Station in Saint Petersburg, he learned that the Mensheviks in various factories and unions had proposed such a delegate body (with one delegate for every one hundred workers) and that elections were already taking place.

From the outset, and at all times thereafter, the Mensheviks had a majority of the politically affiliated among the delegates and possessed overwhelming influence in the Soviet. They elected one of their own number, Zborovski, as its first Chairman. A few days later, in pursuance of their own formula of "broad, non-partisanship," they had him step down in favor of the nonparty lawyer, Georgii Nosar—better known under the pseudonym of Khrustalev—who inclined toward menshevism. Avksentev was made a vice-chairman for the Social Revolutionaries and Trotsky for the Mensheviks. Before the fifty-day Soviet was over, Trotsky was its outstanding leader. His leadership was primarily due to his exceptional eloquence, his swiftness in forming plans, proposing motions, drafting resolutions, inditing stirring manifestoes, but he was undoubtedly helped by his immediate and unreserved espousal of the Soviet and by his relatively interfactional position.

Lenin's writings have suffered a strange fate. Where every word is sacred, to quote the wrong passage at the wrong time may nevertheless get a man into trouble. Official interpreters stress now one part, now another, as political convenience dictates, explain away what is momentarily or permanently inconvenient by editing and footnotes, go slow with the publication and translation of things they think the canonized leader might better have left unsaid. To this day, two decades after his death, the "Complete Works" are not really complete. Here, for instance, are Volumes VIII, IX and X, dealing with the Revolution of 1905 and containing, supposedly, all that Lenin had to say on the 1905 Soviet. A dozen passages seem to attack the whole idea of the Soviet before it was born, but the document which presents his mind in the noblest and most inspiring light as that of a swift thinker reacting to sudden innovation on the part of history, is not here.* Without explanation it was withheld from publication until 1940, then, once more without explanation, it appeared in the Russian theoretical magazine *Bolshevik*. Was it lost all these years? Was it found suddenly in time for the twenty-third anniversary of the October Revolution? Where? How? Was it withheld because of the vested interests of faction? *Bolshevik* offers no explanation. It is vastly superior to anything else Lenin has written on the Soviet of 1905, to his discussion of the Soviet's exclusion of the anarchists, for example (in which he declares that "the Council of Workingmen's Deputies is not a parliament of labor and not an organ of proletarian self-government, not an organ of government at all but a fighting organization for the achievement of definite aims"). Or to his thesis on the Soviet prepared for the 1906 Congress of the united Social Democratic Party, in which he returns to his old distrust of broad organizations.

From the internal evidence it is clear that this remarkable document, unpublished until 1940, was written in Stockholm early in November, 1905, while Lenin had nothing to go by but foreign press reports and a few issues of Russian newspapers.

> I am giving my views—it begins with becoming modesty and tact—as a "foreigner" still forced to write from the accursed distance, the disgusting "beyond-the-frontier" of the émigré . . . without having seen a single session of the Soviet of Working-

---

* References here as throughout, are to the Third Russian Edition of Lenin's Collected Works, the most complete so far published. As this book goes to press, various volumes of a Fourth Edition are beginning to appear. In some ways more complete than the earlier editions, it, too, is incomplete. It suppresses certain writings of Lenin which are uncomplimentary to Stalin or in too obvious contradiction with the present official version of Party history. There has been an especially ruthless suppression of some of the illuminating footnotes prepared by the Marx-Engels-Lenin Institute for the Second and Third Editions.

men's Delegates, without having had an opportunity to exchange opinions with my comrades . . . Comrade Radin in *Novaya Zhizn** is wrong to pose the question:
The Council of Workingmen's Delegates *or* the Party. It seems to me that the solution ought to be:
both the Council of Workingmen's Delegates *and* the Party . . .

Who conducted the strike and conducted it victoriously? The *entire* proletariat, among whom—fortunately in a minority— there were also Social Democrats. What were the aims pursued by the strike? Economic and political at the same time. The economic aims touch the *entire* proletariat . . . the political aims the *entire* people . . . The Soviet ought to *aspire,* to include deputies of *all* the workers, office employees, domestics, unskilled laborers . . . *all those* who want to fight in common . . . all who possess elementary political honesty . . . It does not seem reasonable to me to demand of the Soviet [as the Bolsheviks had just done] the adoption of the Social Democratic program and entrance into the Party . . . Soviet and Party are alike absolutely indispensable . . .

Maybe I am wrong, but it seems to me (on the basis of the incomplete and exclusively "paper" data that I possess) that politically one ought to consider the Soviet as the germ of the *provisional revolutionary government.* It seems to me that the Soviet ought to proclaim itself as quickly as possible as the provisional revolutionary government of all Russia or (what amounts to the same thing under another form) ought to *create* the provisional revolutionary government . . . The Soviet ought to choose a strong nucleus of a revolutionary provisional government and complete it with the representatives of all the revolutionary parties and all the revolutionary democrats . . . We do not fear broadness and difference of shadings . . . rather we desire it, for without the unification of the proletariat and the peasants, without the fighting union of social democrats and revolutionary democrats, complete victory is impossible . . .

In its program ought figure . . . complete realization in fact of the political liberty so hypocritically promised by the Tsar: abolition of all restrictive laws against the freedoms of speech, conscience, press, union, strikes, the suppression of all institutions [such as police, army, censorship] which restrict those liberties . . . convocation of a truly general constituent assembly supported

---

* Radin is the pen name for Knunyantz. His view was the basis of the Bolshevik boycott of the Soviet and then the ultimatum that it recognize the Social Democratic program and "join" the Party. The local Bolshevik leaders changed their mind in two days under the pressure of mass enthusiasm for the Soviet.

by the free armed people . . . real and complete freedom for oppressed nationalities . . . transfer of all the land to the peasants . . .
support of all the measures the peasants themselves have taken
to seize the land, formation everywhere of revolutionary peasant
committees . . .

The word *Soviet,* which has come to be charged with special
meanings and emotional overtones, is, as we have said, merely
the Russian word for "council." It is no different in original intention and flavor from the same word when found in our familiar "Central Trades and Labor Council." Had there been
such a Central Trades Council already in existence, it might
conceivably have taken charge of the Petersburg General Strike.
Even then, it would have had to be enlarged by numerous dele-
gations from hitherto unorganized groups, it would have assumed new powers and functions and been transformed from a
routine body handling day-to-day union matters into a general
staff for an all-inclusive political general strike. When, in the
twenties on our own continent, general strikes broke out in
Seattle and Winnipeg, the participants found it necessary to displace the workaday Councils by special emergency general strike
committees. Labor actions of such magnitude require unified
direction. An authority must be created enjoying the confidence
of the strikers, empowered to spread or limit the strike, to determine its strategy and tactics. Decisions must be made from
hour to hour, even minute to minute. What services shall be
continued so that friendly sections of the public and the participating workingmen and their families may suffer as little as
possible? What trucking and shipping shall be exempt so that
food and milk may be delivered to the workers' homes, so that
garbage may be disposed of, hospitals continue in operation?
(In Seattle and Winnipeg it was a familiar occurrence to see a
garbage truck bearing the placard: "Exempt by decision of the
General Strike Committee.") There are some aspects of public
order to maintain; strike bulletins must be printed to take the
place of struck newspapers; negotiations must be conducted

with other sections of labor, with employers, the public, the authorities; aims must be defined and redefined; decisions must be made on behalf of the entire labor movement. In proportion as the strike is truly general must it assume all sorts of communal, public, governmental and quasi-governmental functions. In Russia, the lack of existing union organization, the political character and the all-inclusiveness of the strike, its spread to every industry, trade, profession, branch of public service and to some 120 cities and towns, the centralist tradition which made the whole country look to Saint Petersburg for leadership, the paralysis of government and the revolutionary mood which expressed itself in the ambition to displace the government altogether—all these gave a magnificent sweep to the functions of the Council of Workingmen's Delegates of Saint Petersburg. It was at once general strike committee, communal administration, organizer of nationwide revolt, temporary parliament of labor in particular and the Russian people in general, rival governmental power. With a little more time at its disposal it would have called into being peasant councils (some sprang up during its existence). Before its fall it was dispatching delegates over the countryside to form additional Soviets (scores had sprung up spontaneously; several had assumed complete local governmental powers) and was issuing a call for an all-Russian Soviet congress. All it lacked was soldier delegates (sporadically a few of these were already appearing) to become a decisive political power, as in 1917.

This all-national general strike had no parallel in labor history. Even before October, the year 1905 had been the greatest year of strikes in the life of Russia (more strikers in one month after "Bloody Sunday" than in the ten preceding years put together). Yet, what occurred now took the government, the socialists, the participants themselves by surprise. A little strike of compositors in Moscow, demanding a few kopeks more per thousand letters set, with pay for punctuation marks, spread by spontaneous combustion through the inflammable materials that had been accumulating for many comparatively quiet months. The war had just ground to a close. Millions of dispirited soldiers were waiting at railroad sidings to be shipped home and demobilized. Many still bore arms and nursed grievances that were soon to flare up in military and naval mutinies. The movements of grain for export were at their height, ships waiting expectant for their freight in the harbors. From printers to bakers to railway shopmen the strike spread; from shopmen to general railway personnel, until 26,000 miles of line and 750,000 rail employees were tied up in the space of ten days. Thereafter, pay for punctuation marks and suchlike economic demands were lost sight of in the general nature of the strike and the political aims it set itself. With the stoppage of the railroads, the whole industry of the country stopped still. Sympathy and necessity combined to close steel mills, textile mills, metallurgical factories, industrial establishments of every kind: such was the strategic nature of railways in the life of a modern country. For the first time in many decades there was no factory smoke on the Russian horizon.

Even "middle-class" intellectuals, professional men and liberal industrialists joined the strike. The Constitutional Democratic Party, assembled in its first national convention, gave its endorsement. The Union of Unions, made up of intellectuals and professional men of all descriptions, refused to enter law courts, laboratories, hospitals, universities, business offices, government offices, declaring themselves on strike like ordinary workers. Most of the employers looked upon the movement with friendly eyes. Some gave their strikers half pay or full pay. After the strike was over, a number of industrialists continued to pay wages to delegates from their factories for the time taken off to attend the further sessions of the Soviet. Wealthy capitalists contributed most of the money for the legal Bolshevik daily, *Novaya Zhizn,* the first number of which appeared on November 9, 1905, and for similar Menshevik and Social Revolutionary journals.

No strike in history in any land has ever been as "general" as this one. On the 23rd, the whole of Moscow, Kharkov and Reval were out; on the 24th, Smolensk, Koslov, Ekaterinoslav, Lodz; on the 25th, Kursk, Samara, Poltava; on the 26th, Minsk, Kremenchug, Simferopol, Petersburg. With the entrance of the capital into the strike it assumed a leadership so decisive that we will have to neglect the explosions spreading elsewhere, to concentrate on St. Petersburg and its Soviet.

On the 26th, the day the first delegates to the Council of Workingmen's Deputies were being elected, the strike embraced, besides the factory workers, drug clerks, court clerks, bank clerks. On the 27th, lawyers, doctors and civil service men declared themselves on strike. On the 28th, the employees of post and telegraph, state banks and finance ministry joined the strikers; the *corps de ballet* of the Marinsky theater walked out; house servants, janitors (*dvorniki*), cab drivers, retail clerks and many storekeepers struck. On the Bourse there were neither demands nor offers. Water supply was partially maintained by locking in the workers under armed guard. At night the city was in darkness save for the blinding glare from a solitary searchlight on the Admiralty Building anxiously sweeping the Nevsky Prospekt. For three days there were no newspapers while the city was given over to the wildest rumors. On the 30th, only the official paper of the strikers (the *Izvestia*, or Bulletin of the Council of Workingmen's Delegates) and the official government gazette (*Pravitelstvennie Vestnik*) appeared, the latter printed by soldiers.

The government seemed to have been seized with paralysis. The Tsar's ministers could not even get to him at Peterhof until they secured a river launch. In widely scattered regions of the country, peasants began "joining the strike" by burning manor houses, seizing crops, moving in on lands. Soldiers "joined" by mutinying against the slowness of demobilization, the conditions of service or the unpleasant duties of punitive expeditions.

On October 30 (October 17, Old Style), the Tsar announced a Duma, civil liberties and a constitution. Here is his own account in a letter to his mother:

> You remember, doubtless, those January days—after "Bloody Sunday"—when we were together at Tsarskoe—they were miserable, weren't they? But they are *nothing* in comparison to what has happened now. . . . It makes me sick. . . . The Ministers, instead of acting with quick decision, only assemble in council like a lot of frightened hens and cackle about providing united ministerial action. . . . One had the same feeling as before a thunderstorm in summer. . . . There were only two ways open: to find an energetic soldier and crush the rebellion by sheer force. . . . That would mean rivers of blood, and in the end we should be where we had started. . . . The other way out would be to give the people their civil rights, freedom of speech and press, also to have all laws confirmed by a State Duma—that would of course be a constitution. . . . We discussed it for two days and in the end, invoking God's help, I signed. . . . There was no other way than to cross oneself and give what everyone was asking for. . . . We are in the midst of a revolution with an administrative apparatus apparently disorganized, and in this lies the main danger. . . .

In such mood, debating the two ways out, accepting the one and longing for the other, the Tsar signed the Manifesto known as that of October 17, charging Witte with the task of executing it and winning the confidence of the people. At the same time there were in his entourage men who thought they understood his inmost desires, as once an English king had been understood by those who murdered Thomas à Becket. Advocates of firmer police rule like D. F. Trepov and Durnovo went into action at the same time as Witte, aided by the fact that the Tsar, like Witte, was of two minds.

The next month and a half were known as the Days of Freedom. More apt would have been, Days of Deadlock. Though the strike could not long survive the Tsar's Manifesto, the

"Strike Committee" did not cease to function. Though a constitution had been promised and with it all sorts of freedoms, the Autocrat, the police, the prisons, the censorship, continued to operate. Lenin (still not in Russia) welcomed as an analysis of "astonishing clarity" Trotsky's characterization in *Izvestia* of the roles of Witte on the one hand and Durnovo-Trepov on the other:

> So a constitution is granted—wrote Trotsky.—Freedom of assembly is granted but the assemblies are surrounded by the military. Freedom of speech is granted, but the censorship exists after as before. Freedom of knowledge is granted, but the universities are occupied by troops. Inviolability of the person is granted, but the prisons are overflowing with the incarcerated. Witte is given us, but Trepov remains to us. A constitution is given, but the autocracy remains. Everything is given—and nothing is given. . . . The proletariat wants neither the police hooligan Trepov nor the liberal broker Witte—it wants neither the wolf's mouth nor the fox's tail. It does not want a *nagaika* wrapped up in a constitution. [*nagaika,* whip.]

In general, it should be noted that the whole attitude of the Bolsheviks toward Trotsky was changing as it became apparent that this twenty-six-year-old stormy petrel had become the outstanding figure of the Soviet, was writing all the most admirable documents on the spur of the moment, preparing all the most welcome motions, making the most moving speeches, doing much of the quick thinking that guided the life of the Soviet in the face of kaleidoscopic change. When the first number of the Menshevik popular daily, *Nachalo*, appeared, the Bolshevik *Novaya Zhizn* wrote: "We welcome a comrade in the struggle. The first issue is notable for the brilliant description of the October strike written by Comrade Trotsky." And Lunacharsky records in his memoirs that when Lenin heard someone say: "The star of Khrustalov is setting; today the strong man of the Soviet is Trotsky," he responded after a moment: "Well, Trotsky has won this by his tireless and striking work."

A general strike cannot continue indefinitely. At best it can only paralyze a government, but, except it develop into armed insurrection, it cannot overthrow it. Meanwhile, prices rise, food grows scarce, wages cease, the strikers themselves suffer. And men can not live forever at fever heat.

The Tsar's Manifesto (drafted by Count Witte) was calculated to separate the more moderate sections of the population from the compact mass of striking workingmen. It accomplished its purpose. Nor were the strikers themselves exempt from pleasant illusion that they had won the freedom they had been fighting for. In vain did the Soviet leaders, Trotsky in the van, seek to instil in them suspicion of the "*nagaika* wrapped up in a constitution." The day the Manifesto became public, tens of thousands of the celebrating population gathered before the building in which the Soviet was meeting. Trotsky stepped out on the balcony, uttered his ringing warning, then, with his flair for the dramatic, he tore up a copy of the Tsar's Manifesto before their eyes. Tumultuously they cheered the act, yet the strike fever at once began to ebb. On October 31, Moscow called off its strike. Next day the Petersburg Soviet had the good sense to set November 3 as the day for orderly return to the factories. The workingmen, loyal to the end, went back impressively in disciplined ranks on the appointed day and hour.

The Soviet's further strategy was directed to the conquest by direct action of the liberties which had been promised. Their first objective was amnesty. Preceded by crimson banners and led by a committee from the Soviet, a mighty procession—unarmed and uneasy—wound through the city with the intention of emptying the prisons. Behind the walls of jails and fortresses, Trepov lined up his men fully armed, while in the palace Witte negotiated anxiously with the Tsar. The news of the signing of an amnesty decree arrived melodramatically at the last possible moment: the unequal test of strength between Trepov and the marching mass was postponed.

Using the printers as spearhead, the Soviet turned next to the conquest, once more by direct action, of freedom of the press. Ignoring the Tsar's censors, they even set up a censorship of their own, refusing to put into type attacks upon the Soviet itself, or slanderous pogrom appeals for the murder of Poles, Armenians and Jews. Then the Soviet took a graver step, prohibiting the printing of a political manifesto of the liberal Zemstvo Congress. The majority of the zemstvo delegates had welcomed the October Manifesto and adopted a declaration against "further disorders." We must leave it to the reader to ponder the problems of "legitimate" and "illegitimate" censorship and the true meaning of freedom. To Trotsky, prime mover of these actions, the case seemed clear enough. "Obviously," he wrote, "they were not hurting in the least the freedom of the press when they refused to print reactionary or liberal slanders." Here was a foreshadowing of the future censorship under the Soviet dictatorship, which would stretch the elastic term "reactionary or liberal slanders" until Trotsky's own writings would be embraced in it. This business of "protecting" the masses against clashing views and the need to think, is an inclined plane down which "progress" is rapid.

The next step in the battle with the Tsar's censors was an announcement by the printers' union that they would not set in type any newspaper which submitted its copy to the government officials for approval. The publishers were delighted to be forced into taking their freedom. All papers, conservative ones included, now appeared with a boxed notice that the issue in question had not been submitted to censorship. They agreed to print touchy items in identical language and if one were suspended therefor, all would suspend. The Soviet had won another round in the conquest by direct action of promised liberties. For six weeks the Russian press was freer than it had ever been in its history, or would ever be again, except for the eight-month period between the first and second revolutions in 1917.

Having won so much by direct action—freedom to assemble, freedom to organize and to strike, freedom of speech and press, and political amnesty—the Soviet now set out to conquer by the same methods the eight-hour day. The Soviet leaders were hesitant; the initiative came from below. This time, however, they could not count on the benevolent cooperation of the employers. To the latter, this was no conquest of freedom but the crossing of the proverbial borderline which is supposed to separate liberty from license. Now they felt sudden closeness to the state, any state. Moreover, was not their man Witte, the man of industrialization and liberal subsidy, quite visibly at the helm?

On the appointed day, November 13, the workingmen quit work in a body, exactly at the end of eight hours. No strike this, just the revolutionary enactment of a more human working day. They had come to work at the accustomed hour of 6:45, had refused the time-honored hour and three-quarters for lunch, staying away from their machines a bare thirty minutes.* At the sunlit hour of 3:15 they left their posts, fresh and exhilarated, roaring "The Marseillaise," marching from factory to factory in a body, pulling out the reluctant. Hereafter the workingmen would have time for rest and recreation, for home and family, for meetings and discussions, for culture and education, for politics and training in the use of arms.

But the employers, with few exceptions, refused to increase the hourly and piece rates to maintain the none-too-big take-home wage. With the same speed as the workingmen had organized previously, now their employers built up associations—directed not against the Tsar but against the workers. Led by the great workshops and offices of the state, they posted notices of dismissal and lockout of those who should take the liberty of deciding their own working hours. The unity of the entire people against the Tsar was at an end. While the Soviet delegates and workingmen were pondering this new turn of affairs, the eight-hour fight got lost in something bigger, for the Soviet voted another general strike.

The issues were once more political. The "constitutional"

---

* The average working day in the capital at the time was ten hours with an hour and three-quarters for lunch, i.e., those who started at 6:15 A.M. got off at 6 o'clock at night.

government of Witte had just declared a state of siege in Poland. At the same time, a short-lived revolt of the soldiers and sailors of Kronstadt (the chief harbor fort defending Petersburg) was put down and the leading participants handed over to a summary field court-martial for trial. Moved by a desire to demonstrate the unity of all the nationalities in this "prison-house of people," and long in quest of some way of binding together the discontented army and the rebellious civilian masses, the Soviet appointed November 15 for a second general strike. Although only two short weeks had elapsed since they had last resumed work, and although the eight-hour fight was still unsettled, the workingmen set out again with amazing unanimity. If anything, their response was more immediate and universal than before. But the employers now exhibited a sullen hostility; the storekeepers, *droshky* drivers, retail clerks, government employees, white-collar workers, ballet dancers, and most of the professional men and technicians were nowhere to be seen. The mechanism of economic, and especially of government life was less paralyzed, the government less frightened than before. On November 17, the executive committee of the Soviet voted nine to six to call off the strike, but was reversed by the general council. But the next day it was so clear that the strike was ebbing that the same general council set its end for the 20th. Still the retreat was in good order and the strike elicited some concessions from the government: the Kronstadt mutineers were transferred from the field courts-martial (in practice mere firing squads) to the regular military courts, and in Poland the state of siege was revoked. Lenin's verdict, written in Stockholm on the day of the Tsar's Manifesto, still seemed to hold good: "Tsarism is no longer able to suppress the revolution; the revolution is still unable to destroy tsarism." But both sides were preparing, according to their resources and vision, for an early day of reckoning.

Attempting to return to their factories, the workingmen found them closed against the resumption of work, on the old issue of the eight-hour day. Confusion set in. Before long the Soviet found itself obliged to let each trade and workshop decide for itself and make such terms as it could for the resumption of work. The weapon of strike was being blunted by too frequent use; the power behind it was being diminished by weariness and hunger in the workingmen's families, and by the growing isolation of the workingmen from other sections of the population. Yet they had reached out toward closer union with the all-important armed forces and had reason to hope that they had made some impression on the soldiers. Many felt that the deadlock must soon be broken somehow, by recourse to arms.

During this time of uncertainty, the forces of reaction were not idle. On the very day that the Tsar granted a constitution, they had rallied around him to defend his throne against his own yielding. Unsure of its troops, the government began to make hasty concessions: increases in pay, extra rations, rounds of vodka, confinement to barracks in moments of stress, shifting of regiments to regions where they were alien to the populace and its aspirations, premium pay for punitive expeditions. Most important of these devices was the playing of one nationality against another—indeed, whenever a government finds it necessary to use troops of one region against the people of another, it is a fair assumption that its case will not bear popular examination. Simultaneously with these measures, the reaction began to organize extra-legal armed forces as shock troops for the impending struggle, forces that were precursors of the secret military groupings, the Blackshirts, Brownshirts, and Storm Troopers of Italy and Germany in the twenties. Under the banner of Holy Russia was gathered together a most unholy and variegated band: the backward, the degenerate, the brutalized, the bewildered, the enraged, the entrenched, the ruined: officers, landowners and gilded youth, demobilized old soldiers and personal servingmen to whom loyalty to the master was the sum of all loyalties, criminals whose police record made them amenable to any instructions, ruined artisans and shopkeepers who were persuaded that the strikes and the eight-hour day were the cause of all their woes, hungry, degraded slum proletarians from the human scrapheap of the great cities, the more illiterate and credulous among the workingmen and peasantry. To the familiar compound of rabid nationalism and national antipathies and social demagogy was added the peculiar Russian component of the Orthodox religious banner and the deep susceptibility to legendary rumor of an illiterate and credulous people. The extralegal groupings were armed by the police, transported to regions where they were unknown, inflamed with drink, protected in their acts of assault, pillage, rape, murder. Their marching song was "God Save the Tsar," their banner the Tsar's image or the holy ikon, their organizations bore such titles as Union of the Russian People, Union of the Russian Land, Russian Orthodox Committee. Their leaflets, printed sometimes in church offices, more often in the secret chancelleries of the police, proclaimed that the war with Japan had been lost because the socialists had been bought by the Japanese and the Japanese by the Jews, that "the Tsar would divide large tracts of Crown lands among the peasants if he could only get rid of the Jews and the Poles," and "Saint Vladimir, who first baptized the people of Russia [in the year 998], has risen from the bowels of the earth and weeps because of the Fatherland brought to shame by Poles and Jews." This last, issued by the Russian Orthodox Committee, bade each recipient make three copies and send them to other villages. "Who has not fulfilled this order within six days will be stricken by grave sickness and affliction, but whoever spreads more than three copies will be granted recovery from incurable disease . . ."*

The workers responded by forming fighting companies of armed men. Funds were collected, many employers contributing. Sporting goods stores were emptied of their rifles and pistols, solitary policemen were disarmed by force. On November 11, in response to the rumor of a pogrom, a veritable fever for arming took possession of the Petersburg proletariat. In the

* The spiritual leader of this proto-fascist religious organization was the priest Evlogi. Forty years later, on September 2, 1945, Ambassador Alexander Bogomolov sat in the first row in the Orthodox Church in Paris while this same Evlogi, a Metropolitan now, said a solemn mass and blessed the new ruler of the Russian state, Marshal Stalin. (New York *Times*, Sept. 3, 1945.)

factories they forged "cold arms," daggers, pikes, brass knuckles, wire whips, iron bars. According to government reports, in a few weeks there were some six thousand Petersburg workingmen organized in motley armed companies, of whom some three hundred formed a better-armed fighting corps, patrolling meetings and the workingmen's quarters in groups of ten. Police raids were organized to confiscate the weapons. In Moscow, by December, there were some hundreds of indifferently armed workingmen, destined to play a fearful and heroic role. In many cities, notably in the Caucasus, the local governments aided directly in the arming of bands for self-defense. There the armed bands were to have a special history of their own.

On December 9, the government, cautiously feeling its way toward the offensive, arrested Georgii Nosar, who, under the name of Khrustalev, presided over the Petersburg Soviet. The Soviet had no answer ready: It could only choose a provisional presidium of three, Yanovsky (i.e. Trotsky), Vvedenski and Zlydnev, and vote "to continue to prepare for an armed uprising." Parvus drafted a Financial Manifesto, issued in the name of the Soviet, of the Peasant League, and the Socialist Parties, calling upon the masses:

> To refuse payment of government land installments and all other payments to the government.
> To demand all wages and salaries to be paid in gold. . . .
> To withdraw all deposits from the banks . . . demanding payments in gold.
> . . . We decide not to acknowledge the debts which, in the form of loans, the government of the Tsar has contracted while it has been carrying on open war against the whole people.*

Eight newspapers published the Manifesto and were suspended by the government. Next day one hundred newspapers did the same, constraining the government to refrain from further

---

* This warning to those who might lend money to the Tsar was the basis of the Bolshevik repudiation of tsarist debts in 1918. The repudiation also included the loans made by the Tsar's government during the World War.

confiscations. There was a run on the banks. Abroad, government credit toppled. The government responded by arresting the entire Executive Committee of the Council of Workingmen's Delegates on December 16. Their last act under Trotsky's chairmanship, as the police were putting them under arrest, was to vote a new general strike and to smash their pistols so that they should not fall into the hands of their captors.

More workingmen struck in Russia during this single turbulent year than in any other country in any year up to that time. The government estimate is 2,800,000 workingmen involved, more than the entire number of industrial workers in the country, meaning that many workers must have struck more than once. The metal workers struck on an average more than three times during the year. In this as in other things, Saint Petersburg had led the nation. But now its workingmen were weary and exhausted. Besides, its most advanced workers knew only too well that this time the strike must end in armed insurrection or not be undertaken at all. They looked at their miserable weapons, and knew they were not prepared. Fresher, more backward Moscow, where the garrison was seething with unrest, picked up the challenge with yet another general strike. The railwaymen joined once more, but—a fateful fact—this time the railroad from Petersburg to Moscow did not close down.

The Moscow general strike, intended as part of an all-Russian general strike, began peacefully enough. The top leadership there had hesitated and had been pushed forward from below. But that leadership, lodged in a Moscow "federal council" of united Bolsheviks and Mensheviks, was arrested the very day the strike began. The national leaders of the Bolsheviks were taken by surprise by what followed, too. They had just called a conference in Tammerfors, Finland, and all during the fateful days while Moscow was in general strike and armed insurrection, they were not in Russia proper. Second-string Moscow leaders and a few from other parts of the country

—Bolsheviks, Social Revolutionaries and Mensheviks—directed and organized as best they could what was in reality a spontaneous eruption. None of the men whose names we have become acquainted with were on the spot at all.

The moral responsibility if not the direct initiative for what happened in Moscow, was above all Lenin's and that of his party, and they did not reject it. From the day he first heard of the fate of Gapon's procession he had been studying military tactics, writing detailed instructions on bombs, pistols, tacks and broken glass to disorganize the mounted Cossacks, barricades, propaganda in the armed forces, the acquisition of arms, the necessity of an armed insurrection. The Mensheviks, a little more hesitantly, had followed suit and *Iskra* had carried precise instructions on barricade fighting. The Social Revolutionaries had added proposals for individual terror. Troop mutinies and naval mutinies and peasant insurrections had contributed to the spirit of rebellion. The great general strikes had given the masses confidence in their power, shaken the government, spread the feeling that perhaps one more exertion, one extra push, might finish the job. Pogroms and defense groups and sporadic armed clashes had added to the fighting mood.

In Moscow, moreover, the garrison had been rife with discontent for some days. Soldiers, even officers, had appeared at workers' meetings to pledge their support. The government had rushed Admiral Dubassov there, fresh from punitive expeditions in other parts of the country. He was one of the die-hards of the stamp of Durnovo and Trepov, spoiling for a showdown by physical force which would terrorize the masses, discredit the Witte arm of the government and undo the Constitutional Manifesto.

The Moscow insurrection had no strategic plan, no plan to assume the offensive, to seize key places, no set date or fixed intention. The strike began peacefully on December 20 and in the first days there were sporadic attempts to woo the excited troops. One regiment left its barracks singing "The Marseillaise," but before anything could be done about it, the regiment was surrounded, returned to barracks, disarmed, and plied with vodka, promises and concessions. Twice Cossack bands were persuaded to disobey their officers and ride off, amid the cheers of the populace. The first sniping shots at troops were possibly fired by provocateurs in an effort to inflame them. The first barricade on the Tverskaya was put up by a jovial population including respectable burghers in fur coats. On the third day there were bloody clashes: barricades began springing up in earnest.

The insurrection was never more than defensive. Barricades were built, but behind them men had almost no arms—perhaps 200 pistols and some hunting rifles to defend a line over ten miles long, against some 100,000 regular troops. Behind the 200 with pistols was a larger number with improvised cold arms, and five or six thousand ready to take up the arms of those who fell. Much of Moscow's population, especially its workingmen, aided with food, barricade construction, information, and sanitary support. The barricades were little more than obstructions to prevent cavalry charges. Fighting was hit-and-run, from doorways and windows and rooftops, around corners and out of courtyards through which retreat was secure. Men fought in detachments of twos and threes and fives and tens, avoiding pitched battles, vanishing swiftly, giving the impression of great numbers. However, once it had become clear that the troops would not join and that the general strike in Saint Petersburg had failed, not for a moment was there any doubt of the outcome. Still, for more than a week, in the Presnaya district, the insurrection held out.

Admiral Dubassov was afraid to use his own troops. Two-thirds of them he considered so unreliable that he kept them confined in barracks; the rest, some five thousand, seemed inadequate to crush the movement. Twice he sent urgent calls to Petersburg for help. Only when it arrived—the crack Semenevsky Guard on the open railway line between the capitals, and other troops that had just been used in punitive duty in the

Baltic Provinces—was he able to go over to the offensive. On the 27th, with the new troops, Dubassov managed to clear the center of the city and confine the guerrilla bands to the Presnaya district, a workingmen's quarter. Then, for three days he bombarded the Presnaya with artillery at long range, indiscriminately. Factories were destroyed, houses set in flames, men, women and children suffered alike. How many were killed and wounded is unknown, perhaps a thousand all told, among them a hundred-odd soldiers and police and eighty-six children. On December 31, when the mopping-up squads went through the Presnaya district, they found that most of the armed fighters had made good their escape. They had to wreak their vengeance on the non-combatant population. Thus the year 1905, which had opened with the Tsar's firing on his petitioning children, closed with the forces of the Holy, Orthodox, Autocratic Government systematically destroying by artillery bombardment an entire quarter of the holy city that had been the traditional capital of Old Russia.

CHAPTER NINETEEN

TROTSKY'S ROUND TRIP

Simpletons and hypocrites urge us to keep within legal limits . . . One would think our lungs infected with an irresistible desire to breathe the atmosphere of solitary dungeons . . . We love our underground as little as the drowning person loves the bottom of the sea . . . But it will not choke us . . . History is a tremendous mechanism serving our ideals. Its work is slow, barbarously slow, implacably cruel, yet it goes on. We believe in it. Only at moments, when this voracious monster drinks the living blood of our hearts as its nourishment, we wish to shout with all our might: *What thou dost, do quickly!*

—FROM THE PREFACE TO TROTSKY'S "MY ROUND TRIP"

The raid on the Soviet Executive netted three hundred prisoners, the most prominent being the acting Chairman, Yanovsky (Leon Trotsky). It is significant of the weakness of the Bolsheviks in the Soviet that there was not one of their leaders among the arrested. For a long time the fate of the prisoners was clouded in uncertainty. While the authorities wondered how the workers would answer the raid on their "parliament," the Minister of Justice was profuse in assurances that they would not be put on trial but had been arrested purely as a "preventive" measure. When the strike called to force their release fizzled, and Moscow's working-class quarter had been reduced to rubble, the government hinted at summary execution. In April, 1906, during the honeymoon period of the convocation of the First Duma, there was talk of immediate amnesty. Thus the fate of Trotsky and his fellow-prisoners wavered between firing squad and freedom until June of 1906, when formal charges were rather hastily drafted against them as fomenters of armed insurrection.

A special high court was set up in medieval fashion out of representatives of the Estates into which Russian society was still officially divided. Before this anachronistic court over two hundred witnesses paraded in motley procession: high military men, officials, workingmen, muzhiks, apartment house *dvorniki* (janitors, used by both the tsarist régime and the present GPU or MVD as spies), provocateurs, tramps, policemen. There were witnesses whose main target was Count Witte rather than the accused; witnesses who took the stand to denounce the government and to call upon the proletariat to free the prisoners and try their prosecutors. Every latitude was allowed in the courtroom.

Inevitably, the young Social Democrat who had begun 1905 by predicting a general strike and closed it by presiding over the last sessions of the Soviet, became the outstanding defendant. With mother and father in the courtroom, the twenty-six year old Lev Davidovich Bronstein addressed his judges for several hours in a "defense" that was an exposition of Social

Democratic views and an indictment of the régime which had put him on trial:

> The strike threw hundreds of thousands of workers out of the factories, awoke them to open political life. Who could undertake the leadership of these masses, who bring discipline into their ranks? The police, maybe? or the gendarmes? or the Security Section? . . . No one but the Council of Workingmen's Deputies. . . . Under such conditions the Council of Deputies was neither more nor less than the self-governing organ of the revolutionary masses, *an organ of state power.* . . . The historic force in whose name the state prosecutor speaks here is only the organized violation of the majority by the minority. The new force, however, represents the organized will of the majority. . . . This difference provided the Council of Deputies with its revolutionary right of existence. . . .
>
> Yes, Messrs. Judges and Representatives of the Estates, we realized *de facto* freedom of speech, press, assembly, inviolability of person—all the things which under pressure of the October strike were promised to the people. But the government apparatus gave signs of life only when it was a matter of tearing the legal conquests of the people to pieces. . . .
>
> Under what circumstances, in our opinion, could the uprising lead to victory? If the troops sympathized with us! So above all the Army had to be won. . . . What is necessary for that? Machine guns and rifles perhaps? Naturally, if the masses had machine guns and rifles, they would have possessed enormous power. But the masses had not, and even today do not have nor can they have, weapons in great numbers. . . . Yet, however important weapons are, Messrs. Judges, not in them does the greatest power lie. No! Not the capacity of the masses to kill others but their great readiness to die themselves—that, my Judges, assures in the last instance the success of a popular uprising. . . . When the troops come to the conviction that the people are ready to fight in bloody earnest and carry the struggle to the end, then the soul of the soldier will and must experience, as in all revolutions, a profound commotion. . . . Even barricades, apparently a mechanical element of the uprising, are of significance in reality above all as a moral force. . . .
>
> The prosecutors demand that you, Messrs. Judges, recognize that the Council of Workingmen's Deputies armed the workers for the direct struggle against the existing form of government. If you ask me categorically: *Was that so?* I answer: *Yes, indeed!*

When he ended, his lawyers crowded around to congratulate him. His mother wept openly, proud of this eloquence which she had but dimly understood, naively sure that acquittal must follow, even some sort of honors for her son. But he and four-teen others were condemned to life-long exile in Siberia; two additional defendants were given short prison terms; two hun-dred and eighty-four of the three hundred were set free.

In prison once more, Leon Trotsky settled calmly down to work. Outside, rebellion and repression raged: pogroms, puni-tive expeditions, field courts-martial, mass floggings, firing squads, peasant riots, holdups of government banks, military mutinies, disarming and slaying of police. But the tsarist prison régime continued astonishingly liberal for all "politicals" who could not be directly connected with acts of terror. Trotsky re-ceived all the books he wanted, wrote, smuggled out articles in the brief cases of his lawyers, was allowed two visits a week from Natalia Ivanovna, who claimed to be his legal wife. For fifteen months, before, during and after the trial, amidst muted alarms and rumors of mortal danger, he lived the life of a studious anchorite. It was a pleasure, he assured Natalia, to work in this quiet place "without any danger of being arrested." For relaxation he devoured French novels. The love for the French novel born in this succession of jails would remain with him to the end. It would be his refreshment on forced jour-neys in an armored train during the Civil War and a solace in exile in Turkestan, Prinkipo, France, Mexico. One of the last essays from his pen would be a generous appreciation of the then little-known young Polish-French novelist, Jean Mala-quais, who had sent him a copy of his first novel, *Les Javanais* ("Men from Nowhere").

In his cell he studied the third volume of Marx's *Capital* and wrote an essay on the Marxian theory of ground rent—token of his deepened interest in the peasant and the land. He ana-lyzed the role of the Soviet and the driving forces that would shape the next Russian revolution. These essays were calculated to defend, deepen, strengthen his conviction of the rightness of the theory of *permanent revolution*. Except for the one on rent, which went astray during a prison transfer, all his writings of this period constitute parts of his *The Year 1905,* published a few years later. It proved to be the most brilliant account from any hand of that memorable year, and one of the greatest examples of eyewitness-participant reporting in all historiography. Published originally in German in Vienna in 1909, it was reprinted in 1922 by the Soviet Government and translated in whole or in part into innumerable languages to serve as a textbook for the study of the year that began with Father Gapon's pilgrimage and ended with the arrest of the Soviet Executive and bombardment of Moscow. After Lenin's death and Trotsky's fall from grace, *The Year 1905* was made the target of elaborate polemics against "Trotskyism," and finally placed on the Index and burnt. But subsequent Soviet historiography has been unable to produce anything to replace it.*

Fifteen months after his arrest, Trotsky started on a journey to "perpetual exile" in Obdorsk up near the Arctic Circle. Fifteen hundred versts (about a thousand miles) separated Obdorsk from the nearest railway line, eight hundred from the nearest telegraph—a remoteness of which the convict would be glad. The prisoners and their heavy military guard traveled from the last railroad stop in forty sleighs, which carried them daily some ninety to one hundred versts toward the north. "Every day," he wrote to Natalia Ivanovna, "we ascend one degree farther into the kingdom of cold and barbarism."

Almost at the very end, when the distance seemed infinite from the nearest telegraph from which an alarm might be sent, he escaped across the snow. Wearing two fur coats, fur stockings, fur boots, fur cap, fur gloves—the outfit of a Siberian *Ostyak*—armed with some bottles of vodka against the dreaded

---

* The complete version is available in German, French and Russian (outside of Russia, of course). Some of the preliminary sketches for it were translated by Moissaye J. Olgin under the title *Our Revolution* (Henry Holt, 1918). All versions are at present out of print. Unaccountably, the Trotskyist organizations, usually so pious in the handling of his literary remains, have not reprinted this, his masterpiece.

cold and some gold pieces which had been concealed in the heels of his boots, he hid in a reindeer sleigh under a load of hay and was driven by a drunken Zyryan guide. A local exile broke a long false trail through the snow for the police to follow, thus giving him several days' head-start. When he reached more traveled trails he posed as a member of a polar expedition, then as a petty official. At last, the Urals, the railway, the Great-Russian frontier, and the comparative safety of semi-autonomous Finland. Here he wrote *There and Back* (known in English as *My Round Trip*). With the money earned by its publication he went on to Stockholm. Natalia and her child joined him in Vienna in October, 1907. He would not return to Russia until the next upheaval in 1917.